Rich Forests, Poor People

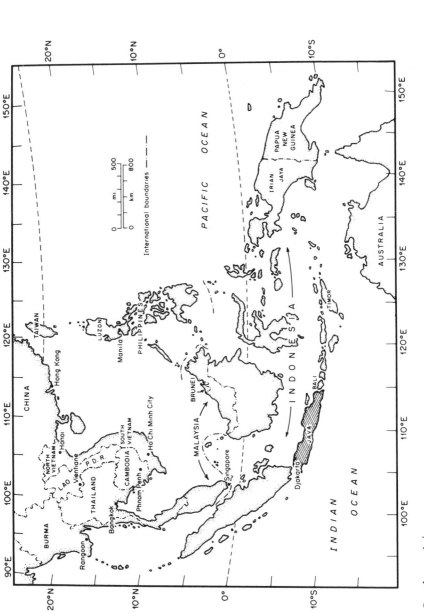

Southeast Asia

Rich Forests, Poor People

Resource Control and Resistance in Java

Nancy Lee Peluso

UNIVERSITY OF CALIFORNIA PRESS
Berkeley   Los Angeles   London

An earlier version of Chapter 3 appeared in *Forest History and Conservation;* earlier versions of the maps and Chapter 3 appeared in *Keepers of the Forest: Land Management Alternatives in Southeast Asia*, ed. Mark Poffenberger (West Hartford, Conn.: Kumarian Press, Inc., 630 Oakwood Avenue, West Hartford, CT 06110, USA, 1990; copyright © 1990 Kumarian Press). They are reprinted here with the permission of the publishers. The colonial-period photographs are reproduced with the permission of the Koninklijk Instituut voor de Tropen, Amsterdam.

University of California Press
Berkeley and Los Angeles, California
University of California Press, Ltd.
London, England
© 1992 by
The Regents of the University of California

First Paperback Printing 1994

Library of Congress Cataloging-in-Publication Data

Peluso, Nancy Lee.
  Rich forests, poor people : resource control and resistance in Java / Nancy Lee Peluso.
    p. cm.
  Includes bibliographical references and index.
  ISBN 0-520-08931-6
  1. Forest policy—Indonesia—Java—History. 2. Forests and forestry—Social aspects—Indonesia—Java—History.
3. Deforestation—Indonesia—Java—History. 4. Social forestry programs—Indonesia—Java—History. 5. Peasantry—Indonesia—Java—History. I. Title.
  SD657.I5P45 1991
  333.75'09598'2—dc20   91-581
                                                              CIP

Printed in the United States of America
9 8 7 6 5 4 3 2 1

Buat Fran dan Asa:
Anggota generasi yang akan datang

CONTENTS

PART V · CONCLUSION

ILLUSTRATIONS

MAPS

TABLES

ACKNOWLEDGMENTS

Support for the research and writing of this book was provided by many people and institutions in Indonesia and the United States. Above all, the Javanese—the forest villagers I lived with and field foresters I met—made this study possible; their trust and generosity can never be adequately compensated.

Research permission was granted by the Indonesian Institute of Sciences (LIPI). My field research was conducted during the same period that I coordinated diagnostic social forestry research in Java for the Ford Foundation and the State Forestry Corporation. The Ford Foundation funded both the fieldwork and six months of writing time. Additional support during the writing phase was provided by a writing grant from the Cornell Southeast Asia Program and a Summer Fellowship from Cornell Graduate School. The Energy and Resources Group at the University of California, Berkeley, provided a desk, computer access, and the camaraderie needed to complete the manuscript for publication. Friends in the Department of Forestry and Resource Management at UC have also given generously of their time to read and discuss ideas about changes in forest management worldwide.

The State Forestry Corporation (*Perum Perhutani*) kindly allowed me to explore its administrative and field policies and procedures, knowing that a sociologist's job is to critically examine institutions. Among others in the Jakarta office I am grateful to Ir. Hartono Wirjodarmodjo and, particularly, Ir. Muljadi Bratamihardja for their good humor and patience in answering my endless questions. In Central Java, Ir. Wahjoedi and Ir. Heribertus Soeharno provided access to their unit and district forests, respectively. Forest district managers in the teak districts (who changed frequently during my visit) also offered their hospitality and time. Both the State Forestry Corporation and the Environmental Studies Center at Gadjah Mada University granted me institutional affiliation; the latter provided office space and staff support whenever I was in Yogyakarta. Dr. Sugeng Martopo was particularly helpful in facilitating my work at the center. Members of the Forestry faculty at Gadjah Mada also provided me with access to data and intellectual support for the duration of the fieldwork. I am particularly indebted to Ir. Chafid Fandelli, Ir. Djuwadi, Ir. Djoko Suharno Radite, Ir. Hasanu Simon, and Ir. Wahyu; their willingness to discuss the details of forest management practice, training, and philosophy gave me many insights into the likely structural and cultural difficulties of implementing the principles of social forestry in Java.

The resources of the following libraries enabled me to develop the historical presentation: the John M. Echols Collection on Southeast Asia at Cornell University, the Forestry Library and the South and Southeast Asia Library at the University of California, Berkeley, the Manggala Wanabakti Library at the Ministry of Forestry in Jakarta, and the library at the Koninklijk Instituut voor de Tropen in Amsterdam.

The fieldwork would not have been possible without the assistance of Sri Mulyaningsih (Nuning). I am in her debt for her outstanding work as a research assistant and thankful that her organization, Dhworowati, convinced her to take part in the study. Discussions with members of Dhworowati also stimulated thoughts about the ways and reasons people use forests. Periodic meetings with the thirteen members of the social forestry research team provided me with an important forum for discussing field research findings as they unfolded. My part-time driver and informal assistant, Bambang, delivered me to remote forests and on several occasions prevented my untimely death on Java's roadways. Chip Barber, Michael Dove, Jeff Fox, Cor Veer, and Freerk Wiersum contributed stimulating ideas and encouragement at various points in the field study. In Yogyakarta, Ida and Shawn Harrington provided occasional refuge from the inevitable pressures of fieldwork. In Ithaca, Siti Fatimah painstakingly coded the household surveys during long and snowy afternoons. Johan Seynnaeve translated some of the more convoluted Dutch writings when I was hurrying to draft early versions of the history chapters. The Cornell Institute for Socio-Economic Research (CISER) supported the computer analysis, only part of which is presented in this volume. Barbara Gaerlan provided access to a computer and a program for making the tables and figures at the UC Center for South and Southeast Asian Studies.

Ben Anderson, Carl Bauer, Milt Barnett, Peter Boomgaard, Walt Coward, Michael Dove, Sally Fairfax, Louise Fortmann, Ramachandra Guha, Jim Lassoie, Nick Menzies, Rod Neumann, Marty Olson, Onghokham,

Jesse Ribot, Takashi Shiraishi, Hasanu Simon, Bill Stewart, Peter Vandergeest, Michael Watts, and two anonymous reviewers for the University of California Press have critiqued chapters or whole drafts of the manuscript. I owe Louise Fortmann a particular debt of gratitude for her comments on three (count 'em) versions. Their comments have been eminently useful; I bear sole responsibility for any remaining shortcomings of the book. My editors at UC Press, Sheila Levine and Betsey Scheiner, have been helpful and supportive at every stage of production; Ben Greensfelder copyedited the manuscript and clarified many vague constructions.

My parents have always made me believe that anything was possible; I am deeply grateful for their love and support. My husband, Bill, has made more than the usual sacrifices in the various stages of this book's completion. Not only did he spend four rainy, muddy months with me in one of the field sites, he also endured long separations while I continued fieldwork and spent endless hours writing and rewriting. In addition, he has learned more about Indonesian forests than he ever dreamed he would when we decided to journey together.

A NOTE ON SPELLING

Changes in the spelling of Indonesian and Dutch names, terms, and words over the past half-century have created a stylistic puzzle in writing this book. The system followed here is: personal and organizational names as well as published titles of monographs, articles, and reports are spelled as in the original; place names and other Indonesian or Dutch words are spelled according to current convention. Thus, the reader will find, for example, the spellings Jepara, Tuban, and Yogyakarta rather than Japara, Toeban, and Jogjakarta or other variants; similarly, variant spellings such as *Boschwezen* and *boswachter* are used.

PART ONE

Introduction

ONE

Structures of Access Control, Repertoires of Resistance

Claim and counterclaim had been the condition of forest life for centuries. . . .
Farmers and forest officers had rubbed along together, in a state of running
conflict, for many decades and they were to continue to do so for many
more. . . . What was at issue was not land use but who used the land: that is,
power and property right.

E. P. THOMPSON, *Whigs and Hunters*

Mantri Kasran used to fire his gun into the air to scare off thieves. People would flee and his assistants would come running. Then one day, about five years ago, he was surrounded while walking near a village in the teak forest. He described his "captors" as "a gang of rowdy teak thieves, some fifty to one hundred strong, many of them wielding hoes, dibble sticks, machete-like knives, and other agricultural implements." They circled around him, cursing rudely. He couldn't fire his gun; it would be just the excuse they needed to attack him, blaming him, as usual, for doing his job as forest guard. Luckily one of his assistants, who lived in the nearby village, heard the commotion and ran to get help. Kasran stalled the mob for what seemed at least an hour, until a logging truck filled with forest police pulled up. He climbed aboard and they drove away very slowly, easing by the villagers, who milled around the truck angrily as it pulled out.

Despite this close call, Kasran says he is not afraid to walk in the teak forest. He doesn't have to look over his shoulder. He has to be brave; he is a forester. But several months after the showdown, he moved his family out of their forest-based home, closer to the capital of the forest district.

He boasted about the incident in late 1984, in reference to the ongoing conflicts between the foresters and the villagers who refuse to understand "the meaning and function of the forest." Returning from a forest development project where some sixty-eight families had been given limited access to forest land for agriculture—in an area with more than four thousand landless rural households—he said, "People's mental attitudes [*sikap mental*] need to be adjusted so they are appropriate to the

3

forest's needs. We [foresters] have to raise people's consciousness about the forest. We need to teach them. The problem is not the forest. The problem is that the people are hungry for land." Then he said, "As a person, I want to help them. But as a representative of the State Forestry Corporation, I must say that we are not a social welfare organization. We are a business—in the business of conservation. On the other hand, it is the task of our whole country to take care of the forest."

This excerpt from a conversation with Mantri Kasran encapsulates the conflict between foresters and forest villagers in Java. Competition over access to land and trees, and over the control of that access, characterizes the relations between these two sets of forest users. Claims and counterclaims, threats and counterthreats, and struggles to support diametrically opposed production-consumption units—forest-based households and a powerful forestry parastatal—are the stuff of forest politics. So is the violence that erupts periodically or underlies the public relationships between the forest players.

Historically, the state, the peasantry, and other external interests have acted out their tensions in the natural theater of the forest. The potential for sustainable management of a given forest is partially a function of the manner in which these players have pursued their interests—and the degree of convergence or opposition between them. Where the interests of states and peasants clash, we often find environmental deterioration, poverty, and ambivalent power relations. The history of state forestry and actual forest use points to the tensions over access and control between the state and the peasantry. These struggles leave their mark by damaging valuable, vulnerable, land-based resources, even in areas where so-called scientific principles of forest management have been in place for more than a century. These are the environmental ramifications of conflict between rural people and foresters.

Sustainable production as defined by a forestry enterprise is not necessarily sustainable from the point of view of forest villagers. The current crises in tropical forests derive from inappropriate institutions, particularly those governing systems of resource access and control. No one source can be blamed for forest depletion or degradation; rather, the deterioration of land-based resources constitutes the culmination of complex interactions between shifting interests. An environmental solution to degradation cannot exist apart from the people and societies who use that environment legally or illegally; degradation itself is a value- and interest-laden term (Dove 1984; Blaikie 1985). Analyses of sustainability *must* include social and political sustainability.

This book describes the history of state forestry policies designed to control forest land, tree species, labor, and ideology in Java, Indonesia, and the responses of forest villagers to those controls. Over time, state-imposed changes in forest access rights have affected not only subsequent policy formation and implementation but also the forms of peasant resistance to state control. In some forests, these changes have caused losses of trees and changed the capacities of certain forest lands to grow those species; in others, forest land has been effectively converted to peasant agriculture. Both conditions are called *deforestation* by foresters. In both settings, deforestation results from conflict, confrontation, and resistance.

Most studies of Indonesian forests have focused on the so-called Outer Islands (which include Sumatra, Kalimantan, and West Irian), where 97 percent of Indonesia's forests are found.[1] Java, in contrast, is known as a rice-producing tropical island. Yet one-fourth of Java's land is legally classified as state forest, and Java is where state forest management began in Indonesia. It is also where precolonial, colonial, and postcolonial state policies have left the deepest marks on the forest and forest-based communities. The island's critical contribution to Indonesia's food supply, its two-hundred-year history of intensive forest exploitation, its high population density, and its differentiated rural social structure create an interesting and appropriate setting for studying the dynamics of center-periphery relations at the interface of forest policy and forest use.

Moreover, timber plantations and the Javanese model of management are being imitated throughout Indonesia and in other parts of the forested tropics. The analysis of the evolution of Javanese forest policy and use is thus relevant not only to the specific problem of forest conflict and degradation on a single island, but also to emerging conflicts in other forested regions. Natural tropical forests are being converted to monocultural forest plantations after damaging episodes of forest exploitation by foreign and domestic firms. The shutting out of rural people and the misunderstanding of the motives underlying peasants' uses of the forest are also being repeated. Ironically, environmentalists' outrage over mismanaged tropical forests has caused some to view Java's forest plantations as exemplars of good management, without understanding their social or environmental history or the political implications of this form of management in Java's social context. Although the forests of Java appear to be the best-managed (according to scientific principles) of all of Indonesia's forests, hard questions need to be answered about the reasons for continued plantation failure and deforestation. Wherever "scientific" forestry has constituted an accepted form of political-economic control, the impacts of these controls on forest-dependent people must be understood as well. Forest-based conflicts in the Amazon, the Pacific Northwest of the United States, and the Outer Islands of Indonesia have erupted also because "science" and societal values did not agree.

The only other recent study to look at state power and local resistance in the context of Third World forest management is Guha's fascinating account of domination and resistance in the Indian Himalaya (1990).[2] Guha focuses on recurring forms of peasant resistance under different forms of state organization, the British colonial state and traditional kingship. As I have done in this study of Java, Guha examines the clashes between opposing world views and material functions of the forest and shows how these contradictory views of rightful forest use have re-emerged in contemporary protest movements by forest-based peasants. Though there are many similarities between the two cases and the analytical constructs of control (or *domination,* the term Guha uses) and resistance, this history of state control of Java's forests is complemented by more nuanced ethnographies of contemporary forms of resistance. Specifically, I show that conflicting notions of legitimacy and criminal action color the actions and ideas of all the contenders for Java's forest resources. As these findings affect all users' and claimants' capacities to manage forest resources, they have important policy implications, which deserve greater attention in future studies of forest conflict.

This chapter presents a theoretical framework for the confrontation between state and peasant interests in the forest. In it I explore the ideology, or "culture," of state authority and legitimacy (in managing forest resources) as an outgrowth of political-economic strategy and structures originating in Europe. The nature of rural people's responses to state policies that restrict forest access derives from local sociocultural and political-economic circumstances, including local interpretations of the cultures and mechanisms of resource control. Both forest-based peasants and the state have constructed ideologies intended to justify their own rights to control forest access. Each side resists structural changes or concepts of management that would confer legitimacy on the other. At a broad level the dynamics of state forest management and local forest use are constrained by the layered structures of resource control and access and contemporary repertoires of resistance. Outcomes—in terms of the ability of the center or the periphery to control the forest—vary according to historical period and geographical location.

The final section of this chapter describes the contemporary setting of the forests where this study of forest-based conflict began.

THE IDEOLOGY AND POLITICAL ECONOMY OF STATE FORESTRY

Most state forest management systems in the Third World have failed to overcome either forest degradation or rural poverty. Indeed, some state systems exacerbate forest degradation because they exacerbate the poverty of villagers living on the edges of the forest. Such counterproductive results are in part due to the colonial-style legal and organizational structures that still dominate state forest management (Blaikie 1985:53). Most Third World notions of conservation and "scientific" forest management originated in the West, under different political-economic and ecological conditions, and continue to reflect Western interpretations of forest productivity and resource conservation by "professional" foresters (Fernow 1911; Fortmann and Fairfax 1985:2).

Forest ownership and laws governing forest use in Europe extend back to at least the beginning of the Middle Ages and evolved in settings as diverse as royal and feudal manorial forests and woodlands owned in common (Mantel 1964:2,10). Both oral and written traditions were important sources of forest knowledge; the latter included local medieval forest ordinances, royal forest ordinances in the sixteenth through eighteenth centuries, and the forestry literature. The earliest forest traditions were likely passed on from the lore and science of the Greeks and Romans (ibid., 9–11), and most early written forest science came directly from the ancients (Meiggs 1982). The precepts of state forestry (forests managed for and by agents of the state) were developed in France and Germany in the early eighteenth century (Mantel 1964:4).

Forest conversion for agriculture had been encouraged under feudalism as a means of increasing production, accumulating capital or goods, supporting feudal lords and the royal courts through tributes, and providing a livelihood for much of the rest of the rural populace (Bloch 1966). As populations grew and the privatization of land through enclosure increased, the loss of forest lands, timber, fuelwood, fodder, and game caused their value to soar. Not only did kings and the gentry worry that their exclusive hunting grounds were in danger of disappearing, they also recognized the potential economic opportunities of controlled forest management. Foresters and gamekeepers had been employed on the lands of royalty, the gentry, and the clergy for centuries, but it was not until 1787 that the first university training program in forestry was established, at the University of Freiburg. Other universities in the German states followed suit in the early nineteenth century, and a national school of forestry was founded in Nancy, France, in 1824 (Mantel 1964:19, 27). Foresters from all over Europe and the United States attended these schools to learn their science. When they returned home or traveled to the European colonies in Africa, Asia, and Latin America, they carried with them the philosophy and methods of state-controlled, or centralized, forest management (Fernow 1911).

The legacy of an American forester, Gifford Pinchot (who studied at Nancy), was a Benthamite phrase that would continue to legitimate state forest management in modern times. Pinchot believed that forests should be managed to provide "the greatest good for the greatest number of people for the longest time" (Dana and Fairfax 1980:72). As Dana and Fairfax point out, however, "The great strength of this view of conservation is that *no one can disagree with its broad objectives.* Its major weaknesses are understanding and applying the concept and *agreeing upon priorities* as theory is put into practice" (emphasis added).

This European-American view of conservation, which has strongly influenced the international community's rhetoric, is important because of its continued influence on Third World forestry policy and structure. While colonial forest officers were trained in Germany and France before establishing and managing the forests and forest plantations in their colonies, many of today's Third World foresters are trained either in these traditions, or in the subsequent interpretations of European forestry applied in the United States (Fortmann and Fairfax 1985:2). For example, both the utilitarian view of forests as a major source of government revenue and the justification of this use as the means of providing the "greatest good for the greatest number of people" have dominated the politics of forestry in many developing countries (Westoby 1987:69). In reality, this mandate has become a justification for absolute state control of the forest resource base and the methods and benefits of its exploitation. Moreover, foresters tend to think of themselves as neutral experts carrying out their science according to the state's will; they rarely view either their own policies or their implementation methods as "political" acts. From the forest dweller's point of view, however, nothing could be further from the truth.[3]

Colonial and contemporary states have often appropriated large tracts of land for forests, agricultural plantations, or major development projects, usurping prior systems of land rights and establishing new land use and resource laws. Oftentimes, this appropriation is justified by claims that the change was in the "common interest" for the "greatest good." Yet Pinchot's notion of the greatest good only abstractly includes individuals living on or near the appropriated land—people who might have radically different definitions of the greatest good and common interest. Tribal people and local peasants gain little from the centralization and transfer of forest control other than occasional work as unskilled or semiskilled laborers on lands they once controlled. While the new forest bureaucracies proclaimed their superior ability to substainably manage natural resources, in many countries land degradation and rural poverty in forest areas began or were exacerbated as a result of the drive of colonial or contemporary governments to control land, forest products growing on that land, and the labor available to work it (Blaikie 1985).

Once classificatory boundaries enclose state lands, official memories of the previous status of those lands evaporate. For example, government officials and ahistorical observers frequently regard overpopulation as the sole reason for environmental degradation on private lands. By ignoring the origins of the spatial organization of populations, they blame the land users alone, without considering the broader contexts influencing the land users' decisions to have more children, cut the forest, or "mine" their agricultural land (Blaikie 1985:58). Foresters have thus criminalized villagers' traditional subsistence activities. They believe local people are acting illegally when they cut timber, remove fodder, farm, or graze their cows in newly planted forest tracts. Even sympathetic observers forget the history of claims to forest lands, calling some people's illegal activities on forest lands "clearly defined case[s] of 'encroachment' . . . in connection with land hunger among more settled agriculturalists, who deliberately enter what they acknowledge to be reserved forest in search of land" (Raintree 1985:13).

In sum, radically different historical and ecological contexts confound the adaptation of forest management systems from Europe. While both colonial and contemporary forest managers have shown different degrees of diligence in implementing land use policies, the structures under which these policies first were imposed are still in place (Blaikie 1985:60). The ideologies of state-controlled conservation that originated in the colonial period also remain, and have intensified since the outburst of world concern about the environment in the 1960s (Humphrey and Buttel 1982) and the reaffirmation of concern in the late 1980s and 1990s. Though government agencies pay some lip service to the need to include indigenous people in designing resource management strategies, a great deal of confusion exists about exactly how to do so without relinquishing the forest service's objective of producing surplus for the state.

To understand the reasons for forest degradation, our analysis must begin with several questions about the broader political economy (Blaikie 1985:73): What is the nature of the state power in managing resources? What are the material interests and ideologies of government organizations and individual agents of the state seeking control of these resources? And how is power exercised? From these questions we move on to an analysis of the nuances of control and resistance. Forest-based conflict and degradation must be studied in historically specific contexts, considering regional political-economic dynamics, local social relations of production, and environmental capacities. Social history is contextual, and local interpretations of broader social processes have their own far-reaching implications (Taussig 1980; Gaventa 1980).

LAND, STATE FORESTS, AND CULTURES OF CONTROL

Rural poverty and "land hunger" have been historically linked to "theft" of forest products or "squatting" on state or corporate forest lands. Land

and peasant access to cultivable land become more pressing issues when states appropriate large bodies of land. In many cases, the state simply denies legitimacy to prior systems of land rights and rights in land-based resources, thus establishing new relations to these means of production. Forest-dwelling people or forest-dependent peasants lose more than they gain from centralized state control over reserved forest or forest plantations (Blaikie 1985:121). Their losses of relative autonomy and forest access are particularly acute when the state uses its control to monopolize resource exploitation.

In general, state power can be observed and understood through its coercive or control organizations by noting where these fit into the state apparatus, the other social forces and groups they are linked to, and their effectiveness (Skocpol 1979:31). These structures and relationships help explain the nature of state control of forests and other natural resources. But it is also important to know what drives the dynamic of state forest control and what gives rise to the state's use of coercion.

State natural resource bureaucracies that directly manage resources on state lands face different types of contradictions in forming policy and performing their duties than agencies that lease resource exploitation concessions to large, often multinational, firms. The peculiarity of a bureaucracy's position increases when it also retains a welfare or socioeconomic development mandate (Bunker 1985). In state production forestry, the government agency may be expected to be a profitable state enterprise, preserve the resource for future generations, prevent environmental degradation, and help develop or alleviate poverty in forest villages. Depending on the immediacy of each mandate at any given time, one or more of these contradictory functions can confound the others. Regardless of which mandate dominates, bureaucrats and other state employees have an interest in maintaining a social order economically and politically partial to them (Skocpol 1979:30; Robison 1986). When social unrest appears potentially explosive, the state and its agents may temporarily work to fulfill the needs and demands of subordinate classes. By "surrendering" incrementally or periodically the state can maintain its power, continuing to control people, resources, and land. Relinquishing control over tracts of land or clusters of resources, however, may constitute the loss of state or agency power in certain contexts. Unwillingness to thus lose power may lead the state to take military or police action in the name of order and control.

Subsequent chapters demonstrate how a particular bureaucratic agency, having organizational constraints imposed by its position and function within the state and its dominant internal dynamic as a state enterprise, has operated in relation to the rural poor and the natural environment. Though its structure differs somewhat, the agency is burdened with the legacy of its colonial predecessors. Moreover, centralizing forces and conflicting interests within the state and the forestry sector have precluded the contemporary resource bureaucracy's effective response to problems at its peripheries, preventing active participation by local people.[4] One result of these failures has been the implementation of social forestry programs intended to renegotiate state resource control, particularly where powerful peasant resistance has threatened state forest revenues.

Any study of state resource control must examine its culture(s) of control, consisting of formal and informal elements. The state's law establishes the bounds of formal control. Terror, torture, or "simple" fear also have characterized traditional and contemporary authority under a myriad of patrimonial, colonial, and contemporary state forms. The rule of law has granted their monopoly to the state (Hay 1975b:25; Sutherland 1979). How separable are the law and the fear the state seeks to instill in a targeted constituency? And which is more effective against encroachment on state-owned resources: the formality of the law or the threat of its enforcement? Moreover, how effective in the long term is a law or mode of enforcement that offends local custom and conceptions of rights?

The law defines and determines the bounds of criminality, but customary laws, practices, and beliefs, or unfavorable material conditions often confound the enforcement of contradictory state laws. Under such circumstances, the enforcement of the state's law becomes a crime in the eyes of the people, an impingement on either what has been described as their "moral economy" (Thompson 1963; Scott 1976) or simply on the perceptions people have of what is right, what is "a just use and distribution of resources" (Kerkvliet 1990:17). In facing these "moral crimes" committed by the state, even a highly differentiated peasantry can mask its class tensions, imparting a Chayanovian solidarity to a normally strained set of social relations. An irony emerges from confrontations between the state and peasantry when the state tries to coerce the peasantry to adhere to state law, and this coercion leads to varied forms of peasant resistance. Coercion has a different effect on laborers extracting resources for the state than it has on other rural dwellers "illegally" extracting resources for themselves. Further, increasing state use of coercion to control resources and rural people can be indicative of declining state power and authority in the face of peasant resistance (Scott 1976:76). Coercion is thus not an end in itself but a part of the evolving process in which one side pursues control over the resources claimed by the other.

FOREST-BASED CULTURES OF RESISTANCE

Poaching has always been endemic in any forest area, and no doubt been coeval with the forests' existence.

E. P. THOMPSON, *Whigs and Hunters*

States try to set the limits of action in the law, sometimes in response to their contentious constituents' activities. The law defines the dimensions of criminality and determines its treatment. Forest law is allegedly intended to protect great tracts of land and resources or reserve them for the exclusive use of certain individuals or groups. Unauthorized users are called "poachers," "timber thieves," or "squatters"; these labels are the ideological creations of such laws of exclusion. Oftentimes, states or their associates and allies politicize the images of forest "criminals," construing unauthorized forest users as outlaws or subversive elements, considering transgressions of forest law to be indicators of a more insidious (and feared) political threat: a threat to the state's authority.

It is important, however, to differentiate between the kinds of political intentions and labels attached to poaching and other state-defined crimes. Peasant politics, whether or not they include poaching, often include protests against losing resource access. If loss of resource access means losing the capacity for basic subsistence, this loss threatens the peasants' own survival and the survival of a way of life. In other words, their motives in using the forest derive from a desire to maintain and control their means of social reproduction. The politics of forest access are not driven by the kinds of macro-political motives often perceived (and feared) by the state—for example, the intention to overthrow the state.

Whether or not they are intentionally breaking the state's law (by stealing wood or appropriating game), peasants have their own notions of morality, rights, criminality, and subversion. Frequently, these differ from the assumptions embedded in state ideology. Against the myriad of possible political-economic backdrops for their actions, peasant acts interpreted as resistance, rebellion, or crime can be construed as constituting specific "repertoires of resistance." Analyzing the components and contexts of such repertoires does not require identification of the resisters' intent. Indeed, intent is far more difficult to identify. Resistance can be analyzed in terms of the dialectic between state controls on the definition of criminality and the actions of peasants within particular material or ideological contexts.

Tilly (1978:390) defines a "repertoire of collective action" as "alternative means of acting together on shared interests." A repertoire of (collective) resistance is embedded within—indeed it is a product of—specific historical and environmental circumstances. The forms that resistance takes depend on the nature and generality of the complaint and the kinds of "weapons" (social, political, or broadly defined technological) at the disposal of the resisters (Scott 1985). Much popular violence, for example, arises in response to violence by a ruling class or the state (Crummey 1986:1). However, the expression of resistance is tempered by the strength of the authority it is contesting, and that authority's repertoire of control. As Scott (1976:195) points out, "the risk of rebellion [is] proportional to the coercive power of the state and its willingness to use that power." Likewise, most situations in which the poor, or the powerless, need to negotiate with powerful states, their agents, their clients, or other powerful figures will be characterized by the tactic of public deference, whatever cultural form such deference might require (Newby 1975:146; Thompson 1975a:307; Scott 1985:284–89).

Some state or class violence is not overt, but surreptitious; sociopolitical controls and power structures can inflict more "silent" forms of violence on the poor or powerless (Watts 1983). Silent or strident, both famine and war can result in rioting, open protest, assassination, and other violent forms of popular response. Alternatively, the circumstances may require the maintenance of a front-stage persona (Goffman 1959) of compliance and passive, or nonconfrontational, resistance.

What determines the forms that protest takes? According to Tilly (1978:390), "the existing repertoire constrains collective action; far from the image we sometimes hold of mindless crowds, people tend to act within known limits, to innovate at the margins of existing forms, and to miss many opportunities available to them in principle."

The "known limits" constraining peasant action must include an awareness of the repertoires of control. As an aspect of control, fear—stemming from memories of past repression and the continued threat of repeated violent repression—silences potentially resounding resistance to change and external control. Even a benevolent aristocracy or the state as patron is backed by violence; paternalism does not revoke the power relationship: when patronage fails, force can be invoked (Hay 1975a:62). Not a few peasantries have learned that revolutionary action most frequently "creates a more coercive and hegemonic state apparatus—one that is often able to batten itself on the rural population like no other before it" (Scott 1985:29). Tilly's explanation is thus a key: Any repertoire of resistance may be simultaneously conscious of and constrained by the social and political limits of collective and individual action.

Other limits are also set by the powerful: the limits of what is publicly and ideologically acceptable social behavior. That which is not acceptable is labeled criminal; this labeling is the prerogative of the state. State appropriation of land, water, wood, and other natural resources redefines the rules of access to these and renders unauthorized access a criminal act. Yet what the state defines as criminal often differs substantially from the peasant definition of crime, and the denial of access to vital resources may loom as the most violent crime of the state toward the peasantry. Sometimes the rage felt by people deprived of resource access derives not from the denial itself but from the reassignment of access to others whose claims are considered invalid (Thompson 1975b: 98). The enclosure policies in Europe of the sixteenth, seventeenth, and eighteenth centuries led to expressions of local resistance or rebellion similar to those documented in colonial and contemporary Asia. Ironically, agrarian conditions in nineteenth-century Prussia, the home of "modern" forestry, and where forest species and lands were monopolized by the state, were remarkably similar to those in Asia:

> Prussian peasants and proletarians in the 1830s, *beleaguered by dwarf holdings and wages below subsistence,* responded by emigration or by *poaching wood, fodder, and game on a large scale.* The pace of "forest crime" rose as wages declined, as provisions became more expensive, and where emigration was more difficult; in 1836 there were 207,000 prosecutions in Prussia, 150,000 of which were forest offenses. [The peasants] were supported by a mood of popular complicity that originated in earlier traditions of free access to forests. [Scott 1985:35, emphasis added]

Forest administrators and forest guards classify forest "bandits" as criminals and, sometimes, as enemies of the state—just as the British did during and after the enclosures (Thompson 1975b:194). Differentiating between forest banditry or "crime" as protest and forest theft for crime's sake or personal gain is particularly difficult when individual acts of banditry or protest are part of peasant survival strategies and linked, simultaneously, to organized criminal networks having quite different motives. In both cases, a defiance of authority is present, in both cases, personal gain is sought. Nor is consciousness a useful criterion for separating the criminal from the protestor or marginal survivor forced into forest banditry. Surely the forest bandit is aware that poaching or tree theft runs counter to state laws—hence the clandestine means of appropriation. To what extent does this bandit consider the symbolic meaning of his or her acts a protest against the material conditions of society or against the criminalization of an age-old survival strategy? To what extent is it simply an extension of that survival strategy in the absence of viable alternatives? As Prochaska (1986) shows for Algerian forest dwellers facing French and British appropriation of their age-old lands, trees, and customs, people's responses to the crimes committed against their livelihoods are freely interpreted by those in power.

Intent alone may be inconsequential. Whatever their intent, the forest dwellers' acts change the forest or land cover, alter the distribution of benefits from the forest, and contest, implicity or explicitly, the state's authority in the forest. The persistence of these claims and counter-claims by different forest users sustains the Gramscian notion that the hegemony of the state (or of the most powerful classes) is never complete. This incompleteness of ideological control accounts for part of the variation in Tillian repertoires of resistance. According to Turton (1986) this variation is a matter of tactics: He depicts peasant strategy as a "middle ground," where repertoires of resistance and rebellion alternate according to the contemporary power of the authorities. Acts of banditry fit within either of these primary repertoires, and, as Stoler (1985:174) points out, are subject to politicization by the state when the occasion suits its purposes.

The question of intent in charges of criminality becomes more difficult to sort out of an act that is only partly a political statement and largely a stab at survival. Whether the actor intends to commit symbolic political-criminal acts or whether the state defines criminal-protest acts as political, and whether these acts take place within the limits of community definitions of acceptable behavior, also influence the bandit's image among his peasant peers (cf. Cohen 1986:470). Taking trees from land claimed by the state and taking them from a neighbor's land are viewed as two entirely different acts by the forest community; one is legitimate, the other is not. This indicates, if not political *motives* underlying the individual's actions, at least the potential for the community's political *interpretation* of a forest villager's theft of trees from state lands. In this sense, community compliance with the act, by protecting the "thief" or feigning ignorance, becomes part of the politics of resistance. In such a context, politicized by both the peasantry and the state, the "bandit" as a popular symbol and the practice of banditry as an outcome of material repression need not remain restricted to regions or time periods in which capitalism is just emerging (cf. Hobsbawm 1959:13–15), but remain salient in regions penetrated long ago by capitalist relations of production.

The criminality of forest or resource-based resistance has other aspects. Peasant resisters can be used or manipulated by powerful others to attain their own ends vis-à-vis the state. These alternate institutions or organizations may have more power and authority than the legal authorities, at least at local or regional levels (Winslow 1975:131). Black market traders or smugglers may take advantage of poor forest villagers, inciting them to "steal" more and bigger quantities of wood or game than they would on their own. The involvement of powerful outsiders does not negate the material foundations of the forest villagers' resistance to state claims on local resources. It only adds to the complexity of understanding and dealing with the circumstances.

There are two major structures of peasant resistance, one based on peasant unity, one on differentiation. (Forms of resistance in response to specific forms of control are discussed in the section that follows.) Cultures of resistance—consisting of ideology, local social structure, and history—are contextual configurations of common peasant response to external controls and state appropriation of resources. Conflict between a village and the state or the state's agents can result in the village's concerted opposition overriding the usual barriers of rural social structure. In essence, all rural classes oppose a common powerful competitor for the forest: the state (Hobsbawm 1959; Thompson 1975b; Hay 1975b). Since colonial times such opposition has surfaced in Southeast Asia as everyday forms of resistance, arson, murder, and outright rebellion.[5]

A second type of peasant response to exclusion from forest lands has been refracted inward, in the increasing differentiation of village society. As population growth and agrarian capitalism (in addition to state or private capitalism in extractive enterprises) increase competition for limited rural resources and laboring opportunities, this differentiation is expected to increase. As in other sectors of agriculture, particularly since the Green Revolution, wealthy and middle peasants have been taking control of more and more private lands, usurping control of formerly common village lands, and taking greater control over forest lands (Wood 1979; Shiva et al. 1982; Cernea 1985; Peluso 1987). Even on lands directly controlled by the state the social relations of production on private lands could mediate the nature of state controls over the forest and forest labor.

These social structural constraints and economic processes accelerate the income gaps between rural classes and may accelerate the proletarianization of the forest-based poor. And, as Hay (1975a) observes (regarding English peasants), "their acts of revenge . . . challenge an historiography that is increasingly complacent about the social harmonies of that society." The same observation might be made about the assumptions of village harmony both during and after the colonial occupation of Java (Geertz 1963). Solidarity and moral economy may be superimposed temporarily on dynamic, differentiated rural communities (White 1983); particularly when the village faces a common enemy or any outsider. Indeed, the differences in the nature of the claim to the forest can make the stakes of resistance significantly different for the rich and the poor.

Both of these structures of resistance, however, may be present in one locale. The ideology of resistance may be appropriated by wealthier or middle peasants to redirect class tensions caused by inequalities of local resource distribution toward the state, the larger and common "enemy" (Thompson 1975a:52; Crummey 1986:141).[6] In this sense, there may be "layers" of resistance that need to be sorted out for various rural classes and groups. To understand the peasantry's justification for the unauthorized use of natural resources requires us first to examine the origins of the state's claim to resources, the process of criminalizing customary resource access, and the potentials for recourse by resource-dependent rural people. We must also break down the village's multiple repertoires of control and resistance.

DEFINING FOREST ACCESS CONTROL AND FOREST-BASED RESISTANCE

> *They clap in gaol, with threats most cruel,*
> *Poor folk who gather wood for fuel;*
> *But let rich loggers go scot free*
> *Who fell and steal the living tree*[7]

The control of access to production forests has three components: control of land, control of species, and control of forest labor. Each of these components can be conceptualized as a type of power resource (Weber 1978:991), or as manifestations of state or corporate power. Ideological control, embodied in the forest laws that legitimate state authority in forests, joins with the other three components to constitute forest access control. Each individual component also has its own significance.

The control of land by the forest management agency represents the foundation of agency legitimacy. Without land, the agency has no power or institutional function. While it is guided by the ideology of the state, the agency retains rights to determine land use, including what species will be planted, how many people will be employed, and how production will take place. In Southeast Asia, land control as a basis of state or state agency legitimation generally originated under colonialism. Precolonial states had less power to enforce restrictions on land use, particularly in regions distant from the seat of government—usually in the heart of the forest (Myrdal and King 1972). Colonial regimes erected structures of administrative and coercive control from which escape was nigh impossible (Adas 1981). Many Third World states have become more coercive since their independence from the colonial yoke. At the same time, the ideological, political, and economic importance of forest land control by the state has increased.

Control of trees on forest land is linked also to the process of agency legitimation. Forestry was traditionally conceived for the purpose of game protection and timber protection (Fernow 1911). Later, a role in watershed protection was added. The planting, maintenance, and exploitation of trees on particular lands often justifies the claim of the forestry agency to that land. Trees cultivated on government land for production of timber, resin, or other nontimber products represent government investments. The profits from their exploitation provide revenues to the state, pay the salaries of the forest agency's employees, provide employment, and help legitimate the role of the forestry agency.

The control of forest labor is important to ensure the profitable exploitation of trees and tree products on forest lands. Forest settlements existed long before the establishment of state forest services in many developing countries. In many of these countries, population growth, skewed distribution of rural resources, and the inability of industrialization to keep up with labor force growth have created large rural labor reserves with minimal political or economic power. Fragmentation of private landholdings in rural areas and rural people's need for cash lead to dependence on forest resources where other income-generating activities are scarce. In such cases the forest agency is able to benefit from semiproletarianized labor on forest plantations. Where smaller tracts of state forest are surrounded by rural or urban communities with many potential income sources, the forestry agency is forced to seek other means of control or to slacken the reins on forest labor. While forest management agencies do not cause these structural conditions, their land, species, and labor control policies are mediated by and may exacerbate the circumstances of forest laborers, preventing them from accumulating sufficient capital to overcome the unfavorable conditions of their existence.

A state forestry agency needs to control land, trees, and labor in order to fulfill three of its roles: government landlord, forest enterprise, and conservation institution. In these three ways, it is a gatekeeper of sorts, assigned to protect property (land and trees) by guarding its boundaries, to guarantee a flow of revenue over the short and long terms by planting and maintaining particular (forest) species, and to protect the environment—inside and outside the forest lands—by following environmental principles for sustained-yield management of the forest lands entrusted to its care. Its protector and producer roles are legitimated by law and policy; its protective functions are implemented by field-level foresters and forest police. The state claims the right to establish the terms of forest access by virtue of these mandates: this is its ideological control.

While forest management agencies are also mandated to manage the forest for the public interest, they do so tangentially to their three primary roles. Many foresters argue that serving those three functions implicitly provides for public welfare. Rarely do they associate public interest with the interests of forest villagers. Nevertheless, state production forestry enterprises have provided opportunities for forest employment and allowed limited usufruct rights to forest lands. Following state ideologies that accompany the legitimation of the state, the agency extends its control to forest-related activities that are supposed to "develop" forest communities, whatever these projects and programs may be called (community forestry, social forestry, village woodlots, and so on). However, the unrelenting tree theft, sabotage of reforestation sites, and rural people's demands to gain or control forest access indicate that forest-related employment falls far short of meeting the needs of forest communities. State agencies rarely, if ever, implement true social forestry projects as Romm (1985) has defined them: projects that transfer control of forest resources to local people.

Much work has been done recently on violent and nonviolent forms of peasant resistance; however, none of these studies has looked at the forms of peasant resistance as responses to specific forms of control over access to resources.[8] I posit that forms of forest resistance parallel or complement the four forms of forest access control discussed above. Forest peasants resist forest land control by reappropriating forest lands for cultivation; they resist species control by "counter-appropriating" species claimed by the state (or other enterprise) and by damaging mature species or sabotaging newly planted species; they resist labor control by strikes, slowdowns, or migration; and they resist ideological control by developing or maintaining cultures of resistance.

Of course the state and those working for or in its interests do not see these aspects of peasant resistance as I have just described them. From their point of view, the forest villagers are "squatting" (on the state's land); "stealing" (the state's trees); "sabotaging" the state's reforestation, harvest, or labor policies; breaking the law by striking; and acting "ignorant" or remaining "backward" by adhering to cultural norms that do not achieve the ends desired by the state or another large-scale forest enterprise, as the case may be. The state's use of such charged words is part of its coercive effort to manipulate public opinion and to "handle" the resisting peasants; as ever, language is a powerful tool in the culture of control. As a result, a complex form of cultural and political interaction develops between the state forestry bureaucracy and the peasantry. Rather than speaking of one side's effect on the other, one side's response to the other, we are talking of an interactive web of actions, reactions, and counterreactions, all embedded in a set of complex contradictions.

In sum, forest degradation and rural poverty are neither isolated nor self-perpetuating conditions. They are, rather, symptoms of resource scarcity, outcomes of agrarian change, and indicators of complex social conflict. Tensions causing degradation and poverty arise from conflict over territory, redefinition of rights and constraints on resource access, surplus appropriation from forest extraction, and the distribution of the surplus extracted. How and why degradation, deforestation, and impoverishment evolve depends on how different interests are negotiated and expressed. The forms in which forest claims are manifested depend on political and sociocultural constraints. As a result, these processes require analysis not only in the political-economic contexts of international, national, regional, and local relationships, but, to the extent possible, from the perspectives of actors at both the bottom and the top.

The winners of this power struggle may ultimately lose a more serious battle. Should the central control structure be too taut, it risks snapping the lifeline of its "opponents" on the periphery. Were this to occur, the users might suddenly decide to ignore all the rules and severely shake the system's foundations. Should the users appear favored in the power balance, the managers may assert greater control by force. Force, coercion, and violence are not merely aberrations from the pattern of the management game: they are real alternatives, the actual use and threat of which shape the posturing of the two sides. As the case of Java unfolds, I analyze the interface between "ideal" organizational rules and collective or ad hoc violence and coercion in Java's forest history.

SETTING

Central Java (Unit I) is the geographical focal point for this study. In this region, the Dutch colonial government introduced "scientific" forest management by the state; since then, it has always been the most profitable of the three forestry units (East, West, and Central Java each constitute provincial units).[9] In 1984, for example, Unit I Central Java showed profits of Rp. 21.3 billion before taxes, Unit II East Java had a net profit of Rp. 8.3 billion, and Unit III West Java had negative returns (Perum Perhutani 1985:14, 43, 45). Moreover, from its westernmost borders with Sunda (West Java) to the heart of the teak forest on its eastern edge, the province includes a wide range of agroecological zones and types of monocultural production forest plantations.

The Forests of Java

To the average observer, the Javanese landscape appears dominated by rice paddies, coconut groves, and fruit trees, with forests situated only on the tips of its volcanoes and accessible on the occasion of an excursion to a park or recreation area in the highlands. In Central Java, few main roads traverse a forest as formidable as those depicted in Javanese myth and theater. Yet during the brief hours spent crossing the old teak plantations, one forgets the bustle and heat of the open agricultural plains. In fact, nearly 3 million hectares—23.2 percent of Java's land area—are politically classified as forest lands,[10] and most of these (like the rest of the island) were once covered in dense forest. Today, one-third of the

TABLE 1.1   Forest Lands of Java, by Provincial Unit and Forest Type
(Hectares)

Forest Type	Unit I (Central)	Unit II (East)	Unit III (West)	All Java
Production	599,255	872,166	567,030	2,018,451
Protection	74,818	334,274	321,996	731,088
Reserve	1,608	158,001	79,074	238,684
Total	655,681	1,364,441	968,100	2,988,223

SOURCE: Perum Perhutani 1981:6.

state forest lands are reserves or protected forests; the remaining two-thirds are for production (see table 1.1).

The State Forestry Corporation of Java (*Perum Perhutani* or SFC), controls and manages the island's production and protection forests; the Directorate General of Forest and Nature Conservancy administers reserve forests.[11] In addition to producing timber and forest products for government revenue, the SFC is mandated to manage production forests to ensure sustained timber yields and to contribute to the welfare of the people.

Teak (*Tectona grandis*) is by far the most economically important species grown on Java's state forest lands (table 1.2), accounting for approximately 92 percent of the SFC's annual income (Radite 1985). Appropriately dubbed the "backbone" of the SFC, teak forest is, on average, eleven times as valuable per hectare as other forest land.[12]

The environmental conditions in which teak grows best are relatively unfavorable to agriculture in Java. The deciduous tree, which grows as high as 40 meters, prefers a climate with a definite dry season of four to six months, well-drained soils containing some calcium, particularly those derived from limestone parent material, and elevations of up to 650 meters above sea level (van Steenis 1981:361). In some parts of Java, where teak grows well, the geologic layers of the earth's crust have folded; those closest to the surface appear to be of volcanic parent material but cover earlier limestone-based strata.

Under both natural conditions and cultivation in Java, teak tends to dominate the forest, making natural teak forest appear virtually the same as monoculture plantation forest. As the forest matures, various tubers and other small plants used for medicinal purposes or food emerge from the forest floor. Monkeys, boar, deer, pheasant, and a variety of other birds and small animals inhabit mature teak forest. Natural springs, some of them seasonal, occur sporadically throughout the forest. Local people generally protect these springs by regular and ritual maintenance.

TABLE 1.2 Distribution of Production Forest Lands, by Production
Type (Percentages)

Production Type	Unit I (Central)	Unit II (East)	Unit III (West)	All Java
Teak	52	65	30	52
Pine	30	22	30	27
Agathis	5	5	3	4
Rosewood	5	1	4	2
Altingia excelsa	—	—	10	3
Mahogany	4	—	12	4
Mangrove	2	—	6	2
Other forest	2	7	5	6
Total	100	100	100	100

SOURCE: Hendro Prastowo 1983:16.

Many of the island's nonteak forests, dominated by tropical pines, but
including rosewood, mahogany, agathis, and some mixed stands of other
species, have until recently been protection forests because of their
slopes. On the lower slopes, agathis and pine plantations are tapped for
their resins (copal and pine resin) and graded or processed for export;
pine is also used in the production of matches, chopsticks, low-grade
lumber for crates, and paper pulp. Within the past five years, some
protection forests have been reclassified as "limited production forests,"
where low-impact extraction of certain nontimber forest products, such
as resin tapping, are permitted. The reclassification has also ensured that
these forests will not be taken out of the jurisdiction of the State Forestry
Corporation and put under the management of the Department of Nature Conservancy. All production forestry activities are within the purview of the SFC's mandate.

There are also plans to intensify production activities in pine forests,
linked to the planned construction of one or more paper or pulp mills
in Java. These plans have arisen in response to the need for the SFC to
diversify its sources of income and not depend so heavily on teak. They
are also intended to change the nonteak management districts from
income consumers to income producers. Delays in the construction of
the mills have so far delayed the implementation of intensive pine
management.

The Forest Villages of Java

Although Java can claim only 3 percent of Indonesia's forests and 7
percent of its land area, in 1985 it housed 67 percent of the nation's 165

million people. In 1900, seventeen years after the demarcation of national forest lands began, the entire island had an estimated population of 28.4 million (Hasanu 1983:21). Nearly five times as many people lived there in 1985 (Republik Indonesia 1989:303). Some 63 percent of Java's population is rural; one-third of the rural populace are classified as forest villagers. Twenty-one million people live and work in villages nestled amongst the montane pine (*Pinus merkusii*) and mixed forests, tucked into irregularly shaped enclaves enclosed by extensive tracts of teak, or hugging the coastal mangroves (Djokonomo 1985:1).

Today, 6,172 Javanese villages are classified as "forest villages," villages set within or beside the state forest lands (Djokonomo 1985:1). The founders of many of these villages struck out into unknown or unworked territories during precolonial or colonial times, perhaps escaping overbearing rulers or seeking new farmland when the older settlements became full (Onghokham 1975; Palte 1983). But colonial foresters set boundaries on peasant settlements and agricultural lands nearly a century ago, after having forbidden them access to the valuable teak trees decades earlier. Thus peasants lost their option to flee overcrowded or oppressive conditions (Adas 1981:219).

Cities and multinational rural industries have absorbed some of the surplus labor from forest villages, but are neither sufficient in number nor attractive enough to accommodate all of it. At the same time, population and political dynamics have shifted the forest labor balance from scarcity to surplus while the distribution of forest resources between center and periphery has tilted the opposite way. As a result of these structural changes, today's managers of the State Forestry Corporation are faced with a different set of management problems than those which plagued their Dutch predecessors, who had to go to great lengths to acquire forest labor (Hasanu 1983:20). One visible outcome of the shifts in the land-labor ratio and in resource distribution has been the devastation of some forest areas and damage to much of the rest.

OVERVIEW

Although relatively few data are available from the precolonial period in Java, precolonial and colonial patterns of forest access, control, and claim still influence Indonesian forest managers today. For example, the notion of the Javanese king's domain is cited to justify forest management by the state. The precolonial and colonial legacies are the subject of part 2. Some similarities are noted between the controls imposed by precolonial Javanese rulers and the United East India Company. As the East India Company took control of more and more forest territory in the first stage of colonial management, there was an attempt to increase the center's ability to enforce controls on villagers' access to teak trees. In the second stage of colonial management, under the Dutch colonial state, state forest management bureaucracies emerged along with supporting ideologies of "scientific" management and forest laws. In this critical period the major mode of control shifted from control of timber and labor to land control. By the time the Dutch left Java in the mid-twentieth century, they had established the structures, ideology, and means of reproducing these in independent Indonesia. In the course of doing this, they also criminalized nearly all traditional local uses of forest land and timber.

Part 3 explores the changes in the nature of the Indonesian state, the contemporary political economy of forestry, and how these altered the practice of forest management. Chapter 4 examines overt and organized forest-based conflict during three recent periods: the Japanese occupation (1942–1945), the Indonesian revolution (1945–1949), and the Soekarno regime (1949–1966). These years, the most violent period in Indonesia's modern history, constitute a quarter-century of widespread forest destruction. The upheavals, however, did not bring about fundamental changes in the basic structure or the philosophical justification of forestry that the Dutch had constructed; in essence, they were only a spike in the otherwise continuous trajectory of Java's forest history. As shown in chapter 5, the primary difference between colonial and contemporary forestry in Java was caused by the destruction of the resource base during the physical and social revolutions. The structures, laws, and practice of state forest management have remained largely the same.

Part 4 presents two case studies of contemporary forms of forest-based resistance to external control, one in each of the major forest types of Java. In most nonteak forests, the greatest conflict occurs over forest land, not the trees. In teak forests, trees are the primary focus of conflict. For each field site, I describe the ecological, social-historical, and cultural circumstances, and the local outcomes of the criminalization of customary forest access rights.

Part 5, the conclusion, considers the need for an integrated approach to forestry as social forestry, including informed political choice in designing forest management schemes. I discuss some current forest policy issues in reference to possible structural and historical obstacles affecting the amelioration of relations between forest-dependent people and forest managers. Each side's resistance to the encroachment of the other on "their" forest as well as the persistence of forest management and of rural social structures that mediate forest access must be explicitly addressed before plantation forest management can be called sustainable.

PART TWO

Traditions of Forest Control in Java

TWO

Gaining Access to People and Trees

THE SAGE: Tell me the story of Java before there were any people.
ISMAYA: At that time the land was all forest, save for a rice field I myself culti-
vated at the foot of Mount Meru. I lived thus for ten thousand years . . . I am
the Guardian Spirit of Java . . . the King and Ancestor of all Javanese spirits
and kings and people.
A JAVANESE LEGEND ALLEGEDLY BASED ON THE *Babad Tanah Jawi.*
CITED IN FOWLER ET AL., *Java: A Garden Continuum.*

Batavians! Be amazed! Hear with wonder what I have to communicate. Our
fleets are destroyed, our trade languishes, our navigation is going to ruin—we
purchase with immense treasures, timber and other materials for ship-building
from the northern powers, and on Java we leave warlike and mercantile squad-
rons standing with their roots in the ground. Yes, the forests of Java have timber
enough to build a respectable navy in a short time, besides as many merchant
ships as we require. . . . In spite of all [the cutting] the forests of Java grow
as fast as they are cut, and would be inexhaustible under good care and
management.
DIRK VAN HOGENDORP, CA. 1801.[1] CITED IN RAFFLES, *The History of Java.*

Thickly carpeting the midsection of Java, from the north coast near Tegal to the shores of Tuban, and stretching inland to points on the southern coast, hundreds of square kilometers of teak enchanted the first Dutch mercantilists and ships' captains arriving in the seventeenth century (Brascamp 1921b:146).[2] Brascamp (1921a:134) called teak "the 'booty' that enticed us to Java," without which "our colonial history would have been much different." Unfortunately, the forests of Java proved not to grow as fast or as ubiquitously as van Hogendorp claimed, and some were exhausted before the end of the eighteenth century (du Quesne van Bruchem 1938a:821–38, 1938b:865–75, 1939:91–107).

From the seventeenth to the twentieth century Java's forests and for-est dwellers have served Javanese sultans and regents,[3] Dutch traders and officials, Chinese businessmen, Japanese war planners, and Indone-sian foresters. But forest people also have exerted some controls of their own. This chapter begins by discussing the probable constraints on forest access felt by Javanese forest dwellers prior to contact with the agents of the United East India Company (hereafter VOC, for Vereenigde Oost-

Indische Compagnie, or "the Company").[4] Scholars continue to debate the nature of rural life during this period. Most pertinent to this chapter are the de jure and de facto claims and controls of the Javanese sovereign and other elites over the forest dwellers' uses of the forest, and the nature of social cohesiveness in forest settlements, specifically, whether it was based on vertical or horizontal ties. I focus primarily on the first of these questions, as others have treated the second question at great length.[5]

The definition of the ruler's domain was important to both the agents of the VOC and the subsequently formed colonial state. The Company made treaties with sultans and princes, not villagers, granting the Europeans access to timber and labor; later, the colonial state claimed to have taken over the governance of the sultan's domains. The conscience of the colonial state was assuaged by the assurances of contemporary political analysts that forest products, forest land, and forest people had "belonged" to the sultan. During the colonial period, however, the expectations and forest access of both indigenous people and the VOC changed considerably.

TRADITIONAL ACCESS TO JAVA'S FORESTS

The population of Java in the year 1600, a decade before the arrival of the VOC, is estimated to have been approximately 3,400,000 (Reid 1984:152). How many of these inhabitants of an earlier era were forest dwellers is impossible to calculate. Yet, though many analysts of early Javanese history emphasize the "crowding" of population into the plains and water-rich hillsides where wet-rice could be grown, other evidence suggests that significant populations lived in the forested hillsides and mountains (Pigeaud 1962:471–72, 486; Moertono 1981:75). Moreover, the percentage of woody forest cover on the island was much higher before the arrival of the Dutch. This forest serviced the luxury and everyday wood needs of Java's kings[6] and commoners (Pigeaud 1962:509–10) and some swidden cultivation was practiced (Pigeaud 1962, IV:494; Dove 1985:13). The massive demands on the forest resources of the island, particularly on its armies of teak, began only with the arrival of the VOC.

In precolonial Java, many forest settlements were far from the effective daily control of any royal court (Pigeaud 1962, IV:390; Moertono 1981:75). This was true particularly for those settlements outside the court's heartland that were not tied to royal appanage lands or religious domains.[7] Moreover, people living at the fringes of court influence or at the crossroads of two or more opposing kingdoms were more able to reject the rules that the distant courts tried to impose. Dove (1985:14) suggests that in some of these areas only swidden, and in others, both swidden and settled wet-rice cultivation were practiced, indicating not only ecological adaptations, but also varying degrees of external influence on the rural social order and the local landscape. As a result of this variation in ecology and relative external control, some communities of forest dwellers on the peripheries of Javanese or Sundanese society may have had more sociological characteristics in common with other forest dwellers of Java than with peasants living in the alluvial wet-rice areas within the same districts. Shared characteristics included the types of community and household relationships to local or distant elites, people's survival strategies in the forest environment, and their de facto governance of access to the products and lands of the natural forest and its various states of conversion.

PRECOLONIAL FOREST DWELLERS

What constituted a forest "village" prior to the nineteenth century would be only partially the same as the present-day concept of a bounded political unit adjacent to or enclosed by state forest lands. Although precolonial and early colonial rural society was described by Dutch anthropologists (and others) as consisting of corporate, self-sufficient, harmonious political units called villages, such closed, interactive units based on territorial boundaries did not exist until the nineteenth century, well after the colonial state assumed control of Java and well after European observers began writing commentaries on their experiences in the Orient (Kumar 1980:577). Even then, it is unlikely that they were ever self-sufficient in terms of being uninvolved with external trade. The myth of the "traditional" closed, corporate Javanese village was created by the Dutch colonial state and has been perpetuated by the modern Indonesian state to facilitate land classification and to legitimate state control of certain lands—including forest lands (Breman 1980:3–4, 10–15). Recent research on the history of Javanese rural structure has shown that the rural landscape prior to and throughout the period of VOC rule was neither temporally nor spatially uniform. In general, society was organized vertically, meaning that a peasant household's relations with its patrons were at least as important as those with its territorial neighbors (Schrieke 1957; Onghokham 1975; Breman 1980; Kumar 1980).

One can imagine a patched sylvan countryside consisting of population concentrations closest to the courts and in the alluvial plains, with forest-enclosed settlements on the slopes of the forested volcanoes, in the hill country, or in the heart of the lowland teak forest. Households settled in contiguous territories did not necessarily pay tribute to the same lord; their allegiance depended on the circumstances of their settlement. Not all forest settlements were egalitarian; many of them probably fol-

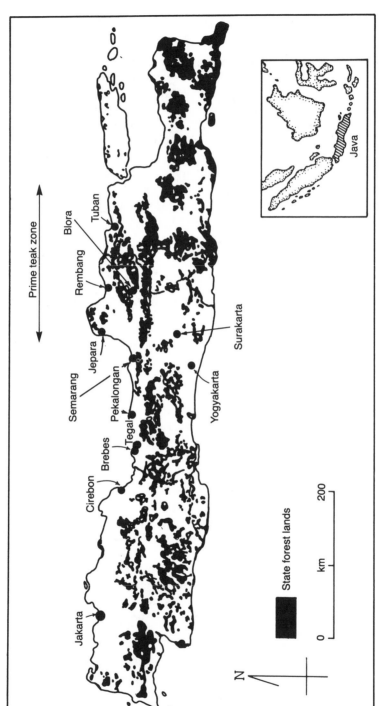

2.1. State Forest Lands on Java, 1938–1990

lowed a pattern similar to that described by Reid (1984:153) for precolonial Java in general: "The pattern was one of large patriarchal households, in which manual work was often restricted to numerous classes of
dependents or slaves."

Why did rural people cut down forests? Primarily, forests were
cleared for agricultural production and occasionally to create grasslands
to attract the animals people hunted for food. In addition, elites required timber for housing, stables, storehouses, and other buildings. In
the teak zone, or areas with access to it, teak was preferred for construction. In much of the prime teak zone in the east-central part of the island
teak would have been the only wood available in sufficient quantities to
provide housing. Teak grows best on Java in this climatic zone with its
monsoon climate and relatively long dry season. The soils here are well-
drained and porous, formed on limestone or other bedrock with considerable limestone deposits. Teak's outward spreading roots, large water
uptake, and broad leaf cover after five years of growth prevent the
proliferation of many other types of vegetation, especially woody species.
As a result, even the natural teak forests in this part of Java tend to look
like monocultural plantations. In both natural and plantation teak forest,
other woods are hardly available; those available are rarely as durable as
teak.

Most forest wood, including teak, was not forbidden by elite claimants
to rural dwellers needing it for housing, fencing, and cooking. Commoners also required shelter, however humble it was compared to the homes
of their patrons. Thus, except in very special cases—a closely guarded
royal forest or a forest with mystical significance—the actual prevention
of local people's use of forests and forest products was virtually inconceiv-
able (Pigeaud 1962, IV:456–57). Where a forest was strategically necessary to a king or other nobleman, myths about the supernatural repercussions of trespassing were spun out as an additional ideological control.

In addition to the fragmented peasant settlements in the forests, other
groups also farmed the forest. Very little is known about the origins or
ways of life of these groups, although there has been some degree of
conjecture in Dutch and Indonesian literature.[8] In any case, it is not clear
if these wandering groups were once a part of the larger society and
expelled or rendered "untouchable" or if they were of different ethnic
origins than migrants from a later period.

The cutting, hauling, and working of teak (sawing into boards, carv-
ing, carpentry) was done largely by one of these groups—the Kalangs.
Forest dwellers and swidden cultivators since at least the Majapahit era,
the Kalangs lived all over Central Java and in parts of East Java, and were
recognized as experts on forest matters (Altona 1922:498). Not only
were they put to work as skilled woodcutters, carpenters, and wood-

carvers in the royal compounds or in the service of lower-level aristocracy, but also whole communities were leased by the sultans and princes to Chinese (and later, Europeans) who had contracted timber rights to sections of the forest or were engaged in shipbuilding. By 1640 Sultan Agung had ordered a number of Kalangs to settle in his royal compound and work for him. So important were the Kalangs as royal woodcutters and woodworkers that when the Mataram kingdom split in 1755, the 6,000 resident Kalang families were divided between the two new sovereigns (de Jonge and van Deventer 1863:2:103).

Kalangs did not mix with Javanese in the same settlements. Aside from probable differences in agricultural styles and corresponding lifestyles, Kalang households were registered because their tribute obligations to the Javanese king differed from those of other rural dwellers. Each Kalang household had to pay a head tax of one Spanish dollar per year, a payment that entitled household members to cut wood anywhere they liked. They also could hire themselves out to private entrepreneurs as long as this work did not interfere with their obligations to cut and work wood for the ruler's warships and palace.

Although the Kalangs performed certain labor duties and paid head taxes to Javanese rulers, they retained a great deal of independence. They would not allow the sultan to regulate their trade; when he tried to levy a tax of 10 percent on all wood sold, they refused to cut any wood at all (Dagh Register Batavia 1681:7/21). The Kalangs, it seems, accepted the sultans' taxes on their persons and labor tributes, but their access to the forest—their source of life and livelihood—had to remain unfettered. The labor services represented both labor control and species control in that a specific species—teak—had to be cut or worked for the king. Controls, however, were loose: where, when, and how they cut the forest was largely up to them (except when ceremonial or sacred pieces of wood of specific dimensions were required by the king). This system conveniently fit with their swidden agriculture; as they cut sections of trees they could cultivate the land.

PRECOLONIAL FOREST IDEOLOGY AND CONTROL

Javanese kings and other elites worked out their arrangements for acquiring wood from the Kalangs and tolerated their swidden agriculture. At the same time, the ideology of the kingdom and the relationships between peasants and rulers reflected the courts' preference for land kept under settled agriculture, as a source of food and surplus to support the nonproductive elements of the state. In this context, the forest in Majapahit lore was conceived as a dangerous environment, populated by evil spirits, yet one which could be conquered and controlled by more powerful good forces such as those represented by the kings themselves (Lombard 1974:476–77; Dove 1985:19). Even the title of the "Babad Tanah Jawi," the Mataram kingdom's historical chronicle, can be translated either as "The History of Java's Land" or "The Clearing of Java's Land." The use of the word "Babad" in the official court chronicle of the kingdom's history indicates the ideological imperative to transform the landscape to one that better served the needs of and was more controllable by the state (Dove 1985:19).

Because the spirits of past kings were believed to remain in the site of a conquered palace, a victorious usurper of power would move the palace to a virgin forest site (Lombard 1974:478). In addition, every year the king and his entourage went on periodic journeys (progresses) throughout the kingdom, traveling through the forest much of the way, as a public display of his royalty and power. The progression through the forest was also a time for the king to collect tributes and maintain his connections with distant settlements over which he claimed sovereignty, and their leaders (Pigeaud 1962, IV:54–55, 78).

Javanese legends tell of aristocrats who leave the peace and asylum of their own or their fathers' kingdoms to confront enemies of both spirit and flesh in the forest: evil gods and goddesses, tigers, snakes, giants, and evil kings. They often meet ascetics in the forest, who advise the protagonists what to do to overcome their enemies. These ascetics have acquired knowledge, power, or enlightenment from their life in the forest, through both personal denial of worldly pleasures and successful confrontations with the spirits and other forest powers. For example, the famous story of Bimasuci finds Bima confronting various trials in the deep forest and later diving into the ocean to confront himself in miniature. The evils of the forest turn out to have been no more than parts of himself—his own demons, as it were. These stories always end with the heroes conquering the external or internal bogeymen and women of the forest and returning triumphant to the ordered and civilized realm. The stories counterpose cleared, cultivated, safe space with wild, primitive, and dangerous space but emphasize the value of both (cf. Lombard 1974:477–78).

KINGS AND COMMONERS: FOREST DOMAIN

In theory, a Javanese king claimed all territory that fell within his realm. Such a claim could not be defined as state land ownership as it would be today; nor did it match European conceptions of property at that time. Under conditions of relative population scarcity, the territory controlled was less of a royal concern than was controlling the people within that territory. People had to be mobilized to produce the surpluses needed by elites to maintain their living styles and realms. As a result, when a king claimed control over a particular expanse of territory, in fact what he claimed was the control of the labor of the land's residents and a portion of the product of their labor (Pigeaud 1962, IV:66, 472; Anderson 1963:48; Onghokham 1976:115; Moertono 1981:111–18).

In exchange for these rights in land, the cultivator was required to participate in compulsory labor services—to help construct roads and buildings, for military service, to open new lands, or to perform domestic labor for the ruler (Pigeaud 1962, IV:470). Compulsory labor was, in effect, a tax on the rights of access to land formally controlled by others, either nobles or local landowners (Onghokham 1975:19). In addition, certain proportions of the yields from these lands might be submitted as tribute in exchange for the rights of access. Naturally, the closer this land was located to the residence of the authority or his officials, the easier it was for the latter to exact tributes from the peasants who worked it.

In this way, both the Majapahit kings and early Mataram sultans did not seek to "own" land in the Western sense but were interested in extending their power by controlling populations who converted forest to agriculture. In lands or territory controlled by these kings, forest or waste land could be cleared by the bondsmen of a ruler, his nobles, the clergy, or others with grants of land. Indeed, rulers were constrained as to how much forest land they could convert to agriculture by the amount of labor they could command to work in remote locales (Pigeaud 1962, IV:471).

The extent of the Majapahit kings' and Mataram sultans' control over labor in remote (forest) areas was debated at great length in the nineteenth and early twentieth centuries by those who wished to justify state control over forest and waste lands and those who believed unrestricted state control violated the traditional rights and customary law (*hukum adat*) of the Javanese people (Holleman 1981:lv–lvii). The "outer provinces" of the Mataram kingdom included the *mancanegara* (external territories) of Banyumas, Madiun, Kediri, and Blitar and the *pasisiran* (maritime provinces) of old Tegal, Pekalongan, Pemalang, Demak, Pati, Jepara, Rembang, Tuban, Surabaya, and Bawean and Madura islands. These territories were generally beyond the court's direct influence and largely unaffected by the royal appanage system (Holleman 1981:151–52). They also contained a considerable chunk of the island's teak forest.

Like rulers and noble appanage holders, people granted rights in land could mobilize their own clients to clear forest for agriculture or to intensify cultivation by building wet-rice terraces (*sawah*) where environmental conditions—and political controls—were conducive to it (Pigeaud 1962:300, 470–72; Dove 1985:13–15). If laborers came from outside the territory, as they apparently often did, giving them rights in the land would integrate them into the settlement area through their vertical ties with those who granted them access to forest or waste land for clearing. Newcomers did not have the same kind of status or decision-making power within a village territory as old-timers or village founders. Nevertheless, they could earn a living. Patrons of any social level could expand their clientele and their political influence by opening new land. Similarly, peasants could clear forest without sponsorship and, in the most remote or difficult access areas, acquire some degree of independence (Breman 1980:31).

Relationships between ruler and ruled or patron and client were not based solely on the exchange of access to land and the promise of protection services for tribute of goods or labor. People in isolated forest settlements during Majapahit rule (which lasted until the fourteenth century) could be "assigned" by the king to create or maintain grasslands in the forest for the royal hunt, and to assist in that hunt when the king arrived (Dove 1985:18). In exchange, the king might "allow" the community access to rangelands for their own hunting or for grazing cattle. This official endowment of forest access rights to the forest dwellers in some areas included rights to cut timber and collect nontimber forest products such as fresh turtle eggs along the forested shores of the southeast coast and wild foods, spices, and medicinal plants (tubers, roots, and leaves) (Pigeaud 1962, IV:494). Of course, as both Pigeaud (1962, IV:456–571) and Moertono (1981:115–18) point out, such concessions were merely token symbols of royal control—given the practical difficulties of enforcing any restrictions from a great distance. By granting access, or at least not restricting it, the kings sought to ensure the loyalty of forest dwellers in case competing elites (equally distant) sought their allegiance.

Forest people could benefit from the king's pronouncement of sovereignty, even though in the daily rhythm of their lives his power was nominal. On the positive side, local people could invoke the king's name if others tried to lay claim to the products of the surrounding forests. The villagers' proclamations of loyalty would influence outsiders' views of the structure of claim and of power, serving to protect the villagers from unwanted interventions. On the other hand, the king's hunting trips could be costly to the keepers of the hunting grounds (and the residents of villages along the way) who provided rice and other foods for the duration of the hunt (Pigeaud 1962, IV:61–64). Belief in the king's mystical powers, however, could cause the peasants to interpret such concessions as honors, provided his requests did not cause great suffering. Moreover, once the king's hunt had departed, local people returned to their de facto control and routine exploitation of the forest and its products.

Rural people could exercise some bargaining power for control of their labor service by moving and switching allegiance to a different lord. Migrations sometimes involved the movement of great masses of people (Schrieke 1957:301; Onghokham 1975:20). Individuals, families, and whole communities moved from one place to another to escape the excessive demands of particular regional leaders; to reestablish themselves in settlements of various sizes after famines, wars, epidemics, or other natural disasters; or to establish an independent existence. Opportunities and incentives for moving were abundant because of low population densities prior to the nineteenth century, the abundance of uncultivated forest or waste land, and the competition between elites for access to labor and produce (Moertono 1981:6). The decision to move or not to move would be influenced by a family's assessment of the costs and benefits of living near their lord or living in a remote corner of a forest claimed—but not patrolled—by that lord. Whether moved by the victor of a dynastic war or forced to flee the depredations of nature or humans, many Javanese peasants migrated prior to the nineteenth-century beginning of colonial rule.

When the agents of the VOC arrived, they made some efforts to deal directly with villagers or wood merchants but could not sidestep the island's noble rulers. As the notion of what constituted domain and the negotiability of domain changed, the usurpation of rural allegiance was also attempted and, at least on paper, achieved by the VOC in some territories.

THE VOC: CONTROLLING TREES AND PEOPLE

Initially, the Dutch wanted not to sell teak, but to use it to build ships crucial to maintaining the power they had enjoyed throughout their "Golden Age" in the seventeenth century.[9] The strength of their navy had made the Dutch the most powerful traders in the world, and Amsterdam was the Singapore of seventeenth-century Europe. The dense, durable teak was among the finest species in the world for ships' timber, and the tall, straight trees, more numerous than people in some parts of the island, made majestic masts for the most formidable battleships. Moreover, teak was reputed to hold up better than European wood (Zwart 1930:974). The prospect of reclaiming seapower, a century after the waning of Dutch supremacy, had thrilled van Hogendorp, and it was little wonder.

Before founding Batavia in 1619, the Dutch had constructed a wharf on an island off the coast, where they built ships through at least the middle of the next century. Teak for construction was shipped from Jepara to Batavia as early as 1622, and from at least 1627 there was a wood market in Batavia supplying both private entrepreneurs and the buyers for the VOC (de Haan 1910, in Boomgaard 1987:6).

Yet the VOC's first attempts to establish itself and acquire the desired products of Java were neither easy nor uniformly successful. Establishing offices, hiring labor, and gaining access to rice and timber required negotiation with the Javanese sovereigns and their officials. Given the VOC interest in gaining immediate access to teak, to places to build ships, and to additional land for offices and storehouses, it would seem that dealing directly with a single, all-powerful "owner" was easier for VOC officials than dealing with the variable usufruct rights of rural people in different parts of the forest. Some, however, did direct business with Chinese traders and other "producers" who sponsored woodcutting. Despite their efforts to bypass the tribute- and tax-collecting rulers, however, no teak could be loaded onto Dutch ships without the explicit permission of a Javanese prince, king, or noble (Brascamp 1921a:147; Boomgaard 1987:7).

Negotiations meant gifts. In 1651, when the first Dutch trade office was established in Jepara to handle the trade in teak and sugar, Governor-General Carel Reiniersz sent a letter to the susuhunan of Mataram explaining the appointment of Dirk Schouten as resident there. Accompanying the letter was a "token of friendship," consisting of expensive treasures from Europe, Persia, and other parts of the world: lace, cloth, rosewater, musk balls, Spanish wine, a diamond ring, black amber, aloes wood, and other luxuries (Brascamp 1920:439). Shortly thereafter, Schouten left on a mission to Persia and was replaced by Jacob Backer, assisted by Bernard Volsch (ibid., 438). The susuhunan waffled between apparent compliance and refusal to allow the export of rice and wood from his region (Brascamp 1921a:146).[10] The sunan's regional officials in the Jepara area also forbade the export of wood from their regions unless they, too, were sent gifts; the governor-general accordingly sent them an elephant (Brascamp 1921a:149).

Eventually contracts were made and deliveries of wood from the hinterlands to the VOC shipyards in Jepara began. In 1677 a treaty between Jacobus Couper of the VOC and Susuhunan Amangkurat of Mataram allowed the Dutch to establish a shipbuilding center at Rembang (Brascamp 1923:640). In accordance with contemporary practice, the treaty put thirty-six villages in the Rembang region in the service of the Company for forest laboring tasks such as logging, hewing beams, and hauling timber (using draft animals, primarily water buffalo) (Brascamp 1923:640). Some of these forest villages were inhabited by the Kalangs. The susuhunan had appointed a Javanese palace noble as the head of the Kalangs, the temenggung of Lamongan. The Company contracted wood through this temenggung but had some difficulties accepting the terms set by the Kalang woodcutters. The problem was that the temenggung could not control the actual exchange of wood for payment; he could only arrange the cutting agreement between the woodcutters and the Company agents. Further, when disagreements over other matters developed, the Kalangs cut back on wood deliveries or did not send them at all.

The Company, of course, wanted to work through a controllable and locally powerful intermediary—someone they could regard as the leader of the Kalangs. But they were faced with a double problem: the woodcutters refused to be bound by contracts—they were prepared only to cut and deliver the trees they wanted to cut—and they were still bound to deliver wood for the sultan. Only in the performance of the king's services did the temenggung have authority to determine where and when they cut and delivered teak. Outside of that, arrangements had to be made directly with the Kalangs. As a result, the Dutch sought to control the Kalang woodcutters by gaining control over or allying with the sultan. Eventually, though the Dagh Register does not explain exactly how, the Kalang intermediary delivered the desired wood to the Company's agents (Dagh Register 1679:425–26; 1680:688; and 1681:159).

From the late seventeenth through the mid-eighteenth century, the authority to control forest laborers gradually shifted. After the 1677 agreement Company agents gained access to Kalang labor to work in the Company's shipyards on the northeast coast. At that time, the sultan still collected head taxes from the Kalangs and influenced their agreements to deliver wood to the Company. After the treaty of 1705 local rulers were required to provide Kalang workers to the Company and were not to exact head taxes; the tax was to be collected by Company agents and paid to the sultan (Brascamp 1923:642). After the agreements of 1743 and 1745, when the northeast coast of Java was ceded to the Company, Company regulations were applied to the administration and control of both Kalang and Javanese communities. By this time, the regents of Pekalongan and Jepara were to handle the administration of the Kalangs, and were responsible for collecting head taxes to be paid to the Company.[11]

Apparently, however, the pressure applied by the temenggung and his assistants to force Kalangs to cut wood for delivery to the Company often rendered the situation difficult. Their threats to chain the Kalangs and send them to the sunan resulted in the outright refusal of the Kalangs to work. The Kalangs expressed their dissatisfaction further by staging a small but symbolically significant attack on the temenggung's customers. In 1770 they attacked the Dutch fort at Joana, killing a corporal and four other people and burning the ammunition storehouse and the resident's rice storehouse. In the quelling of the uprising, ten protesters and ten other people were killed. After this incident, the Kalangs were placed under the administration of the regent of Pati (van der Chijs 1891, 8:654).[12]

The VOC did not restrict its timber deals to Rembang, Jepara, and Pekalongan. In January 1681 a Company agent, van Dyck, had contracted with the three princes of Cirebon to receive deliveries of wood, rice, sugar, and other supplies for the Company. In exchange for the Company's "protection" the princes agreed to supply only the Company (Brascamp 1922b:177–78). By November 1684 the same princes granted the VOC rights to cut specific quantities of wood from the Cirebon hinterland, as well as access to forest laborers (Brascamp 1924a:913). The VOC still had to pay a percentage of every hundred boards cut to the regent of Indramayu (Brascamp 1923:639–41). The amount due the regent was often disputed, with the Javanese ruler demanding 4, 40, or 24 percent at various times. The VOC wanted their agent to negotiate terms similar to those agreed to by the sunan in the 1677 contract—a 2 percent delivery fee. Nevertheless, in Cirebon, the customary tax had been 10 percent (ibid.).

Upon the approval of the regents of Priangan, the forest laborers became subjects of the Dutch resident of Cirebon. These early agreements were of an informal nature, but the people of Priangan were required to begin work immediately in the Cirebon forests (Brascamp 1924a:915). The arrangements were formalized in 1705, when a new contract was confirmed with the susuhunan, ceding the districts of Pamanukan, Indramayu, and Gabang to the VOC, and freeing Cirebon from the suzerainty of the susuhunan. Thenceforth, Cirebon was virtually at the VOC's disposal (Brascamp 1924a:910; 1923:641).

Elephants and English lace were no longer enough to secure the treaties. The Company's intentions were being realized through Javanese rulers or directly; those nobles who refused to follow the path set by the VOC were often replaced. In 1704 Susuhunan Adipatih Anom, heir to the Mataram throne since the death of Amangkurat II in 1703, was replaced by the Dutch with Amangkurat's elder brother, Pangeran Puger. Pangeran Puger, henceforth called Susuhunan Pakubuwana I, was more amenable to Dutch requests. His nephew fled to eastern Mataram, but continued to influence his own network of followers. The Dutch and their favored sovereign fought the real heir of Mataram until July 1708, when he and his family were exiled to the island of Ceylon (Brascamp 1923:640; Vlekke 1960:183).

The VOC became increasingly interested in territorial control but could not impose it uniformly. On July 4, 1705, Herman de Wilde left the north coast for the capital of Mataram with an army of 1,833 "Europeans"[13] and 2,016 "natives," plus the usual artillery, aiming to conquer those districts of the sultanate that had not yet been ceded to the VOC. One of de Wilde's primary goals was to secure access to more teak because so much had been cut along the north coast and the shipbuilding industry was threatened. In the treaty of October 5 de Wilde succeeded in his task. He also obtained permission to move the VOC's coastal headquarters from Jepara to Semarang and reaffirmed its trade monopoly (Brascamp 1923:637, 640).

Wood deliveries remained part of the VOC-Mataram relationship. The forests from which the VOC first acquired timber were those of Jepara, Rembang, Pekalongan, Waleri, and Brebes. Treaties made in 1677, 1705, and 1733 fixed the annual teak quotas to be delivered to Company coastal posts. Beginning in 1733 the quota to Demak was set at 3,000 beams, to Waleri, 2,000 beams, to Brebes, 1,500 beams, and to Jepara, 2,000 large and 2,000 small beams (Brascamp 1922a:133–39). Quotas were determined by the estimated extent of the supply forests and the feasibility of transporting the wood to the coast by teams of buffalo (Raffles 1817, I:181). While the people could only sell teak to or build ships for the Company, rural people and the regents retained their rights to cut the wood they needed for subsistence or for building their own boats. By the early eighteenth century, a water-powered sawmill had been constructed at Jepara, and a wind-powered sawmill at Brebes (Brascamp 1922a:134).

Direct control of the northeastern pasisiran area, later known as Java's Northeast Coast, was relinquished by the Mataram sultan to the VOC in 1743. Later, forested Jipang in the primary teak zone was annexed in 1812 by the colonial state; the state annexed the southern portions of the pasisiran and the mancanegara in 1830 (Hatley et al. 1984:21).

The VOC's control of forest labor was based on treaties with regional Javanese rulers. These treaties gave the VOC access to Kalangs and presumably other forest laborers needed to construct and repair ships or to cut wood. Such forest laborers were exempt both from head taxes and from the nonforest labor services (*heerendiensten*) exacted from the peasantry by regional rulers and the sultan (Brascamp 1922a:131–32; 1923:642). The compulsory forest labor services in the forest districts became known as *blandongdiensten;* the woodcutters were called *blandong*.[14] Boomgaard (1987:13) calculated that the Company employed relatively few corvée laborers each year: about 1,600 in 1776 and 2,200 in 1787.[15] By Daendels's time, in 1809, some 5,050 blandong were employed in the forests.[16]

Local Javanese officials, the regents, mustered the necessary numbers of teak-hauling buffalo from the peasants in their jurisdictions (Raffles 1817, I:181), who then worked under Dutch or German overseers (Brascamp 1922:959). Most overseers had been soldiers working for the

VOC. As early as 1684, however, the Company sent some German wood-cutters to supervise forest activities in Cirebon (Boomgaard 1987:8).

At first, a selective cutting system was employed. In 1777, rather than concentrating efforts in limited sections of the forest, selective cutting was practiced throughout a regency, and payment per beam was made according to its size. Only trees yielding beams of at least 18 Rhineland feet (one Rhineland foot = .3767 meters) and 9 to 10 inches in diameter were felled. The dimensions of the beams delivered from Tegal, Pekalongan, Cirebon, and Pemalang were smaller. Cutting took place in logging sites where the overseers could keep a close watch on the woodcutters. Clearcutting in parcels was not employed until 1801, although it had been suggested as early as 1797 (ibid., 15–17).

Payment for commissioned teak beams, paid to the regents, ranged from sixteen pence for cutting and hauling a beam 18 to 20 feet long and 9 to 10 inches wide to forty-eight stuivers for a beam 31 to 36 feet long and from 13 to 15 inches wide.[17] The regents demanded advance payment for wood deliveries beyond the commissioned quota, which required extra forest labor and cost 50 percent more. Bent wood and other shipbuilding timbers were priced according to weight. Standards for "acceptable" timber quality were set by the Company (Raffles 1817, I:181–82; Zwart 1938:83).

Dragging beams to the coast or a river (for transport to the coast) took three to five days from the closest forests. As the sites became more distant, particularly in 1776 when the susuhunan of Surakarta gave permission to cut in the magnificent forests of Blora, hauling logs to Rembang or Surabaya could take twelve to fifteen days, and the walk back to the forest another five. The effect on the livestock was devastating, and the buffalo population in these locales fell drastically (Brascamp 1920:668; Lugt 1933:30).[18] One Dutch official reported in 1800 the arrival in Rembang of a tree so large that eighty buffalo were used to drag it there; some ten of the animals died en route (Boomgaard 1987:16). This loss of animals affected not only the Company's immediate capacity for transporting timber, but also the agricultural capacities of the peasants forced to use their animals.

Throughout the period of VOC control, shipbuilding remained the primary purpose of VOC-sponsored teak cutting. The wood needs of the shipbuilders were not small. For the largest ships, some 160 feet long, the main mast would measure 94 feet high with a circumference of 26 "palms" around the base. The smallest masts on such a ship measured 26 feet high and were 5½ palms around the base (Zwart 1938:78). In 1779 the Company had a fleet of 104 ships: 56 of 400 lasts (1 last = 2 tons) and 48 of 300 to 350 lasts. Thirty-seven of these were in the Indies that year (Zwart 1938:79). In 1780 Governor van den Burgh estimated that of

Rembang's 3,000-beam quota, some 1,600 to 2,000 beams were used in the shipyard (ibid., 83).

The VOC tried to monopolize shipbuilding rights in the mid-eighteenth century, with varying degrees of success. Java's north coast was heavily traveled by sailing vessels, and Raffles (1817) estimated that 50,000 to 60,000 beams were delivered annually to private concerns. In 1762 both private shipbuilding and the sale of ships to other countries were forbidden (Furnivall 1944:86). Despite the monopoly, private (i.e., non-VOC) enterprises built ships and exported teak. Between 1773 and 1775 permits were available to build ships, but only for ships less than 80 feet in length. On ships larger than 8 lasts, a 10 percent tax was levied (ibid., 87).

As Furnivall (1944:87) pointed out, however, "everything could be arranged."

> In 1774 . . . the Chinese Captain of Rembang got permission to build annually six ships of 20–25 lasts without paying the 10 percent tax. The captain made his living from shipbuilding and thus the government let him keep a sufficient means of living. The 10 percent could also be discounted for ships built (with government consent) for the development of private navigation and commerce. In the 1774–75 fiscal year, this 10 percent tax had earned only 614 Rijks dollars [*sic*].

All this forest cutting was not without environmental consequences. By 1796 forest destruction had become so widespread that the VOC formed a commission to investigate the state of the forests of Jepara and Rembang. The commission recommended halting all timber cutting in the two regions and reducing log quotas in Blora by 50 percent. Despite these recommendations, overcutting of the forests continued (Hasanu 1983:9).[19] Efforts to protect the rapidly depleted forests of the western parts of the teak zone (e.g., Pemalang, Demak, and Batang) by restricting all cutting had been tried earlier in the century, with mixed results (Boomgaard 1987:20–21).

The monetary interests of individual VOC officials conflicted with those of the company they worked for, and were partially responsible for the persistent forest destruction. In 1797 the governor of Northeast Java, P. G. van Overstraten, blamed the destruction of the forests largely on residents who received commissions on the "legal" cut and also sponsored illegal private woodcutting (Cordes 1881:192; Soepardi 1974a:54). The resident of Rembang annually earned 40,000 rijks-daalders (Spanish real) from the cutting of teak forests in his residency (Lugt 1933:31).[20] The official proceeds accruing to this teak-rich residency remained at least this high until the administration of Governor-General Daendels (1808–1811), while in Cirebon Residency the proceeds of wood deliveries under Daendels amounted to 17,000 rijks-daalders annually (Brascamp 1922c:1096). This was not the first time that sanctioned and forbidden forms of teak harvest and sale would cause concern about the fate of the forest.

In addition, logging practices were inefficient and damaging to the soil. Some token efforts were made to replant in the last few decades of VOC control. Even in these rare locales, seeds were broadcast, not sown. Moreover, where no broadcasting was done, selective cutting would have restricted the growth of new trees to those forest gaps where enough light filtered through the canopy to allow germination and establishment of new seedlings.

As the coastal teak forests were depleted and trees had to be sought further inland, private firms gained a competitive edge on the VOC. Private shipbuilders rented forest villages not leased by the Company and bought timber that did not meet Company standards. Private contractors could compete, despite the Company's claims on teak, because they were willing to pay higher wages to laborers for hauling wood to the coast from distant inland logging sites (Raffles 1817, I:182). By 1800 some sixty-seven villages in Rembang, Lasem, and Tuban had been leased to private logging firms, including firms headed by the residents of Rembang and Joana; additional villages had been rented by the sunan to Chinese timbermen (Raffles 1817, I:184–85; Boomgaard 1987:14).

The end of an era was approaching. Both the form of Dutch involvement in Java and the nature of their control over the island's forests would change after the next two decades of changes in the colony's rulers and its forests. After the VOC's bankruptcy in 1796 degradation and poor management (by today's standards) persisted until the arrival in Java of Marshal Daendels (Schuitemaker 1950:38). When Daendels arrived to govern the "new" Dutch colony, the foundations for a "scientific" state forest management system based on land, species, and labor control were put in place.

THREE

The Emergence of "Scientific" Forestry in Colonial Java

Historians have paid too much attention to revolutions and too little to the creation of political stability. . . . Stability, no less than revolution, may have its own kind of Terror.

E. P. THOMPSON, *Whigs and Hunters*

Of all these changes, the restriction of forest use was one of the most galling to the peasants; resources that had always been as free as the air they breathed and that remained close at hand were suddenly being denied to them. Forestry officials might be well-intentioned—though they seemed to be as concerned with forest revenue as with conservation—but their actions deprived peasants of what seemed natural rights. . . . Such restrictions constituted . . . a leading grievance in more than one Southeast Asian peasant movement.

JAMES C. SCOTT, *The Moral Economy of the Peasant*

The nineteenth century was a turning point in forest management and the forms of state control over the teak and nonteak forests of Java. It was then that a bureaucratic, colonial Forest Service drew boundaries between forest and agricultural land—on maps and in the field—and established police forces to restrict people's access to trees and other forest products. Through a process of trial and error, regulations for profitable tree plantation management were encoded in colonial law, as were the philosophies of forest conservation for hydrological purposes. The ideology of "scientific" forestry was embraced by the colonial state and its foresters, while local institutions of forest access and property were gradually phased out of the legal discourse.[1] The ideas of this period, and the impacts of these policies on the lives of forest-dwelling people, remain significant today; the last forest laws effected by the Dutch government were drawn up in the late 1920s and continue to dictate contemporary Indonesian forestry.

This period was also the beginning of the foresters' great concern with their eminent rights of domain over land, timber, and the demarcation of forest boundaries. Their possessiveness is seen today in the persistent use of the terms of exclusion that criminalize customary rights of access to forest products and land: "forest theft," "encroachment," "squatting," and "illegal grazing." Forest dwellers continued to engage in these activities, despite the pejorative labels, in their practice of everyday life. They had to resist the state's increasing resource control in order to subsist, and thus were making, in effect, a political statement. As the twentieth century wore on, peasants continued to counter-appropriate forest land and species. Their actions, and the formalization of the colonial state's self-declared rights to the forest, set the stage for the complex conflicts that continue between foresters and forest villagers today.

CONSOLIDATING CONTROL: THE FORESTS OF JAVA UNDER THE COLONIAL STATE

The VOC was bankrupt by the end of the eighteenth century, largely because of the depredations and corruption of its own officials. In 1796 the Company's directors were replaced by a committee appointed by the government of the Netherlands. As of December 31, 1799, when the VOC's charter expired, the Dutch state replaced the Company as proprietor and administrator. The Batavian Republic inherited an extensive and wealthy colony and assumed the VOC's debt of 134 million guilders (Vlekke 1960:239). From 1808 to 1811, when Holland was under Napoleonic rule, Marshal Daendels served as governor-general of Java. Soon after the Napoleonic annexation of Holland, the English invaded Java. Stamford Raffles served as lieutenant-governor in Java from 1811 to 1815. The English placed William of Orange on the Dutch throne, and on August 19, 1816, John Fendall, the English successor to Raffles, formally transferred Java to three Dutch commissioners-general (Irwin 1967:28–35).[2]

When Governor-General Daendels arrived in Java in 1808, he organized the exploitation of Java's teak forests, passed edicts on appropriate management, and secured the government's monopoly on teak, forest labor, and shipbuilding. For the first time in the colony's history, a quasi-modern government forest service, the *Dienst van het Boschwezen,* was created, with "rights" to control land, trees, and forest labor (Soepardi 1974a:20).[3] At the time, only teak timber was valued for its profits and shipbuilding; thus the domain of this early forest service was limited to lands where teak grew or could be grown.

Four elements in Daendels's system would retain at least philosophical importance through the ensuing two centuries:

The declaration of all forests as the domain of the state (*Landsdomein*), to be managed for the benefit of the state.
The assignment of forest management to a branch of the civil service created expressly for that purpose.

The division of the forest into tracts (*percelen*) to be logged and re-planted on a rotating basis.

The restriction of villagers' access to teak for commercial purposes, allowing them only to collect deadwood and nontimber forest products freely.[4]

In three years, Daendels was unable to secure the apparatus of the state forest management agency. Though his ideas were written down as regulations and carried out in the field during his rule, he was not in power long enough to ensure their continuity. Key components of Daendels's plans changed during the nineteenth and twentieth centuries, namely, the structure of the Forest Service, the scale of its power, and the elimination of the blandong labor services (Schuitemaker 1950:39). Nevertheless, his attempt to implement a kind of a state forest management agency was an important step influencing the Forest Service born in the mid-nineteenth century.

Daendels was determined to manage the teak forests so the colonial state could profit from them for decades to come. He required the inspector general to report any incidents of high-level corruption, slackness in duty, or breaking the oath of office, and to swear "he would never scheme with wood traders, award them wood, or steal wood himself" (Soepardi 1974a:54–55). He also established the first regulations punishing misuse of the forest as defined by the state. The testimony of a "well-known person of good name" that a Javanese or Chinese had been caught "red-handed" or "suspiciously wandering without purpose in the forest" was sufficient cause for imprisonment. The maximum penalties for forest criminals were ten years in prison or the payment of a fine of 200 rijks dollars. Two-thirds of this fine went to the state and one-third to the person who reported the crime. Appeals could be made, but punishments would be reduced only to exile or shorter prison terms (van der Chijs 1896, 15:120–21). These regulations represented a harsh change from previous circumstances, but they were difficult to enforce; no forest police were yet patrolling.

Besides passing edicts concerning the technical aspects of forest management (issued August 21, 1808), Daendels appointed *bosgangers*, or subdistrict forest managers. The bosgangers oversaw logging, replanting, collection of teak seeds, and the girdling of trees the year before they were to be cut (Soepardi 1974a:55–56). Like the forest overseers working for the VOC, Daendels's bosgangers were mostly ex-soldiers (Brascamp 1917:207).

Daendels eliminated all private forest exploitation, and monopolized the trade and transport of teak timber for the state. This meant that all leases of villages and the forests they were to cut for private entrepreneurs were voided as well (Boomgaard 1987:23). In Rembang Residency, forest laborers, their village lands, and the adjacent forest lands were placed under direct administration of a Board of Forests (Furnivall 1944:65). Each woodcutter was given one catty (approximately 1.5 kilogram) of hulled rice a day and a small annual allowance of iron, salt, and gunpowder (Raffles 1817, I:183). The laborers worked eight to fourteen days in the forest at a stretch, during the work season (February to November), and were allowed eight to fourteen days' rest after each period of work (Boomgaard 1987:23).

Daendels's successor during the five-year interlude of English control in Java, Lieutenant-Governor Stamford Raffles, was determined to save money, and dealt a crushing blow to many of Daendels's state forest management measures. He felt that the state was overinvolved in forest management and that the system was expensive and unnecessary. Raffles retracted almost all of the forestry organizational reforms implemented by Daendels. Only in Rembang was a special forest superintendent appointed; in other residencies, the task of forest administration and oversight fell to the residents (Raffles 1817, I:184).

Raffles believed that the Dutch had sponsored the cutting of an excessive quantity of poor teak timber, below the quality required by contemporary shipbuilding standards. Believing that Indian teak was of much higher quality, he reasoned that making Javanese teak competitive within the trading sphere of the British empire would be too costly. Raffles felt the government monopoly on teak sale and shipbuilding created demands on government funds to police its interests. Moreover, he observed, forest laborers were oppressed and lowering wood prices would only cause them greater hardship (Raffles 1817, I:183).

Raffles initiated a policy of reserving the largest and best forests for the state and allowing private entrepreneurs to lease and log the rest (ibid.). Raffles also parceled out forest land as "gifts" to Javanese elites. In 1813, for example, he gave "Raden Adipatty Singasarie Penathan Djoeda . . . and his heirs forever . . . a tract of forestland situated in the District of Brebes [in then Residency Tegal] as a free gift. . . . This land was then [to be] entirely free from cultivation and habitation" (Zwart 1934:547). In his *History of Java*, Raffles was vague about his own conservation measures, but estimated that 40,000 or 50,000 beams could be extracted each year without damage. He was also more lenient in prosecuting forest "crimes." Not only did he want to save money, but he had also relinquished the government's absolute monopoly on teak. Philosophically, this was a major departure from previous state and VOC forest policies.

Another, perhaps unexpected, result of Raffles's "liberalization" of

Daendels's forest management plans was the beginning of a long debate over the meaning of the words used in British treaties with the Javanese sultan and sunan. It remained unclear whether the susuhunan was granting the British rights to timber or to the land on which it grew. The text of the 1811 agreement between the English and the sunan indicates that the sunan's claim to sovereignty over the land was not at that time (and probably not in earlier times) being transferred:

> His Highness reserves to the Honerable [*sic*] East Indian Company the exclusive privilege of felling teak and other timber for shipbuilding, in the forests of His dominions, and H H further engages to supply labourers for that purpose and for the transportation of the same to the limits of H H dominions and such labourers shall in every instance be paid by the British government at fair and equitable rates. ['Het gouvernement en de djatibosschen in Soerakarta," 1917:697]

A treaty signed the next year reestablished British access to timber and labor, while indicating that the sultan retained his rights to the land, or at least his rights to rule a particular territory and its inhabitants. "H H secures to the British Government the sole right and property of the teak timber within the whole of the country *subject to His administrations*" (ibid., 698, emphasis added). Later, Dutch writers of the first set of scientific forestry laws and other colonial legal documents interpreted the control of the Javanese ruler over land or territory as being equivalent to Western property rights, which connote ownership. This interpretation did not allow for the more complex aspects of access to land and land-based resources operating in Java's forests at the time. Local people, regional rulers, and entrepreneurs were engaged in a "layered" system of rights to control or use the forest and its products. This system was flexible and adapted to different needs and different circumstances.

When the Dutch reassumed control of Java in 1816 they adopted some of Raffles's more profitable ideas, but also reestablished the Forest Board of Daendels's time. In 1826 the commissioners-general abolished the Forest Board and transferred control over the forests and forest laborers to individual residents, thus decentralizing control over the forests (Boomgaard 1987:26). Whatever efforts these residents made to regulate forest cutting, however, conflicting objectives from other government sectors accelerated the process. During the Java War (1825–30), for example, the state cut many teak beams and logs in Central Java to build forts and bridges and to block roads (Soepardi 1974a:58–59).

In 1832, under the Cultivation System,[5] the forests were brought under the jurisdiction of the Director of Cultures, though the residents retained effective administrative control over the forests in their own districts (Cordes 1881:212). Teak forests were cut heavily with little regard for logging regulations. The tallest, straightest trees were selected to build sugar factories, coffee warehouses, tobacco-drying sheds, and housing compounds. An extensive road system was built through sections of the teak forest complex to deliver the prized logs to sawmills and woodworking centers (Schuitemaker 1950:40). Luxurious teak homes were constructed for plantation managers and highly placed personnel. In addition, roasting coffee, drying tobacco, and industrial processing of sugar cane from the extensive government plantations required tremendous quantities of fuel. In two regencies of Semarang Residency, 60,000 logs were cut just to build tobacco-drying sheds, while in Pekalongan Residency 24,000 cubic feet of firewood were cut annually for sugar refining. By regulations effective between 1830 and 1836, local people were required to cut and haul wood to the factories. After that year, factories were assigned their own forests from which they were permitted to cut their fuel. Apparently, the factories did very little reforestation. Later, when these enterprises were no longer subsidized by wood deliveries, they split the thick walls of the old sheds to build more sheds or to sell (Cordes 1881:208–10; Departemen Kehutanan 1986, I:67).

Between 1837 and 1840 an average of 16,300 blandongs were employed annually by the state; until 1843 their average annual teak cut was approximately 100,000 logs. Twenty years later this average annual cut had nearly doubled to 175,000 logs (Boomgaard 1987:27), and unauthorized teak cutting, as always, continued. Private shipbuilders, who were legally required to purchase wood from the government, obtained teak from Chinese, Arab, and European middlemen with personal connections in forest villages (Zwart 1930:974).

The other drain on forest resources imposed by the nineteenth-century colonial government was the construction of roads and railroads (Kerbert 1919:626, 627, 647–50; Boomgaard 1987:28). Daendels started the construction of a cross-Java post road in 1808. Railroad construction began in the 1860s, and by 1880 nearly 1,500 kilometers of track had been laid for state railroads and steam trains. West and East Java were connected by continuous rail tracks in 1894, when the line linking Batavia, Bandung, Yogyakarta, Surakarta, and Surabaya was completed (Shiraishi 1989:8).

Forests were cut both to construct and to make way for roads and railroads. Teak trees were cut to size for the construction of sleepers, and fuelwood was needed for the steam trains. Railroad sleepers were also exported; some 280,000 sleepers were exported from Java in 1882 alone (Kerbert 1919:625). Eventually, the State Railway (SS) was given its own forest concession to supply itself with teak.

The construction of railways also facilitated the extraction and transport of teak from the forests ever more distant from the coast. The first forest railroad was built in North Kradenan in 1901 and 1902. By the end of 1912 the Forest Service's own railroads had 600 kilometers of track, and by 1916 about 1,000 kilometers of track (Kerbert 1919:627). In 1909 and 1910 construction of monorails was also begun to transport teak from the forest interior (Departemen Kehutanan 1986, I:149).

In sum, though the foundations of state forest management were being established in the late nineteenth and early twentieth centuries, the power of other government sectors and the progression of colonial extraction were such that the forests' major enemy was the state itself. Technological developments and applications greatly influenced both the power that the Forest Service was gaining in the early twentieth century and the shape of the forest resource from which it was extracting more and more timber. In other colonial economies, such as India, the pattern was one of a triangular conflict between the state's interests in protecting and producing from the forest, industrial wood demand, and forest users' subsistence and cash needs (Guha 1990). In the case of Java, the points of the triangle were similar but different components of the state often opposed each other. Moreover, many of the wood-consuming industries were state enterprises or directly served the interests of the state or of individual colonial officers.

LAWS AND FOREST MANAGEMENT

The 1865 forestry laws[6] are credited with being the first forestry laws for Java. Along with the *Domeinverklaring* of 1870, which declared all unclaimed and forest lands as the domain of the state, these laws laid the basis for "scientific forestry" as it is practiced today. Although the philosophical principles of state forest management had been nurtured for some hundred years or more in the Indies, and elsewhere for millennia (see, for example, Fernow 1911:13–16), there was a difference between the new scientific regulations and the preceding years of declarations and treaties. Land control superseded species and labor control as the key to the state's forest policy. The state did not give up these old forms of control, but as times and the nature of the colonial state changed, so did the modes of forest control.

To recap the events leading up to the creation of the first scientific forest laws: In the half-century after control of Java was restored to the Dutch in 1816, a flurry of regulations regarding forest management had been made and retracted (Schuitemaker 1950:39–41; Soepardi 1974a:49–61). Individuals' usufruct and ownership rights to teak were defined more clearly under the Dutch colonial state. For example, Daendels issued directives[7] stating that teak trees growing on private property or on the private estates (*tanah partikelir*) could be cut for the owner's own use without government permission. But if the teak were transported off the property or sold, a 10 percent tax was due the government (Soepardi 1974a:56). This was similar to the 10 percent tax paid the sultans by the VOC and other renters of forests and forest villages. Subsistence and commercial uses of teak were thus differentiated in policy, with the location of the teak (on private or state lands) creating further divisions in the policy. Teak transport was taxed because it was assumed to be for commercial purposes.

The nature of the Javanese kings' claims on the forest, however, had not simultaneously invalidated local systems of forest use. Such a notion of concurrent rights in forest products and land differed greatly from the systems of absolute domain imposed subsequently by the Dutch. To the Javanese rulers, land had been important insofar as it bore profitable or useful fruits (food, wood) and was worked by subject populations. Territorial control depended more on the balance of power between the king and regional rulers (Moertono 1981:111–14). But as the Company annexed territory, territorial control became more important, and state-imposed controls on forest lands left little or no room for layering local, regional, and statewide systems of claims to forest resources.

Two other aspects of the new colonial state's forest regulations concerned forest villagers. One was the nature of changes in labor requirements, and is treated in the following section on labor. The other concerned the government's limiting villagers' access to the forest to cut wood for household or other uses and discouraging cattle grazing in young stands. The policies on villagers' rights to cut wood were particularly ambiguous.

These latter restrictions were irregularly imposed and easily misinterpreted. In all forests from Cirebon Residency eastward that were not designated for large-scale exploitation, forest villagers and woodcutters were allowed to cut some wood for their own use, but were restricted to logs less than twenty feet long and six "thumbs" wide. Cutting wood for rivercraft, carts, and the needs of regional government was allowed. The cutting of wood for charcoal or teak timber that the government might harvest in the future (an unpredictable variable) was also forbidden. Forest villagers could use waste wood, stumps, roots, and underbrush. If they used wood for restricted purposes, it was to be confiscated and the offender punished (Brascamp 1924b:917–18).

The following sample of these paper regulations illustrates the ambiguity of policies governing people's access to wood. In 1822 *Staatsblad* no. 43 permitted forest villagers to cut fuelwood and timber for house construction or agricultural tools (Cordes 1881:204); this was retracted in 1838 by *Staatsblad* no. 19. In 1842, however, *Staatsblad* no. 5 stated that wood could be cut from the state forests for construction of riverboats and carts (ibid., 211–12). This was augmented by *Staatsblad* no. 26 in 1850, which allowed forest villagers to cut wood from government forests for riverboats, oxcarts, and horsecarts. *Staatsblad* no. 3 in 1851 required villagers to secure permits from local government to cut wood for subsistence uses (ibid., 212). Finally, in 1865 it was decided that forest villagers could take branches, fallen wood, and the wood from forest thinnings for their own use, but in collecting these they had to be "under close supervision" and were restricted to particular forests (*Staatsblad* no. 96/1865) (Soepardi 1974a:61).

The German structures and ideology of "scientific" forest management came directly to Java in the mid-nineteenth century. Both colonial and contemporary foresters define scientific management as that which is governed by a systematic adherence to working plans for cutting and replanting the forest (in forest plantations), according to prevailing principles of silviculture developed through experimental trials over time.[8] The laws of 1865 were the first to describe in detail the procedures by which teak was to be logged, thinned, and otherwise managed: in even-aged stands to be cut over long rotations (eighty to one hundred years). In 1849 the Dutch brought two German foresters and a German surveyor to Java and stationed them in Rembang (Koloniaal Verslag 1849:137).[9] Within five years, the German general manager of this valuable teak forest had established a simple, regulated parcel system that fixed areas to be cut and replanted each year (Lugt 1933:33). These first foresters were joined in 1855 by another German expert, who was made the inspector of forests in 1858. In 1857 four aspiring Dutch foresters from Java were sent to Germany to study forestry (Cordes 1881:224).[10]

The development of scientific forestry laws was concurrent with other changes in the nature of the colonial state and affected the structure of the Colonial Forest Service (*Boschwezen*). It was becoming more and more bureaucratic, the precursor to a contemporary state forest service. Based on laws, using professional foresters trained in forest science to make management decisions, drawing maps of the forest and its other holdings, and policing the forest as a means of protecting state "property," forest management in Java followed the more general pattern of bureaucratization emerging in all sectors of colonial management.

The forest laws were written by a committee appointed by the governor-general in 1860. The committee consisted of an inspector of estates (plantations), a forestry inspector, and an official of the justice department (Soepardi 1974a:60; Departemen Kehutanan 1986, I:74). The roles of these participants were, respectively, to develop a plantation-style management system for timber crops, employing wage laborers from neighboring forest villages; to make sure trees were planted at the proper intervals and that the timing of harvesting, planting, and thinning of the timber crops was in accordance with the trees' potential yield and lifecycle; and to identify crimes (e.g., tree theft or unauthorized cutting, illegal grazing, and setting forest fires) against the states' forest-based property and set punishment for them. Thus, the Dutch planned to "order" the forests for "proper" management, to follow the principles of science in carrying out their work, and to prosecute those who thwarted their efforts at orderliness according to a set of laws of their own making.

Territorially consolidated management of state forests, based on scientific principles and dependent on plantation labor, became the accepted and legal means of forest use. Except for granting local people access to wood thinned in the process of management, and to deadwood or fallen branches, the laws criminalized most traditional forest uses by forest villagers. The changes in the definitions of forest crimes are summarized in table 3.1.

Theft was a particularly nebulous concept and looked different in different settings. For example, the government's wood quotas were cut and shipped to Rembang or Surabaya where officials from other departments clamored for the best cuts. Meanwhile, private firms unable to acquire wood from government sources continued to build ships or handle timber, sometimes selling to government departments, in spite of the state's monopoly. However, bureaucratic procedures were tedious and changed frequently, as did sources of wood, private entrepreneurs' agents in forest settlements, and the means of transporting the trees from the forest. Ship orders had to be filled within nine to twelve months of receipt, barely enough time to acquire timber through legitimate or clandestine sources, to cut and haul the wood, to build the ships, and to send them to the client, with no time to dry the wood sufficiently before construction (Zwart 1930:973). Village contacts, and the networks for illegally cutting and carrying wood to the buyers, were of critical importance to the private entrepreneur. In many instances, the government turned a blind eye to this sort of theft while arresting and prosecuting villagers taking teak for their houses.

In keeping with the land classification processes being initiated throughout the colony, the 1865 forest laws labeled and began measuring the forests under specific types of cover and under different forms of management. For the first time, nonteak forests (*Wildhoutbosschen*, literally, "wild woods" or "junglewood forests"), particularly those above certain elevations or topping the island's string of volcanoes, were included in the category of state forest (Lugt 1933:112). Unlike the teak forests, they were placed under state management for protection, not production.

Teak forests were divided into those which were under regulated management and those which were not (Lugt 1933:33). In teak forests

TABLE 3.1 Criminal Actions in the Forest,
Under Nineteenth-Century Laws

Under 1860 Plans	Under 1875 Regulations
Arson	—
Stealing wood	—
Forest theft	Forest theft
Forest damage	Forest damage
Grazing cattle in young stands	Grazing cattle in young stands
Setting fires in the forest	Setting fires in the forest
Traveling off the roads in the forest with horsecarts, oxcarts, or cattle	Carrying cutting tools off the roads in the forest
Transporting wood without a permit	Transporting wood without a permit
Damaging border markers	—
Cutting without a permit	Transporting wood without prior payment
Selling wood from private lands without paying taxes	—
—	Encroaching on forest land

SOURCE: Departemen Kehutanan 1986, I:75.

under regulated management, private industries bid at public auctions for the rights to cut particular tracts (concessions). Between 1865 and 1874 the number of private concessions increased from seven to seventeen, and private companies were felling some 51 percent of the annual teak cut (Kerbert 1919:629; cf. Boomgaard 1987:31).

Management in these forests was much more intensive than in the others, with the industry being responsible not only for cutting and transporting the timber, but also for replanting. Government foresters handled policing and maintenance of the nonregulated teak forests and the nonteak forests. Government foresters eventually supervised replanting in all forests. By directly involving state foresters in the management of only some of the forests, the state saved money. However, wood theft, fire, and grazing plagued the nonregulated teak forests and nonteak forests, incurring high costs. As a result, in 1874 all teak and nonteak forests except those in the (now greatly reduced) principalities of Surakarta and Yogyakarta were categorized as "regulated" (Cordes 1881:251).

By 1875 another set of forest laws, including regulations on policing and the punishments for various forest crimes, had been put into effect (Lugt 1933:33; Schuitemaker 1950:41; Soepardi 1974a:51,61).[11] Private industry now bid on parcels in all teak forests, not just the best ones.[12] The pace of the timber industry's involvement was slowed by the international depression of the 1880s, causing a drop in the number of concessions, the amount cut, and an 11 percent drop in the proportion of wood cut by private logging companies by 1885. By 1896, however, there were eleven times as many concessions as there had been in 1865 when the forest laws were first passed and they reportedly accounted for 93 percent of the teak harvest (Kerbert 1919:629; Boomgaard 1987:31). Nearly three-quarters of these contractors used clearcutting methods (Koloniaal Verslag 1896:222). These methods were sanctioned by the Forest Service.

The second phase of colonial forest control was well established by the end of the nineteenth century. The state was appropriating forest lands and, like the Forest Service monopoly on the species of teak, forest land appropriation by the state was justified by colonial law. The Forest Service's conservation function was used to argue for state acquisition of watershed areas. Both land and species controls were accompanied by a liturgy of colonial production objectives and conservationism. As we will see, the system of labor control also evolved through this period.

STATE FOREST MANAGEMENT AND LABOR CONTROL

The state's direct control of forest production through forced labor, the blandongdiensten, continued through the era of the Cultivation System, ending with the general trend toward "liberal" policies and the "freeing" of labor to work for wages on agricultural and timber crop plantations. New forms of labor tying began, just after the end of the blandongdiensten, with the initiation of the *tumpang sari* system of reforestation.

The Blandongdiensten and Beyond

When Raffles took over the administration of Java for four short but significant years, he was unsatisfied with the Dutch form of the blandongdiensten, complaining that forest laborers, exempt from head and land taxes, "contributed nothing to government revenue but their labor." He decided that forest workers should be subjected to the same land rents as all other peasants. Rather than paying land rents in cash, however, the forest workers' "wages" were to take the form of tax remissions. The transaction only took place on paper: forest labor was credited in value for taxes due on the agricultural lands worked. At the same time, private timber concerns paid the government a 10 percent tax for any timber they cut and also contracted with local villagers for forest labor—often simply by paying their land taxes (Raffles 1817, I:183; Brascamp 1922b:172).

Under Raffles's version of the blandongdiensten, woodcutters and timber haulers had to work eight out of twelve months a year (April to November),[13] and were under an obligation to guard the forests during the other four months, in exchange for exemption from land rent. Whole villages were responsible for providing labor and buffaloes. According to the policy, half the "working men" of a village were supposed to be left free to work the rice fields at any time during the season.

One advantage to the government of the "new" system was the willingness of the people "in emergencies . . . to lend their own buffaloes to assist those of the government in dragging heavy timber, which could not be removed otherwise without great expence [*sic*], while their children at other times watch and attend the cattle belonging to the government" (Raffles 1817, I:185). Raffles thus created a system for putting all the resources of the forest settlements at the immediate disposal of the government, at a cost (the value of their land rent) less than one-third the potential cost of wage laborers hired to cut and haul the wood.

When the Dutch returned to Java in 1816, blandongs remained liable for land rents and continued to pay them by laboring in the forest. Villagers were still required to provide the quotas of draft animals. However, buffalo that died "in the line of duty" were supposed to be replaced by the government and loggers were provided with axes and other work tools (Hasanu 1983). All villagers also had to help build logging roads. To work off their land rents, an owner of a team of buffalo had to deliver the equivalent of fifteen giant teak trees or thirty-five smaller ones to the log yards. Small wage payments were given out in some forests. In some districts of Rembang, daily wages were 8.5 cents for blandongs, 16.5 cents for group leaders, and 21 cents for the log haulers with a pair of buffaloes (Cordes 1881:215).[14] In other forests, small salt and rice allotments[15] were paid to the workers in lieu of cash (Brascamp 1922c:1097). What percentage of these wages and rations reached the forest laborers is unknown, for it is likely that they, too, were administered through either regents, village heads, or other intermediaries assigned by the Dutch to be representatives of the forest laborers. In most locales, the state's forest production activities had to be subsidized by forest villagers' own food production.

No small number of blandongs was employed. At each regulated logging site, some 100 to 300 woodcutters and 100 to 400 teams of draft animals were employed (Cordes 1881:216). Cordes lists the number of people required for woodcutting activities in certain districts of Rembang in 1865, the last year of the blandongdiensten (table 3.2), but many more men were involved, as the village division of labor provided for the rotation of those in labor service at any one time.[16]

In 1865, as part of the new forest laws and in keeping with the general trend toward liberalization (through private industry's involvement in

TABLE 3.2   Logging and Hauling Labor in Selected Rembang
Districts, 1865

Logging Site	District	Regency	Woodcutters	Animal Teams
Sekaran	Jatirogo	Tuban	150	225
Tambakmerak	Tinawun	Bojonegoro	250	225
Bayangan	Tinawun	Bojonegoro	250	225
Ngawen	Ngawen	Blora	125	100
Blimbing	Panolan	Blora	200	200
Kedongtuban	Panolan	Blora	125	150

SOURCE: Adapted from Cordes 1881:216.

timbering), the blandongdiensten was abolished in favor of a free labor system. The employment of free laborers had been tried as early as 1855 in the Bancar district of Tuban, with the wood being hewn in the forest and hauled through the forest for an average distance of 12 kilometers. The foresters were so pleased with the outcome that they tried the system in three more districts the following year (Cordes 1881:220–21).

As colonial policy and political economy evolved, forest workers were forced to work in the forests in more indirect ways than had been the case when regents or village heads mustered able-bodied men for corvée labor. The abolition of the blandongdiensten created the need for cash to pay the workers' land rents. The land rent owed would no longer be calculated as a shadow price against the value of wages. However, as the state consolidated its forest resources, forest dwellers were increasingly restricted from converting the forest lands to agriculture and from collecting forest products.

Under the new, formalized forest laws, villagers were required to *purchase* wood for housing—an option that few could afford. The limited quantities of timber available for private purchase were still overpriced for the poor. Nongovernment wood extraction and trade went underground. From the government's perspective, anyone taking wood from the teak forests without permission was a thief. Yet to people who made their living by converting the forest to agriculture, and who needed wood for housing and fuel, "stealing" wood was a totally foreign concept.

Although forest villagers may not have realized the vastness of the state forestry organization's control, they were no doubt aware of the limits on their daily use of the once-accessible environment. The demarcation of forest boundaries with stone posts (*palen*) and the formation of a formal forest police force were yet to come to the whole forest, but the preliminaries—forest mapping and the recruitment of state forest officials (*bosbeambten*)—had begun. Punishments and fines were imposed for such forest crimes as firewood collection, charcoal manufacture, woodcutting to build new homes, and grazing cattle in the forest (often the same animals used to haul timber). Under the pretense of liberating the forest people from oppressive systems of labor obligation, the state effectively evicted people from the source of their subsistence. This indirect labor control, enforced by the ever-growing demands of the state on peasant incomes, was at least as oppressive as the blandong system that had bound the peasants for centuries.

Village Rules of Forest Access

A study of native land rights in all the residencies of Java was sponsored by the Dutch colonial state in the mid-nineteenth century and published in three volumes in 1876, 1880, and 1896. The interviews in sample villages were conducted between 1867 and 1869, that is, before the passage of the 1870 Agrarian Law that changed the nature of land ownership and tenure. For our purposes, it is useful to consider the findings of this study in terms of people's access to the forest for clearing, access to forest products, and the ways in which an individual or a household obtained and maintained control over a piece of cleared land. The following discussion on variations in rights of forest access focuses on the residencies of Tegal and Rembang because the villages discussed in chapters 6 and 7 are located in regions that were formerly part of the jurisdiction of these residencies.

Though the dates of village establishment were not reported specifically in these reports, villages where interviews were conducted were reportedly established from "ancient times" to "after the Java War" (1825–1830). In Rembang Residency, villagers reported that their villages had been founded for a variety of reasons: some from overpopulation of parent villages, some established in the wilderness for religious purposes, some established by refugees from upheaval in other provinces. In Tegal, new settlements had been specifically founded by people fleeing heavy labor service in other residencies or regions.

Both in Tegal and Rembang, where land had been cleared for cultivation and abandoned, the clearer retained rights to that land until it had completely reverted to forest. If newcomers wished to work fallow lands not yet under forest cover, they had first to seek permission from the original clearer (Bergsma 1880:74–76, 182). In such cases, powerful local figures, who would today be called "informal leaders,"[17] served as witnesses to claims of tenure rights. In some places, Bergsma reports, a village head or other authority had great control over who cleared land. In others, permission to convert forest to agriculture was needed from a local authority only if the clearer had just come from another settlement or resided elsewhere (ibid., 187–89).

In Tegal, the names of the first forest clearers were remembered in many of the villages surveyed, and these individuals were considered the village founders. Here, clearing began by marking a clearance border and dividing the land among the participants according to their individual agreements with those who granted permission to clear. In some villages, the rights to the land became effective as soon as the land was divided among the clearers and each person marked a share with boundary markers. In other villages, rights would be effective after completion of the clearing; elsewhere, no rights were effective until the lands were completely planted. By the time of the survey, clearance-derived rights included the rights to sell, to pawn, and to rent the land. However, villagers in the Brebes Regency said that these capacities were not original rights, but came only as a result of interaction with Chinese, Arabs, and, of course, Europeans. Clearance rights expired after ten years, on average, if the owner left the village without designating someone to be responsible for the labor and planting obligations inherent in land access (Bergsma 1880:69–76).

In Rembang, forest land was sometimes cleared by groups but the rights to that land were defined on an individual basis—that is, for particular parcels—as were the necessary permissions to clear. As long as the clearer tilled that land, he or she maintained hereditary rights to it (Bergsma 1880:189).

In general, by the time of the survey, many villages were consolidated, corporate entities (but not necessarily closed or self-sufficient) as a result of colonial policy, changed from the vertical structures described by Breman, but by no means isolated (Kano 1982:77). Some 365 of the 808 villages surveyed had some wasteland (*woestegrond*)[18] that was controlled by the village in several ways. First, outsiders, or nonresidents, could not convert wasteland to agricultural land without permission of the village head. In all of Central Java, this permission for an outsider to cultivate village land was not considered a right of permanent access. In other words, outsiders could access that land only as long as they actively cultivated it: if they moved, abandoned the land, or died, they lost the rights to it. Nor did outsiders have rights of transfer. The land reverted to village jurisdiction once an outsider was gone (ibid.). This analysis, however, never clarifies how an outsider could become a permanent insider—through marriage or long-term residence, or other means.

Second, in theory, outsiders had only limited access to the forest products found in the wastelands. Some villages forbade outsiders all access to forest products; others required payment of a tax or a percentage of the collected produce. In practice, however, it was reported that villagers from neighboring villages were often allowed entry and free access to the products they collected. Resident villagers, on the other hand, could collect and use forest products from wastelands as they wished. There were some exceptions, such as *aren* trees (used for making sugar) found on wastelands, which were often divided among all the village residents who performed labor services (Kano 1982:78). The nature of rights in aren trees may have derived from the fact that they grew wild—as is the case in some villages of Kalimantan today. Moreover, rights to fruit trees planted on converted agricultural land that had reverted to forest or waste could be retained by the heirs of the planter.

Kano (1982:42) argues that the prevailing Javanese concept of land ownership at the time of this survey can be understood by examining the role of the community in overseeing the allocation of land. In other words, though people exercised control over the land they worked, the community exerted specific controls. The four main roles of the community were:

1. restricting who could be landowners;
2. setting up land usage rules, including forbidding the sale or other alienation of land;
3. recognizing owners only in the case of someone actively cultivating the land;
4. assuring that the owner did labor services or forfeited his rights in the land. Labor services included *heerendiensten* to the colonial government, *cultuurdiensten* in the forced labor services [or *blandongdiensten* in the teak forest villages], *pantjendiensten* to the Javanese rulers, and *desadiensten* to the village (Kano 1982:42).

In sum, a usufruct or use value connotation of rights in the land prevailed, such that the products of the land—whether natural forest products, products of planted trees, or products of forest lands converted to agriculture—were the concern of the community allocating and regulating access. Land and its products could be used for direct subsistence or for accumulating surplus; but land was not *capital* in its uncleared or "waste" state. Rather, it was a form of insurance against the village's future needs. The insurance was as a potential source of food or income—a means of production. A certain balance was sought between the rights and responsibilities inherent in land control and forest access. The concern in allocating rights to forest or wasteland was the immediate benefit to the user and to the allocator in terms of the labor services and tributes received.

That nearly one-half of the villages surveyed in 1867–69 still had wasteland over which they exercised control indicates that local use rights were significant. As shown below, however, the significance of local rights lay ultimately in their relative power vis-à-vis the increasing power of the centralizing state.

VILLAGE SOCIAL RELATIONS BASED ON
PRIVATE AND COMMUNAL LAND

By the time of the survey, two general types of land were found in most villages: communal lands and individually "owned" lands.[19] Importantly, communal land was not a "natural" social institution rooted in Javanese tradition; it was a rarity in both Rembang and Tegal through the English interregnum (Bergsma 1880:182). People in these residencies had always preferred to own their own land, or to work continuously the plots allotted them by whatever right of usufruct or other local tenure the land was subject to (Bergsma 1880:194; The 1969:68–69).

In the second decade of the nineteenth century, Rembang Resident Van Lawick van Pabst ordered that all wet-rice fields in the regency of Rembang be divided equally among those who performed the blandong services; in some villages this partitioning, a reallocation in effect, had already taken place under the English interregnum government when the land rent was introduced. Those who refused to take part in the compulsory forest services were to lose all their rights in wet-rice land. Most of the time, only wet-rice fields (*sawah*) were divided as communal lands; where these were scarce, the dry-fields (*tegalan*) could also be partitioned annually or every few years (Bergsma 1880:182–83).

Traditionally, land reverted to the administration of the village or settlement area (so-called wastelands) only when people moved or died without heirs. And, during the period in which the VOC was renting out tracts of forest and forest labor for exploitation of teak, migrations were common. Indeed, in Blora, village "possession" of common lands was due primarily to such migrations. With the increasing demands of the blandong system, more individual landowners fled or voluntarily gave part of their land over to the village communal pool. Wet-rice field owners in parts of Rembang and Blora regencies made as much as 25 percent of their fields available to newcomers (Bergsma 1880:184–85).

Although the number of people with rights in land may have increased through the communalization of land, the partitioning was not equal. For other reasons, the "leveling" process suggested by the potential access to communal lands did not eliminate socioeconomic differentiation. Land quality varied. The recipients of poor-quality fields sometimes abandoned them or left them to revert to secondary forest (Bergsma 1880:183). Often the better-off villagers were assigned the "permanent communal" lands, while the rotating shares went to the poorer people or newcomers (The

1969:68–69). In some districts, cattle owners—already better off than nonowners—were given bigger shares when the land was partitioned. This was sometimes because they lost the cattle forced to haul logs as part of the village corvée labor services. In other places, non–cattle-owners were given the most fertile lands to enable them to save enough to buy cattle. This measure was not entirely altruistic; rather, it was sometimes a step toward alleviation of the burdens of the other cattle owners in the village. The fewer cattle in a village or settlement area, the harder each had to work, and the more likely an animal would be crippled or die from exhaustion (Bergsma 1880:182–85).

When the blandong system was abolished in 1865 and replaced by head taxes, the conversion of forest and the commonly held wastelands to agriculture increased rapidly in Rembang Residency, apparently in spite of the forest laws of 1865 and the state's formal claim on all "unowned" forest lands in 1870 by the Domeinverklaring (Bergsma 1880:193). Trends toward privatization of holdings began to accelerate, largely because of the state's claims on unowned land. The corvée labor that once went with rights in land was no longer required. As a result, one means of gaining access to communal land was eliminated. Reportedly, the heirs of some former *sikep* (people with rights in land) who had fled from the hardships of compulsory forest labor returned to reclaim their rights in village land. In their absence, the land had been divided among the remaining sikep and *numpang* (people who worked the land or were dependents, but had no permanent rights in it) to be worked as communal land (Bergsma 1880:193; The 1969:69).[20] Bergsma claimed that their return caused great losses among the poorest and least powerful villagers. However, some returning sikep would have experienced great difficulty in reclaiming their forebears' land rights (Onghokham, personal communication, March 1987), and, except for Bergsma's statement, there is little evidence that shows who actually retained control over the privatized lands.[21]

In later decades, the Forest Service began to mark more and more permanent boundaries around forest and agricultural lands, and the police began to patrol and keep people out of the forest. With the nature of their access to the forest increasingly restricted, people began to realize that there were few opportunities to escape to less oppressive circumstances. This knowledge may have provided even greater incentive to landholders to remain in one place and control as much private and "permanent" communal land as they could.

REFORESTATION LABOR

Controlling forest labor was more difficult in reforestation than logging. Planting trees had always imparted rights to the planter; but peasant ownership of teak trees on state lands was not part of the Forest Service plan. When the German and German-trained Dutch foresters established the rotating system for teak harvest in tracts, reforestation became the art of persuading people to plant trees on state land, an art in which local foresters had little training. At the organizational level, managing forest laborers to sustain decent working relations was not emphasized in the same way as managing teak stands; profits, wages, commissions, and bribes came from cutting big trees, not replacing them. Replacing them, indeed, required paying day laborers hired for each separate task of clearing brush, planting, and weeding for the first few years (Cordes 1881: 268). Foresters working in their individual districts were so isolated, and communications so poor, that each developed his own strategies for reforestation. By trial and error, and with varied degrees of success, local foresters tried to replant their regions' clearcut areas (Lugt 1933:44).

In 1873 W. Buurman began experiments with the *taungya* system, called *tumpang sari* in Javanese and Indonesian—in the forest district Tegal-Pekalongan. It is not clear, but seems likely, that Buurman learned of the taungya system through British colleagues in Burma, where the system is said to have originated (Menzies 1988). Buurman's method (as it was called in the early years) worked as follows: After a forest area was clearcut, local cultivators were sought to clean the rest of the land and plant teak seeds in measured rows of 1 by 3 meters or 1 by 1 meters. Brush clearing and planting teak were usually done between August and September. Between the rows, the planters could grow agricultural crops such as rice, corn, or tobacco for one or two years. Forest personnel had to supervise the planting of seedlings and make sure that the ground stayed clean and the soil loose. The agricultural crops belonged to the planters; they also received a nominal cash fee. Gradually they were allowed to collect fallen or dead wood, but this was not until some time later. Some land did not yield as many or as good crops as other land; higher fees were paid for the lowest quality plots. On the poorest soils or otherwise degraded lands the system failed, unable to attract labor by even high payments, forcing the forester to resort to other means of replanting (Lugt 1933:44–47).

Buurman's system was reportedly equally successful in Semarang, where he was transferred in 1881. Tumpang sari was not widely known or applied to reforestation in Java until 1883, when Buurman wrote a pamphlet called "De Djaticultuur" (The cultivation of teak), describing the method and the local response. The system apparently succeeded best where socioeconomic circumstances were worst; in the districts of Tegal-Pekalongan and Semarang, where he initiated his plan, land was scarce, and the system worked well. For many of the same reasons that laborers flocked to work in remote forest districts, landless peasants sought access to land through Buurman's system. Access to land, even if temporary, was eagerly sought by peasants where land control systems by the state and village elites were particularly harsh. Reforestation laborers who succeeded in replanting a new forest tract were rewarded with access to other, newly opened forest tracts.

By 1912 some 61 percent of reforestation in Java was done by tumpang sari; by 1928 the system's share accounted for more than 94 percent (Lugt 1933:55). Foresters lauded Buurman's method for its economy and efficiency in replanting the forest; only secondarily was it seen as a means of providing land access to poor villagers. Like the other privileges accorded the forest users of Java, access was limited by strict provisions. Forest farmers could plant their crops for no more than two years; most were allowed only one year's use.

The temporary access policy saw the rise of a new kind of forest-dependent rural proletariat. Whole families of landless or nearly landless laborers followed the harvest of teak parcels, building temporary houses of waste wood and teak bark. They were as dependent on forest labor opportunities as on forest land for their subsistence.

The tumpang sari system extended to the forest lands a new form of interdependent farm-forest relationship. By providing the laborers with enough cultivable land for household reproduction, the foresters were able to keep wages for woodcutting low, and planting wages were essentially nonexistent. Like peasant farming on private land, it subsidized low forest wages and kept the costs of plantation teak production low. Tumpang sari had another advantage for the foresters because they controlled access to reforestation plots. Two methods of controlling forest labor were thus established by the turn of the twentieth century: first, by controlling forest villagers' access to forest products for timber-cutting wages or for other uses and second, by controlling access to forest land for agriculture. On state forest lands in general, peasants were forbidden to convert the forest to permanent agriculture; their only chance for farming forest land was on tumpang sari plots.

THE CONSOLIDATION OF FOREST LAND CONTROL

The Agrarian Law of 1870 (*Domeinverklaring*) declared that all land that could not be proven to be owned (individually or communally) by villagers (i.e., land that was not currently under tillage or that had lain fallow for more than three years) was the property of the state. This law provided the basis for the 75-year leases of wastelands to private entrepreneurs for estate development (Boomgaard 1987:37); it also became the basis for the Forest Service's claim to all lands except those under small-scale or plantation agriculture.

Many foresters felt the 1875 forest laws were insufficient, and some gathered to form a team of legal planners to improve the laws. Their revisions, enacted as the forest laws of 1897, established regulations for the internal management of the Dienst van het Boschwezen. The first chief inspector of the Forest Service, Buurman van Vreeden, was installed in July 1897 (Schuitemaker 1950:41; Soepardi 1974a:63). Soon afterward, state forest management was intensified, and small forest districts, called *houtvesterij*, were formed. Each houtvesterij had to have its own ten-year management plan before it was considered officially planned. Districts controlled by private contractors and having only temporary plans were called *bosdistricts*. The first houtvesterij formed was Noord Kradenan, followed by Noordwest Wirosari in 1901, Tudor in 1902, Balo in 1903, and Margasari in 1904 (Schuitemaker 1950:41; Soepardi 1974a: 63). The Dutch again sought assistance in their reorganization efforts from the German fathers of forestry: Five experts in forest planning were brought from Germany in 1909 and five more arrived in 1910. The last teak houtvesterij, the plan for which was finished in 1932, was Gunung Kidul in the sultanate of Yogyakarta.

Two other administrative changes marked this period; both moves consolidated the roles of the Forest Service as controllers of land and forest resources. First, the Forest Service was moved to the Department of the Interior and then to the Department of Agriculture, Industry and Trade; moves that symbolized, among other things, its ultimate concerns with land and commodities rather than people. Second, the forest police, formed in 1880 and originally under the Department of the Interior (*Binnenlands Bestuur*), were made a part of the Forest Service. Partly because the forest police had technical responsibilities besides patrolling the forest for illegal woodcutters and sawyers, the Forest Service had lobbied to have them moved (Zwart 1936:275). Nevertheless, the various police forces were expected to cooperate in monitoring rural people's forest activities. The forest police were authorized to catch "forest criminals," but were not authorized to convict and punish them; for this, they needed the assistance of other police and the justice department (Soepardi 1974b:25).

Subsequent forest ordinances were passed in 1913, 1927, 1928, 1931, and 1934,[22] but after 1927 only minor changes were made, and the 1927 laws are still in effect today. The 1927 laws define the state forest lands (*kawasan hutan negara*) of Java and Madura as follows:

a. lands which are owned by the state, to which other people or parties have no right or control, and on which grow:

    1. naturally regenerated woody species and bamboo,[23]

    2. woody species planted by the Forest Service,

3. woody species not planted by the Forest Service but planted by the state and turned over to the Forest Service for management,

4. woody species planted by order of the state/government,

5. nonwoody species planted by the Forest Service;

b. all lands surrounding the lands stated in paragraph (a) on which woody plants do not grow; as long as those lands are not used for other purposes outside the jurisdiction of the Forest Service;

c. all land reserved by the state for maintaining or extending the forest;

d. all land included in the [state] forest lands when the forest boundaries were established.

These same ordinances define teak forests as land or land parcels:

a. on all or part of which teak trees grow;

b. which have been designated by the state for the expansion of the teak forest, whether that land is currently planted in trees or not.

The drive to intensify management continued until the start of World War II. Intensification meant research and application of technical aspects of forestry, particularly for growing teak. In 1913 the first Forest Experiment Station was established; its purpose was to determine how to extract the maximum timber value from the scientific regulation of the forest districts. Not until 1927 were hydrological, climatological, and very broad social welfare aspects of upland or watershed forests written into law. Previously, the formal function of the Forest Service had been simply to produce revenues for the state from teak (Schuitemaker 1950:42–43). While the indirect values of the forest were discussed in the literature, and the "Junglewoods Forest Service" (*Dienst der Wildhout-bosschen*)[24] was established with these principles in mind, the early framers of forest regulation had not included them in formal forest law.

Members of the Forest Service began in 1925 to seek increased autonomy and authority for the forest district heads (*Administrateur*). They also pushed for intensive planning in the nonteak forests. This led to an administrative split of the service into two self-supporting units: the entirely commercial "Teak Enterprise" (*Djatibedrijf*) and the previously mentioned Junglewoods Forest Service. After eight years (1930–1938) and substantial debate in the forestry literature, an advisory commission was formed and a plan constructed for a united service to manage all state forest lands. The primary objection had been to the difficulty of the state's maintaining the low-value protection forests without the revenue from the teak forests. Compounding the problem, the Djatibedrijf's formation coincided with another major world economic depression, and it was unable to sell its teak profitably. The reuniting of the two services as a single *Dienst der Bosschen op Java en Madura* (Departemen Kehutanan 1986, I:115) marked the end of all forest exploitation by private companies and the vesting of full authority for the production and sale of unprocessed timber products in the state (Schuitemaker 1950:44).

CONFLICTS IN IDEOLOGIES
OF FOREST ACCESS AND CONTROL

As conservation ideologies were used to justify Forest Service control of the uplands, the same notions cloaked the main impetus behind forest exploitation and the Forest Service—the extraction of surplus for the state. While the hydrological functions of montane forests could be scientifically demonstrated, the evolving policy of planting teak everywhere the environment could sustain it could not be defended on the basis of a conservation ideology alone. Teak was to replace nonteak forest species even on land that was very well-suited to agriculture, where other climatic and soil conditions were conducive to its vigorous growth.[25] This policy was meant explicitly to increase future state revenues. As a result, people lost access to the natural forest products when teak plantations replaced them. Moreover, the introduction of teak sometimes resulted in reduced water supplies on adjacent village lands (Peluso 1985). Nevertheless, to many nineteenth-century Europeans the ideology of forest conservation justified state control of key forest lands and masked the reality of production forestry in Java.

By 1870, with the Domeinverklaring, the Dutch had completed their shift in status from that of "tenants," with leased rights to forest products and labor, to "landlords" who controlled forest lands and forest access, thus reshaping the entire nature of forest access control. The villagers lost forever their free access to the forest, the potential autonomy of forest settlements, and important subsistence options. For the poorest, the loss of access to the forest was the loss of a last resort. Squeezed onto the lands designated village or agricultural lands, with little opportunity to change one's status—and little inclination on the part of the landowners to do so anymore—the Javanese lost a certain fluidity in their rural social structure. Forest villagers accepted very reluctantly many of the structural constraints imposed upon them, resisting the foresters and the colonial forest policy in a variety of ways.

RESISTANCE

Resistance to forest policy changes occurred at all the stages in forest history discussed so far: the precolonial, early colonial, and late colonial periods. Onghokham (1975:214–15) identifies three general sorts of Javanese peasant resistance: "long-term expressions of discontent such as migrations, actions against plantations, increases in the crime rate, *Ratu Adil* or messianic movements; explosions of sudden rebellion; and the existence and rise of special sects with different social and religious views of society." All of these were found in forest contexts.

Movements violent and nonviolent, reactions to specific policies or circumstances, did not always involve the entire society but represented crystallizations of broad-based discontent with the structural changes affecting everyday life. The food shortages and famines of the nineteenth century resulted in migrations, movements, and religious revivals all over the island. New taxes and, in some places, new forms of forced labor also stimulated resistance (Onghokham 1975:224–26). The return of the Just King (*Ratu Adil*), who would relieve everyone of the unfair impositions of outsiders, featured in many of these resistance movements, just as it had in precolonial times (Sartono 1972:75, 94–98).

During the precolonial period, one form of passive resistance was collusion among rural people to avoid reporting new forest clearances and thus to avoid the taxes or tribute (Adas 1981:225). These strategies were not equally advantageous to all rural classes (ibid., 226). People with rights in the land, the elites in the rural social order, had the most to gain by avoiding the impositions of royal elites or competing authorities. Nonreporting of newly converted land saved them tribute payments and labor services for their patrons.

In the service of the VOC, Kalang woodcutters had resisted the waning of their autonomy and the increase in external controls imposed on them by Javanese kings and their Dutch allies. Work stoppages and periodic flight into the forest had been modes of resistance to external pressures before the state administrative machine grew stronger. As mentioned in chapter 2, some frustrated Kalangs rebelled by storming a Dutch fort and killing several Dutch administrators. Over the long term, however, Kalang efforts to resist the colonial state failed. Because they faded into virtual oblivion (out of the regulatory discourse as a distinct group and eventually out of local recognition in the forest)[26] it is difficult to know whether their roles as forest "thieves" and "bandits" were not more significant than the blurred historical record will permit us to see.

The loss of mobility and relative autonomy, the hardships of household reproduction caused by the bounding of forest lands and the heavy taxation of the peasantry, and the social processes of resource concentration by elites at the village level resulted in a decline of rural welfare. As The (1967:306) pointed out: "Before long, welfare became a far less conspicuous phenomenon than widespread social malaise in the countryside, a malaise heightened by progressive rural indebtedness in a time of adversity. Not unexpectedly, agrarian unrest on Java, quiescent for some time, gained in intensity after the turn of the century (as testified by the Samin movement and other forms of unrest)."

The Samin movement has been subject to numerous analyses and a complete review of these is not necessary here.[27] However, I will discuss briefly how the Samin movement and other forms of resistance were reactions at least in part to the controls on forest access embedded in the institutional structures, ideologies, laws, and actions of the colonial state by the end of the nineteenth century.

The Samin Movement

When Surontiko Samin began talking to people in approximately 1890, his neighbors in Randublatung and other teak forest villages were ready to listen. Life in the teak forests had become rather strange. More and more, the Dutch were changing the structures of everyday life, in the process causing—whether unintentionally or without concern—a great deal of hardship and misery for the peasants, particularly landowners, of the teak forest.

State forest police had been patrolling for ten years, trying to restrict people from using the nature created by God for everyone. These police spoke of laws about rights to forest land and teak trees and punished people for using them without permission. But these laws were the laws of men—not God. Men—foresters—were putting posts in the ground to mark where the people's land ended and forest lands began. Men forbade access to wood.

Also strange were the new ways in which services were to be rendered. Forest laborers for the state were paid in wages. Labor services for the village head were being replaced by cash collected from the villagers. By the beginning of the twentieth century, farmers even had to pay taxes on things besides land, such as owning or slaughtering livestock, the water used to irrigate their crops, and personal matters such as marriage and divorce. Collecting fuelwood in the forest required the purchase of tickets from these forest police or forest *mandors* (*mandor* means labor foreman; some doubled as police). In some places even the salaries of the forest police had to be paid by the villagers denied access. Land was set aside for their salaries and the salaries of teachers or other outsiders. In addition, while land was being taken away from the common people, village officials in some parts of the teak forest had very extensive landholdings, sometimes 13, 20, 25 bau of land—where average holdings amounted to no more than one-half or one-third of a bau.

The Dutch claimed to be trying to help the villagers, but they imposed "welfare" programs without informing them. The will of the people was rarely, if ever, seriously taken into account. For example, one communally oriented program imposed by the government was to stall cattle together in village stalls. People did not want such a program, they felt it was bad for their cattle, and did not want to trust the cattle to keepers.[28] At the same time, a big irrigation project planned for the Solo River Valley to improve agricultural conditions in the teak forest was canceled. Wouldn't this have improved the villagers' situation?[29]

As the century turned, many people were ready to hear what Samin had to say. By 1907 some 3,000 families were following Samin's teachings as taught by his sons-in-law. Most of his early followers were land-owning peasants. Many of them were descended from the village founders, the forest clearers. Rather than act violently, they personalized the issue with the official representatives of the Forest Service. They refused to speak to the foresters—or to any officials, for that matter—in *krama*, the traditional language of deference. When they spoke in *ngoko*, the familiar form of Javanese, their literal interpretations did not mean the same things that the officials meant when they spoke. Saminists believed that their roles as the transformers of nature into food, the essence of life, gave them equal status to those claiming rights to rule and control forest access. In fact, the state in the name of which these officials acted meant little to the Saminists. The state had not created the wind, water, earth, and wood; long ago the peasant had tapped and transformed them all.

The actions of the Saminists represented a primarily nonviolent reaction to the state's violations of prevailing peasant values; these values centered on access to the forest and agriculture, the preferred livelihood strategy.[30] The movement was born and remained in the heartland of the teak zone of Java, where the Forest Service was also born and where the first boundaries and maps of state forest lands were made. Seeing the forest officials as an obstruction of their inherent right to forest wood and forest land, the Saminists distrusted them. Foresters then and now have believed the movement was directed against them and their control of the forests. No government body controlled wind and water in the way that access to wood and the forest lands were controlled by the Forest Service. Yet the Saminists were not alone in their contempt for external control of their forest; the Saminist movement was rooted in many Javanese peasant traditions.

Samin's followers differed in the types or forms of resistance they practiced. They are most known for speaking in "riddles" or taking a literal interpretation of anything said, but this tactic was neither used everywhere, nor toward everyone. Foresters and other officials were key targets. Some Saminists lay down on their land when the Dutch surveyors came to reclassify communal and salary lands, crying out, "Kanggo" (I own it). Others cut teak despite Dutch efforts to guard the forest. They refused to pay taxes, refused to pay fines, refused to accept wages, refused to leave rented or communal land when their leases expired, refused to participate in the rituals of village reciprocity and the ritual feasts (*slametan*) that accompanied them. Some piled stones in the roads they had been ordered to build. The variation in forms of resistance nevertheless expressed a common discontent with the changes in society.

The Saminists were the most visible of rural protesters in the teak forest during this period.[31] Not until about 1905, as the movement gathered steam, did the Dutch begin to worry. The state was afraid of the ways Saminists expressed discontent—their threats to Dutch claims on authority. The Saminists' refusal to pay taxes and perform village services threatened the colonial coffers, not to mention the preferred orderliness of colonial society. Wherever the Dutch believed the ideas of the Saminists were spreading, they exiled the "leaders" and confiscated protesters' land and other possessions to sell and pay their debts.

What is not explained sufficiently by the literature on the Saminist movement is the reaction of those who chose not to join the Saminists, adopt their religion, or isolate themselves from the rest of society. Many more people than just the Saminists needed and felt justified in using the wood of the surrounding forests. As Dove (1984) points out, the villagers and foresters had radically different belief systems, and also divergent reasons for valuing the forest.

While the Saminists drew together and restricted their interactions with the broader village community, some non-Saminists, particularly village leaders, depicted this withdrawal from society as a betrayal of other village values and norms. For example, when Saminists refused to perform community duties, the village leaders took away simple community rights such as rights to walk on public roads or to work communal lands (Onghokham 1964:40–44). In the later waves of the movement, after 1915, some villages ostracized members who professed Saminism. Such actions may have been as much self-protective as aggressive. While all villagers may have agreed with the economic complaints of the Saminists and felt the strong psychological pressures of the Dutch-imposed social changes (Anderson 1975), many did not agree with the means employed by the Saminists to resist oppressive colonial policies; or perhaps they were simply afraid. Samin and his followers took one path to resisting the changes in the traditional material values of the peasantry; other peasants sought ways to enrich themselves within the new system; still others simply accepted the new circumstances but were demoralized.

The Saminist slogan "the sikep people[32] know what they own" was gibberish to the Dutch, who had known themselves to be "owners" of the forest lands and its trees for decades. Their deals to take possession or control of these lands and the "mercantile squadrons" populating them had been made with sultans, regents, traders, and other accessible Javanese. The Dutch had not bothered to deal with the actual clearers of the forest or the tillers of the land; they did not consider the users' rights. They had their treaties, their laws, and—when needed—their armies to back up their forest claims.

What, after all, were people fighting to retain? For many people in forest communities, their actual use of the forest changed much less than did their legal access. The poorest lost the mobility that had once been something of a weapon against the rich or powerful among them. Whatever their motives, all rural groups continued to take and use teak and other wood from the forest, as indicated in the statistics on forest theft: in 1905 some 45,000 people were arrested for forest crimes, mostly wood theft (Benda and Castles 1969). Villagers could not live without the forest.

In this respect, the Saminist movement can be used to symbolize a long-standing battle over villagers' rights of forest access and foresters' interpretations of their motives. Dutch actions to exile Samin and some of his key followers as subversive elements failed to destroy the movement: even today a few Saminist communities are found in the heart of the teak forest. The government sent an assistant resident in 1918 to report on the Saminist situation and to make recommendations for ameliorating their relations with the government. Perhaps most interesting about the assistant resident's report are his comments on the poor communication between foresters and Saminist communities. Such communication gaps must have long existed between insiders and outsiders wanting different things from the forest. Some sixty-six years later, researchers for the Indonesian State Forestry Corporation would identify the same persistent problems and make recommendations to improve the relations between foresters and forest villagers (Jasper 1918; SFT 1985).

FORESTRY AND PEOPLE: THE CONTINUING DEBATES ON WOOD THEFT

By 1927 the laws and procedures differentiating wood that might belong to the people and wood that belonged to the state were clearly written. All mature teak trees growing on state lands were the property of the state. The state also had the right to tax any mature teak trees sold or transported from private property. Villagers could purchase thinning wood, but each piece, like other classes of government teak logs and boards, had to be marked with a Forest Service stamp. Wood without this stamp was assumed to be stolen. This was particularly irksome when these laws were first implemented because old wood was not marked;

nor would the government stamp remain clear if whole logs were purchased—with the stamp across the round bottom—and then sawn into boards. Not infrequently a house standing two or three years or longer was demolished, the inhabitants punished, and the wood confiscated (Meyier 1903:713).

The forest police began patrolling the teak forests in 1880. With 172 *mantri polities* and their assistants, *boswachters,* the police were the most numerous officials in the forestry hierarchy, and the only level in that hierarchy composed of Javanese.[33]

Though the most numerous, there still were not many of them; it was important, therefore, that they show off their power and authority. The villagers hated the police and their malicious searching for wood. Forest police entered village houses without notice. They looked for standing wood (wood already used in construction) and concealed pieces such as door frames, roofing ribs, boards, and posts that had been "clandestinely obtained" (Meyier 1903:711). Some villagers said that the possession of a piece of teak was punished almost as severely as possession of illegal opium.[34] Also protecting a state monopoly on the sale of a valuable product, the despised opium police could use as evidence remnants of the smell, taste, color, or ashes of the substance found on anyone but the official opium farmer or his agents. Similarly, a forest guard could use the smell of teakwood—particularly aromatic when freshly cut—as evidence of punishable theft (ibid., 712). Forest guards in teak districts today are still reputed to be able to smell freshly cut teak, and to use this skill to find hidden teak.

Some administrators attributed the high rates of theft to teak's costliness, driving people to steal it for their own use and for illicit sale (De boschpolitie op Java onder het binnenlands bestuur 1923:164). Still, the solution proposed was the increase of policing rather than lowering prices or making teak accessible to the people. Some forest administrators and other observers did not approve of such severe restrictions on local people's access to the forest or of the methods employed by the forest police (see, for example, Meyier 1903, Beck 1923, and Becking 1926). However, these liberal attitudes were little match for the increasingly efficient state machine for controlling access to its most valuable forest products.

The interests of the Forest Service and the people were clearly in direct opposition. The latter's use of forest lands for grazing, wood collecting, and—when possible or necessary—as supplemental agricultural fields, was a constant source of conflict between the two sides (Soepardi 1974b:25). By the twentieth century, shipbuilding had ceased to be the primary state use for Java's teak, but luxury wood exports were playing an increasing role in providing state revenue. In 1877, for example, only

860 cubic meters of teak were exported; this represented 1 percent of the total annual cut. Although fluctuating with world political-economic trends over the next forty years (various recessions, trade slowdowns, and World War I), the highest percentage of the annual cut for this period was exported in 1906: some 30 percent, or 65,000 cubic meters (Kerbert 1919:629, 647).

Some scholars and foresters of the time questioned whether forest products generated actual revenues for the government. One critic of the system researched the net profits from forest exploitation in 1903 and found them of little significance because such high production and transport costs were incurred. Even his figures showing the losses incurred in forest exploitation took no account of the wood lost through theft or damage; nor did they indicate the collective individual losses incurred by the villagers whose own subsistence or small-scale commercial enterprises—such as cattle raising, fish breeding, sawmills, wood trade, and construction—were either restricted or forbidden (Meyier 1903:714–15). Other observers questioned the economic rationality of maintaining good agricultural land under teak—a question that foreshadowed the findings (for social welfare as well as economic reasons) of a policy research group some eighty-five years later (de Graaf 1899:914; GOI/IIED 1985b:36–37).

Other hardwoods and bamboo did not grow as abundantly in teak regions as in the rest of Java; thus other types of building materials were not available to most teak forest villagers (Becking 1926:906). Several failed attempts to ameliorate this problem were made, largely because of the limits the Forest Service placed on its own role in the redistribution. For example, in 1918, a regulation for the supply of wood at cost to the "natives" was passed. One forester, Becking, wrote an article encouraging other forest district officers to sell local people teak cut in the course of forest thinning (he had already begun such a program in his district) for use in door, window, and house frames. He also supported the exploitation of woods other than teak for the people and gave preference to the poorest people. The difficulty came in the actual distribution of the wood, which was to be carried out by the village heads. Not a single log was sold under this system, because of conflicts about recipient eligibility and the excessive administrative procedures involved (Becking 1926:906–8). Subsequently, in the 1920s, government timber yards stocked with thinning wood were set up near the big cities to sell timber to local people (Westra 1933:271). However, the poorest people were still unable to purchase this wood because they lacked access to credit and cash was in short supply (Everts 1933:269). Moreover, other government and private businesses were willing to pay the Forest Service's price. The tobacco industry, in particular, became a major customer, rebuilding all its tobacco sheds out of teakwood (Becking 1926:907).

Part of the problem lay in the state's conflicting goals. The political ideology of the period called for the government to provide for people's welfare while making profits at the same time. Welfare programs were designed so the local people paid for any costs through taxes levied on a variety of previously untaxed activities or possessions. But villagers were economically incapable of financing welfare programs, nor was it clear that they wanted such programs, particularly under the terms set by the Dutch government. For example, the Forest Service wanted not only to sell thinning wood to the villagers, it also required the purchase of forest entry permits to collect firewood. People's firewood collection was sometimes limited to two days a week. In some districts, woodcutters were not paid in cash, but with tickets allowing them to collect a certain quantity of waste products from the cut-over forest. Meanwhile, the service sold teak pieces too small for timber classification, and by 1940 industrial-size firewood was the number two revenue-earner for the Forest Service, far exceeding the profits from nonteak timber sales (Schuitemaker 1950:57). The Forest Service rationalized these practices by claiming that most people sold the firewood rather than using it (van der Laan 1933:301). This indicated that people's subsistence uses of the forest could be condoned but their access for commercial purposes was not. The actual effect of these welfare policies was the creation of a labor reserve with very limited legal means of acquiring the cash they needed to subsist.

Critiques of government policy on forest exploitation and wood distribution were common during the 1930s, when the world depression slashed wood exports, particularly luxury woods such as teak. Despite the economic constraints, forest cutting continued. In 1931, 1932, and 1933 only 15,000, 12,000, and 9,000 cubic meters (respectively) were exported, of the approximate annual timber production of 220,000 cubic meters (De nieuwe houtvervreemdingspolitiek 1935:74). The total cut, though below the estimated potential cut of 400,000 cubic meters, was significant, given the depressed economy and market (ibid., 77). Some foresters were proud of the quantities cut in spite of the depression. They boasted that employment rates in forestry remained up (ignoring the fact that wages dropped with the prices), saving the government from providing welfare work for the unemployed. Official reports claimed that demoralization among laborers was low, even though they were forced to accept sharply deflated wages. In the meantime, other state enterprises actually profited from the circumstances. The railways, for example, had inexpensive fuel to run on (van der Laan 1933:293).

Through the 1920s and 1930s the Forest Service continued buying up what it called "critical" land, that is, land in watersheds, with steep slopes, or highly eroded land. Where local environmental circumstances permitted, nonteak land was replanted in teak. Land exchanges were made to consolidate the forest lands; where private individuals were working land enclosed by forest, efforts were made to exchange suitable plots of government land outside the forest. These complicated exchanges often did not satisfy all involved parties; disputes over the relative fertility, size, and location of exchanged lands were frequent (Benda and Castles 1969:223).[35] By 1940, on the eve of the Japanese occupation, the Dutch Colonial Forest Service had brought some 3,057,200 hectares of Java's land under its control (Dienst van het Boschwezen in Indonesie 1948).

SUMMARY: EARLY FOREST HISTORY

As we have seen, prior to the arrival of the VOC, there was a more tenable balance of access to the forest for local people and outsiders with claims on the forest—if for no other reason than that there was a great deal more forest for everyone to use. Precolonial enforcement of restricted forest access was also more difficult, and not necessarily in the interest of precolonial rulers. After the arrival of the VOC, cutting of teak timber intensified, but villagers' access for subsistence was minimally affected, while nonteak forests were virtually ignored by the teak-logging entrepreneurs.

Toward the end of the nineteenth century, a scientific concept of sustainable forest management by the state—for its own profit—began to influence the managers of Java's forests at the same time that this concept was taking hold in other countries. The Forest Service, begun as a production enterprise, extended its custodial role by expanding police activities and formalizing an emerging ideology of conservation by the state. The 1927 forestry laws were the culmination of half a century's trial and error. They represent the entrenchment of an ideology of state legitimacy to control one-fourth the land area of Java.

The means of labor control evolved from the seventeenth to the twentieth century: from the lease of teak forest harvest rights and the labor of teak forest inhabitants, to forced deliveries, to the exchange of labor for land rent remittances, to increased taxation and wage labor in the forest. By the mid-twentieth century, villagers could no longer flee hardship to remote sections of the forest—what remained that was remote? Villagers resorted to furtive means of acquiring building and cooking materials; some accepted small plots of reforestation land for temporary agriculture. Rural agriculturalists who labored in the forest subsidized the state's investment in forestry by producing their own food either on their own lands or on these temporarily accessible reforestation plots.

Forestry policies took away forest villagers' means of helping them-selves; they often made life harder. Both the blandongdiensten and its successor, the "free" labor system, had placed onerous obligations on the people. Reforestation by tumpang sari was developed first for its cost-effectiveness and only incidentally for its minimal, and temporary, welfare-improving potential.

Nevertheless, in the design of reforestation schemes from the turn of the century until the end of the Dutch colonial era, the ideology and rhetoric of "mutual benefit" began to emerge in Dutch forestry litera-ture. By the 1930s, when tumpang sari had become a regular part of reforestation, the Forest Service had begun to speak already of its gener-osity in "lending" land to forest peasants to grow agricultural crops for a year, or sometimes two. The state assumed the role of landlord and land administrator formerly played only by local patrons and Javanese nobil-ity. While the benefits of land and species monopoly accrued to the state, forest villagers increasingly lost legal access to forest land and species. Nevertheless, the notion that state control of forest land and forest prod-ucts was for the sake of the greater good would pervade Indonesian forestry policy long after the Dutch had left.

The closing of the peasants' last frontier and the establishment of a powerful structure of control contributed to the contempt in which the peasantry held state officials, particularly foresters. One form of this contempt was manifested in the Samin movement, but the Saminists were not the only ones who stole wood from government teak forests. The Saminists did not put curses on officials or bar forest police from entering their villages or cemeteries. Such things were done by other peasants. To this day, such cursed spots are found throughout the forest villages of Java and forest officials fear to enter them—even though they are of a different race and nationality than those against whom the curses were originally directed. Tragic tales abound of those who ignore the warnings (see chapter 7) and suffer the consequences.

It has been argued that the same process of changing indigenous social structure by national-colonial policy that took place in nineteenth-century Java is being extended to the rest of Indonesia today (Breman 1980:10; Dove 1984, 1985). Indonesians living in Sumatra, Kalimantan, Irian, Sulawesi, and other islands complain about the "Javanization" of their political structures, cultures, and daily lives. This needs to be under-stood as a complex phenomenon. Besides the Javanese domination of government and Javanese colonization of other ethnic groups' land, what is also happening is the extension of structures and ideologies developed by the Dutch to reorganize rural Javanese life. It is not the precolonial Javanese social structure composed of vertically organized, fluid social relations that is being pushed on the Outer Islands. This

Dutch legacy affecting contemporary Javanization is as much a residue of the Dutch colonial project in Java as were "traditional," closed, corporate Javanese villages.

While most peasant resistance to Dutch colonial forest policy took the form of avoidance, the chaos of life during the Japanese occupation spurred violent confrontations within the forest. Forests, forestry, and forest use were affected dramatically in the midst and the wake of the Japanese occupation. Various uprisings in forest areas occurred concurrent with and subsequent to Indonesian independence. Although tinged with a new nationalism, the postwar Indonesian Forest Service was reconstituted in the Dutch-German mold still familiar, normal, and scientific to the forestry establishment.

1. Man and team of cows hauling teak logs from thinning site, Cepu, 1985.

2. Temporary dwelling built by reforestation laborer in Kaliaman forest, 1985. All the trees shown in this picture were slashed or torn out two weeks after the photo was taken.

3. Cassava harvest from the Kaliaman reforestation site. 1985.

4. Forest villager's forest-edge house and home garden, Cepu, 1985.

5. Unofficial magersaren made of teak leaves and grass, 1986.

6. Forest farmer in Kaliaman forest preparing tumpang sari plot for cultivation, hoeing imperata grass, 1985. Background trees are on private land.

7. Blandong felling girdled teak tree, Jepara, 1985.

8. Blandong making teak posts with traditional axes, late colonial period. (Photo courtesy of Koninklijk Instituut voor de Tropen.)

9. Laborer peeling bark from teak log, Cepu, 1985.

10. Overseer and loggers clearcutting teak, late colonial period. (Photo courtesy of Koninklijk Instituut voor de Tropen.)

11. Transporting teak by ox-drawn carts, Grobogan. (Photo courtesy of Koninklijk Instituut voor de Tropen.)

12. Transporting teak by rail out of teak forest, late colonial period. (Photo courtesy of Koninklijk Instituut voor de Tropen.)

13. Logyard in Rembang, late colonial period. (Photo courtesy of Koninklijk Instituut voor de Tropen.)

PART THREE

State Forests and Changes in State

FOUR

Organized Forest Violence, Reorganized Forest Access, 1942–1966

An open struggle between the forces of state control of forests and local use of them began with the Japanese occupation of Java and continued into the four-year period during which the Javanese fought for Indonesian independence against returning Dutch and British forces. As it turned out, the Japanese occupation of Java constituted only the first part of two decades of battles fought within and over Java's forests. The effects of the violence were felt not only by the increasingly organized contenders for control over the forest (and the state) but also by the forest itself.

The two and a half decades from 1942 to 1967 constituted the most explosive period in Java's modern history; upheaval did not end with the achievement of Indonesian independence in 1949. The physical revolution (against the Dutch) lasted for only four years; social revolution, impelling reconfiguration of national and regional consciousness, raged for decades longer.[1] Both left marks on the forests.

A MODEL FOR CHANGE AND COLLECTIVE ACTION

The violent events that took place in the forests were a function of contemporary forms of political activity. Violence and open expression of opposition were common modes of political expression until Soeharto replaced Soekarno as president of Indonesia in 1967.[2] At this turning point, coming after nearly two years of bloody civil strife and terror, the state recaptured its capacity to monopolize the use of violence.

The Tillys' model of collective violence (Tilly, Tilly, and Tilly 1975: 240–87) helps explain the expression of forest-based violence in Java, the structural characteristics leading to its occurrence, the actions of the foresters as the tenor of violence changed, and the denouement of these decades of collective action. The Tillys contrast "breakdown" theories of collective violence—that is, those built on the notion that structural breakdown and the resultant physical and emotional hardships cause people to take violent action together—with their own theory of "the importance of solidarity and articulated interests" in leading to violent collective action. In other words, they argue that collective violence does not arise primarily from circumstances where strained living conditions cause spontaneous rioting or mob action; rather, it is an expression of power by organized groups with common interests. Violent expression of power by otherwise nonviolent groups is not always intentional. It is often a reaction to the violent response of previously powerful groups in that society—the state and the dominant classes, among others—to the increasing power or assumption of power by new organizations. Violence occurs when the tenor of resistance rises between groups struggling for power—or for control over resources. Depending on the nature of the structural change, states and their agents play key roles in this violence, generally as the repressors of violent or nonviolent collective action aimed at gaining control over the resources controlled by the government.

The Tillys posit the following order of events surrounding the occurrence of collective action: As structural change allows the formation of new groups, the groups seek to gain collective control over resources; as they acquire and use these resources, other groups challenge them either as equals, that is, new groups seeking access to power resources, or as repressors, that is, previous controllers or monopolists of those resources, and collective violence erupts. They also assume

> that the more rapid mobilization [of competing power groups] should lead to extensive collective violence, changes in governmental repressive tactics should strongly affect the level and character of collective violence, highly mobilized groups and groups rapidly acquiring or losing power should be disproportionately involved in violent conflicts, unorganized groups, casual crowds, and marginal people should not. The general level of discontent, the current pace of change, the extent of "disorganization" (as embodied in such phenomena as crime, family instability, suicide, or mental illness) should have little or no connection with the level of collective violence. [Ibid., 245]

Three differences stand out in the case of collective violence in Java's forests. First, acts against the forests, where forest products and lands were appropriated or counter-appropriated, were not restricted to collective actions. A great number of people who were either not organized or did not understand the more abstract objectives of the organizations they joined (beyond the acquisition of trees and land), made claims on forest products and forest land. It is difficult to assess the extent to which individuals who joined political groups understood the implications of their decisions: continued repression of former members of political parties makes the collection of such data impossible. Contemporary informants insist, however, that marginalized people sought what they could from the forest in the mayhem.

The second difference in the Javanese case is that here we are speaking of the physical control of natural resources and ultimately of the rights to dispose of these resources. Though there is some relationship to economic power, these differ from the power resources sought by the contenders described by the Tillys. Political change spurred and created the conditions leading to the seizure of forest resources. Political groups, though having other agendas, used the forest access issue as a way of mobilizing support in forest villages. The foresters who survived the political upheaval remained agents of the victorious factions of the state. These foresters were involved in the ultimate repression of forest villagers who belonged to the political parties most actively mobilized to reclaim forest control. Most important, by the time Soeharto assumed power in 1967, the outlawing of certain political parties and the association of peasant appropriation of forest products and land with particular parties effectively eliminated the Indonesian state's tolerance of many aspects of peasant forest use. The result was the recriminalization of particular forest uses by local people, and the recognition of these acts as criminal by more state agencies than the foresters alone.

Finally, both the breakdown of the state's capacity to control the resources it claimed and the mobilization of forest-based peasants by competing political organizations spurred violent and nonviolent forms of forest reappropriation. Ideologically and structurally, the nature of forest control and forms of resistance were swept up by—and mimicked—the political, social, and ideological revolution of the times. In the jumble of activity and the confusion of changes in the nation's controllers, the repertoire of resistance changed for forest villagers, forest police, and forest managers alike. Notions of forest management, forest access rights, and forest access control also became confused.

THE JAPANESE AND FORESTRY

The Dutch colonial government in Java, and the mystique that had permitted it to rule for nearly 150 years, fell within ten days of the Japanese invasion (Benda, Irikura, and Kishi 1965:61).[3] Forest villagers believed the end had come to the restrictions keeping them out of the forest, a belief that was wrongly construed. Soon forest villagers conscripted for the Japanese forced labor called *romusha* would be spending far more time in the forest at much less profit to themselves. Moreover, most of the people settled in the forest by the Japanese to harvest wood and produce crops for the war effort would be able to stay for only a couple of decades, until the new Indonesian foresters evicted them.

The style of leadership in Java changed under the Japanese from the bourgeois, businesslike "utilitarian calculus of tropical capitalism" of the Dutch to a style marked by "the theatrics and ritual of Japanese imperial and military tradition" (Anderson 1972:31–32). This contrast in style reflected the contrasts of forestry under the two regimes. Some key changes took place under the Japanese; changes that would influence the politics of forest use and state forest management long after the Japanese surrendered to the Allies and left Java. While forestry as they had known it under the Dutch became a morass of chaotic confusion, Javanese foresters working under the Japanese tried unsuccessfully to maintain an ordered and "rational" system of forest management.

Directly and indirectly, the Japanese occupation of Java from 1942 to 1945 had deleterious effects on the island's forests and forestry; the scars of this period are still evident in the distorted structure of today's forests.[4] Many older trees were destroyed, and few trees were planted during the Japanese occupation and the Indonesian revolution. Violent events in the ensuing battles for ideological control of the new state caused significant additional impact.

Chaos and destruction were begun by the foresters themselves, after they heard that Japanese occupying forces had landed and taken over in March 1942. Before Japanese control spread over the entire island, the Dutch embarked on a scorched-earth policy (*verschroeingsaarde-politiek*), in which they burned and destroyed buildings and materials that could be used by the enemy. The foresters wanted to eradicate any potentially useful elements of their legacy and proceeded to demolish their own infrastructure, devastating the sawmills at Saradan (East Java) and Cepu (then privately owned), burning many foresters' houses and forest district offices, blowing up rail bridges across rivers in the forest, destroying forest maps, and igniting logyards full of giant teak logs waiting for shipment (Soepardi 1974a:124).

Forest villagers responded vehemently to the sudden change in the forest custodians. They ransacked remaining logyards, administrators' housing, and the forest itself. The worst destruction took place in some of the most valuable teak forests in the residencies of Semarang, Jepara, Rembang, and Bojonegoro. Some local administrators (village heads and regents) saw the chance to exert their own power and ordered people to bring them the money kept at the forest district offices. Alarmed by the state of the forest and their loss of control, some lower-level Javanese forestry personnel assumed command of their forest territories and issued orders for cutting and planting the forest (Soepardi 1974a:124–25, 1974b:1). These self-appointed mini-commands lasted only until the Japanese arrived in each locale.

Finally, in June 1942, the Japanese Forest Service of Java, called *Ringyo Tyuoo Zimusyo* (RTZ), was established. Becking, the head of the deposed Dienst van het Boschwezen, and some Dutch forest district officers were kept on initially as advisors in the Japanese Forest Inspectorship territories (there were five of these in the whole of Java). Forest areas (*daerah hutan*) were under the jurisdiction of Indonesians with a Dutch advisor overseeing two or three of them. Some Indonesians were appointed to managerial positions (Soepardi 1974b:2). By mid-1943 all Dutch advisors except those at the experiment station, the main office in Bogor, and the Inspection divisions were interned in concentration camps (Soepardi 1974b:7).

From June 1942 through October 1943 the RTZ was part of the Department of Industrial Affairs (*Sangyobu*); in November 1943 because so much teak was required for shipbuilding, it was moved to the Bureau of Shipping (*Zoosenkyoku*). In July 1945 the RTZ was moved again, this time to the Department of War Production (*Gunzyuseisanbu*), putting forests and forest laborers under military control (Soepardi 1974b:2–3). The impacts of this final change in the administration of the forests had little time to take effect, however; six weeks later, the Japanese surrendered.

Timber, firewood, and charcoal were in great demand for the trains, factories, and war-related industries (manufacturing cement, matches, crates). Teak of all age-classes growing near railways and roads was cut and shipped, leaving great gaps in the forests of Pemalang, Balapulang, Gunung Kidul, Gundih, Cepu, Parengan, Madiun, and Blitar forest districts. Forest production in 1943 and 1944 virtually doubled the prewar production under the Dutch (see Appendix D).[5] In 1944 shipbuilding alone consumed an estimated 120,000 to 250,000 cubic meters of the longest and broadest timbers to build 400 to 500 requisitioned ships (Soepardi 1974b:13). In addition, the Forest Service had to provide teak to the shipbuilding company of Nomura-Tohindo (Departemen Kehutanan 1986, 2:9).

In addition to building ships, the Japanese drew on Java's resources in other ways to support their war effort. They rebuilt the Saradan sawmill, but it never reached its prewar capacity. They constructed railways for the transport of wood, goods, and soldiers. Tracks were laid to transport wood from Cepu, Ngawi, Jombang, Saradan, Blora, and Gundih forest districts. Construction delays caused the Japanese to transport logs via the Solo River from Bojonegoro, Cepu, and Ngawi forest districts, the first time this method had been used in decades.

In many locales, whole forest villages were created by the Japanese settling colonies of woodcutters within a forest area to convert the forest to agriculture. In parts of other districts, such as Cepu, some clearcut areas were replanted, but all wood harvests were used in the war effort. No matter what form local forest management took, forest villagers who lived through this chaotic three and a half years today recall the rampant, and ubiquitous, cutting of trees. Everyone took part.

The critical routine tasks of scientific forestry—planting, thinning, maintenance—were all but ignored by the Japanese. There were no work plans. Some Indonesian forest district managers organized replanting on their own. In time their efforts were cut short by their Japanese superiors, most of whom had no training in forestry. In the last six years of active Dutch management (1935–1940) the average annual teak reforestation area was 12,300 hectares and 7,600 hectares for nonteak species.[6] Taking this rate as a "normal" cutting and replanting standard, this would mean that at least 43,000 hectares of teak and 27,300 hectares of nonteak species should have been planted during almost three and a half years of Japanese forest administration. In fact, less than 20,000 hectares of teak and 6,000 hectares of nonteak species were planted in the whole period (Soepardi 1974b:22; Departemen Kehutanan 1986, 2:16). At the same time, forest cutting was taking place at breakneck speed. No one knows how many hectares survived the tumult. At the end of this period, Becking, head of the Forest Service prior to the Japanese occupation and an advisor to the Japanese until their surrender, estimated that teak production would have to be reduced by 30 percent over the next thirty years just to return the forest to its prewar level of quality (Becking 1946, cited in Departemen Kehutanan 1986, 2:17).

The forest villagers bore the brunt of the Japanese excesses in the forest. Vast armies of forest laborers were put to work cutting and hauling timber under the Japanese forced labor system (romusha). Attempting to escape often meant a more rapid death than the starvation that killed many forest laborers. Forest production dropped below pre-occupation levels in 1945, not only because of shortages of tools and transport vehicles, but also because of the repressive conditions the forest laborers endured (Soepardi 1974b:13). Some peasants risked death by planting crops for themselves in newly created forest areas. Villagers and foresters remembering this period say that these peasants were protected by sympathetic local foresters and regents (ibid., 14, 25).

A total of 4,428 hectares of forest land were reportedly allocated to 8,242 peasant cultivators in new forest colonies. More land was occupied without official approval or taken over by the Japanese military for its own use (ibid., 26). Contemporary foresters complain that this practice of "lending" forest lands contributed to people's belief that it was all right to cut down the forest for food production.[7] It is equally likely that the Japanese period fueled people's dormant beliefs in their rights of forest access, particularly during times of food stress. In any case, decades after the Japanese surrendered, their war production policies have led to disputes over land rights between the SFC, the Department of Agrarian Affairs, and individual farmers.

THE REPUBLIC OF INDONESIA
AND THE NEW FOREST SERVICE

Soon after Soekarno and Hatta declared the Republic of Indonesia an independent nation in 1945,[8] Ringyo Tyuoo Zimusyo was changed to the *Jawatan Kehutanan* (Forest Service). Within two months, British troops landed on Java to rescue over a hundred thousand European prisoners of war, to oversee the repatriation of the Japanese troops, and, according to an agreement with the Dutch, to help the latter reestablish their authority in Indonesia (Anderson 1972:133–34).[9] The Indonesians resisted the return of the Dutch authority, and the British attacked and occupied various government buildings, including the Forest Service's main office in Bogor.

As a result of the Allied aggression, the Indonesian Forest Service moved inland to Yogyakarta, where it remained for the duration of the revolution. Wartime virtually cut the connection between the central government and the Forest Service, and the needs of the revolution took priority.[10] This left the Forest Service with a great deal of independence. During this time, foresters were prevented from implementing the Dutch-German management system by sheer lack of service personnel and forest labor; so many people had joined the freedom fighters it was impossible to replant and otherwise repair the extensive forest damage inflicted by the Japanese. Meanwhile, a commission was appointed to translate into Indonesian those Dutch forest laws and regulations ideologically congruent with the goals of the revolution (Departemen Kehutanan 1986, 2:43); virtually all laws, however, were translated word-for-word (Perum Perhutani 1984).

Perhaps most difficult for the Indonesian foresters to resolve were their concurrent desires to return to the orderly and routinized work system of the Dienst van het Boschwezen, and to eliminate those elements of forest management that conflicted with the more egalitarian philosophy sported by the independent republic. Like the Japanese war planners, the Republican (Indonesian) government still needed firewood and charcoal; peasants and others continued to clear forest for agriculture and to cut wood as they needed it. The forest police had resumed patrolling, but were often powerless to prevent forest raiding by impoverished villagers. Eventually, village leaders and the army were enlisted to assist the forest police.

A contradiction had begun to emerge in deciding how to manage the new nation's forests. On one side were the long-term and macro-economic orientations of traditional forestry, in which forests and forest products were viewed as important sources of revenue for the state and, by association, the nation. Moreover, by protecting watersheds and adjacent food-producing lowlands, forests played an important indirect role in the maintenance of large segments of the population. The organization of the Indonesian Forest Service, and some of its major goals, reflected the prewar tradition. Older foresters in particular argued that only a state agency could balance the conservation and production functions of the forest. On the other hand, the people's needs for housing and fuelwood, and land for grazing and agriculture, were an important concern. Many of the younger nationalists felt the needs of people living in forest villages should receive greater consideration in planning forest management than they had under the Dutch. The mixture of values in the new Forest Service often gave rise to differences unresolved by those making forest policy.

At a meeting held in Malang in March 1946, the following objectives were adopted (Soepardi 1974b:46–47):

1. To adapt the organization of the Forest Service to the government's political foundation (*dasar politik*), particularly by shifting the Forest Service's function from the trade/export orientation emphasized by the Dutch and the pervasive forest slashing practiced by the Japanese to distributing wood fairly, inexpensively, and directly to the people.

2. To increase production, prioritizing firewood production for the government railway system and war-related industries.

3. To rationalize Forest Service operations and to repair forest product processing plants.

4. To increase the knowledge of all foresters by establishing forestry training institutions.

5. To help increase agricultural production by reforesting forest lands using the tumpang sari system and, indirectly, by restoring damaged protection forests in watersheds. Also, to enlist the assistance of village leaders and the military to reforest the [reported] 102,000 hectares [of forest land] illegally occupied by forest villagers.

6. To make people aware of the meaning of forestry, by making them realize the importance of laws and regulations. An information-dispersal program was to begin, using radio, magazines, newspa-

pers, short courses, and traditional or religious institutions such as village leaders and Masjumi.[11]

These aims of the new Forest Service, particularly the first one, could perhaps have led to socially and environmentally appropriate forestry. However, divergent management philosophies based on political affiliation and differing interpretations of the Forest Service's functions threw its leadership into dispute. Some foresters perceived a major problem to be that top Indonesian officials had previously worked under the Dutch and Japanese. Adherents of the new nationalism and socialism saw the appointment of these men as inappropriate to the independent state. This perception led to changes being made in forestry administrators, reflecting the changes being made in all sectors of the independent nation's government, partially as a result of the tensions between the younger and older nationalists (Anderson 1972:chaps. 4 and 5; Soepardi 1974b:42–45).

The following incident illustrates this struggle in the forestry context. In November 1945 Soekowijono formed and became the head of the Forestry Youth's Movement (*Gerakan Pemuda Kehutanan*). The movement proposed the formation of a Forestry Workers' Union (*Sarekat Buruh Kehutanan*). Although this union was not originally dominated by Communist party members, Soekowijono's ideas tended to be more radical than those of some foresters preferring a return to the Dutch system. In March 1946 he resigned from the Central Directorship after accusing the other members of still being too oriented toward the past (*beraliran lama*) (Soepardi 1974b:45–46).

True to the new foresters' objectives, at least during the first two years of the revolution, most construction wood (87 percent in 1946 and 81 percent in 1947) was distributed to the local populace. Nearly 70 percent of the firewood cut went to the state railroad service. Fifty-four centers for wood distribution were established in Central and East Java (Departemen Kehutanan 1986, 2:30). One wonders who bought it; few people could afford wood at any price. Inflation meant that teak cost six times as much as it had under the Dutch; even the price of nonteak sawlogs had quadrupled. Teak and nonteak firewood prices had multiplied five-fold (Soepardi 1974b:59).

Despite the changes in its stated philosophy and goals, the "new" Indonesian Forest Service consistently invoked its power and legitimacy and reacted to the upsets on the forest lands in almost predictable "old" ways. Six German and Australian foresters interned in prison camps for the duration of the revolution were released to aid the Indonesian Forest Service in planning to restore forest administration to normal. European professors of forestry were sought to teach in the newly established

Gadjah Mada University in Yogyakarta. Old ties with large-scale Chinese teak wholesalers were reestablished. A forester was placed on the Agrarian Committee formed by President Soekarno on May 21, 1948, largely to ensure that the state kept control over the lands it held as a result of the Domeinverklaring (Soepardi 1974b:80).

As the revolution progressed, the need for firewood for the rail service increased rapidly. In 1947 President Soekarno had requested that the Forest Service make firewood provision its top priority. The foresters launched a massive campaign to alert people to the revolution's need for more firewood, hoping to stir them with nationalist appeals. In addition, forestry officials tried to enlist the help of village leaders and the state police by pointing out the alarming increase in soil erosion and firewood shortage. But the people resisted. The foresters had difficulty recruiting forest laborers to cut firewood. Some village leaders were willing to aid the desperate foresters; others took the side of the people or took the opportunity to capitalize on the lack of forest controls. By 1948 a Special Committee on Firewood had been appointed and President Soekarno issued a government regulation called the "Militarization of the Forest Service." What forest labor could be mustered was mobilized to produce firewood rather than sawlogs (Departemen Kehutanan 1986, 2:29) (see Appendix D).

Though reforestation on a small scale was planned, working conditions precluded its realization. In October 1947 the Forest Service was able to conduct an informal survey of forest conditions in Republican territory. Although survey work was aborted whenever a forest site suddenly became a battleground, foresters managed to measure and mark many forest boundaries in accordance with old forest maps.[12] These markers were meant to remind "squatters" that the Forest Service still claimed the rights to that land (Departemen Kehutanan 1986, 2:28,31).

The public image of forestry and foresters remained unfavorable, perhaps because the upsets of war prevented the implementation of the progressive policies discussed just two years earlier. In August 1948 the Forest Service offices and forests of the primary teak regions were attacked by the Indonesian Communist party and the People's Democratic Front during the Madiun rebellion and suffered great damages. In one incident, a bridge over the Solo River in the heart of the teak forest was blown up. Restorative work in most of Java's forests came to a standstill (Soepardi 1974b:81).

Soepardi wrote that many villagers, strained by the shortages of war, had lost their revolutionary fervor and did not want to work with the Forest Service. This was hardly the only reason for their reticence. These people had a different notion of what the social and political changes brought by war meant. By this time, thousands of hectares of the state forest lands were controlled by landless peasants, many of them former forest laborers, who were as unwilling to give these lands up as to work in the forest under prewar conditions (Soepardi 1974b:64). The Forest Service, reflecting another view of their actions, already labeled these people "squatters" or, more literally, "wild occupants" (penduduk liar).

FOREST DESTRUCTION BY THE PEOPLE

An estimated 220,000 hectares of state forest were destroyed or damaged during 1946. Of these, some 108,640 hectares were consumed by fires (compared with 10,900 hectares in 1938 under the Dutch Forest Service), set presumably by armies and individuals. Approximately 110,000 hectares were occupied by forest villagers or stripped of their timber by peasants and the revolutionary armies for fuel. In some instances, whole "battalions" of armed villagers entered teak forests and removed all the trees for sale or use. In Indramayu Forest District (West Java), 1,300 villagers leveled 117.5 hectares of forest and burned all that remained after hauling out the teak (Soepardi 1974b:60–62).

At the same time that the Indonesian government began returning occupied estate (plantation) lands to the prewar owners (most of whom were European), the Forest Service began evicting the peasants from forest lands. Unions such as the Indonesian Forestry Workers' Union (SARBUKSI) and the Indonesian Peasants' Front (BTI) fought beside the peasants to prevent their eviction. Violent clashes between the foresters, the peasants, and their various supporters often took place. Hindley (1967:172) reported that "in some areas peasants were shot, and in many more the squatters' homes were destroyed, their crops plowed up." Amazingly, foresters were still keeping records of forest crimes. By the end of 1947, some 34,490 forest crimes recorded since 1945 had not yet been settled in the courts. By the end of the revolution in 1949, at least 400,000 hectares, or 14 percent, of Java's state forest lands were allegedly occupied by peasants or deforested by civilian and military wood thieves (Departemen Kehutanan 1986:42).

Why were people only now unleashing their pent-up feelings against the Forest Service and the forest access restrictions imposed for so many years? The apparatus of control was breaking down; at the same time people were more organized, some in armed people's militias. Political violence had been the vehicle of change for nearly a decade. But it was not merely a matter of violence begetting violence. Rather, the circumstances of collective violence constituted a repertoire of collective action shaped by the broader repertoire of the time (Tilly, Tilly, and Tilly 1975:242–43).

While it seemed to the foresters a critical change in the status quo that the stewardship of the state forests was now in Indonesian hands, to forest-dependent villagers there was little change. Restricted forest access, whether imposed by the Dutch, Japanese, or fellow Indonesians, constrained their lives and livelihoods. To forest villagers the restrictions that the Indonesian Forest Service wanted to renew meant a return to the hardships and wood shortages of the colonial period. Teak and other forest species were to be extracted from local forests and sold by outsiders for use elsewhere. Forest boundaries established by the Dutch were to be guarded and local people kept off the forest lands except as laborers working for the state. While many foresters were encouraging a return to Dutch principles, the language of the revolution, whatever party one leaned toward, had been one of freedom and justice for all. Men and women of the forest had gone off to join the fight for independence, and had harbored government soldiers in their forest-based homes as part of their war effort. It did not seem fair that now their newfound freedom would be circumscribed.

At the same time, foresters were responding to the chaos with different objectives in mind. Many Indonesian foresters saw their mission as one that required the return to a "normal" system of forestry, to the regulated system of forest access control they had learned from the Dutch. And, compared to the total disorder and ruinous management of the forests under the Japanese, the Dutch system was much more normal to professional foresters trained in forest science.

AFTER THE REVOLUTION: CONSOLIDATING ACCESS CONTROL

When the revolution ended and the Dutch withdrew in 1949, the new nation still found itself steeped in internal strife. Similarly, battles over the appropriate state forestry ideology and structure shook the foundations of forest management in Java. The Jawatan Kehutanan remained part of the Ministry of Agriculture, as it had been under the Dutch.[13] Until 1957 all forest management was centralized; then, provincial managers took over some decisions concerning the marketing of forest products, forest management, forest exploitation (including labor practices), and forest protection.[14] Policy, however, was still formulated at the center; provincial decisions had to concur with national policy. When the Directorate of Forestry was reorganized into a state corporation, some autonomy of the provincial units was eliminated (Junus 1985:172).

Conflicting ideologies across the political spectrum influenced the state forestry philosophy in the central offices and the field.[15] Various ideas about the relevance of the Dutch forestry system to the needs of the Javanese people began to circulate. Each idea was associated with a political party ideology. According to prevailing notions of political allegiance, acceptance of part of a party's platform was interpreted to mean categorical refusal of all aspects of other platforms. Thus, after 1965–66, when the whole range of Indonesia's political philosophies climaxed in a heated agrarian war, ideas associated with defeated parties' philosophies could be interpreted as subversive.

Until the Guided Democracy period, however, diversity of political thought characterized various state bureaucracies. Different political philosophies were professed by successive ministers of Agriculture (under which Forestry was subsumed), while field foresters working in adjacent tracts followed opposing streams. These ideological divergences reduced the Forest Service's ability to control forest theft and guard forest boundaries; some foresters weren't sure that these should be their goals.

Political groups directly and indirectly influenced the ways people interacted with the forest during the Soekarno period. The four factions most involved with the forest were: (1) Darul Islam and the Islamic Army of Indonesia (*Darul Islam/Tentara Islam Indonesia*), known as DI/TII; (2) the military as a whole and individuals within it who took advantage of their status as the government's armed forces; (3) the Indonesian Communist Party (*Partai Komunis Indonesia*), or PKI; and (4) the "mainstream" foresters themselves, eventually represented by the Indonesian Nationalist Party (*Partai Nasional Indonesia*), or PNI.[16]

DI/TII

The thrust of the Darul Islam movement was the effort to establish an Islamic state in Indonesia. Its strongest bases were in West Java and western Central Java. The movement began toward the end of the revolution and was an outgrowth of the Islamic army element called Hizbullah, which was supported by the Masjumi Party.[17]

The Darul Islam rebels used guerrilla warfare, hiding in the wooded hills of the western half of Java and fighting against the Indonesian National Army (*Tentara Nasional Indonesia*), or TNI. Guerrilla fighting requires cover to be successful, the thicker the better; thus it was in the interest of the rebels to maintain the forest cover. Peasants from areas where DI rebels established forest bases recount stories of friends and family being shot because they cut down trees, cut branches for firewood, or gathered leaves for sale or for fodder. Grazing cattle in the forest was allowed, but on occasion cows or goats were seized by the rebels for food. At night DI patrols entered the villages and demanded contributions of food; anyone who refused or lied about their supplies was shot. The newspapers of the period are full of articles describing the burning, killing, and devastation of forest villages by bands of DI guerrillas.

In some of the hilly forest areas the DI rebels wished to occupy, there were still some communities of forest villagers who had been resettled during the Japanese period. The experiences of these groups and individuals in them varied: Some were able to come to terms with the guerrillas, often providing them the bulk of their food; others were afraid and fled to larger villages, leaving their homes and fields to be occupied and sometimes tended by the DI bands or their sympathizers. In some locales, foresters returned to start reforestation programs in these unauthorized villages and settlements. In what they regarded as a compromise, the foresters distributed seeds to villagers occupying forest land for replanting by the tumpang sari system. In exchange for providing these "squatters" access to the forest land for a year or two more, and the seeds for reforestation, the foresters expected them to leave the parcels and seek other sources of income.[18] They also hoped to win these villagers' sympathies away from nearby DI rebels.

Under the circumstances, these efforts were wasted. Many villagers working lands near the bases of DI activity were too afraid to cultivate either their forest plots or private lands located near the forest. Large tracts of forest land remained untended. Some were taken over by deeply rooted, coarse *imperata cylindrica* grass, others were covered with thick secondary growth, and others were eroded and leached by sun and rain.

Any officials of the Soekarno government, including foresters, were distrusted and often shot on sight by the forest-based guerrillas. Foresters interviewed in some villages explained that during this tumultuous period neither forest nor village officials dared reside in the villages near DI strongholds, let alone go near the forest. In the early 1950s, government action against the rebels increased, beginning more than a decade of upheaval in the daily lives of many forest villagers in West and western Central Java, where the DI rebels were powerful. By day, the peasants had to profess and illustrate their loyalty to the TNI; by night, they had to act the same toward DI/TII.

Disregarding the fear generated by DI, some villagers and officials attacked their camps to avenge DI's actions. In one area, a DI band of 100 had attacked a village, killing five peasants, burning two rice storehouses, two schools, thirty-two homes, and pillaging seventy-five houses. Within a few days, an army of 11,000 angry peasants was organized by local army and police officials and forced the DI band out of the forest (*Harian Rakyat*, June 20, 1957:2).

Ironically, the activities of DI/TII served to preserve the forest, but their relationships with forest villagers were less than convivial. Forest villagers describe the period as one in which everyone was suspicious and suspected. Because everyone had to profess loyalty to both sides, one never knew where one's neighbors' or outsiders' real sympathies lay. Food was short, labor opportunities for those who used to cross the forest were frequently unattainable. The self-reliance that had marked forest villagers through the centuries of enduring the blandong system and other hardships or dangers of living in the forest became crucial for survival once again. The hardships of daily life near the forests where DI was hiding continued until 1962 when its leader was captured.

THE MILITARY

The Indonesian military used tactics that were decidedly harmful to the forest to capture the leaders of DI/TII and rout out other guerrillas. Destroying the Islamic army's hiding places in the forest meant destroying the forest. Other options were limited; whenever battalions approached the forest, DI soldiers saw and shot at them before the army could even locate the guerrillas. As a result, in the mid-1950s, the Indonesian army began retaliatory operations by burning whole corridors and large tracts of forest to force the rebels out and prevent their return. Where Darul Islam rebels were pursued by government forces, a clear path of forest destruction remained—one started by the army to pressure the guerrillas out and finished by villagers who desperately needed something to sell for a livelihood. Although the army chose and implemented its forest-destructive tactics, foresters today blame DI/TII—not the Indonesian army—for the destruction of the forests in which the guerrillas hid.

In addition to a general military strategy to destroy forest hiding places, contemporary forest villagers and foresters recall many incidents in which military personnel (or nonmilitary men posing as such) misused their positions to steal teak. Such individuals drove trucks into the forest, often for several nights in a row, and drove out with full loads of logs. Many hired villagers or worked with other middlemen to acquire logs or charcoal. Given the turbulent atmosphere of the times, many foresters were afraid to take action. The party politics of the period were taken advantage of by these individuals. Labor unions and farmers' organizations supported the peasants and laborers involved in the activities of illegal loggers and military businessmen.

PKI

The activities of the Indonesian Communist Party (PKI) and its affiliated organizations such as the Indonesian Peasants Front (*Barisan Tani Indonesia,* or BTI), the Union of Forestry Workers (SARBUKSI), and the Indonesian Workers' Central Organization (SOBSI) became the most violent and remembered mass actions against the forests, non-PKI foresters, and the forestry establishment.

As described above, during the Japanese occupation and the revolution, thousands of landless peasants occupied the state forest and private estate lands. These peasants were among the first to be organized by the communist organizations. Without legal rights to the land they occupied and with generally few rights in their villages (as landless or land-poor villagers), the squatters were quick to realize the benefits of organization (Mortimer 1974:276,278). Until 1955 BTI was active only in villages adjacent to forest and estate lands (Hindley 1967:172).[19] After the DI uprising ended in 1962, BTI factions entered forest villages in western Java where land distribution was severely skewed or where DI had been harsh on local peasants. There, BTI coordinated peasant activities on forest lands as well as on the private lands of large landholders who had sympathized with DI.

From November 1945 until the end of the revolution, all foresters were part of one union, the Forestry Workers Union (*Sarekat Buruh Kehutanan,* or SBK). Though called a "workers" union, forest laborers were not included as members during the early years (Departemen Kehutanan 1986, 2:70; Soepardi 1974b:45,54). By the end of the revolution, however, the union had begun recruiting forest laborers, and its leadership had adopted much of the philosophy of the left. As in other sectors of the government and society, the following argument was made:

> Although in past years the structure and outlook of our organization [and our] objectives and means of struggle were extremely unfocused, influenced by false and misdirected feelings of love toward the [Forest] Service and the nation, the recent Fourth Congress has given birth to new perspectives and structures [and to] objectives and means of struggle which are resolute and adept in opposing all oppression of the working class which will not end as long as the economic bases of capitalism also have not ended. [Tinjauan Serikat Buruh Kehutanan 1949:9][20]

At this time, the union's acronym was changed to SARBUKSI (*Sarekat Buruh Kehutanan Seluruh Indonesia,* All Indonesia Forestry Workers Union) and thousands of forest laborers were recruited.

By 1962 SARBUKSI claimed 250,000 members, including forest administrators, rangers, and laborers.[21] The union was further strengthened after affiliating with the communist All Indonesia Workers' Central Organization (*Sentral Organisasi Buruh Seluruh Indonesia,* or SOBSI). Many forest villagers who had access to tumpang sari land for reforestation, or who were hired as day labor for reforestation (*cemplongan*), belonged to BTI as well as SARBUKSI. BTI membership grew from an estimated membership of 360,000 in 1953 to an enormous enrollment of 5,654,974 by July 1962, a number they claimed represented 25 percent of the adult peasant population (Hindley 1967:165–66).[22]

The less radical foresters broke off from SARBUKSI and formed a new Forestry Workers' Union (*Sarekat Buruh Kehutanan*, or SBK; Departemen Kehutanan 1986, 2:70). They also formed regional organizations to "advance their members' science and knowledge" (ibid.). Later, when these regional organizations joined together, they began publishing forestry journals.

As the decade progressed, SARBUKSI influenced many policies affecting forestry workers within the bureaucracy and in the field. SARBUKSI branches argued for peasants' rights to the forest land they occupied; they also supported promotions and salary raises for lower-level forestry officials.

Enterprise Councils (*Dewan Perusahaan*) were formed in each forest district, each with a representative from SARBUKSI, to deliberate on and form policy. When the forestry leadership of the district wanted to take action against employees, particularly those affiliated with SARBUKSI, the information was passed to other SARBUKSI members and letters of protest sent to the central Forestry administration in Jakarta, the provincial legislature (DPRD), and the national legislature (DPR). For example, when the Forest Service tried to cut its expenditures by cutting out the traditional New Year's bonus for reforestation labor in Magelang Forest District, the regional SARBUKSI representative met with the administrator and demanded payment (*Harian Rakyat*, September 17,1957:2). SARBUKSI members also lobbied to prevent the promotions of foresters unsympathetic to the interests and politics of the PKI and SARBUKSI and by association, unsympathetic to the demands made by and in the name of forest laborers and peasants who had appropriated forest lands.

Informants today say that even in forest districts where most foresters were SARBUKSI members, the Forest Service as an institution was deplored by the communist affiliates. It was depicted as an extension of a colonial bureaucracy that had not changed the social relations of forest production by eliminating its colonial style of land control and forest production. SARBUKSI and the other communist affiliates were not alone in their accusations and actions against the Forest Service, however.

Occasionally individuals raised bands of activists around a forest-related issue or incident and acted to undermine both the SARBUKSI and the Forestry positions. In Nganjuk, for example, when foresters were clearing undergrowth from damaged forest land before replanting, a village leader organized a group of farmers to cut down adjacent forest and agricultural crops planted by forest farmers on 328 hectares of forest land they had been assigned for reforestation by tumpang sari. When the forest farmers protested their losses to the foresters, the foresters insisted that the lands they had ordered cleared were the 50 hectares adjacent to the 328 hectares already under cultivation. Further investigation of the incident showed that the village head had promised "attacking" farmers that the land would be divided among all those who took part in the "clearing." The PKI daily paper reported that the foresters were not at fault in this incident. Rather, the village head had created a disruptive situation, pitting farmer against farmer (*Harian Rakyat*, May 8, 1957:2). The village head took advantage of local people's negative feelings toward the forestry establishment.

While SARBUKSI played a major role in fighting for the rights of so-called forest squatters and forest laborers, it is unclear how much it planned to involve forest laborers and peasants in forest/watershed/land conservation in the long term. This was largely because the vortex of the power struggle and the activities of the PKI were in Jakarta. Part of their political strategy included depicting the heads and agents of Forestry as the enemies of the people in cartoons, slogans, and articles. Later, this strategy was turned around to the advantage of the non-SARBUKSI members of the forestry establishment.

Polarizing the issue, the conservative foresters associated political ideology and actions with opposing land uses and capacity to protect the environment. On one side stood the actions and politics of SARBUKSI, the PKI, and BTI. Pro-agriculture, anti-forestry, they were depicted as enemies of the environment who would lead Indonesia down the path of environmental destruction and crisis. On the other side, the foresters argued, traditional forestry offered the only means of environmental protection that could simultaneously serve the state and provide for the greatest number of people: Forests protected irrigation systems and water supplies, aided food production, prevented erosion, supplied local wood needs, and generated state revenues.

On the surface, this depiction appeared to be true. As long as forest lands were legally controlled by the state, SARBUKSI and BTI made the forestry issue into a land issue, as the PKI leaders felt this would draw the most peasant support. They also encouraged the counterappropriation of teak. BTI and SARBUKSI stated that farmers should exchange occupied forest land needed for hydrological purposes for land outside the forest, and on occasion offered to reforest barren land, but it is not known whether any action was taken.[23] Their comments, even as reported in the PKI's daily, come across as little more than lip service to the very real need for careful management of certain critical lands by whoever controlled those lands (*Harian Rakyat*, November 5, 1957:2).

One result of this apparent lack of an environmentally sound, alternative forest management plan by the PKI/BTI/SARBUKSI contingent was the lack of a strategic ideological angle to justify the occupation and use or control of forest lands by forest laborers and other peasants. According to party ideology, local people's rights to this land were based not on their ability to manage it under forest or mixed tree and field crop cover, but on their inalienable rights to a means of production. This concept was often vaguely interpreted as meaning any land could be converted to agriculture. Such a vague interpretation sounded attractive to land-hungry peasants,[24] but it was politically unacceptable to a forest department built around concepts of forest control justified by the traditional forestry ideologies of environmental protection and revenue earning (production). The PKI thus won some fleeting victories—through the sheer numbers of people supporting squatting rights—in political organizations, in the national and local legislatures, and in the military. In the long term, however, state power in the peasant-state struggle over control of the forest lands doomed the would-be peasant claimants and their supporters to lose at least the legal battle. As it became clearer which groups would win and lose the broad-based political struggles at the national level, people's power at the forest village level waned. It is likely, however, that the traditional forestry ideology of environmental protection through centralized state control of trees and land would have won no matter which party line was victorious in Jakarta. Without a specific plan that considered both environmental and social impacts of forest use, the political manipulation of the forestry issue would not have sufficed in the long term.

THE POLICIES OF THE FORESTRY ESTABLISHMENT

The Indonesian Forest Service had inherited some three million hectares of land from their colonial predecessors, but much of it had been severely damaged. Exposed lands, particularly in the limestone hills where the island's best teak grew, were liable to be ruined by erosion and exposure to the harsh dry-season sun unless some vegetative cover was restored. Steeply sloped forest lands, and those where the soil depth was shallow, had to be reforested rapidly to prevent topsoil loss, siltation of downstream irrigation channels, and decreased soil productivity.

The Forest Service had other reasons to replant forest lands in teak, pine, dammar, and other forest species. Land control had been the basis of the Forest Service; the tension between market demand for forest products, the control of access to these products, and the regulation of forest labor that harvested and maintained these products had historically been key components of its structure. The destruction of the wars had upset the ordered management system of the Dutch under which most foresters had trained. Moreover, squatters were claiming large sections of the forest lands, often winning the sympathies of powerful people who had interests in agricultural conversion.

Further, the state's loss of forest control, especially of land valuable primarily because it possessed the environmental characteristics favorable to high-quality teak, would mean the loss of power and profits. Political parties and organizations aiding forest laborers and peasants, as well as other government agencies, including the Department of Agrarian Affairs, the departments of Agriculture, Plantations, and the Interior, could gain from the Forestry Service's loss of land and power. As under the Dutch, particular tree species indicated the classification of the land on which the trees were planted and the government body which would control that land.

Foresters writing today, all of whom survived the political upheaval of the period, describe this time as one in which the interests of forestry were not served. For example, the Committee for the Development of Forest and Agricultural Regions (*Panitia Pembangunan Wilayah Hutan dan Pertanian*) was established in 1951 to handle the "squatter problem." The members of this committee represented various government agencies, the military, and agricultural services. After two years, the head of the Forest Service reported that the committee constantly thwarted the Forest Service's interests in the land disputes, even though these interests had long been written into law (Soesilo 1953). Some members of this contemporary agrarian committee apparently disagreed with the system of forest access control imposed by the Dutch, and hoped to change it under the new Indonesian government. The forester's remark echoes the dissatisfaction expressed in 1875 by the newborn Dutch Forest Service about the joint committee writing the forest laws.

In the field, foresters tried to forge bonds with police and military men to guard the forest. Where such cooperation was possible, the forest police reported success in guarding the forest. But whenever it ended, as it would always have to, they couldn't keep people from taking trees. Often, as described above, individuals in the military, the police, or local village administration worked against the forestry establishment—and not always because of their personal or party politics. Even the guns that teak forest police began carrying in 1962 were of little help in deterring thieves. Many forest police feared that shooting a thief would lead to allegations of needlessly violent actions against the people and mass reprisals; injuring someone or threatening to do so had led to the deaths of colleagues.

The foresters also worked with Department of Information officials to convince people of "the meaning and functions of the forest" as the state defined it. Tree crops that could be grown in home gardens were promoted for use on marginal land. Religious leaders, youth groups, and women's groups were mobilized to teach farmers the importance of tree crops for home gardens. Foresters participated in committees for tree garden crops at various levels of provincial government. Although it is not discernible from the materials available on this period, presumably foresters worked with activist groups in their own political parties. Where political ideology apparently did not match the forestry principles being promoted, both foresters and the peasants they were teaching and mobilizing must have been conflicted or confused.

Despite the various forces pulling government departments apart, there was one ideology on which many government officials agreed: The "real" problem in implementing their plans to reforest damaged forest land was the rapidly increasing population and the proportionate increase in the number of poor and landless peasants:

> In my opinion, this problem cannot be solved simply by moving people who illegally clear forest land to other places on Java . . . [in addition to or instead of] . . . exchanging land outside the forest lands [for occupied forest land]. The reason is that this does not . . . reduce the population density on Java which causes the thirst for agricultural land and forest products and the shortage of employment opportunities and which is, in fact, the underlying cause of forest destruction and illegal clearing of forest lands. [Soesilo 1953:142]

The chief of the Forest Service argued correctly that the redistribution of the forest lands for conversion to agriculture could only temporarily solve the problems of the landless peasants. With Java's population increasing by approximately 600,000 every year, an army of landless peasants consistently augmented those currently clamoring for access to the forest lands. But he used this unhappy fact to argue another conservative position toward forest land and its illegal occupants: that it was unreasonable for the Forest Service to find nonforest land to exchange for these forest lands. The conservatives were hesitant to consider the reasons for peasants' presence on the forest lands—whether the Japanese had placed them there or individuals had taken advantage of the chaos of wartime and moved onto the forest lands of their own accord. They also disdained any notion of peasant rights to those lands or of the foresters' objectives and duties in the wake of the revolution. They were, after all, working for the greater good, "The People" [*Rakyat*] of Indonesia. In the view of the forestry establishment, peasants who farmed forest land without permission were squatters who obstructed this goal and exacerbated two additional, aggravating problems: the theft of wood and illegal grazing in young forest.

The head of the Forest Service went on to say that between 1950 and

1953, the average annual value of teak logs lost to the state Forest Service through theft was Rp. 8 million; this accounting did not include the potential value of the lumber and other wood products from these logs, or their value had they reached maturity. Further, he added, at least 120,000 hectares of forest lands had been damaged or destroyed by cattle, implying that this figure was in addition to damages sustained during wartime. These two problems were compounded by their invisibility; they were normal peasant activities. Well-intentioned foresters were in a quandary: they hesitated to upset peasant livelihoods, of which cattle were an integral part, yet they did not want cattle to graze in young forest. They also did not want to return to the Dutch system of constructing iron or barbed wire fences around newly reforested tracts. The most difficult contradiction experienced by postindependence Indonesian foresters was that they were not supposed to be (nor did most of them want to be) so harsh as their predecessors.

Soesilo suggested that the best means of relieving the pressure on the forest resources was a combination of three approaches, namely, (1) to resettle squatters and people occupying Japanese-created forest villages off Java, making them the highest-priority target group for the government's transmigration program; (2) to industrialize other economic sectors, hoping to absorb more un- and underemployed forest villagers; and (3) to intensify agricultural production and increase rural labor demand in the private sector. Meanwhile, the agrarian laws upholding state forest control should be reviewed and foresters should return to their business of reforesting, harvesting, and maintaining the forest (ibid., 140–42).

Two things are striking about the Forest Service chief's concept of the forest problem and its solutions. First, foresters need not acknowledge any institutional blame for having monopolized land and teak or for the service's methods of land, tree, and labor control. Second, the problems of overpopulation, land hunger, and so on were not ever attributed to the service's colonial predecessors, and were believed to fall outside the purview of the foresters' mandate. No connection was made between people's contemporary material circumstances and impacts of past forest policies.

Rather than engaging forest villagers in forest management or other action solutions, conservative foresters labeled people occupying forest lands "squatters," an illegal and thus criminal status, which somehow justified sending them to the Outer Islands or making other sectors responsible for their employment. It was not a new strategy. Sultans and regents of the eighteenth and nineteenth centuries labeled their political competitors "bandits" to justify their exile or elimination. At the village level, when the Dutch decided which local strongmen to make village heads, the others were relegated to the category of bandits, outlaws, or brigands (Moertono 1981). The same ideological tactic was used when the Dutch deposed rivals to the sultan's throne, or when Dutch and English ships labeled their competitors, the Bugis, "pirates" (Reber 1966; Warren 1975). The criminalization of customary rights or claims has been an effective political tool throughout Southeast Asia and the rest of the world (Adas 1981; Cohen 1986).

The structural changes required to change the production relations in forestry and improve social relations between the Forest Service and forest villages, briefly recognized during the revolutionary period, were never made. Conservative foresters never made the critical switch from "the trade/export orientation emphasized by the Dutch . . . to distributing wood fairly, inexpensively, and directly to the people" (Soepardi 1974b:47). The political polemics affecting postwar forestry caused the relations between forest laborers and forest managers to polarize even further. As the decade progressed, the tenor of party relations and labor relations reached a crescendo of conflict and confrontation. Latent Dutch forestry ideology grew stronger among frustrated foresters who did not adhere to the ideals of the parties trying to increase the political power of peasants and laborers by expanding their legal resource base to include the state forest. One could almost describe the conservative foresters' activities as retreat and regrouping—seeking strength from activities of the colonial past in familiar organizational surroundings.

After the revolution, for example, the Forest Service still employed Dutch advisors in the departments of Technology and Foreign Relations. At Gadjah Mada University, Dutch and German foresters taught traditional forestry as they had practiced it in Java and other tropical colonies, or their own countries, before the war. The government wanted to develop its capacity for industry, and forest industry was no exception. When they requested FAO assistance in designing industrial forests, the FAO sent an Austrian expert to Indonesia for a year. Other Europeans came in the same period to help establish pulp and paper industries. The ECA (Economic Cooperative Administration) and Eximbank (Export and Import Bank) provided funds to build or rebuild the seven industrial sawmills on Java, for finer processing of teak (Departemen Kehutanan 1986, 2:48,52).[25]

While Europeans were helping lay plans for the future of industrial forest development in Indonesia, the Indonesian foresters were restoring the infrastructure of prewar Dutch forestry that had been destroyed—the houses (1,682), offices (50), logyard shelters (50), sawmills (2), logging roads (1,500 kilometers), railroads (800 kilometers), and bridges. They also began some mechanization of forest production and forest product transport (ibid., 52).

Despite the antiforestry activities of the political parties and debates in the parliament, many of the traditional tasks of forestry were carried out. Foresters felt an urgent need to regain control of the forest lands, to develop their industrial capacity, and to earn revenues. Their production fervor overpowered Becking's admonishment about restricting forest harvests over the upcoming thirty years. Production of sawlogs in 1950 (432,179 cubic meters) and 1951 (490,722 cubic meters) nearly met 1940 levels (551,854 cubic meters). Rather than sacrifice revenues, the chief forester remembered, it was better to postpone the demands of rural people on the forest

> for the sake of forest conservation, new inventory and new business plans had to be made. It was estimated that in the upcoming years, wood production would not exceed 500,000 cubic meters per year.[26] This was because tree-cutting had gone over its limits, much damage had been inflicted on the forest, and insufficient forest maintenance was possible during the Japanese occupation. *Therefore, the forests of Java would not be able to fulfill the needs of the population for wood.* On the other hand, the population was continually increasing. Forests outside of Java have great potential but the situation and conditions there still preclude their immediate exploitation.[27] Transport infrastructure, labor, and other matters still present significant obstacles. [Soesilo 1953:140, emphasis added]

Although "people's wood auctions" (*lelang rakyat*) were held periodically in the forest district offices through the 1950s, the days when some 80 percent of wood sales went to the common people were gone. Only 0.7 percent of construction wood, 0.3 percent of firewood, and 0.1 percent of charcoal were sold at these auctions (see table 4.1). Only forest villagers were eligible to buy in these forums and wood traders were not allowed. Some people's wood was restricted to subsistence use by the buyer. Offering prices could not run higher than Rp. 12,000 per cubic meter (compared to minimum opening prices of Rp. 12,000 per cubic meter for wood sold at "small auctions" and minimum opening prices of Rp. 60,000 per cubic meter for "large auctions" held at the provincial auction centers for the best wood) (Departemen Kehutanan 1986, 2:55). Whole villages could purchase wood for their construction needs or firewood, but in 1955, these two categories accounted for less than 0.5 percent of the wood distributed by the Forest Service. Small traders designated as wood distribution aides (*pembantu distribusi hasil hutan*, or PDHH) bought (at 20 percent discount) another 2 percent of the construction wood to distribute in remote villages. Much purchased wood was likely not used for the average poor household's construction or fuel needs, but for wood-consuming rural industries such as lime manufacturing or tobacco curing, whose users constituted a different class of rural

TABLE 4.1 Distribution of Wood Products Sold by the Forest Service,
Java and Madura, 1955

Means of Sale	Sawlogs Cubic Meters	%	Firewood Cubic Meters	%	Charcoal Cubic Meters	%
Export	11,875	1.9	—	—	—	—
To state railroad	34,531	5.4	443,967	49.7	—	—
To other govt. services	15,096	2.4	23,082	2.6	2,330	4.4
To village distributors	13,019	2.0	1,432	0.2	230	0.4
Discount to villages and other organizations	2,002	0.3	66	—	35	0.1
Out of hand	337,819	52.8	352,430	39.4	32,445	60.6
Large auction	172,508	27.0	28,761	3.2	1,195	2.2
Small auction	47,432	7.4	5,024	0.6	1,135	2.1
People's auction	4,663	0.7	2,705	0.3	4,045	0.1
To forestry employees	237	0.1	35,556	4.0	16,115	30.1
Total	639,182	100.0	893,023	100.0	57,530	100.0

SOURCE: Jawatan Kehutanan R.I. 1956, Laporan singkat hasil usaha Jawatan Kehutanan 1950–1955 (Departemen Kehutanan 1986, 2:56).

dwellers. Small-business people could buy wood "out of hand" (*dibawah tangan*) from the forest district, but again, this option was usually not possible for poor villagers.[28] Out-of-hand sales accounted for more than 50 percent of the construction wood and nearly 40 percent of the fuelwood sold that year. Wood sold at large auctions constituted the next largest proportion of the total and was used by furniture manufacturers and other large wood consumers. It is highly unlikely, in fact, that poor villagers ever purchased wood.

Ten-year technical plans (called *Rencana Pengaturan Kelestarian Hutan,* or RPKH) for planting, harvesting, and maintaining forest districts were begun for areas experiencing the least conflict. Old maps were obtained[29] and the foresters marked the boundaries of the most valuable forests in the hopes that this would deter squatters or peasant encroachment (*bibrikan*) from private lands onto the forest lands. Foresters allowed people to stay on land they were farming if they could prove ownership; like the Dutch consolidating the forest lands, the foresters were particularly concerned if the land in question was an agricultural enclave within the forest; an unconsolidated forest was more difficult to manage. The only legally binding form of proof, however, was a written certificate of title or the equivalent, a rarity even on long-established agricultural land.

In some Japanese-created villages, the peasants had already constructed irrigated rice terraces, fish ponds, housing compounds, and schools. Forest villages that had already erected such infrastructure, particularly irrigation systems,[30] received some favor; often the provincial government became responsible for finding land to exchange. Yet, while some foresters admitted that the peasants who had been placed in the forest by the Japanese had a different kind of claim to the forest land they worked than those who occupied forest land of their own accord, the potential loss of territory to the Forest Service impelled foresters to resist changes in land control standards that differed from those set by the Dutch.

Foresters today believe that a key problem in rebuilding the forest during the Soekarno period was the lack of a unifying ideology within the Forest Service, the government, or the rest of society (Junus 1985). This began to change under Guided Democracy, when the tenor of political life changed and regulations strengthening the traditional forestry position were passed, establishing the base for forestry's great power under Soeharto's New Order government.

In the wake of the losses forestry was suffering from collective political action and marginal peasants acting individually, foresters sought to regain legitimation for their control of forest lands. In 1960 a law was passed[31] stating that a squatter could be evicted from state land without court order. Military authorities were used to remove those who refused to leave (Stoler 1985:156). The legislation was a coup for the traditional-authoritarian method of forestry; its enforcement foreshadowed the future of forest access control in the name of the state.

This legislation was followed by a reorganization of the Forest Service in 1961. A State Forest Enterprise, called *P.N. Perhutani*, was formed. By now, Soekarno's Guided Democracy policies were gaining strong ground, as was the military; but divisive political orientations precluded complete forest control by the forestry establishment—indeed the establishment itself was still divided. Consequently, P.N. Perhutani never achieved the degree of success its successor, the SFC, did. Although P.N. Perhutani was mandated to produce foreign exchange to help finance reforestation and supply forest products to industry, the political situation was not yet conducive to its conducting business as a business (Junus 1985:173).

THE CLIMAX: FOREST-BASED AGRARIAN WAR

The showdown between the conservative forestry viewpoint and the PKI-backed peasants materialized in the unilateral actions of the 1960s described below. Supporters of the forest peasants, however, vacillated between wins and losses even before this.

In 1956 peasants laying claim to forest lands were permitted to appoint their own representatives to negotiate their claims with forestry officials. This law[32] was an extension of a 1954 law providing negotiation rights to squatters on private estate (plantation) lands. Both laws came about in response to demonstrations and other activities of militant squatters' groups that led to the shooting deaths of five peasants squatting on estate lands in North Sumatra. While the BTI complained about some aspects of the laws, the concession was seen generally as a victory for the peasants (Hindley 1967:172).

In the ensuing months, the Forest Service took stock of its lands. Large areas were being converted to private agriculture and the idea of exchanging occupied forest land for private land gained ground. The concept was not new; it had been suggested in the early postwar years as one alternative (albeit an unpopular one) to the squatter problem. One attractive aspect of a land exchange program was that it shifted some responsibility to other government agencies that controlled or influenced the disposal of land: the Department of Agrarian Affairs, other departments in the Ministry of Agriculture, and the Department of the Interior. It thus seemed a victory for both the forest peasants and the Forest Service when the military chief of East Java pronounced in August 1957 that squatters who had claimed forest lands prior to August 1 of that year would be provided with other land outside the bounds of the state forest lands. Peasants claiming forest lands after that time would have no rights to those lands (*Harian Rakyat*, August 9, 1957:2).

These concessions were apparently considered insufficient because by 1964, the PKI and BTI were encouraging the peasants to engage in "unilateral actions" (*aksi sepihak*). Peasants occupied lands belonging to large landowners, private estates, or the Forest Service, and cut down trees on forest lands and plantations. While a full description of this campaign is beyond the scope of this chapter, some of the factors leading up to it are relevant.[33] Most critically, the tenor of resistance changed, as did the responses evoked from government officials outside PKI-affiliated organizations.

The key change in PKI strategy was the active mobilization of the peasantry in the land reform movement. Aidit, the head of the PKI, reported to the Central Committee in December 1963 that radical land reform—the confiscation of all landlord landholdings and the free redistribution to poor and landless peasants—should be the focus of their new revolutionary offensive. With the peasants slated to be the vanguard of subsequent radical actions, it was important to raise their political consciousness and reorient them from traditional patron-client loyalties to organization by class.[34] The unilateral actions, in turn, were meant to stimulate the Department of Agrarian Affairs, which had been slow in carrying out the already passed Land Reform Law.[35] Peasants were to control the courts of justice and try landlords and officials who were reticent in implementing land reform.

Until the initiation of the unilateral actions, the major thrust of the PKI strategy had been an alliance with the PNI. This strategy was not abandoned, but pushed into the background in favor of direct political involvement of the peasantry. Rural conditions were certainly ripe for it, and Mortimer's synopsis of these is worth quoting at length:

> There is evidence that conditions in the countryside had deteriorated markedly in the preceding months. The late 1963 harvest in Java had been heavily depleted by the worst drought and rat plague in living memory, and accounts of privation were common. Aidit himself in his report of December 1963 mentioned that "the people are now eating virtually anything edible," and in the following months various sources drew attention to misery on a huge scale. Reuters News agency reported on February 16, 1964, that in Central Java, where the crop failure had been particularly severe, one million people were starving; in the district of Wonosari between two and six people starved to death daily; and the deputy governor of Central Java said that 12,000 people were being treated for malnutrition and 15,000 families had deserted their barren rice fields. The crisis was not confined to Java: Antara [the official government news service] detailed that 18,000 people were starving in Bali and that there were serious rice shortages in South Sumatra. *Harian Rakyat* reported on February 18 that people were selling everything including their children.
>
> Despite such evidence of widespread rural distress, the Djakarta press contained no references during this period to food riots or other forms of overt social unrest in the villages or small towns that were unusual in their size or extent. [Mortimer 1974:300–301]

Today, forest villagers and forest officials remember this time of subsistence stress as one in which forest dependence accelerated among the poor. The flight response—migration to the forest—was triggered in a modern context for a traditional reason. I visited one forest village in 1984 to which the village head said that some 15 to 20 percent of the residents had migrated in the wake of a 1963 famine in the mountains south of Yogyakarta. In other villages people sought sustenance in the forest, some living off wild roots and tubers, others selling whatever teak and firewood they could obtain.

It was not only the deteriorating social conditions that led to the mobilization of the peasantry, however; it was also the growing strength of the PKI and its rural organizations. As it gained power, the PKI became more visible and more daring in its approach, holding mock trials, seizing land, organizing rallies, and generating slogans. In the forest, resistance took on the character of open confrontation.

Some of the most extensive unilateral actions took place on forest land. Groups of peasants, sometimes numbering in the hundreds or thousands and reportedly mobilized by BTI or the PKI youth group, *Pemuda Rakyat,* entered the forest lands. They would then proceed to divide the land among the peasants. Oftentimes, these groups encountered forestry employees who generally were reported as trying to stop them; sometimes sympathetic foresters tried to stay out of the conflict. Incidents often involved injuries to foresters or peasants; in many cases, foresters' or others' houses or offices were attacked and ransacked and money was stolen. In some cases, the communist factions justified their actions by saying that local foresters aggravated forest land disputes through some mismanagement prior to the incident (*Harian Benteng,* October 21, 1964).

Foresters sometimes responded confrontationally as well, replacing BTI-backed forest farmers against their will with forest laborers from outside the village. In other instances, farmers claimed land rights under the squatters' provisions that had permitted continued occupation of land farmed since the Japanese period. Some local foresters were reputed to be exacting bribes from reforestation laborers for access to forest plots (Departemen Kehutanan 1986, 2:109). BTI defended the farmers' claims by citing government policy to increase national food production. Famine, they pointed out, was ravaging the countryside[36] (Mortimer 1974).

As SARBUKSI and the PKI grew more powerful, other political elements stepped up their activities. At the same time, an Islamic Forestry Workers Union formed (*Sarekat Buruh Kehutanan Islam,* or SBKI) and affiliated with the Indonesian Islamic Workers Union (*Sarekat Buruh Muslimin Indonesia,* or SARBUMUSI).

In facing the growing strength of the Communist party and its affiliates, Islamic and other noncommunist political groups in the Forest Service moved to strengthen their ties with members of other government bodies. One forester who lived through this period as the head of a predominantly communist forest district recalled the progression of strategies that the PNI faction applied to the task of overcoming the power of the PKI.

First, they strengthened the position of the SBK by expanding membership, particularly of foresters who were already civil servants (*Pegawai Negeri*), thus strengthening their organization's capacity to influence local policy implementation. They also consolidated their efforts with those of regional legal authorities primarily to accelerate the processing of forest crimes through the courts. This had been problematic from their point of view because SARBUKSI members frequently coordinated the handling of these crimes. Some 3,000 cases in this forest district alone remained untried in 1964.

Then, the anti-PKI faction held mass trials in villages where theft and illegal occupation of forest lands were most common. Each mass trial addressed hundreds of individual cases a day. Officials from the state police, the judiciary, and the public prosecutor's office were enlisted to assist in the process. After the trials, local forest police confiscated and sold allegedly illegally acquired wood. Hundreds of supposedly illegal teak houses were torn down and auctioned off. Convicted offenders were sentenced to three months in jail. This faction of the Forest Service had become strong enough to see that employees involved in the theft of trees or sympathetic to the peasants' occupation of forest land were severely reprimanded or fired. Not surprisingly, those fired were primarily SARBUKSI members. These outcomes were possible largely because the forest district head and some of his key staff members were PNI, NU, or members of other parties unsympathetic to the PKI.[37]

SARBUKSI and other groups reacted by trying to discredit the leadership of the forest district, sending letters to other organizations and government bodies in the district and the national legislature. In early 1965, the BTI held a mass meeting in that district and sponsored a unilateral action in which approximately 200 peasants rushed onto the forest lands, slashed teak seedlings, and planted food crops. The foresters enlisted ANSOR[38] and MARHAEN youth groups to help round up and bring to trial some 150 peasants. According to the forest district head, they overburdened the prison facilities and had to be divided among the jails of the area (Blora, Rembang, Jepara, Pati, Kudus). As soon as their short sentences were over, however, they took part in political agitation once again.

The ascending power of the left, including organizations backing poor forest peasants who challenged the forestry establishment, was terminated by the events following September 1965. An alleged communist coup was attempted,[39] provoking a counterrevolutionary movement by the right. The events preceding this attempted coup, its failure, and the involvement of other governments are beyond the scope of this discussion. Nevertheless, the events that followed it left a searing, permanent mark on the people whose lives and livelihoods were tied to the forest.

After the attempted coup, since then known as the 30th of September movement (G30S) in reference to the counterstrike, many of the people who had posed problems for the Forest Service—squatters, forest laborers in communist-affiliated organizations, and black market teak traders—were killed or interned in camps for political prisoners.

Islamic groups, the army, and youth groups were mobilized by the counterrevolution to find and kill anyone known or believed to be a communist, including anyone affiliated with a communist organization. SARBUKSI members who were not killed or exiled were fired permanently from the Forest Service; their children are still regarded with suspicion today. Whole forest villages of Islamic faithful were mobilized to attack PKI-affiliated villages. In some areas, hundreds of PKI supporters were taken into the forest, shot, and buried in mass graves. One village girl reported watching a truck loaded with wailing people, hands tied and piled one on top of another, as it was driven through the forest to an isolated spot where they were "disposed of." Everyone remembers the rivers running red. Many forest sites thought to be haunted became even more frightening to villagers traveling through. To this day, there are sections of the forest that the survivors of the debacle will not traverse. The event's fearful memories serve to help contemporary foresters protect Java's forests.

SUMMARY

As we have seen, conflict over access to forest lands and products exploded into open resistance movements and peasant refusals to obey forest laws and policies. The sustained growth, intensity, and openness of the forest-based opposition to the forestry establishment resulted from increased solidarity and strength in the organized numbers of people opposed to the ideology and political-economic controls of the previously dominant forestry establishment (Tilly, Tilly, and Tilly 1975:244). These organized movements were both offset and aided by the breakdown of the century-old tradition of forest control.

When, for example, the Dutch foresters first began to destroy the infrastructure of forest exploitation in an effort to deter Japanese use of the forest, the forest villagers took it as quite a different sign. The action became a signal that the old forms of control were being released, and in their absence, villagers rushed to openly claim wood or territory from the long-forbidden source. At the beginning of this period of structural breakdown, collective action involved violence against the forest (by forest villagers pursuing their subsistence needs).

More violence occurred as the forest villagers organized into interest groups. Whether Islamic or communist, peasants were increasingly organized into formal groups with particular ideologies, interests, and goals. During the revolution, much of the violence these groups participated in was aimed at the Dutch, directed not only against their persons but against their property and symbols as well, including the symbols of forestry: thousands of offices and homes, hundreds of kilometers of rail tracks and roads were destroyed. This violent expression of power emerged not from breakdown and desperation but from solidarity and organized resistance in the form of an attack on what the state forestry organization and its agents had stood for.

After the wars, organized forest resistance was integrated into political party platforms whose legality permitted people the freedom to openly express the forest politics that derived from the conditions of their existence, whether poverty or religion or simply a different view of human rights was the driving force behind their membership. The ideologies and tactics of various parties and organizations operating in the forest were localized versions of larger struggles for power at the national level.

Foresters were caught in a bind of contradiction, participants in the ideological struggles to define their future roles in Indonesian society, but also struggling to maintain the resource base that was crucial to their individual and common futures. Whatever ideology they professed, by the time this period ended no cohesive alternative plan for involving forest villagers in forest management had emerged from even the most radical foresters. Thus, the immediate predecessor of the SFC continued to appear colonial in nature to forest villagers and officials in other government agencies. And, in the final, most violent years of this period, the foresters played the Tillian role as repressors of collective action, as agents of the state that made the kinds of claims resisted by the organized Javanese: claims on land, trees, labor, and ideology.

Another relationship between organized and unorganized resistance must be noted here. Organized collective action facilitated unorganized, individual, autonomous actions having similar cumulative environmental effects. At the same time, this unorganized sector provided the organized action groups—political parties—with a source of indigenous ideology that facilitated their organizational capacity. In this way, the two styles of resistance were not only complementary but intertwined. Complicating matters further, the postwar Forest Service and the foresters faced their own ideological contradictions. Individuals waffled between their political commitments and their professional chagrin at the deterioration of their source of power, profit, and legitimacy. Above all, the state needed an income-producing forest sector.

Control of access to the forest lands was more than a state ideology and a legal configuration throughout this period: it was manifested in the political platforms and daily activities of individuals in all the major political parties and organizations throughout Java. Thus both the solidarity-producing effects of external threat and the divisiveness of ideological opposition were present. Only by waging outright war on these opposing factions—within and outside of the Forestry structure itself—was the mainstream, traditional forestry philosophy of control reinstated.

Today, the war begun by the Dutch and complicated by the Indonesians continues. The vestiges of past battles remain but the forest villagers' tactics are more clandestine now, forced underground by the fearful memories of the recent past. The state, on the other hand, is openly buttressing its paramilitary capacity to protect its forest resources.

FIVE

State Power to Persist: Contemporary Forms of Forest Access Control

The sanction of the state is force, but it is a force that is legitimized, however imperfectly, and therefore the state deals also in ideologies.
DOUGLAS HAY, "Property, Authority, and the Criminal Law"

The reorganization of the SFC under Soeharto's New Order and the economic growth thrust of the New Order state characterized Forestry's initial reappropriation of the forests of Java. The key questions examined in this chapter are whether and to what extent Indonesian forestry is new and different under the New Order. The answer, as described below, is "not so new." The contemporary political economy of forestry has combined with the tenets of scientific forestry, laid down by the Dutch in Java and recognized worldwide, to legitimize Javanese foresters as skilled technicians who play major roles as police in rural Java. The structures, laws, ideologies, and labor policies shaping foresters' management strategies are essentially the same today as under the late Dutch colonial state. The manner of realizing their functions has become more repressive, more militaristic. Both historical and contemporary aspects of this culture of control have influenced the ways villagers regard and respond to local foresters. Villagers' responses have, in turn, created contradictions for field foresters who must control village forest use on a daily basis.

The current culture of forest control is more intense than that prevailing in the seventeen years following Indonesian independence or under the Dutch. The SFC exerts more stringent control in three ways: through the militarization of the forest protection system, the coupling of the principles of Pancasila[1] with scientific forestry, and the initiation of community forestry programs. These "changes," however, are little more than new forms of old control mechanisms. What has, in fact, changed since the Dutch regime are the condition of the forest, the absolute number of people living in the vicinity of the forest and dependent on it for a living, and local strategies for gaining access to land and other village resources. The first of these was discussed in chapter 4; the other two are discussed in chapters 6 and 7.

In this chapter, I examine the persistence of colonial characteristics in their Indonesian form: the composition and role of the SFC, the role of forestry in the political economy of Indonesia, and the misconnection between scientific forestry and the social and economic needs of local people. I also look at how the SFC has tried to address these constraints through repressive and preventive approaches to forest security. The conclusion is that the persistence of colonial forms of forest management is legitimated by three "old" ideologies: (1) that state forestry serves the greatest good of the greatest number of people, (2) that scientific forestry is an efficient and rational form of resource use, and (3) that promoting economic growth through forest production for the state is the key component of the forester's role. These ideologies neither match local people's views of the forest, nor contribute to forest villagers' development.

OLD AND NEW IN NEW ORDER FORESTRY

How does the structure of the contemporary SFC resemble that of its colonial predecessor? The organization is composed of technical forestry specialists, forest police, and administrators. These officials view their primary objective as the production of teak and other forest products; they are a business run by principles of capitalist production. Like its colonial predecessor, the SFC has been mandated by the state to scientifically determine ecologically sound uses of the forest lands it controls, to market forest products, to allocate forest labor, and to oversee forest villagers' welfare. Like their colonial counterparts, contemporary foresters disdain local people's ecological knowledge. They exert control not only over the scientific ideology of forestry but also over forest land, species, and labor. Both colonial and contemporary foresters have claimed that indigenous forest users are backward and ignorant of "the meaning and function of the forest." Foresters also disclaim the political sophistication of forest-dwelling people who recognize the power struggle over natural resource control taking place.

The SFC is an autonomous state corporation mandated to produce revenues to support itself and provide 55 percent of its profits to the National Development Budget (GOI/IIED 1985a:11). While its predecessors, the P.N. Perhutanis[2] of East and Central Java, had been state corporations (*Perusahaan National*), neither was powerful nor autonomous: their operating budgets came from the central government to which they also submitted all revenues (Junus 1985:174).

After the addition of West Java in 1978, the territory controlled by the SFC mirrored that controlled by the Dutch Forest Service in Java, except for enclaves of forest land disputed by peasants placed there by the Japanese or occupying the land since the revolution. To briefly recapitulate the organizational history since the establishment of the New Order in 1967: In 1969 the New Order's Ministry of Agriculture was established,[3] under which fell the Directorate General of Forestry. In 1972 the Perhutanis of Central and East Java were legally joined as separate production units of Perum Perhutani. The *Perum* form of state enterprise functions as a government nonstock company, with its own budget, subject to ministerial approval.[4] Until 1983 the SFC answered to the minister of agriculture; in that year, forestry became a ministry in its own right (ibid., 173–74). The Forest Service (*Dinas Kehutanan*) of West Java was made part of the SFC in 1978.[5] Forests in the Special Region of Yogyakarta are not part of Perum Perhutani, but have retained Forest Service status.[6]

Since 1967 four changes have been made to make SFC management more efficient and facilitate forest control. First, many forest districts have been made smaller, and an effort was made to form forest districts exclusively of teak or nonteak species. Second, the emphasis on teak has been maintained but foresters recognized the need to expand nonteak production and diversify the SFC's revenue base. Third, fiscal management procedures have changed. Income, rather than being managed at the Forest District (KPH) levels, is managed more centrally by the units and the central office. Export earnings are managed in Jakarta. Proceeds from wood auctions, contracts, and individual sales remain within the unit (Perum Perhutani 1981:28). The wealthy, teak-producing districts subsidize the management of nonteak districts, protection forests, and low-production teak districts. In addition, teak-rich Units I (Central Java) and II (East Java) subsidize teak-poor West Java (interview with Chief of Unit I, November, 1984).

Management Constraints at the Field Level

Most forest land in Java is administered by the SFC for either full or limited production purposes.[7] Figure 5.1 diagrams the SFC structure of command.

The smallest management unit is controlled by a mantri, and is called a "forest police resort" (*Resort Polisi Hutan*, or RPH). Some RPH, particularly in nonteak forests, contain forest areas of 1800 to 2500 hectares. Each year, several hundred hectares of the RPH may be slated for intensive management activities such as reforesting, tapping, logging, or forest maintenance. These duties, plus the more time-consuming task of forest security, are the responsibility of one mantri, assisted by an average of four mandors. Mandors are assigned specific functions such as

Board of Directors
President Director

Dir. of General Administration   Dir. of Production   Dir. of Marketing

Personnel   Finance   General Admin.   Security & Agraria   Planning & Public Rel.   Production   Industry   Marketing

Division Heads (Bureaus)

Unit Heads
I. Central Java   II. East Java   III. West Java
→ Forest District Administrators (*ADM/KKPH*)
→ Assistant Administrators (*Adjun ADM*)
→ Forest Subdistrict Officers (*Asper/KBKPH*)
→ Forest Guards (*Mantri/KRPH*)
→ *Foremen (Mandor)*
Planting, Logging, Resin Collection, Security
Mandors' Assistants
→ Work Group Leaders, Heads of Forest Farmer Groups (*Kepala Kontrak*)

Forest Laborers (Buruh)
Forest Farmers   Loggers   Tappers   Other Labor

Figure 5.1. Structure of the State Forestry Corporation and Its Relation to Forest Laborers

planting, logging, or tree nursery supervision, and double as forest police. Some, particularly in the teak forest, are full-time forest police. Theoretically, one planting mandor is supposed to handle 25 hectares of land under reforestation, meaning he must supervise 50 to 100 reforestation laborers (in tumpang sari). Some planting mandors must oversee 100 or more hectares of land, and have little time for anything else. In teak forests, where the RPH on average cover 800 hectares, forest control is more intensive but more complex. Forest police generally patrol in pairs or threes both to reduce their vulnerability to attack and to be prepared for action should they discover a band of teak thieves.

While the demands on field personnel are increasing, their numbers are decreasing. For example, the total number of SFC employees in Unit I declined by 16 percent from 1979–83, but 41 percent of the total reduction came from the daily wage employees (pekerja harian lepas), all of whom are mandors (calculated from Perum Perhutani, Unit I 1983: 10). For those who kept their jobs, the prospects for promotion were poor: not only was the number of civil servants (pegawai negeri) reduced by 30 percent in that time period, but the qualifications for achieving that status increased, as did limitations on the total number of civil servants.

Unlike forest laborers (buruh), mandors are considered part of the official SFC hierarchy; they are provided foresters' uniforms and expected to conduct themselves accordingly, whatever their employment status or salary level. This means that even though they may be lepas (independent), they still represent the agency and its interests. All mandors are on twenty-four-hour call. Usually they work nine to twelve hours a day and must be available for special patrol duties. All mandors work long hours; those ranked as daily wage laborers work for low salaries and receive no pension. In 1984, starting mandors were paid Rp. 700 a day. Daily wage employees with seniority received only Rp. 1,200 a day.[8] Permanent wage employees receive a monthly salary but no other benefits such as retirement. The best benefits are enjoyed by civil servants, followed by company (SFC) employees (pegawai perusahaan). Where reforestation is under way, mandors typically have access to a forest plot they either work themselves or sharecrop. Villagers with no other sources of income—either from land or wages earned by other household members—cannot afford to work as forest mandors. Because mandors are forced to seek other sources of income in order to continue working for the SFC, they are in fact subsidizing the SFC.

Like army personnel, forestry officials of the ranks of mantri and above are periodically relocated to prevent subjectivity in carrying out their official duties. Mandors, however, are usually assigned in their home villages or nearby RPH. Experienced mandors have the advantage of familiarity with local social and environmental constraints. Yet, in many ways this lowest level in the forestry hierarchy is under the greatest pressure. Mandors are part of local kin, class, and community networks as well as part of the forest bureaucracy. As government officials in the village they enjoy some local status; as foresters they are ranked lowest in an extremely hierarchical power structure. Overworked and underpaid, it is not surprising that mandors are tempted to accept favors from villagers or to "sell" access to forest lands. Mantris also fall prey to temptation, but they have fewer material reasons. Minimally, mantris are ranked as company employees and earn significantly higher salaries and benefits than their counterparts in other government agencies. Many of the types of incentives recommended for reducing corruption are part of their normal employment package.

Indonesianization has not changed the basic structure or function of the SFC, although it has been cast in the form of an efficient, modern, capitalist enterprise. Its "personality" in the field, from the perspective of forest villagers, remains that of a foreign institution seeking to control the extraction of local resources. The nature of loyalty on the part of the field foresters has changed, however, to a loyalty based on a recent history of intensely nationalist ideology.

New Order Ideology and Forest Control

Upon the establishment of the New Order, important changes were made from the orientation of the national government under Soekarno. First, economic development was given priority and facilitated by Foreign Investment Law no. 1/1967. Second, the basic state philosophy of Pancasila was elevated to the status of a sacred ideology,[9] while any ideology, philosophy, or idea connected with outlawed parties, especially the PKI and its affiliates, was considered anti-Pancasila.

After the establishment of the New Order, foresters affiliated with outlawed political groups and parties were fired. Most were barred from future government employment, some were interned.[10] Since then, an unwritten but subtly enforced ideological pressure has begun to be imposed: foresters, like other government officials, are expected to support GOLKAR (the major "party" of the bureaucracy)[11] and its interpretation of Pancasila. Less important in the earliest years of the New Order, this possessiveness of the national ideology has grown with GOLKAR's power, with the growth of military power, and as the state has become more stable. The bureaucracy has assumed the roles of both policeman and judge in ensuring that activities, organizations, or individuals remain true to its interpretation of Pancasila (Robison 1986). Loyalty is shown through membership: in many forest districts, membership in

GOLKAR is one of the prerequisites to promotion. As one forest mantri explained, "the government [i.e., GOLKAR] does a little bit for us, we must do a little bit for the government." Foresters are expected to recruit new members. In some areas, reforestation laborers must be members of GOLKAR in order to gain access to reforestation land.

This singularity of political affiliation combines well with the ideology of forestry that held together the forestry bureaucracy under the Dutch and has tended to cement the forest services of the world. As in other forest services of the world (Kaufman 1967), the field foresters of Java possess an esprit de corps almost unmatched in other branches of government service. Javanese foresters—even those who complain about the pay or their chances for promotion—suggest that their common experience of isolation binds them to each other. Located at great distances from their counterparts, and often faced with dangers from hostile physical and social environments, individual field foresters serve the state differently than other state bureaucrats. From their earliest forestry training days they are told they have "one common goal and one common destiny" (*satu tujuan, satu nasib*).¹² This common philosophy and the philosophy of scientific forestry are used to legitimate land, species, and labor control.

In Java, as elsewhere, scientific forestry emerges in planning the management of timber and other "traditional" forest products such as pine resin and copal. These products are produced, factory style, in industrial tree plantations. Since the worldwide revolution of scientific forestry in the nineteenth century, forestry bureaucracies, including those in Indonesia, conceive of "traditional" forest products as those which resource bureaucracies (or companies) are most effective at producing. These "traditional" products are products extracted on a large scale and tend to be used in industry rather than for household consumption. (Timber is used in both, but the housing industry can absorb the higher production of this style of exploitation.)

In conjunction with their appropriation of the notion of traditional, foresters have demoted the broader definition of the word to one that implies backwardness. This denigration of traditional forest activities by swidden cultivators, peasant farmers, or rural peoples in general has become a tool in the battle over the forests. The latter's interactions with forests, which tend to be directed more toward nontimber than timber products, are publicly derided as being inefficient or destructive. In fact, they are disdained more because they threaten the bureaucracy's more "rational" use of the resources (in the neoclassical economic sense of the word). In Java, as in other countries with forest management bureaucracies, traditional scientific forestry is legitimized in forest law and justified by two other universal notions in resource management: that of management for the greatest good and that of the superiority of (Western) science to other forms of resource management.

To realize this ideology, three types of forest control have persisted since the Dutch controlled the forests: land, species, and labor controls. Their contemporary Javanese forms are described below.

Forest Land Control

The one-fourth of Java's land area classified as forest land corresponds nearly exactly to the land controlled by the Dutch Boschwezen before the Japanese occupation of Java. "Forest" or "forest lands" in Indonesia, as in many other countries, are political, not biological, definitions. Forest lands were defined as part of the Dutch Forest Laws of 1927 and 1932 and translated for inclusion in Basic Forestry Law no. 5 of 1967, still valid today. In the early part of this century, Professor Dr. Ir. van Arstson calculated that some 30 percent of Java's land area *should be* under forest (Prastowo 1983; GOI/IIED 1985b:34). While this figure was based on the characteristics of Javanese topography, contemporary foresters tend to interpret "30 percent forest land" to mean the political boundaries, not the actual forest cover. In calculating the amount of land under forest, they do not include privately owned woodlands, home gardens, or plantation lands under tree cover.

To illustrate: At the SFC's 1984 annual business meeting, the director of production (Soerjono) stated that the operational goals of the SFC should be "to retain the current forest lands and as far as possible to increase the forest land area in order to achieve the ideal [30 percent] proportion to the [total] land area [of Java]" (Perum Perhutani 1985:134). Moreover, while foresters frequently state that the 30 percent goal of land under forest has not yet been achieved, they avoid stating that at least 25 percent of state forest lands are not under woody cover.

Some forestry documents indicate dissent from this mainstream view, more in accord with the calculator's intent. A staff member in the Central Java SFC planning office calculated that at least 30 percent of Java is covered in woody species by adding all land under private home and forest gardens, plantation lands, and state forest lands (Perum Perhutani, Biro Perencanaan Unit I Jawa Tengah 1983). Moreover, by totaling the amount of land the Central Bureau of Statistics recorded in the land use categories of state forest lands, estate lands, and woodlands and tree crops in 1985, we find some 32 percent of the land was in the state forest lands or under forest cover (calculated from BPS 1988). PERSAKI (the Central Java branch of the Indonesian Association of Forestry scholars) calculated that approximately 25 percent of Java is under tree cover. They accounted for the 25 percent of state forest lands categorized as

"empty land," adding the remaining 75 percent to the area under plantations, and (a conservative) 20 percent of the home gardens (PERSAKI
1985:8).

Having codified and legitimized its control of the forest lands in the
law,[13] the SFC has control over all activities on forest lands. Mining, the
collection of rocks, limestone, or firewood, and conducting any kind of
research within the forest boundaries require formal SFC permission.
"Police security activities in the forest, or forest security, according to
Government Regulation No. 28, 1985, are designed to secure and guard
the rights of the state to the forest lands and forest products" (Djokonomo 1986:5).

The principle that the forest lands are restricted to general access
requires the territorial forest officer to control the traffic of people and
goods from, into, and within the forest lands. So-called preventive measures to control territory and protect the property of the state include
patrolling the forests (because "the forest lands are closed to anyone who
has no need to be on them"), becoming familiar with the territory, and
getting to know the people who live near the forest (ibid.). Some means
of "civic control" are checking the permits of students, scouts, tourists,
and researchers using the SFC/forestry facilities for pleasure or research.
Other security checks include checking forest product transport passes
and supervising people "who have a traditional relationship with the
forest" to ensure that they obey regulations. Finally, whenever officials
from other parts of the government bureaucracy (civilian or military)
enter the forest, they must also check in with the local SFC officials (ibid.,
9). Failure to do so causes the forestry officials to register verbal or
written complaints with their counterparts or superiors in the responsible agencies.

Where preventive activities fail to protect the SFC's territory effectively, repressive action is permitted. To exert territorial control, the SFC
has several policing mechanisms and institutions: the forest police (*Polisi
Hutan*, or POLHUT) who operate at the mandor level, the PCK (from
Polisi Chusus Kehutanan: Special Forestry Police), and the PJJ (*Patroli Jarak
Jauh*), or long-distance patrols also called BRIMOB, like the mobile bri-
gades of police and military that they imitate. The PJJ operates as a sort
of SWAT team in the forest. The first of these controls had counterparts
under the Dutch; the second originated under Soekarno; the third is the
creation of the SFC. The main way that territorial control has changed,
then, has been in the intensity of police activities, particularly the militarization of the process.

Differences between management of teak and nonteak forest districts
lie in the type, style, and degree of forest access control implemented by
the forest police in the forest district. Being of more value, and produc-

ing enough income to justify greater costs, teak districts employ more forest police of all kinds and levels, and, in most cases, involve more intensive policing. Teak forest police have less territory to cover than forest police in nonteak districts, and PJJ squads operate where large-scale teak theft is a perennial problem.

Each level of the forest security system also carries with it a different degree of prestige, freedom of action, and impact. The regular forest police function as cops on the beat—the "beat" in this case being either the teak or nonteak forest. Police patrol the forest lands, watching for illegal collection of firewood (for example, from live seedlings or trees), improper collection of teak leaves (only mature leaves—the less desirable ones—are allowed to be collected), destruction of new seedlings, illegal grazing,[14] illegal charcoal manufacture, or signs of tree theft and damage. Forest police and their immediate superiors, the mantris (forest guards), usually work with village informants who report illicit logging plans, times and places illegally acquired wood will be transported, or the hiding places of stolen teak.[15] As mentioned earlier, forest police often double as either logging foremen (*mandor tebang*), planting foremen (*mandor tanam*), or tree nursery (*pembibitan*) foremen. Because local foresters are not located out of their home areas, they often have access to extensive information networks.

The special forest police (PCK)[16] are ranked at the mantri's level. Each forest district has a certain number of regular PCK, who as a rule do not operate in the same area all the time, but come in to investigate theft, and occasionally to patrol. Both mantris and PCK officers receive at least three months of training in police methods and basic criminology. Both mantris and PCK are authorized to carry guns in the teak forest, making them an additional armed service, along with the police and the military.[17]

In some teak forest districts, mantris spend as much of their time engaged in high-powered security activities—stakeouts and the like—as in planning reforestation, logging, thinning, or forest labor organization. One of the most popular stakeout methods is called *tunggu manuk*, or "waiting for the bird," in which a forest guard camps with his mandors—forest police and others—at a different spot in the forest every night, patrolling at random various entries and exits into the forest lands. One forest guard told me he used snakes over which he cast a spell, ordering them to guard the "four directions" of a highly susceptible, valuable section of the teak forest. While his approach is obviously an extremely personal one, it is not uncommon for forest guards and mantris to use traditional Javanese talismans and formulas for catching thieves on specific dates and times, according to their own Javanese birthdays.[18]

The long distance patrols are paramilitary operations. A typical operation unit consists of the following: a special four-wheel-drive vehicle and an SFC driver, a unit head, about five PCK (or fewer PCK plus some representatives from the local army post), and the regular police. Everyone but the driver is armed. The vehicle is driven into a forest area based on informants' information. A kilometer or two from the site, the vehicle stops, the passengers descend, and they scatter in teams after synchronizing watches and agreeing upon a meeting time and place. If nothing is found within a certain time period, the operation is called off. If they find wood and capture the thieves, they bring them back to the forest district office. It is an understatement to say that PJJ squads are not highly regarded by local villagers. One driver described an experience he had while waiting for the squad to return from a sweep operation, in which his car was stoned, and another in which the car was nearly overturned by angry villagers.[19]

An SFC policy paper written by the corporation's General Administrative Director (*Direktur Umum*), who oversees, among other things, forest security and agrarian affairs on forest lands, states:

> Based on the political map of the Island of Java, [we see that] a portion of the working territory of the State Forestry Corporation lies in the Red Belt and the Green Belt areas, or in other words, areas formerly influenced by G.30S/PKI and DI/TII. This problem [*kerawanan*] [with these areas] is aggravated by unfavorable geographic conditions, i.e., that these working areas are often isolated and communications are difficult. These troublesome circumstances strongly influence the success of the SFC's efforts to manage the forests and forestry [*sic*] there. . . . Conscious of the burden of implementing these tasks and the strategic position of the State Forestry Corporation in serving the country and in the development of our people, particularly within the scope of [our] participation in directing sociopolitical security and safety in Java, an island which has traditionally [and] historically acted as a barometer of political hegemony and power in the archipelago, all SFC troops are expected to play fundamental roles as Security Agents capable of detecting political, economic, social, cultural and military troubles [*kerawanan*] among the people, even more so as we approach the 1987 elections. . . . Unlike other businesses . . . the SFC has a special mission related to the conditions of the territory it manages. These conditions have resulted in the SFC's being an enterprise with two functions. [Djokonomo 1986:1]

The politico-military function of the agents of the SFC as controllers of territory has led many field foresters to view themselves as modern-day heroes of the state. Similarly, one subdistrict administrator (*camat*) in the teak forest likened his job to that of a sheriff in the Old West. Higher officials in the SFC encourage such feelings among their field personnel. As were the VOC's soldier-foremen in the forest, modern-day field foresters are construed to be the field troops entrusted with the protection of the state forest resources. Their field duty is "justified" by the SFC's political mandate to control land and the foresters' conservation mandate to achieve or maintain some balance in forest ecosystems. This conservation ethic is both acceptable to certain contemporary international interests and congruent with the philosophy of their profession as foresters. Thus field foresters embody one of the dual functions marking the philosophies of many branches of the Indonesian state. ABRI (the armed forces) is given the double function of maintaining national security and developing the people. The foresters are guardians of the state's capital.

Species Control

The Dutch, in declaring a monopoly on the teak timber trade, were the first to exert strict species control on timber products of Java. They also institutionalized the modes of species control. Species control on Java has two purposes: to consolidate claims on certain lands as forest lands and to ensure a state monopoly on the first-order trade of the single most lucrative forest product on the island.

At the 1984 annual meeting of the SFC, the head of the Production Division stated, "As a company we must grow and to grow we need to produce more and to produce more we need investment, and our heart is the production of forest products. Therefore, the development, maintenance, and production of forest products must always increase in order to spur growth" (Perum Perhutani 1985:102).

The linkage between scientific forestry and species security in state forest management is exemplified by the following passage, written by the General Administrative Director (*Direktur Umum*) for the SFC: "Security activities *implemented through technical forestry* are a means of protecting and securing the longevity and integrity of the forest lands and the trees on those lands, by managing them in such a way as to achieve an ecosystemic balance, both among the components of the forest itself and between the forest and the environment around it" (Djokonomo 1986:5, emphasis added).

Teak (*Tectona grandis*), pine (*Pinus merkusii* and other varieties), rasamala (*Altingia excelsa*), and copal-producing trees such as agathis are among the species designated as forest species. Trees considered agricultural species include coffee, rubber, and fruit trees. The forest species classification means that large-scale cultivation is controlled by a forestry agency, although individuals may cultivate these species on private land. The Department of Plantations (an agricultural department) does not intercrop teak or pine with coffee or chocolate on (agricultural) plantation lands. Likewise, the SFC is normally not supposed to intercrop rubber or other species on the forest lands for the uses of the SFC.[20]

Tree tenure is part of species control strategy. According to tradition in many parts of Java, tree planters have certain rights in the trees they plant and sometimes to the land under or around the trees (Bergsma 1880). To avoid conflict over trees on forest lands, and to establish state rights of ownership, the SFC and its institutional predecessors have always provided the seeds or seedlings of all trees slated for forest production. When seeds are planted, as is the case with teak, planting is expected in exchange for access to reforestation land (tumpang sari). When seedlings must be planted, usually with their roots encased in mycorrhizae-enriched soil packets, the forest district pays farmers for carrying them to the plots from the mandor's house or a nearby drop-off point. Alternate row forest crops, such as *Leucaena leucocephala*, are planted as seeds by the reforestation farmer. All living parts of the major species belong to the SFC, although villagers are allowed to collect the leaves from teak trees over ten years old.[21] Mixed tenure arrangements for the branches or leaves of alternate species are common, but the SFC tries to retain ultimate control over their disposal. For example, where leucaena is planted, the foresters, not the farmers, are supposed to determine when it may be cut for fodder or fuelwood, and the trees at 10-meter intervals must be left standing for seeding and boundary markers.

The SFC also controls which agriculture species farmers may plant between the rows of forest species. Tree crops are not permitted because they take too long to mature, they shade the major crop, and they might establish land claims by the forest farmer.[22] Even fast-growing trees, such as papaya, or tree-like food crops such as banana, are not permitted. Banana in particular is discouraged because its broad leaves shade the forest species. Cassava is supposed to be forbidden because it is believed to drain soil nutrients and destroy soil structure. Because of its importance as an emergency crop for the farmers, however, many field foresters allow farmers to plant cassava around their plots' perimeters. Dry-field rice, corn, peanuts, and other field crops, or vegetables where agroclimatic conditions permit, are encouraged because they do not compete with or threaten the trees. They are also the easiest to clear when the first stage (agricultural) of tumpang sari is over: once the trees have been established for two or three years, they shade the ground between rows and prevent economic production of the farmers' field crops.

Marketing rights are the other component of species control. For teak, because of its value, the SFC imposes strict controls affecting even teak grown on private lands. Teak may be grown on private lands for private use by the grower, but if it is sold or transported off the grower's land, a fee (called a *pantong* in one part of Central Java) must be paid to the SFC.

All teak shipments by the SFC, by trucker contractors, or by individuals must be accompanied by traveling papers valid for twenty-four hours. Under certain circumstances, villagers' access rights to teak on state lands include rights to dispose of some of the by-products of logging. This was exemplified earlier in the discussion of the rights of the blandong to the small branches of the timber trees he cuts. Nevertheless, by selecting particular products and production techniques for its major forest products, the SFC influences the benefits forest villagers can gain from the forest. A simple illustration of this influence is in the customary manner of cutting teak trees. Until the 1950s or so, teak trees were chopped and sawn at a height of one-half to one meter above the ground. The blandong had traditional disposal rights of the stump; he could either take it or transfer his rights in it to other villagers. Since the intensification of forest exploitation, the stump height has been progressively reduced; trees are now cut approximately 1 inch from the ground. Some blandong, or those to whom they transfer their "rights," dig up the stump and sell it, make charcoal from it, or use it as firewood. The smaller stumps are of less value to the woodcutter.

Species controls imposed by Indonesian foresters include classification systems, tree tenure, and marketing restrictions; all of these controls originated under the Dutch and have become more strictly enforced in recent years. As pressures on the resource base increase, the SFC is becoming increasingly efficient in the appropriation of surplus from its remaining resources. Maintaining controls on particular species ensures both a more efficient form of large-scale production and the increasingly skewed distribution of legal access to major forest products.

Labor Control

Like the controls on forest land and species, the SFC's controls on forest-related labor derive from the structures of access to labor opportunities imposed by the Dutch. The systems of reforestation (by tumpang sari and day labor) originated with the Dutch, as did the logging rotations, the use of forest villagers' draft animals for hauling logs, and the resin tapping systems in pine and agathis forests. Where labor opportunities are scarce, or when land ownership is skewed, selection of laborers based on their relative compliance with SFC policy becomes a kind of control; the threat of losing access to needed income can be used to quiet a dissatisfied laborer.

However, the change in the total population since the Dutch period has created a new kind of contradiction in controlling forest labor. Though population data referring exclusively to forest villages at the time of the 1930 census are not available (because "forest villages" was not a census category), some simple calculations illustrate this point. The population of Java in 1930 was approximately 42 million (Manderson 1971, cited in Hasanu 1983:21). By 1985 the population was approximately 105 million, 63 percent of which lived in rural areas. Even if we assume that 90 percent of the 1930 population lived in rural areas, the increase in the number of rural people over this period would have been 56 percent. In some forest areas where other employment opportunities are scarce, this increase created a sizable labor reserve.

Rural labor reserves increase also as a result of increasing concentration of agricultural land. Higher population densities lead the SFC to make different policy decisions regarding labor, which may in turn have unintended impacts on the forest. For example, the plentiful availability of temporary labor enables the SFC to cut the costs associated with long-term commitment to state employees. However, many people engage in illegal forest-related activities because of the low and irregular wages of much forest employment and because there are not enough jobs for everyone. Many forest villages are far from other nonfarm earning opportunities. Insufficient employment for this labor reserve means people seek income from the forest in other ways than through formal, or authorized, forest labor. Thus, it could be argued that more people remain outside the direct control of the SFC; without hope for authorized employment, they seek sustenance in other ways.

State policy requires that the SFC use labor-intensive methods of exploitation where labor is in surplus because Java's rural industries, the service sector, and agriculture cannot absorb enough of the island's growing labor force. In order to justify mechanization, primarily the use of chainsaws, the SFC must argue that labor is in shortage.[23] Nevertheless, chainsaws are being used in some teak districts to accelerate production, even though labor is available or the physical conditions of the site are suited to manual logging.

A different kind of contradiction emerges in less-isolated forest areas: forests near urban areas, agricultural plantations, vegetable-growing regions, or rural industries. In such places, the higher wages and returns to labor in these industries attract more of the rural labor reserve. A day's wages on a tea plantation, for example, may be twice as high as a day's potential income from logging. While this means less pressure on the forest, it decreases available labor. Though this decrease should cause the SFC to become more competitive and raise wages and benefits, instead the circumstances are used by forest managers to justify the use of chainsaws and reduce their labor demand. In the case of reforestation, mechanization is neither practical nor politically feasible. In sum, the kinds of factors affecting the availability of forest labor, the relative control the field forester can exert over that labor, and the pressures on the forest resource base by unauthorized uses of the forest vary by region and socioeconomic context. Formal labor for the SFC, and some informal uses of the SFC lands, are subject to controls through policies and regulations. Access to laboring opportunities is controlled by field foresters. On Java's forest lands, formal labor includes reforestation, logging, tapping, maintenance, log-hauling (by individuals, groups of men, or cattle), and seedling transport. All forest laborers are paid in wages or in kind, usually calculated on a piecework basis, either for logs cut, split, or hauled; for resin collected; or for an area cleared of brush and secondary growth. In the case of reforestation by tumpang sari, laborers are paid a nominal contract fee, as they were under the Dutch. In 1985 this fee was Rp. 5,000 (US$3.03) for the length of farmer tenure, usually two or three years. Their major form of remuneration comes in the form of access to plots of forest land for a certain period of time. This kind of payment lends an informal aspect to formal labor, giving forest laborers access to non-timber forest products—in this case agricultural products—rather than a share in the major product, namely, the trees planted. Other similar arrangements include the rights to dispose of stumps in logged-over forest and the rights of the blandong to the small branches on the teak trees he cuts. No forest laborers are permanent employees; all are classified *buruh lepas* (literally, "free laborers").

The SFC controls some informal forest labor by the issuance of permits or by granting informal permission to use the forest. For example, lime producers need permits; burning limestone means not only digging on forest lands but also cutting wood for fuel. Forest laborers and other villagers also obtain nontimber forest products from the forest lands, including firewood and fodder, wild game, leaves, rocks, limestone, and charcoal. They also graze cows and goats in the forest. While the percentage of households with members formally earning wages from the SFC varies widely among forest villages, most of these informal forest uses are universal and not limited to people within certain economic classes. Grazing on forest lands is supposed to be regulated and not allowed in young forest under ten years of age. Only dead wood is allowed to be taken for fuelwood, and only the old leaves on older teak trees are allowed to be collected. All these regulations are meant to preserve the integrity of the forest.

For forest villagers, both formal and informal activities are important to household economies. In most areas, forest villagers are compelled by the limits on local formal earning opportunities to seek informal income on the forest lands. Informal activities have the advantage of independence: the fuelwood collector, for example, decides himself or herself where and when to collect and answers to no mandor. As we will see in chapters 6 and 7, villagers' informal forest labor is most difficult for the SFC to control. Fuelwood collectors frequently cut live branches or saplings because there is not enough dead wood for fuelwood needs. Villagers graze their cows in young forest because there is more for the cows to eat. They cut the youngest teak leaves because they are more supple and preferred for wrapping. Social norms cause foresters to have greater difficulty denying women access to fuelwood or keeping children from grazing in restricted areas. In sum, though the nature of the controls and the controlling regulations today are similar or identical to those under the Dutch, their implementation is increasingly confounded by the increasing informal demands on the forest.

Though the basic components of control have not changed since the Dutch were the foresters, changing structural constraints have required a more intensive application of their principles by contemporary foresters. Javanese foresters persist in maintaining these controls, but their effectiveness is waning.

NEW PROBLEMS IN NEW ORDER FORESTRY

The forestry apparatus and its contemporary sociopolitical context differ in two major respects from the time that Java was a Dutch colony. First, the SFC and Forestry sectors are more powerful at the national level than were their predecessors the Dutch. This is because of their greater autonomy: The SFC is a parastatal organization and Forestry is a ministry.[24] The political economy of teak production has changed because all wood destined for export must first be processed in-country. In the timber source areas, however, the extractive nature of forest industry shifts the balance of major benefits outside the region. From the point of view of local people, outsiders—no matter that they be Indonesian rather than Dutch—are still trying to control their local resources.

Second, because the forest was damaged during the political upheaval between 1942 and 1966, repairs and damage control have become more critical components of forestry strategy since 1967, partially explaining the heavy-handed approach taken by the SFC in forest security. The two approaches to forest security are repressive (paramilitary) and preventive (economic development) measures. The SFC's mandate to oversee the development of forest villages is taken within the context of forest security. Externally conceived, with objectives to benefit the SFC more than the villagers, village development efforts have hardly touched, let alone improved, forest villagers' lives.

Both these changes have been subsumed under the broader production orientation of the SFC. They are thus manifested as echoes of the more powerful mandates rather than equal pillars supporting the SFC in a changing context. They are discussed in greater detail below.

The Political Economy of Teak in Java

As we have seen, the power of the SFC in contemporary Indonesia stems from the structure of the state itself as well as from the SFC's guardian and production roles as a parastatal corporation. This is why it is important to understand how production forestry fits into the general political economy of Indonesia. It is also important to understand the social organization of forest production at local, regional, and national levels as a means of understanding the impact of structure on actors at each of these levels.

Forestry, the second largest sectoral earner after oil, consistently contributed 12 to 13 percent to foreign exchange earnings in the 1980s (Tarrant et al. 1987:1–20). Depending on the world market for timber and the policies affecting the whole Indonesian timber industry, some 3 to 6.5 percent of Indonesia's timber comes from Java. Java's timber is primarily teak. World demand for teak remains high, and Java is among the top three producers in the world, the other two being Thailand and Burma. In 1984 teak exports alone provided 1.9 percent of the nation's foreign exchange earnings from forestry (Perum Perhutani 1985a:90; Republik Indonesia 1988–89:354). That same year, the SFC contributed US$5.9 million in taxes to the Indonesian budget.

Teak forest makes up one-third of Java's state forest land and one-half of Java's production forest, yet provides 92 percent of the SFC's total income (Perum Perhutani 1985; Radite 1985). Teak is managed by the SFC as part of the three million hectares of state forest land under SFC control. The SFC controls all access to forest land, retains a monopoly on the domestic marketing and transport of raw teak, controls all formal forest labor, and controls much forest village development.[25]

Most changes in the political economy of teak since the Dutch period are functions of the SFC's structure as a capitalist enterprise. All exported teak must be processed in some way before export. There has been some flux in the volume of teak timber produced each year, but the general trend has been an increase. In 1969 some 520,000 cubic meters of teak sawlogs were produced; by 1986 production had risen to 798,000 cubic meters (Republik Indonesia 1989:354). Part of the increase can be attributed to wood-saving practices such as cutting trees closer to the ground, more use of thinned wood (particularly in age-classes 5 and over), and improved technology for using pieces formerly discarded as waste, for example, by making parquet for floors. Part of the increase is also attributable to forest district managers' incentives to produce more than the annual targeted quantity or to reach quotas set before losses from teak theft have been accounted for.

Indonesia's recent focus on the development of nonoil revenues has caused the SFC to aggressively pursue a minimum 4 percent real-growth target every year (Perum Perhutani 1985:7). It has achieved this goal by restricting the number of civil servants and mechanizing some forest operations—even in labor surplus districts (Hasanu 1983:91; Djuwadi 1985:41).[26] The nonoil export development push has also led the SFC to improve the quality of the teak conversions[27] it exports (Perum Perhutani 1985:7, 37).

State and private enterprises in Indonesia have integrated (at the national level) the steps in extraction and processing of major natural resources such as timber and oil. Some parastatals such as the state oil company (Pertamina) and the SFC have remained relatively autonomous of foreign investment, compared to, say, the timber extraction industry in the provinces of Kalimantan and Sumatra (Robison 1986).[28]

Nevertheless, national policy sometimes has adverse effects on the earning capacity of the SFC. For example, from 1980 to 1983, Indonesia imposed a phased ban on log exports in order to stimulate domestic wood-processing industries. Though directed primarily at rapid deforestation problems and the loss of value-added to timber companies with logging concessions in the Outer Islands, this policy also affected the SFC. At the time of the ban, the SFC stood to gain more by exporting raw logs, which had export prices two or three times higher than domestic prices in the 1970s. The SFC has no monopoly on the marketing of processed teak, and given the high costs of establishing teak-processing industries capable of producing world-class wood products, economic incentives for industrial transformation did not exist. For at least the short term, the government's domestic industrialization policies reduced the SFC's earnings. In fact, the cost of producing wood products of competitive export quality has been stated as a major reason that most Java teak is sold domestically (B. Muljadi, personal communication 1985).

The long-term attraction of exports, however, is the higher value: though less than 8 percent of the volume cut was processed and exported by the SFC in 1984, these exports contributed some 21 percent of the SFC's income, a threefold increase in as many years (Perum Perhutani 1985:28). Of course, only the highest-quality timber can be used for export products and the amount of high-quality teak is limited.

The benefits of industrywide integration are not felt at the local level, and the dominance of forestry in local employment structures has created an extractive economy (Bunker 1985). Six SFC sawmill/wood-processing industries are located within the teak zone of Central and

East Java, but three of these are in towns or urban areas outside the extractive zone.[29] Much teak furniture for the domestic luxury market is produced by private entrepreneurs in Surakarta, Semarang, Jepara, and Surabaya—cities that border the teak zone but are far from the source regions and rarely provide employment for forest villagers. By law, private conversion of teak into furniture or boards is not permitted within nine miles of the forest borders and never in villages enclosed by the forest boundaries. This policy has been in effect since 1972 and aims to discourage unauthorized forest cutting.

What are the problems associated with the system? First, the extraction of the raw material itself is becoming increasingly expensive because of failed reforestation efforts, depletion of the older plantation trees without equal replacement, and unrecovered losses due to war damages (Peluso 1985; Teguh 1985; SFT 1985). Second, most of the biggest remaining trees (old growth) are in the most remote locations and are therefore the most costly to cut and transport (Perum Perhutani 1985:9). Third, few, if any, undisturbed hectares of forest plantations remain. As Hasanu (1983:88) points out, much thinning is now done without official sanction by local people. The potential production of a hectare of teak forest land is clearly declining. Recent estimates place the average value per hectare in Central Java's teak forest at one-quarter of the potential value; in East Java, average value per hectare is one-fifth its potential (B. Muljadi, personal communication September 1985).

The cumulative effect of tree losses on the forest structure is shown in Figure 5.2 (calculated from PERSAKI Cabang Jawa Tengah 1985b:47). Figure 5.3 shows what an ideal forest plantation would look like: an equal distribution of trees in eight age-classes over an eighty-year rotation. The ideal figure assumes no disturbance from human or other sources.

The primary sources of income for the SFC are the Central and East Java teak plantations planted and maintained by Dutch foresters in the late nineteenth and early twentieth centuries, and tracts of original forest that have not been cut in known forest history. Tracts to be clear-cut within the decade are represented by age-classes 8–12,[30] which in 1984 constituted 6.1 percent—together with the hectarage from the MR (underproductive) category—of the province's productive teak forest. In 1982 some 8,000 hectares of Central Java's forest land remained in age-classes 9–12. These are the oldest old-growth trees, well beyond the normal cutting age. They contain more wood and represent a considerable subsidy to the "normal" income from clearcutting trees in age-class 8.[31] Between 1982 and 1984, 38 percent of the area in age-classes 9–12 was harvested (PERSAKI 1985). The most dramatic drop was in age-classes 11 and 12, from 2,700 hectares in 1982 to 203 hectares in 1984.

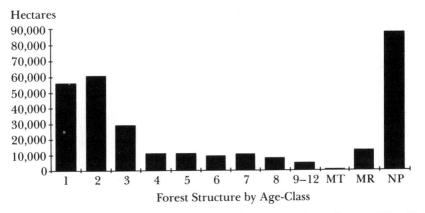

MT = Masak Tebang (ready to cut); MR = Miskin Riap (underproductive); NP = Unproductive or nonteak producing land within a designated teak forest

Figure 5.2. Teak Forest Age-Classes and Unproductive Forest Land, 1984, Central Java

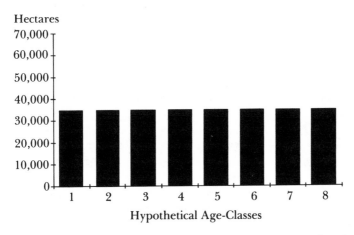

Figure 5.3. An Ideal Teak Age-Class Distribution (Plantation Forest)

The clearest illustration of the unsustainable nature of the current teak production system is the tremendous skew between the young, nonproductive forests and forests in which thinned or clear-cut trees have substantial economic value (age-classes 5 and older).[32] Figure 5.4 collapses the age-classes of the Central Javanese teak forest in 1984 to demonstrate that the area of unproductive and nonteak producing teak forest exceeds the area that will be clear-cut within the next forty years. I

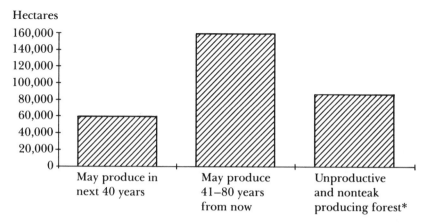

Hectares

*Includes SFC's categories for empty land, unproductive teak land, land unsuitable for clear-cutting, and land unsuitable for teak.

Figure 5.4. Potential Production of Central Java Teak Forests (based on 1984 data)

have overestimated the amount to be cut in the next forty years by assuming that all the forest in the poor increment category (MR) will be harvested.

As Figure 5.4 shows, if no political, social, or natural disasters disturb the current stocks over a forty-year period, only 19.6 percent, or 59,549 hectares, of the Central Java "teak forest" will produce teak timber by the year 2022. Given the history of conflict in Java's forests, the probability that the forest will remain undisturbed is virtually nil.

Figures 5.2–5.4 illustrate the limited potential for maintaining current levels of teak extraction. Why has this happened, in spite of a strong commitment to scientific forestry for sustained-yield production? The problems started with the forest-based conflicts of the years 1942 through 1967. In addition to the difficulty of rehabilitating these lands, there are three reasons current patterns of forest extraction have become unsustainable: foresters are overextracting teak, forest farmers are keeping much of the forest under agriculture, and organized forest theft networks are depleting stocks. Let us consider each of these in turn.

Pressures on foresters to overcut.   Normally, the area logged each year is one-eightieth of a teak forest district. State pressures for the SFC to increase real income by 4 percent each year, coupled with tree losses due to theft or standing stock damage, have caused forest managers to add supplementary logging tracts to their one-year plans in order to meet the market quotas determined in ten-year plans. Additional cuts come from forests that would not normally be logged until succeeding years. Both field and administrative foresters talk about the difficulties of meeting quotas from certain tracts and the necessity year after year of adding supplemental cuts. In speaking of the sustainability of a management plan, there can be no such thing as a "supplemental" tract in a forest when plans are made for harvest rotation. Cutting into a future tract means depleting future stocks and reducing future income. In some districts where trees have grown beyond the eighth age-class, local foresters have somewhat more leeway for supplemental cutting; because few trees remain in these age-classes, this option will soon be gone.

De facto forest conversion to agriculture. The second stress derives from the variation in land and resource control during the eighty-year rotation cycle of the tree plantation. As explained earlier, reforestation in Java is primarily by the *taungya* system, or *tumpang sari,* introduced in the latter years of the nineteenth century. This type of agroforestry for plantation establishment is initially dominated by the agricultural components (one to three years) but taken over by the forestry-tree components for the long term (twenty years or more under pine, forty or more years under agathis, seventy-eight years or more under teak). In teak forest, this means that much of the forest land in age-class 1 is under a mixture of agricultural and young tree crops, while age-classes 2–12 are essentially teak monocultures. During the first period, the forest farmer largely controls the land and it is his or her daily activities that determine the health of the trees. After the two-year tumpang sari period, control returns to the foresters. Dense population around most forest areas precludes most tumpang sari farmers from moving to freshly logged blocks after successfully reforesting others—other villagers will seek access to nearby tumpang sari sites. Thus it is in the farmers' interest to keep the land under the first stage of tumpang sari. The disproportionate amount of land in age-class 1 (Figure 5.2) is thus a crude indicator of repeated reforestation failures.

The outcome of these contradictions has been that tumpang sari farmers effectively control 6 to 10 percent of state forest lands in Central Java.[33] Forest-based relations of production have also been influenced by village social systems, thus by 1984 the organization of labor on reforestation lands in several forest villages studied had begun to resemble that of adjacent agricultural lands.[34] Sharecropping, the sale of access rights to reforestation land, and the advance sale of tumpang sari crops were common in many forest villages, even in SFC community development villages (see chapter 6) (Peluso 1986; SFT 1985). Wage labor was also common. These patterns of access distribution have implications not only for the nature of power and control in forestry, but also for the roles of those who have traditionally controlled access to reforestation lands, the field foresters. They also strengthen elite villagers' power vis-à-vis the state on the lands it claims because the state must convince them to plant and maintain trees. In this way, village internal politics and state-peasant relations influence the sustainability of Java's forests and forest management system. (This subject is explored further in chapter 6.)

Forest "crimes." The third pattern of forest extraction threatening sustainable management is forest *crime,* that is, the cutting of wood or use of the forest (for grazing, burning, charcoal making, or other purposes) without the explicit permission of the state resource controllers (the SFC). There are various levels of this type of forest extraction, ranging from individuals cutting seedlings for fuelwood, to groups working together in a village, to the organization of a whole village under formal and informal village leaders, to a larger-scale black market network connecting forest villagers with wood processors. This last supplies teak furniture industries with an estimated 40 to 50 percent of their raw wood. Powerful operators working from outside forest villages have manipulated local circumstances (need for cash income) and SFC policies to their advantage. (This aspect of forest degradation and village resistance is discussed in chapter 7.)

The conflicting interests of foresters and forest villagers have been exacerbated by the confrontational tactics used by the forest police, also a carry-over from the Dutch period, generally creating tense relations in forest villages. Though the contemporary political climate precludes villagers' overt opposition to state forest policies, the evidence of village resistance to state control is reflected in the figures on teak theft and forest damage.

Table 5.1 shows that a high rate of peasant teak extraction has persisted from colonial times to the present. Given the security implications, crimes may in fact have been underreported. Significant rises in the incidence of forest crimes were recorded before the onset of the worldwide depression in 1929. Forest theft has been worse under the Indonesian foresters than under the Dutch, generally remaining high through the 1960s, 1970s, and 1980s. A sharp drop was noted in 1966, the year when many forest squatters and laborers organized by communist groups were killed in the agrarian war. By 1974 theft was on the rise again, reaching an all-time high in 1982, the year the PJJ operations began. Though theft declined in 1984—a fact that foresters attribute to the cumulative impacts of paramilitary forest policing since 1982—the rate had risen once again by 1986.

Teak theft undermines state controls and often results in land degradation. Although patches of forest land where trees have been stolen

TABLE 5.1 Recorded Forest "Crimes," Selected Years, 1918–1986

Year	Total Cases (All Forests)ᵃ	Tree Theftᵇ	Area Damaged (Hectares)ᶜ
1918	27,218	18,910 cases	n.a.
1923	17,154	12,372 cases	n.a.
1928	74,928	11,892 cases	n.a.
1933	45,507	n.a.	n.a.
1938	52,528	37,189 cases	n.a.
1962	41,102	263,699 trees	12,945
1965	36,809	221,470 trees	24,844
1966	21,311	109,258 trees	6,663
1967	28,447	157,837 trees	38,865
1968	22,170	97,553 trees	3,851
1974	n.a.	153,838 trees	9,461
1979	n.a.	203,702 trees	28,451
1982	n.a.	245,217 trees	70,428
1983	n.a.	130,788 trees	41,721
1984	n.a.	64,727 trees	7,700
1985	n.a.	72,816 trees	10,496
1986	n.a.	126,419 trees	6,679

SOURCES: *Verslagen van den dienst van het Boschwezen in Nederlandsche-Indie over het jaar 1921–22, 1927, 1929, 1933–36, 1938–39;* Direktorat Djendral Kehutanan, *Statistik 1968;* Perum Perhutani 1981; Perum Perhutani 1985; Perum Perhutani 1987.

ᵃIncludes tree theft, damage to standing stock, illegal grazing, charcoal manufacture and transport, wood transport without permit, forest conversion to agriculture, and collection of forest stones.

ᵇMost recorded crimes occurred in teak forests, but in the years for which disaggregated statistics are available, crimes in nonteak forests accounted for as much as one-fourth of the total. Pre-1978 data do not include West Java.

ᶜDamages include forest fires, unauthorized grazing, and forest conversion to agriculture.

may be reforested after the remaining trees are logged, soil damage due to exposure affects the land's capacity to regenerate teak. Where theft or soil impaction by cattle grazing on designated reforestation tracts are recurrent problems, the degradation is obvious in bedrock exposure, lack of vegetative cover, or the growth of gnarly, deformed teak trees. The SFC also considers the conversion of forest land to peasant agriculture as a kind of forest degradation. Like the state, the peasants' goal has been to retain control over land. Unlike the state, peasants regard forest converted to agriculture as improved rather than degraded land.

Although growth and production continue to be important to the political economy of forestry in Java, the indications are that neither the resource base nor the social system will be able to sustain them at the same levels as in the recent past. At the ideological level, the concern about future trends has been mated with the SFC's mandate as a quasi-development agency, responsible in part for the well-being and economic development of forest villages.

FORESTERS' RESISTANCE TO STRUCTURAL CHANGE: EFFORTS TO DEVELOP FOREST VILLAGES

Ideological commitment to the alleviation of poverty and to village participation in forest management has not been backed up by as much planning and thought as traditional forestry pursuits. Thus at the field level, two types of solutions have emerged: ad hoc adaptations to field circumstances by field foresters and SFC-planned forest village development projects.

The Ad Hoc Approach

To deal with the difficulties of implementing broadly conceived policies in widely ranging local circumstances, field foresters often adjust forestry policy on an ad hoc basis. Some of this is for the sake of getting a job done or to benefit local people. Other adaptations are no more than self-enrichment or self-empowerment schemes developed by disloyal field personnel.

The documentation of a wide range of field-adapted management systems indicates that many forest security problems stem from the responses of officials to the inadequacy of forestry laws and structures, the current forest situation, and their own interest in the current system. The fact that they are taking steps independently and that these actions are leading to additional forest losses echoes some of the problems of forest management under the VOC. What differs most profoundly is the contemporary ideology of sustained-yield management entrusted to the state and its agents, the field foresters. The failure of some foresters to observe the high standards of professional performance set by their own colleagues has led directly to villagers and others ignoring the rules as well.

Research in West and Central Java in 1984–85 (SFT 1985; Peluso 1986) identified three forms of ad hoc policy adaptations by field foresters: the adaptation of the agroforestry technologies permitted on forest lands (adapted species control), the adaptation of the allocation system of reforestation land (adapted land control), and the reallocation of funds within local budgets (adapted labor control). Each of these is considered briefly below.

Agroforestry on forest lands. SFC policy on crops permitted on reforestation plots specifically aims to preclude interference with the growth of the main species. Crops believed to drain soil nutrients (e.g., cassava), to damage the soil structure, or to increase erosion potential are not to be planted. Cassava, however, which is said by foresters to have all these adverse effects, is a low-input, low-risk crop for farmers in many areas. Most foresters know it is futile to forbid all cassava planting on reforestation lands. Instead, they try to regulate the planting pattern, allowing the farmer to plant cassava around the plot's perimeter. When forest farmers show discretion by following these directions, foresters may tend to be more lenient on other matters.

Allocation of tumpang sari land. Tumpang sari land is supposed to be allocated to poor forest villagers to give them temporary access to land for a livelihood. However, in many forest villages of Java, forest villagers complain that favoritism is shown in selecting forest farmers; that access to forest land is "sold," "rented," or "pawned"; that the most fertile or valuable tracts are allocated to wealthy villagers or outsiders; or that irrelevant or unfair criteria are used to select farmers, such as the prerequisite that forest farmers prove they use birth control (SFT 1985). In addition, people have been refused access to tumpang sari land if they refused to work without pay at jobs that are usually remunerated, such as clearing land for *cemplongan* planting,[35] transporting seedlings to the forest, building shelters for the mandors, or helping build roads in the forest. People who will work without pay are said to be more "cooperative" than others, more loyal to the SFC—just as clients are supposed to be willing to work under any circumstances for their patrons. People clamor over tumpang sari access nearly everywhere the forest soils are cultivable.[36] Some field foresters take advantage of intense pressures on agricultural land for personal enrichment, through reforestation scams which have the most potential for enrichment of the foresters.

The reallocation of funds in local budgets. Periodically, a forest manager (district, subdistrict, or smaller) feels a need to change the allocation of funds in his budget. If unforeseen costs arise in implementing a new program, or wages have to be increased or supplemented in order to compete with other sectors (rarely done), funds might have to be sought from other budget items. Sometimes a production system is changed; for example, chainsaws may be purchased to replace manual saws for logging (Djuwadi 1985). Cost differences are made up by substitution of "voluntary" labor for paid labor. Social forestry field researchers noted the nonpayment or postponement of forest laborers' wages (Peluso 1985; Teguh 1985); the failure to pay tumpang sari contract fees (ibid.); reduced wage payments in logging operations, resin collection, and seedling transport (Djuwadi 1985; Peluso 1985; Radite 1985); and discrepancies in the way project funds were distributed (Djamali and Zulfi 1985). Signatures or thumbprints were found to be forged on official documents certifying that payments had been received by laborers (Djuwadi 1985).

Obviously, budget adjustments often indicate illegal appropriation of funds by someone in the forestry hierarchy. In one shocking—though perhaps not unusual—case, a field forester reported a remote section of healthy forest as degraded, recommended targeting for reforestation, and sold the rights to the plots to local villagers. No one would have been the wiser had there not been a trained forester conducting research in that site (Teguh 1985).

Some management compromises aid entire forest-edge communities; others transfer benefits into the pockets of individuals, including formal or informal village leaders and forestry personnel. For example, permitting cassava cultivation on forest lands may benefit poor and rich farmers alike, whereas the unauthorized sale of access rights to fertile forest plots benefits only the "sellers" and the buyers who can afford it. Sometimes the good and bad aspects of local adaptations are linked. For example, a field forester may allow villagers informal access to the forest lands to collect firewood or to farm small plots in exchange for their silence about the forester's involvement in illegal activities or misuse of funds. If wages for forest labor fall below local standards, field forestry personnel may allow forest villagers to collect larger sizes of firewood than usual, or turn a blind eye to the cutting of living saplings for fuel (Djuwadi 1985). These types of ad hoc adaptation may benefit local people but generally lead to increased forest degradation.

Although upper-level foresters are aware of bureaucratic constraints at the field level, they view these contraints as the price for efficient production and centralized control. Structurally, the SFC has sacrificed its capacity to make site-specific policies. Accurate reporting of both problems and ideas from the sites is complicated by the top-down hierarchy of the forest bureaucracy and the dependence of field people on their supervisors for promotion recommendations. Afraid of being judged inadequate, or in some cases fearful their illegal actions may become known, local managers and field personnel (asper, mantri, mandor) conceal management problems or local policy aberrations. Although central, unit, and district managers make regular field trips, they can be led past difficult access locales having serious, but concealed, problems.

Early Efforts at Social Forestry

Social forestry, known in the 1970s and early 1980s as community forestry, was initiated in the 1970s by the SFC with minimal foreign assistance and advice. In the most recent of its programs, the SFC invested some 5 percent of the corporation's net earnings in community forestry projects every year (B. Muljadi, personal communication 1985). Despite this financial commitment, most of the SFC's community development projects did not succeed in alleviating poverty or stopping forest encroachment as intended. Some of the failures were attributable to the isolation of pilot projects that were never extended beyond the experimental stage (either within or outside of target villages) and structural flaws preventing the projects from addressing both the short- and long-term needs of the village poor (Peluso and Poffenberger 1989). The projects changed neither the terms of forest access nor the nature of SFC control.

The underlying goal of SFC community forestry activities has been to control forest access by reducing local people's forest dependence. It is part of the "preventive" aspect of forest security and thus fits into the SFC mandate to provide "service to the general interest which is manifested in the conduct of territorial control duties, including the tasks of territorial development and the development of the people" (Djokonomo 1986:1).

Problems have arisen in the interpretation of "the people" and in the justification of prioritizing forest production for the state before direct local forest use. Loosely defined, "the people" refers both to those living near the forests and, more broadly, to the population of Java. The SFC acknowledges its responsibilities to both groups but distinguishes between the means by which it will fulfill those responsibilities. The SFC claims to work in the interests of the entire populace by guarding the forest's integrity, keeping it under tree cover, keeping production costs low, and making forest production profitable for the state. To the smaller group, the 21 million forest villagers, the SFC allocates informal access rights, and selected villages are provided opportunities to participate in community development activities. Securing forest villagers' welfare is not viewed as a means of contributing to the welfare of the entire nation.

To deal with the management problems they faced in the field, SFC foresters designed various development plans such as the Prosperity Approach and PMDH (*Pembangunan Masyarakat Desa Hutan*, or Forest Village Community Development). Though implemented under the guidance of two different president directors of the SFC, both programs worked in much the same way. Various pilot projects included beekeeping, small-scale animal husbandry, and importing silkworms to produce silk on mulberry tree plantations. Fruit and fuelwood seedlings were distributed and check dams were constructed on private village lands. Unfortunately both programs failed to meet the broad and difficult goal of relieving local pressures on the forest by alleviating poverty.

These forest village development programs were developed by central forestry planners without inputs from either forestry field personnel or forest villagers. The abstract goals of the SFC were congruent with the New Order's ideological objective of achieving "a Pancasila society." For the most part the programs were not geared to the specific needs or constraints of particular villages: labor availability, marketing constraints, and so on. This contributed to their ineffectiveness.

As is usual for community development projects of this sort, horror stories abound in the field about government-provided livestock dying, lack of markets for honey causing people to abandon their new beehives after a few months, demonstration plots functioning more as showcases for visiting dignitaries and the press than as sources of seedlings and ideas for local people, the refusal or fear of local people to participate, and wealthy farmers capturing project benefits. There are also some stories of partial success, where the foresters' efforts were sincere and supported by other officials and informal leaders, and in which local people cooperated based on trust. However, even those projects that succeeded in reforesting some areas or improving working relationships between village leaders and the SFC have not reported reductions in the forest dependence of poor forest villagers.

A key component of both programs was the MALU strategy, so called after an acronym for *mantri* (forest guard) and *lurah* (village head).[37] The program was to serve as a functional substitute for a forest extension service, which does not exist in Java. Subdistrict level agricultural extension agents (*Petugas Lapangan Pertanian,* or PLP) are supposed to work with field foresters in extending information about tree crops to farmers in addition to performing their agricultural extension duties. One PLP is generally responsible for agricultural extension in some ten to fifteen villages and has minimal time available for tree crop or forest extension. Mandors and mantris are supposed to provide incidental extension information in the field.

The MALU approach has been problematic because it is more a means of controlling forest access than a development mechanism. The program was established to achieve SFC objectives of asserting authority over forest lands. MALU was structured to promote cooperation between the SFC and village leaders, and aimed to reduce the tensions that had sometimes characterized the two groups' relations in the past. By linking the village leaders to the SFC through a village development program, the SFC hoped to gain more control over forest villagers. In other words, it was a coalition strategy to link two elite or power groups to give foresters more direct control over villagers, who are technically outside their jurisdiction. In this way, the program reflected the tactics used by the colonial state to secure the loyalties of local leaders through patronization and formal legitimation of their local positions (Sutherland 1979; McVey 1982; Anderson 1983). Thus, the MALU program served a parallel function, as an indirect form of labor control and bureaucratic orientation. Where village leaders already felt tied or oriented toward the state, either as former members of the military or supporters of GOLKAR, it seems to have been easier for the local mantri to engage the village leader's cooperation.[38] Where this is not yet the case, as in some villages having histories of unpleasant relations with colonial or contemporary foresters, or whose leaders are involved in the black market for teak and have their own interests in forest control, the MALU strategy has failed to achieve the SFC's intentions of protecting the forest. Overall, however, it has institutionalized a more positive relationship between village heads and foresters. This has fit the broader state strategy of unifying ideologies and structures of control by different components of the state.

As the class and power alliances grew stronger between bureaucratic elites in different branches of the civil service, the gap between these elites and the peasantry widened. Mantris and mandors had never been taught to work with villagers as development agents, community organizers, or even extension agents. Training in the forestry school or in short courses focuses on technical forestry and forest security. Forest guards were often chosen from among the toughest members of the community who were not afraid to confront those infringing on the state's claimed property. This was not conducive to the evolution of mutually beneficial alliances between poor or average villagers and the local foresters.

Although their community development literature acknowledges poverty as a marginalizing force and a threat to the integrity of the forest, it has been difficult for foresters to prioritize poverty alleviation in village development efforts by targeting and maintaining a commitment to poor villagers. Community development is secondary to other aspects of the SFC agenda. In the opening comments to a workshop on forest village development held in 1982, the president director said: "The first goal [of the SFC] is to improve the potential, effectiveness, and role of protection forests in protecting land, water regulation, environmental quality and esthetics. The second goal is to preserve germ plasm from the danger of extinction. The third goal is to increase the function and benefits from forest lands for social and economic needs" (Perum Perhutani 1982:i). Furthermore, the maintenance of the SFC's income is, not surprisingly, paramount, although in the same breath the director talks of both increasing revenues through traditional and modern forestry science and decreasing poverty: "The attitudes and skills of foresters should upgrade minus areas to plus [areas] and increase the SFC's income so that it does not stop at 60 billion [Rupiah]/year. With various efforts, the SFC is targeting a 5.7 percent annual growth, for example with technological innovations (seed and seedling selection), and targeting the decrease of forest villagers' poverty by 1 percent per year for the period ending in 1985" (ibid., 2). Achieving village development or well-being is not treated as being complementary to the traditional practice of forestry. The two goals are implemented as different and incompatible parts of the agency's mandate. Though the ideology sounds nice, the reality has not materialized: "Forestry Development . . . is meant to eliminate life below the poverty line and simultaneously to improve the welfare of forest villagers. In this way it is hoped that by the year 2000 there will no longer be life below the poverty line and there will only be self-sufficient villages [*desa swasembada*] working towards the National Development goal to manifest PANCASILA villages" (Perum Perhutani 1982:i).

The emphasis of these projects remains on the adoption and spread of new technologies rather than the socioeconomic effects of their adoption. Thus there is no reduction of rural income gaps and no lowering of rates of forest dependence. The actual establishment of "Pancasila villages"—if they are to be self-sufficient—requires difficult political choices both in the production and allocation of the surplus from forest exploitation. It may not be possible to serve both village self-sufficiency and revenue generation by the SFC from the same forest. The SFC has not yet made these choices, nor has the state given it the opportunity or the means of doing so. Meanwhile, the SFC "drops" seedlings and livestock (goats and chickens) into target development villages, where they are distributed by its new allies, the village leaders—who confound the poverty-alleviation goals of the program by distributing them to their kin, clients, or other local elites (SFT 1985). Even within the context of the separate development program, no structural controls have been applied to check the local social processes allowing rural elites in many sites to capture these new benefits. This is the most difficult part of village development; it has also been the least examined in community forestry projects. Theory and practice remain miles apart.

In addition, social controls and class loyalties constrain the field forester. Arriving in the village with a new economic tree species, he may be met by curious elite progressive farmers cheerfully offering to plant the new varieties on their lands, or teasing him about giving them a few samples. Thus new seeds or seedlings run out before being distributed to the poorer farmers. When seedling supplies are limited, helping better-off farmers plant trees in part confounds the project objectives of keeping the forest intact by decreasing the forest dependence of the village poor. Like family planning programs that count acceptors instead of users, forest development programs that count seedlings dispersed rather than distribution patterns are missing the point. The forest-dependent people remain dependent or are marginalized even further.

Changing aspects of the Indonesian political economy have recently contributed to the agency's openness to contemporary conceptions of social forestry. Until the mid-1980s, Indonesia's development budget was fueled largely by the export of its own natural resources, particularly oil. Because oil contributed 70 percent of Indonesia's foreign exchange earnings, the state could be selective in accepting development loans and advice. Since the drop in oil prices, however, the development budget has also suffered. Between 1982 and 1987 the percentage of GDP contributed by oil decreased by 50 percent. The nonoil sectors, including forestry, increased by 25 percent but total revenues dropped. Accordingly, government expenditures were reduced by a dramatic 23 percent (Tarrant et al. 1987:1–20).

Despite the expenditure cuts, the Soeharto regime retains its ideological and financial commitment to development. To make up for the depletion of natural resources, the government has been forced to depend more on outside sources for development funds. Between 1982 and 1987 Indonesia's total external debt increased by 41 percent to some 45 percent of GDP (ibid.). Given the forecasts for the tenure of Indonesia's oil supplies (the country is expected to be a net importer by the year 2000), unless nonoil exports can make up the difference caused by the oil gap, this dependence can be expected to either grow or remain as high as at present. The ultimate effect will be a regime more susceptible to the demands and conditions set by international funders. As international funders increase their attention to issues of social welfare in, for example, the vicinity of major natural resource extraction sites, the priorities of the natural resource agencies will also have to undergo some change.

An in-depth discussion of the most recent social forestry programs goes beyond the scope of this chapter, but is discusse 1 briefly in chapter 8. (On early phases, see Barber 1989; Peluso and Poffenberger 1989.) Though they have the potential of making state forest lands more productive for everyone, recent reports indicate a similar reluctance of foresters to give up their traditional controls and a renegotiation of forms of control by both foresters and villagers.

SUMMARY

Since the beginning of the New Order, the SFC has changed little, either structurally or ideologically, from the Dutch style and objectives of forest management. It is still oriented toward production for export and luxury domestic markets and still views village development efforts as tangential to its true purpose: to practice scientific forestry for the benefit of "the greater good" through the vehicle of the state. The SFC manifests this purpose in its structure and function as a state enterprise, maintaining the "field personality" of a paramilitary forest control apparatus staffed by forester-technicians-police and allied with other security forces and local officials. It legitimates its activities by laws written by the Dutch in the 1920s and 1930s and translated, word for word, after Indonesian independence. Forestry has appropriated both the national ideology of Pancasila and traditional Western conceptions of state forestry as science. These structural, tactical, and philosophical elements have combined to create the contemporary culture of forest control in Java.

Other similarities to the colonial forest service include explicit policies of exclusion from the forest lands, the requirements that peasants perform "voluntary" labor, called forced labor in another time, and the SFC's power as a state-within-a-state prior to and after the revolution and subsequent social upheaval. Foresters maintain social distance from the poorest or most forest-dependent villagers and keep physical control of the forest through both the show and use of force. Most of the SFC's land, species, labor, and ideological forms of control have counterparts in the colonial period.

Most problems with social forestry in Java have stemmed from the foresters' failure to release control and negotiate real changes in power and forest access mechanisms. Preventive and repressive approaches to forest security—the two-pronged attack—were developed to secure the forest for traditional scientific and state revenue-earning uses. The separation of community development efforts from routine forest production lies at the root of the program's failure to successfully reforest and develop the area. However, the response of the forest-based peasantry to the routine forestry approach and to the efforts at community development are forcing the SFC to reconsider its position and renegotiate, no matter how reluctantly.

PART FOUR

Peasant Power to Resist

SIX

A Forest Without Trees

If we are condemned to talk always in terms of politics, we should perhaps begin to see politics not just as policy outcomes with consequences over decades or centuries, but also as experience and meaning within the ephemeral framework of men's lives.

BENEDICT R. O'G. ANDERSON, "Millenarianism and the Saminist Movement"

Pak Muasa had his own mini-forest on the 500-hectare tract of state forest land being reforested these past two years. He and his twelve children controlled some 10 hectares between them, managing these lands almost as if they were their own, planting fast-growing fuelwood species, papaya, banana, cassava, hill rice, maize, and groundnuts. They also controlled one of the few plots near a year-round stream—in the dry season a trickle—and were able to plant cucumber and long beans in the dry season while most of the cracked clay earth in this "forest" baked under the sun, cropless. While teenaged boys frequently cut the cassava leaves growing on other forest farmers' plots to feed their own goats, no one dared cut the leaves of plants on Pak Muasa's land. Besides the fact that someone from the family was usually working on one of the contiguous plots, the villagers were generally wary of Pak Muasa's *ilmu*, his personal power. He had used his power to walk the tightrope of survival during the height of the DI crisis, working as an "independent" intelligence operator for the government officials afraid to face the DI army. Another proof of his power was exhibited in his numerous healthy progeny and his rare ability to keep two wives, in relative harmony, within the same house. He was both "elected" (by a 5 percent margin) the head of the reforestation laborers (*kepala kontrak*), and selected to do the job by the mantri. For this status he claimed the traditional right of first choice of tumpang sari plots, and he chose the most fertile valleys in the hilly forest for himself and his sons' and daughters' families. He also worked with the mandors collecting fees in cash and kind from the forest farmers. For every Rp. 2,000 he collected, he kept Rp. 1,000. He possessed no land of his own but had acquired power through fasting, pilgrimage to sacred spots in Java, and meditation since he was a young man. He knew the four directions to seek help when Kalianjat village was experiencing a drought or other trouble. He also had prophetic dreams. In one of these, a recurrent dream, he was walking through the forest and arrived at a beautiful house. When he opened the door, it was full of gold. Pak Muasa was never afraid of his future. His internal power had been manifested on earth in twelve strong grown children, good health, and the power to make the right connections with the foresters.

Pak Mustafa also worked every day on the forest lands. He went mainly to collect fuelwood to sell, while his work on his tumpang sari plot was frequently rehabilatory. As usual, he had been given a quarter-hectare that was subject to frequent landslides; half of it had slid away within months of his allocation. This tract of forest in the foothills of an active volcano, Gunung Slamet, was subject to frequent seismic activity. He had to walk a good hour and a half to get there, and was thus loath to mix the dung from his one goat with the poor soils of the forest: he was always afraid the land would shift and any crops would be lost. Though he didn't expect to get a good plot, he always requested one, and planted it at least in cassava.

His main source of income was from sales of firewood, which he collected in the scraggly teak stand, from the SFC's leucaena plantings, or from people's gardens. During the rainy season, it was easiest to buy the rights to wood on someone's private fuelwood lot, collecting enough wood to sell over a couple of weeks' time, or to seek wage labor on someone else's land outside the village; this gave him immediate cash. Recently, the foresters were cracking down on fuel and fodder extraction, even though the villagers had planted the leucaena trees. They had met him one day on the muddy path back to the village, angrily grabbed his yoke, and smashed the fuelwood he had spent all morning cutting. They took his *parang* (knife) as well.

Mustafa's wife, with their three children aged two, four, and eight years, rarely traveled the distance to the sweltering forest plot; his eldest son was in school and there was no one to watch the children at home. If they went out, they preferred the cooler hour's walk through the tree gardens owned by their neighbors to the one-eighth-hectare plot of mixed fruit trees, cassava, and corn that they owned. Though just a small *kebun,* the various fruit trees provided them with quick cash or foods to cook with their meager portions of rice each day. On her way home, the wife collected branches of firewood for cooking. Pak Mustafa's young family will not mature in good health; his second child died before the age of three, unable to suck even the thin milk from his mother's breast. The family was neither heir nor kin to power or wealth, and lacked the right connections to the local controllers of forest access.

KALIANJAT

This chapter focuses on Kalianjat village, located beside a 2,000-hectare tract of forest currently designated for pine production. (Kalianjat is a pseudonym, as are the names of other villages, small towns, the forest subdistrict, and people mentioned in this chapter.) Kalianjat villagers know that the Indonesian government claims Kaliaman forest but refuse to regard the forest lands as national property off limits to their long-term access.

Two tendencies that would seem to run counter to each other were observed in Kalianjat. Within the village, there are struggles for forest control between poor and rich villagers. At the same time, the village unites in its resistance to external forces trying to control the forest; at present, this is the SFC. The first, internal conflict is part of a broader pattern of village differentiation. Struggles over private land and a highly skewed pattern of land distribution in the village make access to the forest lands critical to the village poor and an additional means of capital accumulation for the wealthier villagers. Oftentimes, forest policy or the actions of local foresters increases village divisiveness along class lines. The factors influencing villagers' forest use decisions vary according to class. Villagers' status and economic assets affect the nature of their relationships with the foresters who mediate formal forest access.

The more powerful force is the general opposition to any outsiders—individuals or institutions—that try to control the forest. This can be seen in their analysis of the meaning of their village's name (the pseudonym reflects values similar to those of the original name): *aman* meaning "safe" or "secure," while *kali* means "river" or "stream," the source of an element essential to human survival. Kalianjat peasants today see Kaliaman forest in the context of its historical function: a source of refuge and life. Although their reasons for and degree of forest dependence differ, people of all strata in this village use forest resources and have a strong interest in keeping the forest lands in the reforestation stage—that is, under a tumpang sari system. By keeping most of this forest land under tumpang sari, the villagers as a whole retain a greater degree of control over the forest lands and over the local foresters than they could if it were under mature pine forest.

In the first half of this chapter, an analysis of the village structure of access to land shows how some class tensions are relieved by access to extensive tracts of forest land for tumpang sari. In this section, Blaikie's notion of "access qualifications" (1985:123) is used as a tool for understanding how people are able to engage in various income-generating activities. Blaikie defines access qualifications broadly as "entry costs" (ibid., 7) but includes both economic (e.g., access to credit or surplus capital) and noneconomic criteria such as kinship, patronage, residence in particular geographical areas, or membership in particular social groups. Each household or individual makes decisions to engage in various agricultural and nonagricultural activities depending on the qualifications of employment and the characteristics, qualifications, or connections of the household or individual.

The second half of this chapter looks at the history of village confrontations with external forces. This is an interpretive history, recounted by the villagers themselves, except where comparisons to limited available archival materials are noted. The de facto conversion of the forest to agriculture, started by villagers under the tensions of war and maintained through strife and peace, provides physical evidence of the battered peasant-state relations in this forest village. Contemporary peasant-state relations seem to indicate an empowered or "winning" peasantry for at least the past twenty years. But this victory is tempered now, and will be in the long run, not only by class but also by the power of individuals to manipulate structures of forest access in both traditional and modern ways.

THE FOREST SETTING

RPH Kaliaman (Kaliaman forest)[1] is located on the Central Java side of the border between Central and West Java. When the Dutch finalized the boundaries of the state forest lands in the 1920s and 1930s, they exchanged government land outside the state forest for private plots inside. This "new" forest was under the jurisdiction of (and named after) Kaliaman village.

According to the people who cultivate the forest, extract fuelwood, or graze livestock on its open lands, Kaliaman forest has always belonged to everyone living on its borders. Their common ancestors converted the natural forest to swidden agriculture and tree gardens, their legends of origin derive from constant interaction with the forest, and their contemporary livelihoods depend on their access to the forest. They call it a *hutan tumpeng*, likening it to the mountain of rice (*tumpeng*) that symbolizes sustenance in ritual feasts celebrating the critical junctures in people's life cycles. At least six villages, located in three different subdistricts and consisting of an unknown number of hamlets, use the forest lands of Kaliaman. All lie in the southern half of Brebes District, and except for one, these villages are subsumed under a single forest subdistrict (BKPH) in West Pekalongan Forest District (KPH Pekalongan Barat).

The planned function of Kaliaman forest, which has been designated as a pine production forest by the SFC since the early 1970s, is the production of fast-growing tropical pines (*Pinus merkusii*) to supply pulp.

A pulp factory was slated for construction on the south coast of Java in 1990, the result of a joint venture between Japan and Indonesia. Before harvesting the trees for their pulp, the SFC plans to tap pine resin (*gondorekum*) for at least ten years.

The forest consists of low hills (150–200 meters above sea level) with soils composed of mixed volcanic and limestone parent material. Slopes range from 5 to 50 percent. The clayey latosols, litosols, and regosols are highly prone to erosion during the rainy season and severe cracking during the dry season. Between 1978 and 1982 annual rainfall averaged 3,145 millimeters, with rain falling primarily from October to May.[2] Temperatures range throughout the year from 20°C to 30°C.

While this forest may represent sustenance to the villagers, it has been a forester's nightmare for forty years. In 1983, 59 percent—more than 1,090 hectares—of the 1,851-hectare RPH was classified "unproductive empty land," covered in thick clumps of choking *Imperata cylindrica* and *Saccharum spontaneum* grasses. Some 551 hectares (27 percent) were still planted in teak, but the occupation and the wars had rendered it a poor quality teak: crooked, discolored, sprouted from stumps, and growing at irregular intervals—deformed reminders of the forest's previous designation as a teak plantation. Another 205 hectares (11 percent) were sparsely planted in tropical pine trees, most just a few inches high, and intercropped with tumpang sari food crops. In 1983 and 1984, 213 and 208 hectares, respectively, were officially opened for reforestation by the SFC. Local forest farmers planted rows of pine and leucaena for the SFC in exchange for temporary cultivation rights to that land. This reforestation program was at least the fifteenth in twenty-two years. After all this, only a few clumps of pine stand 2 or more meters high. Sitting sentinel on the highest hilltops or beside streams filled with water all year long, these trees were protected by nature from the arson fires that have ravaged this forest since 1972. No state agency has been able to wholly reforest this tract of forest land since the Japanese occupation.

THE FOREST VILLAGE

Accommodating a population of roughly 7,750 villagers in 1,340 households, Kalianjat is divided administratively into five hamlets. Lying due east of Kaliaman forest, Kalianjat's village lands are bordered on the west by the well-traveled two-lane road between Tegal and Purwokerto. The village is hidden from the road by dense mixed groves of coconut palms, fruit and nut trees, clumps of bamboo, rows of fuelwood trees, and other assorted greenery. Paralleling the road, and cutting through two of the hamlets making up the village, railroad tracks lead from Purwokerto, Yogyakarta, and points east to Tegal, Jakarta, and other towns on the northwest coast of the island. Until 1979 only a footpath led the 3 kilometers from the main road to Kalianjat's residential "center," and until 1983, when rocks were used to harden its surface, this footpath-turned-road consisted of red clay passable by motor vehicles only in the dry season. Big trains traveling to busy cities thunder through, and single-engined, two-car trains chug along the tracks to local stops between Purwokerto and Linggapura. Few stop to load or unload passengers or cargo in Kalianjat.

Nevertheless, the train tracks have been the villagers' major footpath and contact with the wider world since their completion in 1918. They lead to a roadside village and its market 2 kilometers away, the first stop on the way to the bustling Gunungaji market, another kilometer down the road toward Purwokerto. Every morning from before dawn until midmorning, a steady and surprisingly silent stream of villagers from Kalianjat and its neighbor to the east bob, shuffle, tramp, or waddle the 2 kilometers to the roadside market village, their gaits depending on the nature of the loads they carry. Along these tracks also walk laborers from the villages seeking day labor in nearby fields or construction sites, or setting out for several weeks or months of labor in Jakarta, Bogor, Bandung, or other cities.

The traffic runs largely one way. Except for the government officials and extension workers who are forced to stop occasionally in Kalianjat on official business, and a few itinerant traders, few outsiders visit Kalianjat. Despite the stream of agricultural and forest products into Gunungaji and the nearer village market, many business people of these market villages consider Kalianjat a "wild place," "deep forest," a hiding place for monkeys, snakes, scorpions, spiders, and unfriendly forest spirits. They also know it as one of the forest villages that a battalion of DI soldiers occupied over the course of some fourteen years.

The social and environmental history of Kaliaman and Kalianjat bear on labor relations and political life in the village today. Early institutional impositions on villagers' rights and means of access to the forest continue to affect their interactions with the forest and foresters. Before turning to the village's history, however, we need to consider how the structure of access to local land resources affects villagers' perceptions of and use of the forest.

CONTEMPORARY CONSTRAINTS ON VILLAGERS' LAND-USE DECISIONS

Access to Village Land

Of the 755 hectares of land under the administration of the Kalianjat lurah, 64 are classified as "irrigated by simple technologies" and "rainfed" land (*sawah*),[3] 453.7 are dry-fields (*tegalan*),[4] houses and garden lands occupy 216 hectares in the residential section of the village, and 21 hectares have miscellaneous common uses such as cemeteries, paths, old grazing lands, and state reserve lands.

Kalianjat villagers also use four types of nonforest state land: *tanah are-are, tanah GG, tanah SS,* and *tanah erfpacht.*[5] Tanah GG is legally provincial land that can be taken back by the state. Tanah SS is land bought by the railroad company at the beginning of the century. It borders the railroad tracks to a maximum 10 meters on either side and the railroad controls its disposal, renting or sharecropping the land to villagers. The tanah erfpacht, locally called *persil,* was plantation land rented by the Dutch to Dutch planters who never reclaimed it after the war. The plantations were originally leased for seventy-five years and by 1985 these leases had not officially expired.

Explaining land distribution in Kalianjat is complex because so many Kalianjat villagers buy land, particularly paddy land, outside the village. In the neighboring village of Kaliaman alone, the village head estimated 200 of the village's 450 hectares of paddy land were owned by Kalianjat villagers. His Kalianjat tax collector said 139 Kalianjat villagers own Kaliaman paddy land. Kalianjat villagers also buy dry-lands outside the village for planting in tree crops or as a form of savings. In contrast, the lurah of Kalianjat reported that only one nonresident owned Kalianjat land.

These circumstances led to some conceptual problems in analyzing land tenure data and in determining their meaning for an analysis of village class structure and capital accumulation. I decided to include land owned outside the village because understanding the distribution of village land alone would not explain capital accumulation in agriculture. Moreover, other types of land—particularly the former plantation and reforestation lands—become available periodically and play an important role in the household economy, as shown below.

While the selling price for paddy land that can be double-cropped is still higher than for dry-lands, dry-land prices are slowly catching up. Trees planted on a plot increase the plot's value. Some dry-fields, particularly tree gardens that produce year round, are valued more than most local wet-fields, which yield only one substantial rice harvest annually. Labor and capital inputs tend also to be lower for tree gardens than for paddy, while returns can be very high. Most early studies of Javanese peasant farming were in villages on alluvial plains where paddy cultivation predominated (or irrigation for Green Revolution technologies was possible), and researchers tended to treat dry-fields as universally less valuable than wet-fields.[6] But as one wealthy peasant in Kalianjat repeatedly instructed me, "Tree crops provide the peasant's 'salary.' Every month I harvest coconuts and the leaves of *mlinjo* [*Gnetum gnemon*], and at intervals I harvest other fruits. Seasonally I harvest rice and other field crops, but it is the monthly collection of my tree crops that gives me the cash I need to cultivate other crops, to pay the laborers who help me, to buy my family's needs, and to buy more land."

Both wet-field and dry-field values vary according to irrigability or crop mix, but such variation could not be noted in the figures. Because local use of the word "pekarangan" was not restricted to home gardens, we filtered people's answers on these questions and recategorized them according to the standard definition. In the "tegalan" category were included any dry-fields, mixed gardens, or forest gardens not directly adjacent to a house.[7] Home gardens or house yards were recorded as "pekarangan." In the tables below, the term *cropland* includes all agricultural land except home gardens. *Total agricultural land* indicates cropland and home gardens minus the area actually occupied by the house. The figures show *controlled land* rather than *owned land*, although most farmers did not pawn or lease land out or in during the period covered by this survey. Land control was calculated by subtracting land that was sharecropped, pawned, or rented out from the total land owned by the household and then adding land sharecropped, pawned, or rented in.[8]

In 1984, at the peak of reforestation land availability, the addition of forest land pushed some people over the subsistence line and allowed others to accumulate some of their surplus. To fulfill basic subsistence needs, an average family of five requires 0.7 hectares of dry-land, or 0.3 hectares of irrigated land, or 0.5 hectares of mixed land (Soedarwono 1979; Billah et al. 1982). As table 6.1 shows, 58.1 percent of households in the sample controlled no more than 0.5 hectares each of private crop land (all agricultural land except home gardens). This group, moreover, owned less than one-fifth of the total land controlled by sample households. At the same time, while only 15 percent of the sample controlled more than one hectare of private cropland, they controlled some 41 percent of all the private cropland controlled by the sample. Home gardens slightly altered this skewed distribution (table 6.2) but approximately 25 percent of the sample lived in houses with home gardens owned by their parents.

Reforestation land had the most dramatic impact on the land base available to Kalianjat villagers (table 6.3).[9] The reforestation land reduced by 27 percent the proportion of the sample with less than 0.51 hectares of private land and increased by 23 percent the number of people controlling more than 1 hectare (see figure 6.1). Since the availability of forest land enables more people to subsist, live more comfortably, or accumulate capital, all village classes have a material interest in keeping the forest under reforestation. However, an analysis of the for-

TABLE 6.1   Cropland Controlled by Sample Households, 1985
(N = 74)

Size of Holding (Hectares)	% of Sample	Total Area Controlled	
		Hectares[a]	%
0.00–0.10[b]	27.0	0.12	0.35
0.11–0.25	16.2	2.01	5.91
0.26–0.50	14.9	4.19	12.32
0.51–0.75	18.9	8.77	25.79
0.76–1.00	8.1	4.93	14.50
1.01–2.00	13.5	11.83	34.78
More than 2.00	1.4	2.16	6.35
Total	100.0	34.01	100.00

SOURCE: Kalianjat Household Survey, August 1985.
[a]Mean = 0.46 hectares; median = 0.37 hectares.
[b]The Indonesian census classifies owners of less than 0.10 hectares of land as landless.

TABLE 6.2   Private Land Controlled by Sample Households, 1985
(N = 74)

Size of Holding (Hectares)	% of Sample	Total Area Controlled	
		Hectares[a]	%
0.00–0.10	23.0	0.60	1.56
0.11–0.25	13.5	1.69	4.41
0.26–0.50	16.2	3.74	9.76
0.51–0.75	18.9	8.56	22.33
0.76–1.00	10.8	6.89	17.98
1.01–2.00	16.2	14.44	37.67
More than 2.00	1.4	2.41	6.29
Total	100.0	38.33	100.00

SOURCE: Kalianjat Household Survey, August 1985.
[a]Mean = 0.53 hectares; median = 0.40 hectares.

est access data by quantities of private land owned showed that nearly half of the sample households with more than a hectare of private land worked tracts of forest land larger than a half-hectare. The opposite was true of the most land-poor segment of the sample. Some 23 percent of the sample were virtually landless, controlling 0.10 hectares of private land or less (including home garden land),[10] but only 6 percent of these worked more than half a hectare of forest land.

TABLE 6.3   Total Land Controlled by Sample Households, 1985
(N = 74)

Size of Holding (Hectares)	% of Sample	Total Area Controlled Hectares[a]	%
0.00–0.10	4.1	0.03	0.05
0.11–0.25	2.7	0.39	0.60
0.26–0.50	20.3	4.92	7.62
0.51–0.75	17.6	8.06	12.48
0.76–1.00	14.9	9.35	14.47
1.00–2.00	35.1	32.82	50.81
More than 2.00	5.4	9.02	13.96
Total	100.0	64.59	100.00

SOURCE: Kalianjat Household Survey, August 1985.
[a]Mean = 0.87 hectares; median = 0.79 hectares.

Better-off peasants also dominate certain nonforest state lands. The two hectares of tanah are-are in the village were formerly village common grazing land but are now planted in fuelwood species "owned" by three or four (wealthy) local families. A former lurah sold the rights to these families in the early 1960s. The tanah GG is currently planted in food and fuel crops by one of the village administrators for his household's use. Information on who rents tanah SS from the railroad was not available.

The tanah erfpacht is not controlled only by well-off peasants, but is accessible to rich, poor, and middle peasants. In 1963, people from villages surrounding the 422-hectare tract began informally cultivating this persil land. The government gave 125 hectares of this land to the national cavalry in 1983 for a horse-breeding ranch, and much of this has been reforested in fodder-producing species. Among Kalianjat villagers, those in the hamlet closest to those lands tended most to have claims on persil lands. They retain these claims by keeping them under field crops or by planting fruit trees. Peasants from other forest villages also farm the persil lands. One section of about 15 hectares is disputed by the SFC—which claims it as part of the forest—and Kalianjat peasants who claim it has always been private land.

Kalianjat peasants don't think of access to the forest in terms of "doubling the village sample's median landholding." Rather, they express their views as one peasant did, saying, "The life of the people of Kalianjat almost completely depends on the reforestation land (tanah kontrak)." Because the doubled landholdings pushed so many people out from under the 0.7-hectare poverty line, we have evidence of the reality of their perceptions.

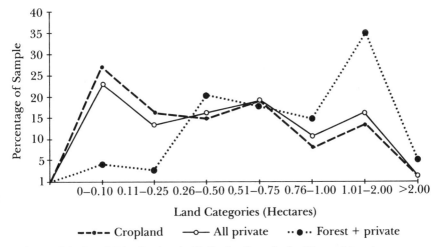

Figure 6.1. Land Distribution in Kalianjat Sample, by Type of Land

Off-farm employment is increasingly important to household incomes in Java (White 1989:296), and Kalianjat is not an exception to this. However, people still prefer to think of themselves as *tani* (which translates as peasant or farmer) if they have access or control over any agricultural land. When asked about their primary occupations, even the landless who had some tumpang sari land would refer to themselves as *tani kontrak* (*kontrak* being the local term for the reforestation lands) rather than *buruh kontrak* (laborer on the forest lands). One of the legends about the founders of their village, Nini Kolong and Kaki Kolong, is that their hands were perpetually curved inward, as if they were never meant to release their hoes. Whether they earn more income from their nonfarm activities, whether they are wealthy peasants or barely subsisting forest farmers, people associate the good life with that of the tani.

Production Relations on Village Lands: Land and Tree Tenure

Kalianjat peasants have actively produced for the market since at least 1967; earlier opportunities for commercial sale of their products have been available since nearby agricultural plantations were established some four to five decades earlier. Labor relations are highly commoditized. Many parents pay their grown sons and daughters wages to work on their plots, even when the sons and daughters are part of the same household (defined here as eating from the same pot of rice).[11]

Most privately owned agricultural land is owner-operated. Some 77 percent of all wet-fields, 97 percent of all dry-fields, and 72 percent of all home gardens are owner-operated. The few sharecropping arrangements reported by sample villagers had been made between parents and their grown children.[12] The only village land we heard of being leased out was the lurah's salary land (*tanah bengkok*).[13] Villagers explain that although sharecropping and leasing land used to be common, wage labor has dominated production relations in agriculture since approximately 1967. Poor villagers complain that the richer villagers think only of money and profit, while the wealthier villagers simply say it is impractical to rent out land.

Some land is pawned out, usually in exchange for gold. The landowner pawns out his or her land as collateral for borrowing gold. The same amount of gold must be returned in order to reclaim the land. This system protects the gold-lender from cash inflation and pays "interest" in the form of harvests from the land. Wet-fields, dry-fields, mixed and tree gardens are pawned. The pawners may or may not have rights to harvest tree crops on the land but would not have the option of cutting down the trees. According to the 1960 Agrarian Law, pawning agreements are limited to seven years, after which time the government has determined that the value of harvests will have reasonably exceeded the value of the gold, and the land is to be returned to the owner. However, informants in Kalianjat reported pawning land for as long as fifteen years. Others reported that they could never return the borrowed gold and lost the land. This process has been a major reason for land transfer in Java (Soentoro et al. 1976; White 1983) and has caused tumpang sari land to be transferred as collateral as well (SFT 1985; Peluso 1986).

Trees on Private Lands

Trees belong either to the land owners, the tree planters, or to persons designated by the planter (e.g., a son or daughter). Some farmers bequeath their trees and the land where they are planted to different inheritors. As such, the land recipient may not harvest the fruit or cut the tree without permission from the owner. While land and trees are more commonly inherited together, the possibility of separating the two indicates the value accorded by local people to certain trees (this practice was reported for coconut and mlinjo trees).

Neither firewood nor fodder can be collected without permission or purchase. Some people plant whole gardens in firewood species and sell the rights to the harvest of the wood, which must be completed within a set time limit.

Because trees still indicate claims to land, peasants historically have been prevented from planting their own trees on forest lands unless the seeds or seedlings were provided by the SFC and its institutional predecessors: The foresters did not want to serve customary claims that the trees belonged to the planter. Despite these restrictions, some Kalianjat peasants have planted papaya trees and firewood species on their forest plots.

Access to Forest Land

In Kalianjat, nearly all forest land is reforestation land or potential reforestation land, which is opened periodically, in tracts based on ten-year forest district management plans. Each year, different areas are available for tumpang sari, the dominant system of reforestation. In the first half of the 1980s, quite a bit of land was opened for reforestation: 124 hectares in 1982; 213 hectares in 1983; 208.5 hectares in 1984; and 109 hectares in 1985 (BKPH statistics 1986).

In the absence of comparable surveys from the early years that tumpang sari was opened, we cannot know for sure how much land was owned by the people who worked tumpang sari plots in previous years. However, the survey conducted in 1985 showed the participation by sample households in selected reforestation activities over the past twenty-two years. The percentages of the village sample that participated in reforestation in five of these years are shown in figure 6.2. Participation was highest in 1984, perhaps owing to the unusually large amount of land opened in 1982 to 1984. More typically, 40 to 50 percent of the sample took part in the reforestation programs. Interestingly, though tumpang sari was officially closed in 1979 (see below), nearly 20 percent of the 1985 sample had cultivated forest plots distributed by local foresters in 1979 (see village history below).

In theory, forest villagers living below the poverty line who are "hard workers" are to be given priority for cultivation of tumpang sari land (Perum Perhutani 1982:6). However, in forests where the demand for land or labor opportunities is high, local foresters have changed the qualifications determining access by prospective forest farmers.

In Kalianjat, as in most other villages with which we had contact, field foresters expected forest farmers to perform forest-related labor voluntarily, calling it *gotong royong* or *kerja bakti* (mutual assistance; labor of service);[14] those who refused to "volunteer" were often refused plots when the area opened for reforestation was limited. This was not the case in Kalianjat in 1982 to 1985 when extensive tracts of land were opened for reforestation. Anyone, regardless of voluntary labor participation, income group, or past relations with the foresters could obtain tumpang sari plots. In other years, however, this was not the experience of Kalianjat farmers.

Though better-off peasants are not supposed to get priority for tumpang sari land, they often do. Middle and better-off peasants in

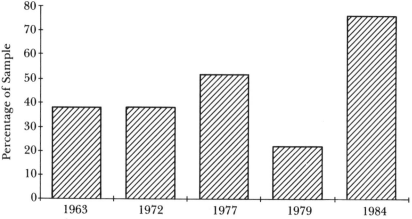

Each of these years marked an important change in SFC policy for Kaliaman forest:

1963   First teak reforestation after DI
1972   First pine reforestation experiments
1977   Trials mixing Calliandra with pine
1979   "Unofficial" opening of forest lands
1984   Over 500 hectares of Kalinusu under tumpang sari

Figure 6.2. Tumpang Sari Cultivation, in Kalianjat Sample, in Selected Years

Kalianjat had acquired plots as extensive as 2.5 hectares in the most fertile locations: in the depressions between hills and nearest rivers. Field foresters justify their allocation of tumpang sari land to better-off peasants by claiming poor peasants are "lazy" or better-off peasants are harder workers and more clever than the poor ones. However, the "diligence" of the better-off peasants on their own lands is more a function of their having the capital to purchase inputs such as fertilizer and pesticide or to keep animals to produce organic fertilizer. On forest lands, they have capital to purchase access to the best plots, to hire labor if necessary, and to supplement the plot with inputs. Better-off peasants can pay labor to work their private land while they take part in *kerja bakti* or work the forest land. Poor peasants must choose among these activities and household survival comes first.

Along with good relations with the forester, capital is an important access qualification for cultivating more than one forest plot. A peasant household with capital can hire laborers to do part of the work on one or more plots of forest land while a poor peasant household is limited to its own family labor. Labor inputs for cultivation on the forest lands are high. Clearing, burning, and hoeing a quarter-hectare tumpang sari plot in Kaliaman forest requires an average of 40 to 60 man-days[15] (160–240 man-days per hectare). A second hoeing done prior to planting absorbs an additional 20 to 30 person-days per quarter-hectare (80–120 person-days per hectare). At a daily wage of Rp. 600 for men and Rp. 500 for women, plus a midday meal for any laborer, the minimum cost of preparing a quarter-hectare plot is Rp. 34,000 plus sixty meals. The staple served must be white rice (corn-rice, though a common local staple, is not acceptable as a supplement to wages), and payment must be in cash at the time the labor is performed. Moreover, little or no reciprocal labor among the poor was reported or observed during this research.

Household Reproduction and Capital Accumulation from Reforestation Activities

The disposal of crops grown on forest lands—their use for subsistence or sale—reflects the patterns established with privately grown crops, and figures into the household's reproduction and accumulation strategies.

Peasants in different land-ownership categories do not benefit in the same way from the forest lands. McCauley (1985) and Stoler (1975) have shown that Javanese peasants decide to plant particular species and crop mixes according to the total amount of land to which they have access. Better-off peasants plant more tree crops, experiment more freely with agroforestry combinations, and are in a position to undertake riskier ventures in search of greater profits. Peasants with access to small quantities of land tend to give priority to food production, unless they earn sufficient income from other employment.

However, access to tumpang sari land, particularly if it is perceived as available for several years, extends any household's total agroforestry system and affects planting decisions. The availability of tumpang sari land (authorized or unauthorized) and related wage-earning opportunities since 1963 have extended the total land base of many poor Kalianjat peasants, allowing them to plant more tree crops on their small dry-field plots or in their home gardens.

Wealthy and middle peasants benefit more from access to tumpang sari land than do poor peasants, particularly when they gain access to large or numerous plots. For wealthy peasants, access to tumpang sari plots may allow them to keep part of their private land fallow and continue to harvest tree crops from these lands while growing food on the forest lands. Alternatively, they may use all their land and hire additional labor to work it, in the process producing enough of a surplus to buy more land. Access to tumpang sari land also ensures a steady food supply, which allows them to experiment with new tree and field crops on their private lands. Having access to more working capital may cause them to raise small animals such as goats, whose organic fertilizer can be used with or instead of chemical fertilizers. Goats are also a source of quick cash, of meat for annual or life-cycle rituals, and of the capital of patronage: poor villagers or their children can be hired to care for the goats in exchange for half the offspring. Goat raising, moreover, is subsidized by access to the forest lands: everyone who collects goat fodder collects the bulk of it from the forest lands.

Middle peasants tend to follow production strategies similar to those of rich peasants. Some feel more deserving of tumpang sari land because their own holdings are smaller than those of the rich. Many middle peasants keep goats. This allows them to use goat manure for fertilizer, giving them higher yields from their forest plots, and thus some surplus capital to buy more goats. Some middle peasants hire laborers when labor demand peaks in the agricultural cycle. As long as tumpang sari land is available, they are positioned more favorably than their poorer neighbors to accumulate surplus from the forest and purchase more private land, sometimes moving up in economic status. Several Kalianjat households are well-known for becoming rich from having had access to tumpang sari land rather than from inheritance.

Poor peasants are rarely able to purchase fertilizer, although some accumulate enough capital to buy a goat or two. As long as fodder is available from the forest lands, raising goats costs nothing but the farmers' own labor. A major difference, however, is in how that goat serves the poor peasant's household economy and the household's land. Many poor peasants reported selling their fertilizer to other forest farmers, thus enriching another's land at the expense of their own. Some need cash, and dung supplies are regular enough to provide small cash sums every few days. Others have such poor plots, or such a distance to walk to their forest plots (up to 7 kilometers from the village in 1985) that they feel it is not worth the labor investment. Some, given poor nutrition and resultant low energy levels, complain of being too tired to work if they have to first carry heavy loads of fertilizer such distances. Thus their persistent poverty contributes to the cycle of land degradation and results partially from the structure of access to reforestation plots.

The grim scenario that leads to the further impoverishment of poor peasants and their land is repeated on the forest lands. Where farmers can only afford to plant cassava, poor soils grow poorer with each year, particularly if they are not replenished. Eventually even the quantity and quality of the cassava declines, reducing the food base of the peasant household and of its goats. Not being able to produce enough food on the forest plot to ensure the reproduction of the household, the peasant must buy rice and a few other bare necessities. The peasant may be forced to sell the goat to avoid its dying and total financial loss. The peasant seeks cash through wage labor. Wages are spent on subsistence and cannot be used to purchase inputs to improve the productivity of the forest plot.

Many foresters have said that it is natural that the kinds of benefits derived from tumpang sari differ according to the economic circumstances of the forest farmer. They view the fact that wealthy peasants with tumpang sari land provide wage-earning opportunities to the poor peasants as beneficial to the latter and themselves. After all, the point of the reforestation scheme is to plant trees. This attitude ultimately thwarts the foresters' goal of reforestation. Wage-earning opportunities are rarely sufficient to extract poor villagers from poverty. They supplement their low earnings by stealing wood or planting soil-degrading crops. Whatever their motives in allocating the best plots to certain people, these foresters are effectively responsible for exacerbating an already difficult situation.

Production Relations on Forest Lands

Land tenure and labor relations on forest lands were beginning to reflect those on private lands in Kalianjat. Rights to cultivate land are sold, rented, or sharecropped out by forest farmers assigned their plots by one way or another. Pawning, however, was not reported on forest lands. When forest land access rights are transferred informally between farmers, standing crops must be purchased before the right to cultivate the land they occupy is transferred to the buyer. Land perceived as more fertile (land in valleys rather than on hilltops) brings a higher price. As on private lands, periodic hiring of day laborers is the most profitable means of land cultivation for the official forest farmer. Those who can afford it employ this system before sharecropping or transferring the rights to cultivate the land to someone else. The costs of production, even on a quarter-hectare of land, are so high that some of the poorest farmers are forced to sell their rights to the land. These families have neither the capital nor the family labor to prepare and plant the land in time for the rains.

Access to Trees and Other Crops on Forest Lands

Among forest villagers, different attitudes prevail toward the unwritten rules guiding rights to harvest food crops, food crop residues, and tree crops on forest lands. Food crops are indisputably the property of the planter. Livestock owners or tenders may request permission from the cultivator to harvest leaves and stems left after the latter has harvested peanuts, sweet potatoes, banana trees, cassava, or other crops. Sometimes a prospective crop-residue collector will assist the forest farmer in harvesting the food part of the crop in exchange for access to the leaves and stems.

The fuelwood species planted as an alternate-row tree crop for the

SFC, *Leucaena leucocephala,* also produces leaves that make excellent fodder for cows, goats, and water buffalo. SFC policy requires that the leucaena trees at 1-meter intervals remain uncut to provide seeds and border markers; those planted in between can be cut at periods determined by the forester for the use of the forest farmer. In practice, some forest farmers insist on cutting any leucaena, others are willing to leave the 1-meter markers.

Not all forest farmers own goats or other livestock, but the ones who do rarely cut leucaena from their own plots. Among most forest farmers, there is an understood agreement that leucaena leaves on trees with or without the 1-meter markers are free for the taking whenever the person assigned to the plot is not there. This allows the cultivator to both contribute to the village "supply" of fodder and honestly tell inquiring field foresters that his leucaena was stolen by an unknown culprit.

Persil Lands

The allocation of cultivation rights to persil lands is distinct from that of forest or private land. The access to and rules about persil lands may reflect the rules of an earlier time when land was not "owned." Technically, persil plots cannot be sold, as private lands can, but the crops to be planted are selected by the planter. The rights of access to the crops are sold, however, and people make a specific distinction between selling land and selling the crops. Two other systems for gaining access to the persil lands were reported. Some informants said anyone can plant persil if there are no signs of prior claim such as standing field crops or fruit trees. Others said that access was gained through a former plantation foreman, a peasant who lives in a neighboring village. This man told them which plots were available and supposedly advised them on the relative fertility of certain sites.

Over time, the conditions of access through the foreman have changed, though more in terms of their public practice than in their impact on the distribution of the yield. The remnants of traditional forms of resource access are being combined with the contemporary mores (or local interpretation) of the Pancasila society. When people first started cultivating the persil lands—in the years following the DI uprising—the lurah of Kaliaman met with all the cultivators after every harvest. The cultivators brought portions of their harvest "to express their appreciation" for the right of access to these lands. Many cultivators also offered some of their harvest to the labor foreman at the meeting. Today, the foreman says, these meetings with the lurah have stopped, although some cultivators still bring tokens of their appreciation—from one-tenth to one-third of a harvest—to his house and to the Kaliaman lurah. Public displays of tribute donations are becoming less and less appropriate. It is likely, however, that the persil lands have been used less in the last few years only because of the availability of tumpang sari land.

Once a person has cleared the land and begun planting, he or she has exclusive rights to its use and its produce. When a transaction between two parties interested in transferring use rights to this land occurs, whatever monetary exchange takes place is not based on the land itself. Rather, a price is set according to what crops are standing on the land when it is transferred. Similarly, an inheritor inherits the crops and the rights to use that land, rather than the land itself. For example, one villager said she bought a rice crop on a hectare of persil land for 20 grams of gold three years ago. Another cultivator paid Rp. 40,000 for the rights to cultivate one-half hectare of persil land planted in cassava, other tubers, banana, and papaya. Improvements to the land, such as construction of simple irrigation canals, increase the transfer price as well. Though the labor investment in unowned land is unusual, some farmers are willing to try to improve the cropping potential of the land in the short term.

OTHER INCOME-EARNING OPPORTUNITIES AND ACCESS QUALIFICATIONS

Forest-Related Employment

Most forest employment in Kalianjat is related directly or indirectly to reforestation activities. Types of forest-related employment include petty trade of snacks and wholesale purchase of crops on the reforestation lands, assisting the mandors in various capacities, transporting seedlings, and the collection of teak leaves, imperata grass, and fuelwood on the forest lands. Small-scale traders tramp through the tumpang sari lands every day, buying papaya and bananas regularly, seasonally buying tubers and other staple food crops. Other traders sell snacks to people while they work. The SFC also buys leucaena seeds from forest farmers.

The head of the forest farmers (*kepala kontrak*) and his assistants (called *kepala kelompok* or "group leaders") receive no salaries but customarily are allocated one-half hectare of tumpang sari land, a quarter-hectare more than the official amount usually allocated to forest farmers. In Kalianjat they also are accorded first choice of forest plots. With the recent opening of hundreds of hectares in Kaliaman for reforestation, the kepala kontrak cultivated as much as 2.5 hectares himself at one point, with another 6 or 8 hectares cultivated by his sons and sons-in-law. Additional income comes in kind from forest farmers. At harvest time, forest farmers donate part of their harvest from tumpang sari lands to those who allocated them land access. This informal tribute is collected and divided among the kepala kontrak, the mandors, the mantri, and the lurah, all of whom feel justified in receiving it because "the people feel they should show their thanks." The amount a forest farmer donates depends on the size and relative fertility of his or her tumpang sari plot and the crop's yield that season. When crops fail, as the second maize crop of the 1984–85 season did, donations are not collected. If donations are not brought to the house of one of the officials mentioned above, the kepala kontrak or a mandor usually drops in on the household after the harvest. Though it may not be spoken, the reason for the visit is generally understood.

The Kalianjat villagers subsidize reforestation by paying for labor to carry seedlings to the plots from the village or by doing it themselves. Pine seedlings are dropped off by trucks at the mandor's house and must be transported to the forest plots. The seedlings are packed in plastic packets containing mycorrhizae-enriched soil to help them adapt to the transplanting environment. In Kaliaman, forest plots are located 3 to 7 kilometers from the village. A man can carry about fifty seedlings per trip, complete with soil and protective plastic bags. Women carry about thirty seedlings per trip.

The SFC district office is supposed to pay wages for seedling transport because it is a heavier labor investment than simply planting teak seeds. The official wage due forest farmers for transporting seedlings is Rp. 2.0 to 2.5 per seedling, or Rp. 1,668 to 2,058 per quarter-hectare plot (with 834 seedlings per quarter-hectare) (KPH Pekalongan Barat 1985). Kalianjat forest farmers said they had never been paid by the SFC for seedling transport. Later, the mantri and the asper confirmed this, saying that the money was reallocated to pay transport laborers where the seedlings were grown and to pay for the truck because the amount allocated by the forest district for these purposes was insufficient. However, the asper had never informed the district of this shortage of funds for wages; in fact, he boasted to his superiors that he could cut their costs of reforesting Kaliaman.

To plant a quarter-hectare plot, placing the seedlings in 3- by 1-meter rows, a man must make seventeen round trips, a woman twenty-nine round trips. In other words, to plant a quarter-hectare of tumpang sari land in pine seedlings, men travel 102 to 238 kilometers and women working alone travel 164 to 392 kilometers. Forest farmers who pay village laborers to transport the seedlings pay by the day. The wage for a half-day of carrying is Rp. 750. For carrying and planting, the wage is Rp. 1,000. One woman hired a man for two days to plant an eighth-hectare plot; some men said they could plant a quarter-hectare plot in just two days. The carrier often discards part of the protective soil on the way to the forest. This not only lightens the burden, it also reduces the survival rate of transplanted seedlings, and ultimately prolongs the time that the land will have to be kept under tumpang sari.

Another lucrative, but grueling, forest-dependent occupation is the collection and sale of teak leaves. The best leaves are those from young trees; these are also the most disputed by the foresters. Older leaves crack easily when used for wrapping, and sell for less in the market. At the time of the research, we knew of four households, two of which were female-headed, who collected teak leaves from the old teak stand. In general, Kalianjat villagers consider collection and sale of teak leaves an absolute last resort, when no other income-earning opportunities are possible.[16] On the other hand, some leaf collectors said they preferred collecting teak leaves to doing agricultural labor. These four families, however, were among the poorest in the village.

The remnants of Kaliaman's teak stand lie more than an hour's walk from the village-forest border. During the rainy season, collectors walk to and from the village over slippery and deep clay "paths" carrying bulky bundles of leaves. With the dry season comes a longer walk over the crackly hot, unshaded hills and a longer search for marketable leaves. One family that provided us six months of household income data collected leaves on alternate days. Both husband and wife collected and loosely bound the leaves for about six hours, after walking to the forest for one-and-a-half hours. The return trip took two hours or more, under the burden of the leaves. At home they spent four to six hours folding and rearranging the leaves for efficient transport by *pikul* and *gendong*.[17] On the same night, they would leave around 2 A.M. for the Gunungaji market. By approximately 5 A.M. they arrived at the far end of the market with their leaves, having traveled some 5 kilometers from home. They sell all their leaves to their regular buyer for Rp. 2,000, pocket the Rp. 150 that she gives them for the bus trip home, and walk the distance instead. Usually they rest a day and a night before going to the forest again.

Fodder and firewood are collected for household use as well as for sale. Fodder is rarely sold, but in those sales reported during the research period, a pikul of leucaena, cassava, and other leaves from fodder-producing species sold for Rp. 500. Firewood is collected on reforestation land, from persil plots, from the old teak stand, and from home, mixed, or forest gardens. Marketable firewood species include *Leucaena leucocephala, Gliricidia, Acacia villosa,* and *Tectona grandis.* Many more species are used for home consumption. A pikul of firewood sells in Gunungaji for Rp. 800 to 1,200, depending on the species.

Imperata grass is used by forest farmers when they clear their plots for shelters or to build roofs for goat pens in the village. A limited market for imperata exists in Kalianjat but most forest farmers build shelters of the grass as they cut and clear their tumpang sari land during the dry season. A man-sized pikul of imperata sold in the nearest village market for Rp. 1,000 during the rainy season of 1985, and for Rp. 600 during the dry season. Some grass is collected for fodder by the few villagers who own cows, but no farmers were found during the research period to be managing plots of reforestation land to produce imperata grass for cow fodder (cf. Dove 1984). How does one gain access to these types of forest-related employment? Aside from reforestation land for cultivation, the qualifications are relatively simple; daily working capital is needed only by wholesale produce buyers. Working for wages in some cases requires a personal connection—through kinship or patronage. No capital or special connections are needed to collect teak leaves, imperata grass, or fuelwood—just a parang (field knife) and a tolerance for heat and long walks carrying heavy loads. For tumpang sari, farmers with large forest plots need capital to pay wages; everyone must pay unofficial user fees in cash or kind to the foresters, the lurahs of Kalianjat and Kaliaman villages, and the kepala kontrak.

Local Nonforest Employment

Nonforest employment in the vicinity includes farming, agricultural wage labor, carpentry, petty trade, livestock trade, pedicab driving, construction, coconut sugar production, midwifery, and civil service. The access qualifications for nonforest employment vary as do those for forest employment. Some occupations require high capital investments. The livestock trade, for example, requires significant initial capital or credit. Employment in the civil service requires education, which has its own capital demands—unofficial entry fees, uniforms, books, and so on. Access to government employment requires unofficial fees and political connections. Petty commodity production and trade require working capital.

Wage laborers often seek opportunities outside of Kalianjat because of the village's scarcity of paddy land, which absorbs more agricultural labor than dry-field agriculture. Paddy land is abundant in surrounding villages. Kalianjat peasants who own paddy land in Kaliaman and other "paddy land" villages hire laborers from those villages as well as from Kalianjat. Since 1982, when much tumpang sari land was opened, wealthier peasants have complained that there is a shortage of Kalianjat laborers willing to travel across Kaliaman forest (a fast-paced walk of 1.5 to 2 hours). A few young boys from Kalianjat work as live-in shepherds for large landowners with water buffalo in nearby villages.

Women as well as men do nearly all kinds of agricultural tasks, but economic class determines the kind of labor they do. Women from better-off families, for example, are less likely to do land preparation, whether for their own land or for wages on others'. Most of those who work for wages on other villagers' plots own the least land of their own. The most common pattern is for both husband and wife to labor on others' lands. Some 39 percent of sample households in all land owner-ship categories worked as teams. The overwhelming majority of these— 69 percent—controlled a quarter-hectare or less of private land. Some 45 percent of sample women worked in other villages as agricultural laborers, while 47 percent of sample men worked as agricultural laborers in other villages and the market town. Women also made significant contributions to the cultivation of reforestation plots: of all sample house-holds with forest plots, 91 percent of the female spouses of household heads and female-headed households, and 91 percent of male house-hold heads worked regularly on the forest lands. In addition, 29 percent of the children in these households worked on the forest plots. We also found that 37 percent of the women and 35 percent of the men had worked for wages on other villagers' forest plots.

Rice transplanting and weeding is primarily a woman's task; men make seedbeds, plow, or hoe fields. Hoeing, planting, and weeding in dry-fields, persil, or tumpang sari lands are done by both men and women. Members of both sexes harvest tree crops such as mlinjo and other fruits or leaves that require climbing the tree. For land prepara-tion, women's wages are about Rp. 100 lower per half-day (16.7 percent), and the meals served the women laborers are smaller.

Bamboo is sold for use within the village or brought to a major city on the north coast by agents with trucks. Bamboo cutting and transport are men's tasks; 1985 provided ample labor opportunities for laborers in the study hamlet. In January 1985 a buyer from this city arrived in Kalianjat, made contact with a local man to act as a broker, and began to buy bamboo from local people. The bamboo owner is paid Rp. 200 per stalk (only mature stalks are taken) and the person who cuts the bamboo is paid Rp. 30 per stalk. The rate for hauling one bamboo pole 2 kilometers to the main road is Rp. 200 for medium-sized poles and Rp. 250 for thicker ones. When it is sold locally, buyers may carry the bamboo them-selves from the owner's garden and thereby pay only the purchase price and cutting fee. When they hire transport labor within the village, the wage averages Rp. 100 per pole, but may vary for long distances. Bam-boo haulers earned from Rp. 1,000 to 1,600 a day. The local labor fore-man working with the buyer said that each day about twenty haulers were employed. The year we were there, reportedly only the second year that bamboo traders had come to Kalianjat from Brebes, many men opted to stay in the village and earn cash by carrying bamboo rather than seeking construction jobs in Jakarta.

Both men and women work as petty traders, combining the Central Javanese and Sundanese patterns.[18] Most field and tree crops are sold with minimal, if any, processing. The major market for Kalianjat produce is a village market, 2 to 4 kilometers' walk along the railroad track from the various hamlets of Kalianjat. Although nearly every family in the village owns at least one coconut tree and one mlinjo tree, neither mlinjo nor coconut is processed locally into higher-priced commodities. Only cassava is sold processed. Traders estimated that some 60 percent of the cassava produced in the village is made into *gaplek* (peeled, sliced, and sun-dried cassava). Although slightly more labor is required to produce gaplek, the burden of transporting it to market is reduced approximately two-thirds by sun-drying the strips for five full sunny days. In addition, the price differential is significant, with cassava selling for Rp. 50 a kilogram and gaplek selling for Rp. 200 a kilogram. Other locally made cassava products include cassava flour (*aci*), various types of cassava chips (*mangleng, sriping,* and *jelutot*), a snack made from grated and steamed gaplek (*tiwul*), fermented boiled cassava (*tape*), and boiled, sweetened, and mashed cassava (*getuk*). Cassava-rice (*nasi oyek*) is made by only a few families who recently migrated from a mountain village.[19]

In addition to local labor, some unmarried women work in Jakarta for one or two years as household servants and return to the village to marry, live, and work. After marriage, women rarely leave the area or seek work that requires overnight stays away from their families. Men tend to migrate for shorter periods of time—one to three months—returning to the village during peak periods in the agricultural and forest-planting cycles. Men migrate for seasonal labor outside the village before and after marriage, some coming home to the village every three weeks, some going away only once a year (usually the month before *Lebaran*, the Muslim New Year). Some reported migrating to work since the time DI occupied the forest nearby, when they were under great pressure to join either DI or TNI. People said that the number of men who migrate seasonally varies according to how much tumpang sari land is opened for reforestation.

In sum, the forest lands of Kaliaman are critical components of the survival strategies of Kalianjat villagers. The land opened for reforestation in 1982 and 1983 nearly doubled the whole village's stock of dry-field agricultural land. This official access to more agricultural land has had various effects on the livelihood strategies of the local peasantry, at least temporarily changing migration patterns and pushing many people out of poverty for the short term. Access was not denied to those who were already well-off, however, and several better-off peasants have taken the opportunity to strengthen their own household economies by purchasing access to a well-placed and substantially sized forest plot. Thus, rich and poor have a common interest in maintaining the village's access to forest lands, though for different reasons. As the following section illustrates, the control villagers feel they have achieved—and need to retain—over these lands is perceived as a natural extension of the history of their tense relations with outsiders.

LOCAL FOREST HISTORY

The forest history of Kaliaman, as interpreted by the Kalianjat villagers, puts a different slant on the history of forests and forestry in Java presented earlier. It is constrained in that it derives from villagers' collective and individual memories of events that shaped the forest and the production relations around the forest until forty years after the Japanese occupation. The memories of times before the occupation were the most clouded, and already subject to multiple interpretations as they were handed down. But two themes recurred as the villagers told their history, whether in individual or group discussions: their concern with the forest as part of their resource base, no matter how administrators classified it, and their hostility to any outside or internal forces—whether individuals or institutions—that have tried to keep them from the forest.

Forest and Village Land Use Before 1911

Kalianjat and Kaliaman forest were located where the outer fringes of several kingdoms of old Java met: Mataram to the east and south, Rajahgaluh to the west, and Cirebon to the north. The local myths, language, cultivation practices, and land-use history all reflect a mixture of cultural influences from what are today the provinces of Central and West Java. The early settlers remained largely autonomous in their daily affairs, far from both the centers of power and the prime locations for intensive agricultural production. During the period the villagers call "the age of lurahs" (*jamané lurah-lurah*), local people, not outsiders, allegedly rose to local power.[20]

The forest itself was not subject to claims by powerful outsiders. One of the former lurahs called the forest before the first conversion to teak *hutan otonom* (literally, "the autonomous forest"): "People could take as much wood as they wanted. In the old days you could build a whole house, 9 by 6 meters, from one *laban* tree [*Lagerstroemia speciosa*, Pers.]; sixty wide boards to cover everything but the roof. There were foresters then, but they didn't keep us from the forest; moreover, there was only one per subdistrict. Most importantly, the wood was for the people."

Kaliaman was originally a mixed tropical forest, composed of woody species such as laban, *Ficus* spp., and *bamboo ori,* wild tubers such as *sluweg* (*Amorphophallus* spp.), and medicinal or spice plants such as wild *kunir* (*Curcuma xanthorrhiza*) and *temu lawak* (*Curcuma xanthorrhiza Roxb.*). Some forms of swidden cultivation persisted until about 1911, when the Dutch government began securing the forest lands' boundaries and registering people's land holdings for taxation.[21] Prior to 1911, no paddy land was found within the village; semipermanent dry-fields, swiddens, and grazing and wallowing lands (for water buffalo) predominated.

Precise evidence of the villagers' "rules" regarding forest conversion for swidden cultivation is not available and oral and written accounts differ. Writing in general about Tegal Residency,[22] for example, Bergsma reported that the person who converted forest, or his descendants, had ultimate rights to land as long as it was kept under cultivation. Leaving the land fallow for more than a certain number of years (usually ten years in Bergsma's sample villages) could result in the person's loss of the land claim (1880:76). People felt no need for written proofs or formal land registers—demanded later by the Dutch government—"because the rights of clearance and age-old [land] rights were respected by everyone" (ibid., 77). If two people claimed the same piece of land, they would try to settle the dispute themselves or go to a village leader who had served as a witness or agreed to arbitrate. The arbitrator either granted the land to one of them or took it from them both (ibid.).

Village informants insist that land was not "owned" permanently, as it is now, but that usufruct rights prevailed. Kalianjat villagers are not specific about the number of years land could lie fallow before a claim expired. The custom probably varied according to the circumstances, as other customary law had (Breman 1980). Today villagers say land left fallow for a few years could be cultivated by anyone; no permission was necessary. Moreover, anyone who wanted to could use the forest, taking whatever they needed. Old people remember a strip of fruit trees that used to form a circle around the natural forest, suggesting some sort of individual claim on either these trees or the land they were planted on. While the land was not under cultivation of field crops, anyone could freely graze their livestock in the forest, including among the fruit trees.

Partly because of the lack of paddy land in Kalianjat and the abundance of paddy land in surrounding villages, many people in Kalianjat kept water buffalo. Water buffalo were both the means and the form of capital accumulation. The richest families in the village owned great herds of water buffalo (some allegedly owning up to eighty teams at one time). Other households kept two or three animals of their own; some cared for the livestock of others. Many Kalianjat villagers tended cattle owned by paddy cultivators in Kaliaman and other neighboring villages. Caring for others' livestock could lead to the acquisition of one's own: local livestock-tending arrangements generally included provisions permitting the tender to claim one of every two offspring. During the land preparation season, Kalianjat cattle owners rented out their cattle to land owners in the paddy-growing hamlets in Kaliaman and other nearby villages. These rice-cultivators concurrently hired Kalianjat draft animals and the labor of their owners or caretakers. A team of water buffalo hired to plow 1 *bau*[23] of land cost 4 to 5 *geding* of paddy (threshed, unmilled rice). One geding equaled 62 kilograms of paddy, making the price per bau 248 to 310 kilograms of paddy. Working several bau a year could earn the buffalo owner enough rice for his family for the year. As a result, the owners of large herds neither required land to obtain rice, nor did they need to make swiddens to subsist. Cattle owners with smaller livestock holdings supplemented their yields from swidden cultivation and the rental of their animals. Those without livestock made swiddens or labored for other peasants or livestock owners.

The above account, compiled from oral histories recounted by the villagers of Kalianjat, corroborates a written account in the *Adatrechtbundels* (Commissie voor het Adatrecht 1911:158). A committee reporting to the welfare commission on land rights in villages in this vicinity and in other parts of Brebes and Tegal observed the following:

> [In Tegal] one can borrow cattle from friends or kin when needed because no land leasing is done here. With a team of buffalo one can plow two bau because the cattle must be returned in fresh and powerful condition. Cattle are also exchanged locally and the agreement is customary. For example, A who has no cattle has one bau of land. B also has one buffalo and one bau. A rents a buffalo which both B and A can use but B pays no rent because he has a buffalo. The rental price is 6 pikuls of paddy [for one buffalo], valued at f.9 (9 guilders) which is paid immediately after the harvest. In addition he [the renter] sends a *tumpeng, ketupat, lipet*,[24] a pair of coconuts, a chicken, two bamboo containers, and other items worth a total of f.0.50.
>
> There is no leasing of the land [in Brebes]. Most of the time the rental price of cattle is paid in paddy, negotiated after the harvest. Cattle that are needed are rented from elsewhere. A team of buffalo rented for three months a year at 12 pikuls of paddy per team is payable immediately after the harvest. One pikul of paddy is equal to approximately f.2.0 [2 guilders]. It is an exploitative practice.

Whether or not these were exploitative practices would depend on the value of money and the amount of paddy received. Certainly a peasant who depended on rice for subsistence might value the payment in kind (paddy) more highly than the cash value accorded the rice by the writers of this document.

Forest Controls, 1911–1942

The Dutch began imposing direct controls on Kalianjat forest land and species in 1911. Major Dutch sugar and indigo plantations were farther north, and turn-of-the-century maps show that the natural teak forest stopped some kilometers north of Kaliaman. From 1911 to 1918 agrarian officials assessed land for taxation, consolidated the state's forest lands by exchange, and forbade swidden cultivation. Legal transfer of land ownership now required proper documentation and payment of administrative fees.[25] Also during this period, construction of the railroad traversing Kalianjat began.

While forest consolidation progressed, it is unlikely the forest villagers realized the foresters' ultimate motives to permanently bound the open access resource and plant it in tree species to which they would have no access. Land was understood in terms of its various uses. Uses often changed. Grazing areas could be transformed to cassava gardens and then to tree gardens, or the reverse. Hillsides on which trees or grass once grew might be dug away until the land could be irrigated and streams diverted to create paddy fields. A plot could be used as a wallowing hole for water buffalo, or the red soil could be "mined" for clay to make bricks. Alternatively, trees or crops could be cleared to build a house.

When the newly acquired state forest was marked by posts, the Dutch initially permitted the collection of wood and other products but forbade conversion to agriculture. The Dutch consolidated their claims to forest land by exchanging enclaves of agricultural land in the forest for other land. At this time, they also acquired the fruit tree zone for conversion to state teak forest. The law said that the Dutch state was to be paid for wood taken from the natural forest. In practice, however, wood collected in the vicinity of Gunungaji was rarely paid for because the Dutch considered it worthless (Commissie voor het Adatrecht 1911:182).

Outside the forest, villagers claimed ownership of land they farmed but lost access to fallow land unless they paid the taxes. Peasants with large herds of buffalo claimed large tracts of land. Capital accumulation and the sustenance of their households were not problems for them, even when the state took greater control of the forest lands. They could pay land taxes in rice, earned by hiring out their cattle or by working their animals on their claimed lands. People today say that peasants with few or no cattle were afraid to claim land on which annual taxes were due. For them, cattle raising alone was a less expensive option because keeping cattle did not require owning a lot of land: cattle could graze on the forest lands and the state tax on cattle was less than the tax on land. Thus as swiddening became more difficult to practice, peasants chose either land or livestock strategies, or combined both to their greatest advantage—as long as they could pay the taxes.

Kalianjat peasants began constructing irrigated fields (paddy land) when Dutch land classification limited them to permanent agricultural systems. Most of the dry, hilly lands of Kalianjat were not conducive to natural irrigation. Owners of land along the village's two rivers began chipping away the cliffs on the banks of the rivers. By 1918 about five hectares of paddy land had been created by this system they called *gugur gunung* (literally, breaking down the mountain).

People planted corn and cassava in their dry-fields. Cassava had been introduced at the turn of the twentieth century by the Dutch planter who rented several hundred hectares of land from the colonial state to grow cassava and coffee. As part of the agreement, the planter obtained usufruct rights to the land and permission to use local people to plant cassava and coffee. Peasants intercropped these commercial crops with their own food crops. The planter bought the cassava and was given shares of the other crops. The climate was not suited to coffee, the major crop, and the cassava processing plant in Gunungaji was so far from the plantation that people did not want to carry it there. Though the project failed after three years, people continued to cultivate the land. Cassava made its way into the people's cropping systems.

In 1939 another Dutch planter, Theodorus Bernardus Thomas van de Laar, rented more than 420 hectares of land in the same area from the Dutch government.[26] As previously, the people planted a certain quantity of lemon grass (*Cymbopogon citratus*) for the plantation and intercropped it with food crops. Peasant cultivators sold the lemon grass to the factory and sharecropped their food crops at a 2:1 farmer-factory ratio. After the war, the planter never returned to the plantation. These plantation lands became the persil or tanah erfpacht of today.

In 1937 the Dutch Forest Service determined that teak could grow as well in Kaliaman as in the rest of the forest district to which it belonged. Their decision was part of a general plan to maximize forest profits by converting all natural forest on Java to teak where environmental conditions were suitable.

The Dutch assigned two foresters to Kalianjat to oversee the labor involved in converting Kaliaman to monoculture teak production. People today remember the Dutch foresters' allocation of access to the forest as being more fair than that done by foresters today. According to people who took part in the conversion, the Forest Service deliberately selected poor peasants to cut the natural forest in exchange for the right to sell or use the wood and to gain temporary access to the land. No wages were paid these first forest farmers. Some 120 peasants were hired from

Kalianjat to clear and plant 30 hectares in teak and agricultural crops. Each household received only one-quarter hectare. Kalianjat villagers were at first suspicious of the Dutch intentions. But the first harvest from the nutrient-rich soils of the newly converted forest was so abundant that people clamored to participate in the second clearing. This time, said informants alive at that time, wealthy peasants bribed the foresters to gain access to the second 50 hectares of Kaliaman forest slated for planting in teak.

Kalianjat villagers speak of the 1930s as *jaman berontakan* (the time of upsets), referring, perhaps, to the overturning of their former life styles. Patterns of access to the forest and private lands, the amount of land opened for cultivation, and the restrictions on access to some parts were all new. These upheavals were punctuated by natural disaster when, in the early 1930s, earthquakes shook the area for approximately three months. Some houses were flattened, landslides occurred, and hot water from subterranean streams bubbled up through the soil in some farmers' fields. To everyone who speaks of them, the land upheavals and the resulting microchanges in land use symbolized the broader societal upheavals rocking the forest settlement for some two decades. Until 1937, when foresters came to live in the village during the conversion of the natural forest, the villagers had never had to deal daily with outsiders directing land affairs inside village territory. Outsiders had always lived outside. One farmer-philosopher summarized the building tensions quite simply: "The Dutch wanted to tell us what to do, but people from Kalianjat don't like to be told."

Japanese Occupation

During the Japanese occupation, the forest became a source of emergency food in a time of crisis. The Japanese ordered Kalianjat villagers to clear more forest to plant food and industrial crops. Food yields were distributed by the Japanese only, and many were taken to feed the Japanese army. Villagers remember having no chance to plant food for themselves. They were dependent on what they were given and on wild tubers that could be found in the secondary growth near the old lemon grass and cassava plantations.

In order to survive, people were forced to cut down their *aren* palms (*Arenga pinnata* Merr.) and boil pieces of the inner trunk to eat. Many people were starving; children had the distended stomachs symptomatic of malnutrition. Lacking food, poor people sold cattle or land. Sometimes they traded their land for cattle and exchanged the cattle for food. The owners of larger herds managed to survive without selling all their buffalo and began converting their accumulated capital from cattle to land. One former livestock trader said two buffalo bought him half a bau of good garden land in the residential area of the village.

The Japanese also introduced tree crops for planting in home gardens: castor oil plants (*Ricinus communis*), guavas (*Syzyginon aquenon*), cashews (*Anacardium occidentale*), and some firewood species (e.g., *Acacia villosa*). Edible tubers and medicinal herbs that once grew wild in the forest also found their way into privately owned gardens, replicating on private lands the food-supplying functions once served by the forest.

Water began to be a problem, particularly in the dry season. Local people associate water shortages with the replacement of the natural forest by teak, remembering that the various types of ficus native to the forest had always "attracted" water, or at least had not monopolized it. Until then, there was also what people called "black forest" (*wana ireng*), or forest that had never been converted to agriculture (but was used as a source of wood and other products). Village water from springs, streams, and rivers had been plentiful year-round before the forest was converted to teak.

Rebellion and Resistance

Hardship and food shortages plagued the villagers of Kalianjat long after the Japanese occupation. Dutch foresters returned to the village in 1947 and in 1948 and reembarked on a reforestation program. By the end of 1948 the Indonesian revolution had intensified and several branches of Hizbullah, the Islamic army, formed in the Kalianjat vicinity. People continued to farm the forest but abandoned all efforts to plant trees for the state. Nevertheless, some of the teak planted in 1937–38 had grown tall in the decade since the conversion.

After the defeat of the Japanese in 1945, a civil war broke out between Hizbullah and the nationalist and communist factions of the Indonesian army. The forest and the forest villages became battlegrounds. Many Hizbullah soldiers were village natives. Hizbullah, and later, Darul Islam, occupied the forest, taking it back from external forces in a symbolic sense. Until 1951 local people cultivated the forest lands. They say they were not afraid of Hizbullah and DI because the movement had not yet become radical; it was mostly local folks. Islam was a common cause that much of the village could organize around.

By 1951, however, the ideological battle between DI/TII and the Indonesian state had become irreconcilable in its intensity. Government forces from Yogyakarta arrived and were stationed in Kalianjat and a neighboring forest village. Former members of Hizbullah joined either government forces or DI/TII. The DI/TII forces, many of whom were now from outside, began to refuse villagers access to some of the forest lands. Once acknowledged as "insiders," DI began to act as hostile outsiders, demanding or stealing foodstuffs and livestock from the local people and killing anyone who refused to cooperate. DI soldiers entered the village at night in groups of ten or twelve and knocked on doors. Failure to turn over food could mean immediate and bloody death.[27]

> Of course we supported DI: if you didn't you died. You woke up every morning and felt lucky if you made it to the evening. DI hid behind trees or corners where they knew people passed when coming from the market. They took everything you bought. If you reported them, you were killed.
> We also supported the government: each day government soldiers came into people's houses and threatened to burn them down if the owners were caught hiding DI there.

DI also polarized the Islamic majority and the minority who only acknowledged Islam but were lax in their practice of it. At the time, however, people would not openly commit in public to one side or the other.

> DI came and took away people's food: yet they claimed to be "orang Islam [Islamic people]." What kind of Islam is that? Real Islam means *selamet* [well-being]. Taking people's food is not selamet. It is simply not right to take food in that way. If they had won the war, they would have shot anyone who didn't want to pray five times a day. What kind of Islam is that?
> Which side did I support? That's easy. By day, when the government soldiers asked me, I was for the government. By night, when DI came to my door asking for food, I was for DI.

In the mid-1950s government soldiers parachuted into Kaliaman forest and burned out the DI "nests." These soldiers worked with local people to cut down forest trees. One former air force commander we met claimed responsibility for burning a swath through the forest from Gunungaji to a remote subdistrict town some 26 kilometers further inland. As the area around the study hamlet became safer in the late 1950s and early 1960s, everyone—the army, local villagers, and outsiders—appropriated teak trees. Local people needed to replace their houses, bombed or burned during the anti-DI operation. Some exchanged teak for cash or food from traveling entrepreneurs. The army also assured people that things would soon return to normal, which to the peasants meant resuming farming and control of their lives. By 1962, when the last DI company was captured in the forest bordering the northern tip of Kaliaman, most of Kaliaman's teak was gone.

Jaman Aman (*The Safe Period*)

Kalianjat villagers refer to 1962 as the beginning of "the safe period" (*jaman aman*). Village life returned to a kind of normalcy. The forest and other lands once again became accessible for grazing and for agriculture.

There was a short period that was not so safe, at least for residents of the paddy-growing villages near Kalianjat. From 1965 to 1966 Islamic Kalianjat villagers actively hunted BTI and PKI supporters with the army and Masjumi. There were only three supporters in Kalianjat; they were not killed but imprisoned. There were plenty of laborers in the alluvial rice-growing villages around Kalianjat, trying to reclaim land from the wealthy, primarily Muslim, peasants. The rich villagers, those who had descended from the large herd owners of past years, led the attacks from Kalianjat; they mobilized the poorer and middle peasants, in the name of Islam, to oppose the "atheistic" forces of PKI and BTI. There are many possible reasons they thought it important to participate, and to have help: wealthy Islamic peasants in neighboring villages, some of them kin by descent or marriage, were being attacked or killed, and competition for land was at its height. Many of these peasants also felt the need to reestablish credibility with the government: as a former "nest" for DI, the village was being watched. They would not renounce Islam but could show support for the victorious forces of the state. At the end of the period, many of these better-off villagers bought some of the rich fields left behind by those killed or chased away in the bloodbath.

The safe period was marked by the return of men from the army or the city to the village, the intensification of mixed and home garden cultivation, the increase in tree crops, the grazing of cattle on the imperata fields that now occupied the forest lands, and a decrease in the average marriage age. During DI, people put off marriage until age 25 to 29; life was too uncertain. In the late 1960s, young people aged 13, 14, and 15 married and built houses next to their parents'. Village informants claim the village "began to get crowded" (*mulai ramai*) in this period; there were fewer deaths, more births, and more opportunities to cultivate land.

In 1963, for the first time since DI occupied the forest in 1951, tumpang sari was attempted by P. N. Perhutani. Teak seeds were distributed but people rumored they were not required to plant them on the forest lands: planting was to be voluntary (*sukarela*).[28] Many people planted the seeds on their private lands.

The availability of forest lands and the former plantation lands for food production and grazing stimulated people to plant more trees on their private lands. Some land-poor and landless villagers from Kalianjat crossed the "imperata forest" to labor in the rich paddy fields of Kaliaman and other villages with irrigated agriculture. Middle and well-off peasants of Kalianjat bought paddy land in these villages and employed landless or land-poor laborers from Kalianjat to cultivate it.

Resistance Without Rebellion: The New Order

Local people used the forest to graze water buffalo, cows, and goats until 1967, when forest security became much stricter. Foresters no longer allowed grazing in the forest, and were particularly strict in newly planted areas. After twenty years of bloodshed and fear surrounding the forest, people were afraid to openly oppose state policy. Although few Kalianjat villagers had been victims of the PKI purge, the memory of the violence remained. So did the memory of their neighbors' fates when they resisted the demands of DI.

In response to these tighter controls, many villagers sold their large livestock in 1967 and 1968, investing their profits in land or trips to Mecca. As the population grew in peacetime, private lands within the residential area were filling up with houses and tree gardens; so were formerly common grazing lands. By 1970 few people kept large livestock, and those who did kept them in their gardens.[29] Even well-off villagers were unable to maintain the extensive land-use strategies required for raising the large herds preferred by their grandfathers.

As part of the plan to intensify forest management, the SFC split the 85,000-hectare Pekalongan Forest District into two districts, West and East Pekalongan.[30] At the same time, Kaliaman was taken out of Balapulang District and made part of West Pekalongan. When the foresters changed the district borders, they changed Kaliaman's forest type from teak to pine to match the dominant species in the rest of the district and facilitate forest management.

In 1972 the first fast-growing pines (*Pinus merkusii*) were planted in Kaliaman. Tracts for pine reforestation by tumpang sari opened and closed for the next few years. Agricultural use of the forest lands not being reforested was forbidden and this prohibition was strictly enforced.

At approximately the same time, frequent fires broke out on the forest lands. The villagers erected what Scott calls a "quiet barrier of feigned ignorance" between themselves and local foresters (1985:32). The anonymity and common loss of access bound the otherwise stratified village in common enmity against the agents of the state. As fires flared on the forest lands, "no one knew" who started them. Between 1976 and 1981, seventy-three fires were recorded, causing nearly Rp. 11,000,000 in damages (see table 6.4). The anonymity also confounded the foresters: How were they to take action against unidentified opponents?

All but a few stands of pine cut off by streams from the main forest were destroyed in these forests. No one was arrested although crude homemade fuses found in the charred remains proved that arson was usually the cause of the fires. The foresters' reports cited arson for most

TABLE 6.4 Fires in Kaliaman Forest, 1976–1981

Year	No. of Fires	Hectares Burned	Losses (Rp.)[a]
1976	27	814	1,726,550
1977	6	124	354,000
1978	1	4	315,000
1979	14	211	1,417,200
1980	1	41	205,000
1981	24	428	6,694,500
Total	73	1,622	10,712,250

SOURCE: BKPH statistics, 1986. (Full table given in Peluso 1988:282–83.)

[a]In 1976 the exchange rate was Rp. 415 to the dollar. A devaluation of the rupiah in late 1978 lowered the rate to approximately 623. After the devaluation of late 1980, the rate dropped to approximately Rp. 1,000 to the dollar.

of the fires; others were called "accidental," the result of carelessness when a forest farmer was burning grass to clear his plot on a windy day. Each time a fire occurred, excited crowds of people gathered to watch from adjacent fields. The foresters sought people's help, but many villagers eluded them or feigned fear of the flames. Some feared open defiance and followed the mandor's orders to fight the fires. One man expressed the common sentiment:

> Yes, sometimes there are fires here that maybe are set by people, and with those fires, the trees die. But that means kontrak will be opened again. If there is a fire, people are glad to see it. When the mandor asks for help to put out the fire, people purposely go slow so the fire doesn't go out. Sometimes they even throw burning branches on to the tree tops to kill them. Even the smoke will kill these pine trees.

Kaliaman forest became notorious. Mandors and mantris from other RPH were on constant alert for Kaliaman fire duty. Those not called to help remember climbing the slopes of Gunung Slamet to watch the blaze below. To field foresters, posting in Kaliaman meant an almost inevitable resignation to failure. In this forest, the foresters could control neither the lands, the crops, nor the people.

CONTEMPORARY REFORESTATION: PEOPLE AGAINST FORESTERS AND FORESTS

Pine and red calliandra, a fast-growing firewood and fodder species, were planted in Kaliaman in late 1977. The president director of the SFC at that time, Ir. Soekiman Atmosoedarjo,[31] said red calliandra was planted to serve both environmental and social purposes, as a rapid, nitrogen-fixing groundcover for "exposed" forest lands and as a source of fuel and fodder for forest villagers. In Kalianjat, however, both foresters and local people recall that villagers were forbidden to cut calliandra. Foresters said it was planted to rehabilitate the soil and check forest degradation. Villagers said the foresters wanted it for themselves. Asked about this local discrepancy in implementing central SFC policy, Ir. Soekiman explained that some forest district managers remained "rather fanatic" about traditional forestry and did not understand the policy's goal—or purposefully chose to misunderstand it.

The atmosphere was already tense between the villagers and the foresters. Both groups wanted to control the forest lands on their own terms. This boded ill for the fate of the calliandra and pine. In spite of increased security measures (more guards) in Kaliaman, first leaves and branches, then the trunks of most trees, disappeared. By 1979 nearly all the forest had been burned in forest fires. Also in that year, the director general of Forestry publicly declared that no "empty land" remained on Java's forest lands. "Regreening" had been achieved in the forest, so no reforestation programs were needed. Most Kalianjat villagers thought the moratorium on tumpang sari was a punishment for having stolen and burned the government's trees.

This left the foresters a great deal of latitude to individually manipulate local forest access. Tumpang sari did not resume officially until 1982, but in 1981 local field foresters unofficially opened what they called "pre-reforestation." In exchange for rights of access, they collected fees from local people to cultivate forest plots. Some "sold" the standing trees on forest plots to prospective cultivators.

By 1982 the anomaly of the Director General's statement was translated into a series of crash reforestation programs throughout Java, including Kaliaman. Field foresters now had to find laborers to reforest nearly 400 hectares by tumpang sari in two years. They feared that their history of conflict with local people, evidenced by the unending fires, would be an obstacle to getting people to plant pine seedlings with their agricultural crops on the forest lands.

The foresters pursued a number of strategies. First, they offered tumpang sari plots to some thirty families from another district who had helped kill wild boar in Kaliaman forest several times. Second, the foresters sought the assistance of local farmers and the village leaders with whom they had ties.

Anyone, in fact, could obtain a plot of any size. Foresters offered plots to peasants with large landholdings, who they thought would do the job and not dispute the land. Many people took on two, three, or four large plots. Foresters allocated tumpang sari land to female-headed households even though women without husbands or adult sons are usually discouraged from such activity by foresters, who claim women are unable to properly prepare the land for cultivation—ignoring the frequent involvement of village women in all agricultural activities on private lands.

To appease local people, the field foresters (the mantri and the asper) also submitted a proposal to the SFC, suggesting the extension of tumpang sari tenures from two years to five. Before Jakarta approved their proposal, the foresters told prospective forest farmers their contracts would extend for five years. When Jakarta almost immediately refused the request as too radical, the foresters did not inform the people. Two years later, when the foresters began to close down tumpang sari, people were outraged (but not surprised) that the promise had been broken. The village headman requested an extension, and the foresters, fearful of the consequences of early closing, granted them another year. They also collected Rp. 1,000 per tumpang sari plot to "pay for the extension" and another Rp. 1,000 per plot as "a tax on their crops."

The next year, no extension was granted. On the hot, dry day that the following year's reforestation plots were distributed, an angry crowd began gathering early. For weeks, the tension in the village had been almost palpable, in the sharp gossip about the mandors, the new mantri, and the new asper. The forester was late. When he arrived at noon, tempers were short. He granted only a third of the requests for plots, and gave out only quarter-hectare plots because the total area slated for reforestation that year had been reduced. Some wealthier peasants grumbled that it was not worth their while to work such small plots; some middle peasants were disappointed at the implications for expanding their own land bases. Some of the villagers gathered there admitted to having secured a plot already, by private arrangement with the kepala kontrak or one of the field foresters. They resented the need to do this, as well. Although their reasons varied, all villagers harbored negative feelings toward the foresters.

People did what they could to protest and foil the past three years' reforestation efforts. As usual, when transporting seedlings from the road to the forest, carriers discarded the mycorrhizae-rich soil along the way, condemning the seedlings to eventual death. They planted cassava, banana, and papaya on their reforestation plots, despite restrictions on these crops. They cut leucaena leaves and wood at will, rather than waiting for the foresters' approval. But they only exercised their "rights" when hidden by the night.

They also told tales of almost supernatural struggles between local forest users and the foresters. Stories such as the one about a fuelwood cutter drawing on inner power and striking a blow powerful enough to send the forester who challenged him flying across a forest stream were a source of great amusement to listener and teller alike.

Sometimes people resisted openly. One night after one of the poorest widows in the village had had her teak leaves confiscated and slashed to pieces by the new mantri and a mandor, an angry group of young men went into the forest seeking revenge: "We tore every plant from the mandor's forest plot. We slashed the leucaena, pulled out the pines, trampled all the food crops. But the mandor and mantri didn't dare show their faces, let alone try to stop us."

When the tumpang sari plots were closed in 1985, field foresters feared another rash of fires. Instead, the villagers slashed or carried off all the leucaena and ruined or uprooted the pines. Within days, the forest soils once covered with healthy leucaena and largely free of imperata grass were choked with it. Many villagers turned their anger against other forest farmers by stealing ripened bananas, papaya, cassava—whatever they could carry away. No fires were ignited but rumors circulated every day that they might be. Forest farmers ordered to perform "voluntary" forest labor walked off the job, in the process leaving behind their new tumpang sari plots. The foresters were forced to hire day laborers and to work with them clearing the imperata and planting new pine seedlings.

More than anything else, these villagers used the powerful tool of anonymous—but unanimous—protest against the outside forest controllers, reminiscent of similar class-transcending movements by eighteenth-century English peasants. Refused access to the game and other natural products of Cannock Chase, the English villagers

> hated the [game] keepers, the laws, and many of the Justices of the Peace. They also hated the [lords] with a violence that was forced underground by the law and by fear, that was often calmed by charity, but that also surfaced in those isolated, anonymous acts of revenge which were among the few free expressions of the labouring poor. . . . Such acts were the traditional weapons of the powerless against the great. They do not appear in the court records because the offenders were never caught. Few can ever be certainly identified as expressions of wide discontent because their authors spoke to the enemy in a language of symbolism so dependent on personal context that we can rarely recover it. [Hay 1975b:253]

What is most intriguing about the nature of forester-villager relations in Kalianjat is the way shifting alliances have been made. We saw above how differentiated the village is in terms of access to private land and how access to reforestation land has changed this in recent years. At the same time, traditional alliances among the power and economic elites— the foresters, the Islamic elite (primarily wealthy villagers who have made the Haj), and the village officials—have interacted with the structure of forest access and given some large landholders even larger land bases. Thus, while unquestionably providing temporary relief to the village poor, the opening of tumpang sari land in Kaliaman has also widened the existing gap between rich and poor.

Are class alliances really shifting? Despite the income gap, members of all strata want access to forest land and view foresters as common enemies in their quest to control that land. They worked together to prolong access to tumpang sari land by foiling successive reforestation schemes. All of them tell stories about their negative experiences with foresters, all object to the attitudes of the foresters, all claim that foresters are dishonest, all laugh at the impotence of the foresters fighting forest fires, and all cheer fellow villagers who extract forbidden booty from the forest lands.

However, poor and middle peasants point out that their wealthy neighbors consistently emerge from the chaos of political crisis as powerful as ever: Rich villagers paid TNI to capture and return their sons in DI/TII alive; they purchased land left in other villages when PKI supporters were slain; they purchased the land and cattle of Kalianjat villagers who could not survive the hardships of the Japanese occupation and the remaining cattle of those who could not resist the controls on grazing imposed by SFC foresters.

At all points, the better-off villagers have used an ideology of solidarity and common interest to mobilize the poorer villagers. Community religious leaders took advantage of the vestiges of patron-clientism and cross-class loyalty to Islam. For a short period, Islam (through DI) gave them a powerful alternative they could organize the poorer villagers around. But the DI opponents of the state eventually excluded the villagers from their fields and the forest. They made themselves into outsiders and lost much of their local support. Villagers "repaid" the outside government forces that helped rid them of the DI/TII threat by participating in the communist hunts of 1965–66. Once this debt was repaid, however, they wanted to reestablish their autonomy.

However it has emerged, or whoever is controlling it, a common culture of resistance to outside forest control overlays the class differences in Kalianjat. This resistance is not fueled by incipient macropolitical motives to overthrow the state apparatus (see Thompson 1975b:163; Scott 1985:31), it derives from a strong desire to maintain autonomy. Kalianjat villagers are demanding access to a traditional source of sustenance—the forest—that helped make some of them rich and took the edge off poverty for others. By participating, actively or passively, in the repeated foiling of reforestation, they are reclaiming what they perceive as their traditional rights in the land from a series of hostile outside interventions.

CONCLUSION: POLITICAL, ECONOMIC, AND IDEOLOGICAL
SURVIVAL STRATEGIES

The case of Kaliaman forest, and its users in the village of Kalianjat, illustrates how peasants can exert power through land-based resistance and maintain state forest land under agriculture—to their common benefit. It seems that although their technical level of "firepower" is lower, the villagers of Kalianjat are ahead in the struggle to control the forest lands of Kaliaman. Access to forest land, however, and the types of benefits gained with that access, is mediated by class. Those with capital can gain access to better lands and can invest in more profitable forms of cultivation.

The decisions foresters make in allocating access to this land are critical to the shape of the local political economy. Field foresters are thus the focus of much of the tension in state forest lands today. Foresters often assist the better-off or otherwise powerful peasants because they perceive them as most able to get the job done. However, these same peasants use the foresters' affiliation with an external institution competing for control of the forest to deflect the poorer peasants' dissatisfaction and anger.

It will take more than a new crash reforestation program to reforest Kaliaman. The tension in Kalianjat will not be resolved by the methods attempted repeatedly in the past forty years. Such a resolution may take a complete turnaround in structure, behavior, and ideology, and perhaps the sacrifice of the SFC's plan to make this a forest productive for the state.

SEVEN

Teak and Temptation on the Extreme Periphery: Cultural Perspectives on Forest Crime

I prefer working in a teak forest where the trees are different sizes—not all big and not all newly reforested. Why? Ya, because it's much easier to steal them.

A LANDLESS BLANDONG

I don't care what any of them say. It's not possible to steal teak, on a large or a small scale, without an inside man.

AN ASPER IN A PROFITABLE TEAK SUBDISTRICT OF KPH CEPU

When a new mantri comes on, we watch him. When we discover his weakness, we use it to bring him down. Everyone has a weakness. Everyone. And we always find it out.

AN UNAUTHORIZED TEAK BROKER

Foresters are fond of commenting that in the teak forest they have two headaches, land and trees, while in nonteak forests their main headache is land. Yet the primary focus of control and resistance efforts in the teak forest is the teak itself, because the bounds of the forest have been defined for the longest time in the teak zones and because much of the conflict over access to land—forest or private—was so violently handled in 1966. This is not to say that the teak districts do not have their share of Japanese-created forest villages and hamlet-wide land disputes with the SFC; nor that the occasional poor family is not given access to a hidden plot of forest land by a field forester willing to bend the rules. But land in the teak forest is simply not as valuable as other forest land—the famous volcanic soils characterizing Java's mountain forests are a far cry from the limestone soils of the teak zones. Moreover, the backbone of Java's forest economy is teak, and various types of black and gray markets in teak are thriving; thus the foresters' protective efforts, and the efforts of villagers and outsiders to outsmart the foresters, focus largely on the trees.

In the eyes of the Indonesian state, cutting and selling teak without state authorization has been a crime for over a hundred years. Customary uses of the teak forest—ranging from its conversion to agriculture to

the cutting of wood for local construction, for fuelwood, or for sale—
have thus long been considered by the state to be crimes against its
property.

Unlike the SFC, teak forest villagers do not regard their unauthorized
acquisition of teak as a "crime," in the sense of being something morally
wrong. While they know that the state regards it as a crime against state
property, for them the appropriation of trees from the state forest lands
represents no moral dilemma or social stigma. On the other hand, the
unauthorized appropriation of a neighbor's property—a chicken or part
of a crop—is socially unacceptable and regarded as theft, a crime, a
breach of village solidarity. Cutting down the tree of a neighbor on his or
her land is likewise an unacceptable act. As discussed below, the economic and ecological constraints of the region in which they live—
largely created by the system of forest access control designed by the
Dutch and maintained by Indonesian foresters—preclude agriculture
and employment in teak plantations as the sole source of subsistence.
Teak is the most accessible and valuable natural commodity forest villagers can acquire and market. Its appropriation, for some, is simply a
matter of survival.

This chapter describes village resistance in the form of "counter-
appropriation" of teak by the villagers who plant it, harvest it, or live in
the midst of it. *Counter-appropriation,* Scott's term (1985:34), is more fit-
ting than "theft" because villagers feel no remorse in taking this wood
from the state forest. The combination of the villagers' need for additional income and the high price of teak have attracted professional
black market wood merchants and other unauthorized teak brokers.
Working through village entrepreneurs, village officials, or even field
foresters, these intermediaries purchase or provide hiding places for
appropriated teak. The involvement of both villagers and black market
entrepreneurs, with their different motives and methods of acquiring
teak, confuses efforts to control access to maturing teak. At the same
time, the more organized element manipulates local resistance efforts
and alters some of the implications of Scott's model of passive resistance.

Nearly every forest village has it share of teak thieves (as the government labels them) and protective networks, which include many or all of
the village residents. Those villages labeled *rawan* ("troublesome"; literally, "dangerous") by the foresters pride themselves on their ability to
resist SFC control. Others are more cautious of their public stance, particularly as the specter of the PKI massacres has not yet subsided. Outside entrepreneurs pressure individual foresters either to participate in
the counter-appropriation of teak or to turn a blind eye when the villagers do. Outsiders also take advantage of and try to perpetuate the culture
of resistance that dominates life in the teak forest. Gambling and prostitu-

tion, common to both "frontier" societies and contemporary resource colonies, are supported by outside financiers who make local people indebted to or otherwise dependent on them. In this manner, the resistance of the forest villagers to one sort of external control makes them vulnerable to another. In neither case are they able to emerge from poverty; in neither case do they actually take control. The state's confrontational policies and tactics actually fuel the illusion that the villagers have greater control if they choose to break the government's law. In fact, like the Javanese villagers who fled the depredations of one feudal lord for the lesser demands of others, these villagers are manipulated no matter what "choices" they make.

Two major conclusions can be drawn from this case study of forest reappropriation. First, in many teak forest villages, the counter-appropriation of teak is a way of life, embedded within local culture, economic imperative, and everyday politics. Second, despite the motives of people to resist external control, village appropriators are used by outsiders on both sides of the law who accumulate capital at the villagers' risk. The interactions between villagers, foresters, and outsiders are so intertwined that bigger issues of long-term forest sustainability get lost in the labyrinth of public and private transactions.

THE SETTING

Districts and events referred to here fall within the prime teak zone of Central Java, particularly the teak forests of the administrative districts (*kabupaten*) of Jepara, Pati, and Blora. Jepara, Pati, and Blora were, for the most part, parts of Jepara and Rembang residencies in their various territorial incarnations under Dutch rule. The eastern districts of the old Rembang Residency, Bojonegoro and Tuban, are now part of East Java.[1]

The teak belt of eastern Central Java is a hard landscape: mineral-poor (except for the calcium that seems essential to producing good teak), predominantly limestone-derived soils and bedrock make farming difficult. The teak trees dominating the landscape are tall, dense, and valuable. To outsiders and officials assigned there, the inhabitants of the teak forest districts have always been known for their resilient individualism, their general disrespect for authority, their propensity to appropriate resources claimed by the state, and their fierce loyalty to fellow villagers in opposing would-be conquerors and controllers.

INCOME AND EMPLOYMENT IN THE TEAK ZONE

This case study illustrates what happens when a densely populated agrarian society lies in the midst of a valuable teak forest and access to that forest is tightly restricted by outsiders. The teak forest is the major source of off-farm employment and yet doesn't provide enough authorized labor opportunities for everyone to take part in.

Access to agricultural land in the teak zone is limited, even more so than in other forested areas, and the quality of the paddy land is generally poorer than in other districts. In the district of Blora, 44 percent of which is classified state teak forest land, only 24 percent of the total land area is suited to paddy.[2] Much of this is rainfed and produces only one good rice or maize crop a year.[3] Some 30 percent of the land is under dry-field agriculture. With an average population-to-land ratio of 389 people per square kilometer, this teak-dominated district would seem less crowded than much of the rest of Central Java, which had an average density of 742 people per square kilometer in 1980 (BPS 1981:45). However, it is not uncommon for a subdistrict's land to consist of 75 percent state forest, making agricultural density the more relevant statistic. The ratio of people to agricultural land in this kabupaten, subtracting the forest lands not legally accessible to the forest villagers, yields an average agricultural density of 716 people per square kilometer.

Rendering the situation even more difficult for the people squeezed onto these lands is the poor quality of the agricultural lands, the restricted availability of irrigation facilities (or potential for irrigation), and the resulting low potential for labor absorption compared to the irrigated farming systems of Java. On average, a hectare of land in Cepu annually yields 3,700 kilograms of paddy rice (which amounts to approximately 1,300 kilograms of hulled rice), or 3,100 kilograms of dry-field rice (*gogo*) (approximately 1,000 kilograms of hulled rice), and 970 kilograms of maize and possibly 140 kilograms of other crops such as cassava, groundnuts, soybeans, sweet potatoes, or mung beans (Kabupaten Blora 1982:173). One hamlet head estimated that a family of five cooks 1.5 kilograms of rice and 1 to 2 kilograms of maize per day.[4] Even if agricultural land were owned equally throughout the district of Blora, in which most of Cepu is located, each household in 1982 would have averaged 0.724 hectares (dry and paddy fields combined) (Kabupaten Blora 1982:5, 36). This would not have been sufficient land to produce their food needs. Of course, land distribution is far from equal; some forest hamlets have no paddy fields at all, and a hypothetical hectare is 2 to 10 times more than most landowning families own.

Location in the forest affords residents occasional opportunities to work tumpang sari land, which is nearly always dry-fields. Foresters point out that this access to additional agricultural land is an important contribution to the local land base. While the temporary access to reforestation land undoubtedly aids some people's subsistence, its overall contribution is minimal. In 1982, for example, only 719.15 hectares of forest lands in Blora District were under tumpang sari, that is, in the first two years of the teak plantations' eighty-year life cycle. This amounted to less than 1 percent of the district's total agricultural land and about 0.5 percent of the total land area.[5] As a simple contrast, some 6,805 hectares in this district serve as salary lands (*tanah bengkok*) to village officials.[6] These lands represent 7 percent of the total agricultural land and account for 14 percent of the total paddy land—in other words, the best land of the region, usually irrigated and capable of yielding two or three crops a year (Kabupaten Blora 1982:5,16). Compared to salary lands, tumpang sari land—which generally gets only one good crop a year, sometimes yielding a smaller second crop—produces at least 25 to 50 percent less per hectare, and yet these smaller plots must support more people. As tumpang sari plots are generally divided into quarter- or half-hectare plots, in 1982 the number of people farming the 719.15 hectares of forest land would range from 1,438 to 2,876, with an average plot of one-fourth to one-half hectare. With 295 villages in Blora, the number of officials using the 6,805 hectares of salary lands could range from 1,000 to 2,000, depending on how many officials in each hamlet had access to salary land and whether or not salary land was available for the officials in that village. Depending on the official's rank, he or she would work 1 to 10 hectares, sometimes even more.

Tumpang sari land is worked either by people living in villages near the reforestation site, or by rural people who live in temporary housing called "base camps" (*magersaren*) for the two years the land is under cultivation. These magersaren are either planned or spontaneous communities that remain for only the duration of the reforestation period. As part of the Prosperity Approach program, temporary housing was set up for forest laborers. In Cepu Forest District, twenty magersaren were built or rebuilt at various times between 1974 and 1985.[7] These magersaren consist of wooden houses, usually constructed of mahogany, measuring 6 by 5 meters and set 5 meters apart, built in clusters or rows of twelve. One house is usually occupied by a mandor. In addition, a small Muslim prayer house (*mushola*) is adjacent to the site. The wooden structures were built to provide temporary housing for forest laborers, primarily those employed in reforestation sites, both to replace the houses of teak leaves built by laborers in the past and to permit them to "guard" the reforestation sites.

In spite of these efforts, houses of teak leaves and bark still line the edges of reforestation sites and the term *magersaren* is used by local people to refer to both the SFC-built structures and the leaf houses. Some of the inhabitants of these houses are among the poorest of the rural poor, without any land or cattle of their own, while others are temporary residents with some dry-land and houses of their own in other villages, and perhaps a cow or two for hauling teak. Oftentimes the SFC allows a magersaren community to remain longer than the two years allotted for reforesting teak forest tracts. For example, the forest laborers may be allowed to reside longer if a new logging or reforestation site is opened nearby. Barring these occasional divergences from SFC policy, after two years the magersaren base camp houses are broken down and moved, sometimes followed to a new site by the same resident forest laborers.

One such magersaren in the heart of the Cepu forest district was found to house some sixty-two residents, three to seven per household. The residents, called *pesanggem*, as are tumpang sari cultivators, came from seven different villages. Five of the households owned at least one cow; one household had four cows, all of which were tethered in back of the tiny structures by night and grazed in the forest during the day. Each pesanggem had been alloted plots of tumpang sari land of one-fourth to one-half a hectare.

The food produced on this reforestation land was hardly sufficient to earn a living. All of the residents earned cash from other activities: making and selling charcoal for Rp. 750 to 1,000 per pikul, selling firewood for Rp. 100 per small bundle (about Rp. 1,500 per pikul), hauling timber to pick-up sites for approximately Rp. 1,000 to 1,250 per day, selling teak leaves for Rp. 2,000 per pikul. Some pesanggem owned some village dry-land under other crops. Most had small gardens beside the magersaren house, or at least some trellised vines of squashes and gourds.

One pesanggem living with his wife in a leaf house adjacent to the wooden structures claimed to have lived in eight different sites since Dutch times. He had never been a logger and said he was too afraid of the law to cut teak illegally. Each day his wife collected two large gunnysacks of grass from the forest and from fallow village lands to feed their cow, and fed their six goats three bundles of cassava leaves. They had taken a loan this year at the insistence of the mantri in order to plant a new hybrid variety of maize on the forest lands: the loan was for fertilizer, seeds, and pesticide. Whether their harvest was good or not, they were liable for the loan.

The man and his wife had sold their house in the village but kept a half-hectare of dry-fields there. They planned to bring home the bark from their current shelter to build a new one when their time here was up. The man complained that whereas the Dutch had allowed pesanggem and blandong to bring home wasted teak for their own use, now the SFC wanted it all. Moreover, though the crops were much less profitable here than the teak, the mandor still collected about 200 ears of corn from each pesanggem family at harvest time. He expected it as part of his service; the mandor wasn't so well paid and the old man could understand his need. But 200 ears was nearly 20 percent of the crop if a persil of 0.35 hectares were planted in maize. It wasn't easy for the pesanggem, either.

Nontimber earning activities available in the forest are critically important to the economies of all teak forest villages, particularly during the dry season. Women collect and sell roots and medicinal plants during the dry season, or collect wild tubers and varieties of *Amorphophallus* spp. (*iles-iles*) for household consumption. Men and women earn small amounts by thinning young teak for the SFC (Rp. 1,250 per day for a few days at a time), making charcoal illegally (Rp. 35 per kilogram in the village or Rp. 70 a kilo in the town), or by cutting deadwood and old tree trunks into firewood and selling it for Rp. 100 per bundle to the drivers of logging trucks—who resell it for Rp. 300 per bundle in the marketplaces near the drop-off points for their logs. One man can pikul or bike approximately fifteen bundles of firewood in one trip to the roadside where the logging trucks will pass. A vanful is worth Rp. 5,000 in the village; this would sell for Rp. 25,000 in Blora. Costs include Rp. 10,000 to rent the van and approximately Rp. 2,000 to tip the guard at the sentry post. These prices are from an area where much of the forest has not been logged recently and where there are still many stumps left from the old logging days: as late as the 1960s, teak trees were felled about one-half meter above the ground. Other forests would not have so much deadwood. Men also earn money by trapping and selling pheasants (sold for Rp. 50,000 each for adults), monkeys (Rp. 35,000), or songbirds (Rp. 5,000 to 100,000 depending on the bird's voice), or by leading hunting expeditions when wealthy Chinese or prominent military or civilian bureaucrats come to the forest to practice their sport. These hunters will often pay tips for services rendered. On occasion, men hunt and sell wild meat (boar, deer). The presence of wild animals—and the income they provide—is also dependent on the nature of the forest cover. Gambling and prostitution are other sources of income and loss.

The collection and sale of medicinal plants is generally considered a poor person's occupation. However, when logging and reforestation activities are not available in the immediate vicinity of the village or when changes in forest cover decrease the supply of certain plants, forcing prices higher to conform with demand, better-off people are not as ashamed to participate. In one village where there had been no nearby logging activities for some five years and the last adjacent reforestation area had been closed for three years, the hamlet head, his wife, and their daughter collected medicinal plants to sell to a trader who periodically sought them in the village. The trader, incidentally, was the wife of a (low-paid) forest police mandor. At the time, three years before the interview, the various medicinal roots and stems found in the teak forest sold for Rp. 35 to Rp. 500 per kilogram, depending on their availability. By 1985, the prices ranged from Rp. 200 to 800; most having tripled, some increasing by sixfold. Prevailing agricultural wages illustrate the relative value of these activities: In 1985, a morning's planting (6:30 A.M. to noon) of rice or maize was paid Rp. 100 plus breakfast snacks (i.e., no rice); a day's planting labor brought Rp. 200 plus lunch and a breakfast snack. A morning's ploughing (which requires the ownership of at least one cow or water buffalo) would bring Rp. 1,000 plus breakfast snacks in the rainy season and Rp. 750 plus breakfast snacks in the dry season. In addition, access to agricultural labor opportunities, particularly planting, requires some kind of relationship with the landowner. The number of agricultural labor opportunities in the hamlet would be reduced by the extent to which smallholders exchange reciprocal labor. This was quite prevalent in this hamlet. Access to medicinal plants and other forest products, however, was open to whoever found them first. Their availability is dependent on the stage of forest succession and the fact that there is forest cover.

Migration may help land-poor households survive. Whole households or just a few members move seasonally or permanently to another rural area or a city. Individual migrants may send back regular remittances or accumulated savings in the form of gold jewelry sometimes carried home over the New Year holiday. Transmigration, the solution that most foresters wish more villagers would choose, is often imposed by district and subdistrict quotas. A village head is informed that he or she must submit the names of a certain number of households for transmigration; if no one volunteers, households are selected to go. Some villagers fear transmigration until someone they know experiences it firsthand and either returns (for good or on visits) or gets word back. One woman said the people in her village used to think those designated as transmigrants were taken out of the village and shot, a gory commentary on the nature of the local history. Village heads are pressured either directly or by circumstances to recommend landless villagers or those known to be involved in teak appropriation, essentially to be rid of the problems. Depending on the nature of the transmigration site to which people are sent, the end result of the action may be quite successful or a disaster.[8]

Formal labor in the teak plantations is relatively well paid, when it is available. To illustrate: a logging site in Cepu measured 24.6 hectares and was divided into 2-hectare blocks. The site was planted in 1887 (probably one of the first tumpang sari plantings) and the trees girdled in 1983. As is the practice, the girdled trees dried standing for two years. The wood production target for this site was 2,056 cubic meters of sawlogs and 514 stacked meters of industrial firewood. In addition, smaller branches would be taken by local people for firewood. During the logging operations, the following workers were employed: one mandor, seven pairs of blandong, five animal skidders who each brought a pair of buffalo or cows, and two laborers to carry and stack wood near the pick-up point. Labor opportunities were also available to the logging truck drivers and their assistants, generally two of them per day, and to two or three log loaders and unloaders. Everyone except the mandor and the drivers who worked for the SFC was paid on a piecework basis. Skidders were paid by the distance the logs were dragged, blandong by the size of the trunks felled and cut, loaders by the volume of wood loaded and unloaded, drivers and assistants by the trip and the distance traveled if the truck were privately owned; those employed by the SFC were paid salaries and a premium per truckload. Young blandong reported earning Rp. 2,000 to 3,000 per day on average; older ones, Rp. 1,000 to 1,500. Skidders earned approximately Rp. 1,000 to 1,500 per day; loaders, Rp. 425 per cubic meter split between the number of loaders (a truckload would hold 4 to 6 cubic meters); depending on the distance, a driver would receive Rp. 980 to 1,720 per cubic meter and/or a premium of Rp. 1,000 per trip. His assistant would receive a Rp. 500 per-trip premium.

Forest laborers, even loggers, are never considered permanent employees; they are all temporary labor. No permanent payroll for the loggers exists—none is expected to stay throughout the season. Even when they do, they are relisted each two-week pay period. Blandongs coming from faraway villages are the worst off.[9] They pay their own transport to the logging site unless they happen to be near the road passed by the logging trucks. Most sleep in guard houses with a logging mandor or the forest police patrol; some seek shelter in nearby village houses or a magersaren. Forced to buy meals at foodstalls set up in the forest by nearby villagers, the itinerant blandong loses part of his source of reproduction—he doesn't have access to the cheaper food that his wife can cook to support him. Some bring rice, if they have any, from home. Between the money he spends on food, cigarettes, and the inevitable card games, a logger can lose a significant portion of his earnings during his employment sojourn. Some loggers return home on pay day to give their wives some of their earnings.[10]

Given both the number and population of teak forest villages (3,000 villages with more than 10 million inhabitants) and the practice of rotating teak harvest sites on an eighty-year cycle, it is not possible for all forest villagers to work full time every year for the SFC. To work full time, laborers would have to move every year or two. Because logging sites are not adjacent from one year to the next, such moving often requires traveling great distances. The poorest of these laborers, living in magersaren of wood or leaves, *do* follow the teak harvest and form a forest-based rural proletariat. These people are arguably the poorest—and most state-dependent—of Java's rural poor. Many forest laborers have some, albeit in small quantities, of their own land to work. Yet, as part of a more general pattern of Javanese peasant survival strategies involving significant inputs from off-farm earning opportunities (White 1989), forest employment is an important element.

The SFC clearly benefits by having an available labor reserve that is part peasant and part proletarian, whose food production and other income-earning activities subsidize the SFC's low and irregular wages. Thus, the peasant-proletarian remains dependent on the SFC for critical wages, but can usually squeeze by when those wages may not be available. A fully proletarianized forest labor force would be extremely expensive. Ironically, because it provides temporary labor opportunities to many forest villages on a rotation basis, the SFC claims to provide substantial rural employment. Yet the type of employment it provides is insecure, irregular, and subject to arbitrary mediation by controllers of access to those opportunities. Moreover, the forest industry benefits doubly by making forest land available temporarily for agriculture. Because the cultivators are obligated to plant trees on that land, any improvements they make to the land or to their crops—such as the addition of fertilizer or compost—will simultaneously benefit the state's tree crops.

As Stoler has pointed out for North Sumatra (1985:190, 208), households in a plantation economy may actually "prefer" semiproletarian to full proletarian status, clinging to the image of being peasants by part-time participation in agricultural activities on village or forest lands. The household conceptualizes and presents itself as a peasant (farming) household, whether or not it can reproduce itself on the land it has to cultivate. Maintaining access to agricultural resources masks their dependency on their logging wages or food produced on forest land as well as on the authorized collection of nontimber products and the unauthorized appropriation of teak. Moreover, the physical barriers to agricultural (or industrial) expansion in the villages increase their dependence on formal and informal forest-based employment, and their dependence on field foresters as controllers of access to many sources of forest income.

Tallying the employment figures of the logging site above, we would find twenty-eight workers employed there at a time. If 374 hectares of forest were logged in 1983 (KPH Cepu 1983a:5) with the same levels of employment, this would amount to some 420 workers in the entire forest district employed in logging. The district had a 1981 population of 525,952 (KPH Cepu 1983b:13–14). If half of these are men, and half again are between the ages of 15 and 50,[11] this yields a potential logging labor force of 131,488 men. Not all these men may desire logging employment, but no more than 420 can find it. As a result, when household income from logging, thinning, reforestation, nontimber forest product collection, and other off-farm employment or remittances are insufficient additions to agricultural income, forest villagers appropriate teak.

EXTERNAL DEMAND, LOCAL PRODUCTION

Teak is appropriated and sold through unofficial channels, a black market stretching from forest-edge communities to the major cities of Java. Collectors may be organized on a long-term basis, cutting teak when the opportunity arises or the conditions are auspicious, or they may be organized on an ad hoc basis to fill a specific order. In addition, all forest villagers cut teak for subsistence uses, including shelter, fencing, and fuelwood.

Which villagers are involved in the illicit production of teak? Teams of woodcutters chop teak trees in the forest, saw them into boards in the forest or at home, and transport the wood to hiding places. Before selling it, they treat the wood so it loses its fresh aroma and appears old. There are various methods of treating wood to age it, including soaking it in diesel oil, burying it underground for several months, wiping it with soil, or painting it. The woodcutters or other villagers remove the teak from its hiding places when an order comes in, saw it into boards if this hasn't already been done, and carry it through the forest to drop-off points late at night. Their way is guarded by lookouts traveling parallel paths through the forest and inside the village or city bounds at either end. Oftentimes a local mystical advisor (*dukun*) calculates the best time to cut or transport wood and provides mantras, amulets, or herbal formulas for protecting nocturnal woodcutters at work. More secular individuals work "magic" by paying off certain foresters and military guards at the entrances to main roads. Still others construct teak cabinets, tables, benches, and chairs. Some villagers provide storage space for boards or logs behind false walls in their homes, under their dry-fields, or in extra rooms built onto their houses. Local women act as decoys, as the actual appropriators, as marketing agents, and as troubleshooters in case husbands, brothers, or boyfriends get caught. Nearly all villagers, including formal and informal leaders, are necessarily involved in withholding information from untrustworthy outsiders about the who, when, where, and how of unauthorized teak appropriation and marketing.

NETWORKS

There are two kinds of networks through which processed or semiprocessed teak is taken out of teak forest villages, one sanctioned by the law and the foresters involved in it, the other illegal. The fact that one of these networks is technically legal is a key element confounding teak forest security and one of the reasons that the other networks persist. The first kind of network is the aboveground one through which teak houses are sold; the second, the underground network for exporting illicitly sawn timber out of the forest and forest villages. Teak is overwhelmingly the most common building material in the primary teak zone. Of 8,659 houses in one subdistrict of Blora in 1982, 8,514, or 98 percent of them, were constructed entirely of teak (Kabupaten Blora 1982). In addition to the fact that teak acquired locally is the least expensive housing material, neither clay for brickmaking nor bamboo for woven walling is found in significant quantities in the natural environment.

People sell their houses for various reasons: some families move out of the village, most often because they transmigrate or have no land or other means of making a living in the rural area; others do it for quick cash to pay for gambling debts, weddings, circumcision feasts, or other events. Because there is no legal basis for refusing people the right to sell their houses, foresters and district officials have been forced to deal with a complicated set of regulations governing the selling and transport process. There is also a lively demand for teak houses, generated by the expense of acquiring enough newly sawn teak to build a house. Many old teak houses in forest villages are quite large and contain considerable quantities of timber—at the time of their construction boards were cut much thicker than they tend to be today. Whatever the reason for the sale, the transaction usually takes months and involves permissions and transport papers from offices at various levels of the administrative and forest districts from which the house originates and to which it is destined.

Equally complex are the networks for carrying teak timber roughly sawn into boards, window and door frames, or posts, or made into cabinets, buffets, and other furniture. In this case the permissions involved are illicit and made on a personal, rather than an administrative, basis. A larger and more diverse labor force is employed at any one time in these enterprises than in the sale and transport of teak houses, although some of the personnel in both sorts of networks may overlap. More local people benefit from the black marketing of teakwood products than from house sales and probably than from legal employment in teak production and government processing; participation in this labor force is not subject to the same seasonal constraints and access controls as legal logging and reforestation, nor are the cutting sites rotated in the same manner as planned sustained-yield logging.

Selling one's house is not against the law, thus the housebroker is never acting illegally. Indeed, the system's structure protects those who profit most and risk least. When a teak house is sold legally, either the owner or the broker distributes envelopes containing tips to foresters up to the Forest District office level, to officials at local military or police posts, and to bureaucrats in the civil administration offices who process the paperwork. The amount tipped depends on the recipient's status, local custom, and the size of the house. One housebroker bought a large village house (containing 8 cubic meters of teak) in the heart of the teak forest for Rp. 500,000 in 1984. She sold it for Rp. 1,200,000 to a businessman in Blora. In addition to the cost of the house and its transport, she and her partner-husband gave what she called "commissions" to four village officials, four kecamatan officials including the police, four or five people at the asper's office, and all the field foresters. Among others, she paid four mandors Rp. 2,500 each, the mantri Rp. 5,000, the asper Rp. 10,000, the village head Rp. 20,000, the village secretary Rp. 10,000, and the hamlet head Rp. 5,000.[12] These tips, though not official, are common parts of the entirely legal transaction of selling one's house.

What is illegal is the unauthorized collection of teak to build a replacement dwelling after a house sale. The whole process puts the field forester in a contradictory position. Field foresters derive small benefits from the legal sale of houses but bear much of the responsibility if the houses are replaced. Villagers are also at risk for they must find, cut, saw, hide, and transport the wood and rebuild the house. They are the most dependent on the income of the sale and reconstruction but can go to jail if caught rebuilding.

Middlemen or women act as intermediaries who organize the retrieval of hidden teak, are contacted by outsiders for teak, hold or distribute money to the woodcutters and other forest villagers, and take care of tips or payoffs, when necessary. Many of these intermediaries, who live in forest villages or forest-based towns such as Cepu, Blora, Pati, or Jepara, have other means of economic support. They may be large landowners or traders in other types of goods, including other types of forest products besides illicit teak (such as charcoal, fuelwood, and wild game). Such individuals possess the kind of working capital and status necessary to make contacts with bureaucrats and well-off customers. Their local power may derive from the brokerage of other state services, from their control of seasonal employment, or from their roles in connecting the village with other product and labor markets. Having both the economic power and the dependent clientele that such power implies, they are also influential in local politics. As a result, many intermediaries have both the political connections and the economic backing to handle accidental discovery.

Who buys teak from houses? There are both long-term, big-time brokers who sell many houses and ad hoc purchasers who are not interested in the responsibilities or risks of long-term business. In the latter category are included people who buy teak houses for themselves, family members, or friends. While these buyers perpetuate the demand for unauthorized teak, they do so in absence of the kinds of motives driving the major brokers. In the former category are often people from various walks of life also involved in the upper echelons of teak marketing and manufacture. Their primary occupation may be in the military or civilian bureaucracy; they may be business people. Their personal and professional connections allow them to either negotiate deals with local foresters or to discourage local foresters from obstructing a deal's completion.[13]

Longer-term brokers may participate in the networks described in the following section. Short-term or ad hoc brokers also need access to information about what is available in the village as well as credibility or legitimacy with outsiders who buy or connect them with buyers. In one set of village transactions, for example, the village head's ex-wife (with whom he was still friendly) bought a house in one of the hamlets when a number of people transmigrated; she sold it to the friend of a subdistrict official. This was her only transaction, however, at a time when some seven houses were left behind. Although she paid Rp. 20,000 for eight laborers to break down the house and load it onto two trucks, none of the officials was paid the usual commission. Local people said that illustrated the lurah's power, adding that even the asper was surprised (kaget) to see the trucks carrying the wood out. On another occasion, the asper himself served as a broker for a house for his brother. In this case, he not only passed out envelopes to every local official and the head of forest security for the forest district, he summoned them all to the house site to officially receive their envelopes and passed out boxes of sweet and savory snacks at the same time. Everything was done according to custom and law.

THE OTHER NETWORKS

As in other spheres of their work, field-level foresters face great contradictions concerning teak theft. In order to keep their jobs, they must at least superficially make efforts to protect the teak from thieves. Many field foresters truly believe their mission is to protect the teak for ecological reasons as well as for the business interests of the state. Sometimes, however, they are forced either by their own inability to resist the temptations of profit or by the secret sanctions and threats made by powerful outsiders interested in obtaining illegal teak. Whatever their reasons, foresters generally acknowledge that teak theft requires participants inside the formal control structure in order to be successful. The most common operations depend on having at least one insider at the field level, but they can also involve high-level employees of the forest district's security, marketing, or production operations.

A typical extraction network would be organized as follows. Village woodcutters cut wood when they can, working in groups as small as two or as large as fifteen, depending on the size of the trees or boards they plan to cut and carry away. Smaller trees can be shouldered and carried by one or two men, larger trees require the combined efforts of six to twelve men. Sawing boards or posts on location in the forest increases the risk of discovery in the forest but allows one group member to act as transport labor, carrying away boards as they are sawn. The saws are kept quiet by placing rubber or a banana tree trunk against the metal saw. If discovered in the forest, the woodcutter cannot be charged if he runs away before being captured.

Any wood that is not for an immediate order is hidden. Hiding places vary within and between villages and affect the quality and availability of the wood. Sometimes wood is hidden in cemeteries or other spots that have curses on them forbidding the entrance of foresters, officials in general, or anyone that can be considered a *priyayi* (aristocrat or upper-class person). When timber is buried under cultivated fields (usually dry-fields but foresters' reports on stolen timber show that paddy fields are also hiding places), it must be done at the beginning of a planting season, preferably while farmers are plowing and preparing their land, so the digging arouses no one's suspicions. Boards and posts are buried approximately one meter below the surface and crops are planted above them. When the boards are dug up, preferably in the transition period between the cropping seasons, the time underground will have aged the wood somewhat, and, the cutter hopes, eliminated the telltale smell of freshly cut teak. These boards and posts may then be sold, used to replace older, drier wood taken from a standing house, or used for double-boarding someone's house or barn. Double-boarding allows the householder to sell off the inside or outside walls of the house without making the change obvious to patrolling foresters; all houses in the teak forest are registered. Sometimes newly cut or recently dug up wood is whitewashed or painted to make it look older before double-boarding.

Whenever an order comes in, arrangements are made to get the teak out of its hiding place and out of the village without any obvious change in the appearance of the village. The law precludes someone simply taking apart a house and selling it without permits. For this reason, villagers double-board their houses, selling the interior while leaving the exterior standing. Alternatively, villagers may collect wood over time in their own or someone else's house, between false walls or in a barn, for example. Transporting it out of the forest village may be done by transport laborers traveling by night on foot or by hiding the boards in a modified transport van. The floor of the van is layered with boards over which are piled sacks full of firewood, agricultural products, or charcoal (also illegal to make but legal to market). The best and longest pieces have to be hand-carried because they would protrude from such a van. Every forest village surrounded by or bordering on teak forest has guards posted at all roads leading to and from the village. When a van pulls up to the sentry's post at the entrance to the forest, if the military or forest police sentries offer no objection, the van may pass with minimal inspection. If necessary, a tip is paid; this is often customary whatever the commercial cargo may be. The costs of transporting the teak, including tips, fuel, van rental, and labor, are borne by the buyer, indirectly through the charges imposed by various intermediaries.

When new forest police are assigned at the post, they may insist on an inspection. To preclude this, having found out in advance that the guard would be a new one, the driver may tip more generously than usual, or add a sack of charcoal or firewood. Sometimes, particularly on such occasions, a young woman is brought along to flirt with the guards as they inspect the van or to deliver the tip and keep their attention momentarily. They play on the expectations of the roles played by foresters and forest village women, so much so that foresters speak constantly of the need to be strong enough to resist the local temptations.

In some places in the late 1970s and early 1980s, teak appropriation became more confrontational, unusually so, given the extent of local involvement in the PKI massacres of the mid-1960s. Boisterous groups of fifty to one hundred men traveled into the forests and cut whatever teak they wanted. Unless by accident, field foresters or forest police officers rarely confronted such groups even though they carried side-arms. Mandors, mantris, and higher forestry officials had ugly confrontations with village mobs in the forest, some of which ended in death or severe injury of the forester. These incidents, and the disadvantage at which they placed the foresters, were a critical reason for the formation and deployment of the integrated sweep teams of army, police, and foresters. Villagers' open opposition and crimes against state property "legitimized" the state's use of force, particularly when field foresters were being attacked or killed.

One assistant forest district manager mentioned an unsettling incident he had observed as a district planner in the late 1970s:

> I was in ——— to check on some reforestation sites. I saw a man walk by with a teak log and thought he was a blandong. Then I wondered where they were cutting; the annual plan didn't include logging in this area. I called over a mandor and asked him which block they were logging or thinning. The mandor said they weren't doing any this year. I was surprised and asked about the log that had just gone by. The mandor said,

"Oh, that was a teak thief." He didn't dare stop him, though it was broad daylight. Neither did I.

Mantris and mandors beaten up or killed by crowds have been victims of agricultural implements such as hoes or sharpened dibble sticks. Other villagers wielded the machete-like knives (*parang*) owned by every household. In 1986 a mantri was killed and another seriously injured while trying to confiscate wood in a local version of a sweep. One version of the event reported:

> The foresters had sent letters to the village head several times, never receiving acknowledgement. One day the mantri was given a tip that a great deal of wood was being held in a known thief's house and would be moved out of there soon. There was still no reply from the village head, so a group of four: the mantri, a PCK, a mandor, and a policeman from the sub-district went to the village head's house. He was out. It was late for such a visit, around 10:00 P.M. Contrary to policy, the group proceeded to the house of the alleged thief. His wife answered without opening the door, said her husband wasn't home and that she was afraid to open up. The team then went to a local food stall to wait. Within minutes, the food stall was surrounded by a group of angry village men carrying agricultural tools. They entered the food stall and attacked the four men. Two managed to run away and get help. One hid far enough under the table to evade the attackers. The mantri was beaten to death.

Even in the wake of such blatant anti-Forestry actions, the foresters were not able to reclaim the property of the state in an openly violent way. Although foresters in the teak forest carry guns, the threat of using them is a more powerful weapon than their actual use would be. Killing or shooting a peasant, especially one in a group of angry woodcutters, could have violent repercussions. Foresters and Forestry are already criticized by members of the Ministry of Agriculture, scholars, and provincial administrators as being "too colonial." Outright aggression on their part would fuel these arguments and reduce the foresters' current strong position in the courts. Even in as powerful a ministry as Forestry, it is to the SFC's advantage (though not necessarily to their liking) to appear powerless to act in some situations.

Perhaps fortunately for the foresters, the early 1980s saw an acceleration in other types of crime. Though not directly intended to do so, the state-sponsored "mysterious killings"[14] served to frighten many forest thieves as well as eliminating petty criminals, thugs, gangsters, and others perceived to be threatening social and political stability. Some major forest thieves were eliminated (partially because of their other crimes), and the disposal of petty criminals in the forest is believed by forest officials to have deterred other would-be teak thieves. At first the victims' corpses were left where they had been killed, or dumped in visible or public places to serve as gruesome warnings to others. However, objections by middle- and upper-class families (waking up to find dead thugs in their front yards) led to a change in the policy. The bodies were subsequently dumped in the forests. Foresters often had to oversee their removal or burial.

In interviews, managers of teak districts and security officers at the unit office neither endorsed nor protested such actions, except for the roles they were forced to play in the bodies' disposal. They did, however, maintain that many of the big teak thieves—including some powerful network organizers—were involved in other criminal activities, providing "sufficient reason" for their elimination in this manner. They pointedly suggested that the mysterious killings had radically reduced teak theft rates in 1983 and 1984. (According to Perum Perhutani [1986:78], losses from forest theft in Java declined from Rp. 3,403 million in 1982 to Rp. 1,624 million in 1983, Rp. 880 million in 1984, and Rp. 389 million in 1985.) Unfortunately, from 1985 to 1986 the rate of theft increased by 50 percent (*Kompas* 1986), indicating that the sources of the problem had not been eliminated.

There is, of course, a great deal of local variation in the degree of violence that villagers are willing to use in seeking to regain control over the wood of the forest. Though the strategies—to both resist and control—may be more or less the same, the tactics differ. And wherever these teak appropriation activities are played out, it is difficult to draw lines between the so-called sides.

CULTURES OF CONTROL AND RESISTANCE

Throughout the years of colonial and postcolonial control, teak forest villages have retained a frontier atmosphere. The men are tough; the women are tough. All go to extremes to prove it, evidenced by excessive gambling, prostitution, teak appropriation, or other behaviors extreme in comparison to a more universally understood Javanese type. In other words, the refined adjectives used to describe the ideal Javanese personality rarely suit a native of the teak forest districts.[15]

Most residents of the teak forest districts have also hardened of necessity. Their parents and grandparents were pioneers, although not because they never knew feudalism (cf. Scott 1985:61–62). The teak forest is known for having been a refuge for groups and individuals opposing control by the old "centers" of power. Villagers are proud of this heritage; many are equally proud of being simply *wong cilik* (little people). To illustrate the power of this position, they point to the curses on sacred sites preventing the entry of officials and others of the upper classes.

The teak forest districts are liberally peppered with cursed sites, curses which were declared long ago yet are powerful enough to deter people from entering today. It was common to collect stolen wood in one village having a cursed cemetery before transporting it for a big sale. When the BRIMOB squads came through, they went straight to the cemetery on a tip and confiscated two truckloads of stolen teak. Whether the tip was from a friend or foe of the foresters is debatable. According to local accounts, the mantri on the operation was stricken with an upset stomach on the way home and died that night. Whether the story is actually true does not matter as much as the fact that local people believe it is true: it is repeated frequently by villagers ranging from the hamlet head to landless laborers. Even telling the tale is a form of local resistance to outsiders treading uninvited on village territory (Ives 1988).

Today, these people's toughness has become an envelope, a means of precluding control by the "refined" and powerful outsiders they have fought for centuries. Resistance as everyday politics has become a form of exerting control.

INDICATORS OF RESISTANCE: CRIME AND PUNISHMENT

In October 1984 some 5,484 "forest criminals" were waiting for their cases to be tried in Central Java. These criminals had been caught in earlier months of 1984 and in years previous, but their cases were backed up due to the overwhelming number of arrests and indictments.[16] Things were so confused that some of the indicted individuals had already served their requisite three months in jail without trial because they had been caught red-handed with stolen wood (Perum Perhutani Unit I 1984:49). The SFC reportedly spent Rp. 12,504,152 on long distance patrols (integrated village sweeps) (ibid., 47). For their efforts they recovered some 581 cubic meters of mediocre-quality saw timber (for the most part roughly sawn into posts and boards) and 81 stacked meters of teak firewood. In 1984 they also confiscated thirteen saws, three axes, six cabinets, and nine unidentified pieces of evidence, and arrested 658 suspected teak thieves. These arrests and confiscations were no more than a drop in the bucket, as table 7.1 illustrates.

CHANGING THE RULES AND TAKING CONTROL

As we have seen, a successful black-market operation involves the active or tacit participation of one or more mantris or mandors. Even if the forester's participation has been verbally ensured, however, the network protects itself by identifying other "weaknesses" in the forester's career or private life. Should the forester feel remorse or fear when his terri-

TABLE 7.1 Thefts and Forest Destruction in Central Java, 1979–1984

Type (Unit)	1979	1980	1981	1982	1983	1984 (to Oct.)
Standing stock (no. trees)	96,581	139,206[a]	84,233	10,020	50,072	17,101
Sawlogs (cubic meters)	6,388	21	11,337	28	57	1,805
Firewood (stacked meters)	1,414	327	646	121	16	791
Forest slashing	24+	37+	22+	19+	46+	1+
(hectares+trees)	23,211	6,326	0	825	129	0
Fires (hectares)	4,889 (+1,569 trees)	3,483	881	24,274	14,040	1,466
Grazing (hectares)	268	299	158	156	424	176
Squatting (hectares)	7,165	17	37	137	26	5
Disputed lands (hectares)	n.a.	n.a.	n.a.	n.a.	n.a.	2,474[b]
Natural disasters	180+	200+	119+	1,813+	222+	91+
(hectares+trees)	56,095	34,616	41,359	2,701,903	62,648	24,747

SOURCES: Perum Perhutani Unit I 1983, 1984.
[a]64,214 teak and 74,992 calliandra.
[b]Not including some 113 hectares of disputed forest lands planted in coffee at Colo, Pati.

tory begins to disappear tree by tree, the network needs a trump card to prevent his throwing in his hand. Such tactics are not unusual by any means, they are the well-known tools of organized crime; they have also been used by political and social resisters the world over for centuries. In the teak forest, involving foresters in the culture of naughty behavior is a tactic that works to the advantage of the "other side," and one that can be pointed to by the foresters to rationalize their straying from duty. When foresters' pride in the performance of duty is displaced by discovery of involvement in illegal teak networks, they can claim that their *budi* (spirit) was not strong enough to resist temptation. While on one level they may lose a certain amount of status by being reprimanded, on another level they are almost willing victims.

Accompanying these political tactics are myths and legends that recall and champion the little guy's manipulation of field foresters, even when the real manipulation of all sides derives from outside. These tales sport ancient themes of mortal difficulties in avoiding temptations; only individuals with powerful magic can overcome them. Elements of popular and traditional culture are also woven into the myths, imbuing an everyday situation, a ritual event, or a casual encounter with the potential for explosion into a "mystical" experience leading the forester astray. Mystical power is believed typical of particular districts, of certain villages, or of areas within the forest. Besides temporarily derailing the loyalties of the foresters, these tales provide the people with an ideology of access to power greater than that represented by the forester; namely, the state. In the imagination of the powerholder, it becomes possible both to overcome the forester on the earthly plane and on some intangible plane to overcome the state.

Both foresters and local women talked about women tempting foresters to disregard their guardianship duties, with a strange mix of pride and embarrassment at their involvement. Such beliefs have long been embedded in the ideological history of the area, as exemplified by three stories told about women of the teak zone in different historical periods. In one, which a prominent villager told me, people from his village and an adjacent village were not allowed to intermarry. His village had been founded by runaways, outcasts, and thugs, while the neighboring village had been founded by an ascetic. The people in his village were loath to let their criminal and magic secrets out; at the same time, their women were very beautiful and attractive to many men. One day, the ascetic in the other village had been tempted by a local woman while he was fasting. He wanted to continue his calling and detested his weakness. He swore that no one from his village could ever marry a woman from that village. So it has remained until today.

A second story, told by a Dutch forester posted in Java in the late colonial period, tells of the women of a village along the Lusi River who were notorious teak thieves. Not only did they take part in cutting the teak, but they swam downriver with it, in the nude, to preclude the foresters' interference. Should a man try to stop one of them, they would claim he had done wrong by her. He would then have to face the angry villagers wherever she was caught.

Finally, whole regions, such as the north coast of Java around Jepara or parts of the hinterland of the old court city of Surakarta, are places where it is believed that beautiful women seek magic to control men. Legends of powerful and beautiful women hark back to colonies of women ascetics and the guardian spirits of prostitutes. While some of the women living in these districts do not use their power to material advantage, others may use it for self-enrichment or work with men who wish to control others. According to forest lore, few foresters can resist their advances. These women "distract" local foresters while their husbands are "working" in the forest, they also go to work after a husband or boyfriend has been captured for theft, approaching superior officials and enlisting their assistance in convincing the local forester that he should release their men.

The ultimate weakness is earthly—money—and the temptation of many a forester has begun or ended with the promise of quick cash. For mantris or aspers, the temptation to sell access to the SFC's most valuable trees should be overridden by the very favorable circumstances of their jobs. Mantris earn salaries of Rp. 150,000 to 225,000 per month, are provided with housing by the SFC, are guaranteed pensions, and have access to credit to buy motorbikes. Aspers have higher salaries and credit to buy cars. In short, mantris and aspers are granted many more benefits than other civil servants of comparable job status.

Nevertheless, the community price of status and position is high. Because he is a forestry employee, others in the community expect more of the mantri: he generally pays a higher entrance fee for his children to register in school, the ritual feasts he hosts must be more expensive, his wife and children have to wear more expensive clothes, and so on. For those who cannot juggle these expectations, or who have no additional sources of income (e.g., land or other businesses), the financial strains only add to the temptation of illegal offers. Unfortunately, the community generally believes the field forester is making extra money on the side, whether or not it is true.

Mandors, on the other hand, have the least recourse from misplaced community perceptions of wealth. Though mandors are on call virtually twenty-four hours a day, their average pay is completely inconsistent with the community role assigned them. Some mandors have been promoted to civil servants (*pegawai negeri*), and some are company employees (*pegawai perusahaan*)—both of whom earn realistic salaries—but these are in the minority. Many more are on a daily or monthly wage basis (*pekerja harian lepas* and *pekerja bulanan*). In 1984 and 1985 many mandors were earning between Rp. 16,000 and Rp. 26,000 a month, with no housing benefits, no official credit, and no pensions.

Mandors, as discussed earlier, are selected from among the local population, and thus have the closest ties of kin and other obligation to the local people. Local people, consciously or not, pressure the mandor to help them, for, despite his low salary, people consider him to be powerful. Indeed, he is powerful in the local community: he selects people to cultivate tumpang sari plots, to log, to thin, and to earn other income through forest labor. At the same time, he is only too aware that the work available through the SFC is rarely enough for the entire community to be employed and that other opportunities for forest villagers are limited. He is a key controller of forest access.

The forest mandor, therefore, generally has three contradictory self-perceptions generated by the communities of which he is part. In one, he views himself as an individual working for an important cause (in this case the protection of the state's forests), backed by a powerful, legitimate organization, and preceded by a long history of courageous individuals working against difficult odds to keep the forest intact and producing.[17] In this pursuit, he is joined by a brotherhood of others in the same circumstances, who feel great pride in withstanding the physical and social hardships of their occupation. In the second view, the mandor sees himself as a traditional, although small-scale, patron who controls access to land, trees, and labor opportunities. As such, he has a "clientele" that must be kept happy but also kept in their places. The third perception emerges from his role in the household, as a wage-earner with little time to participate in agricultural or other income-generating activities. Given the constraints set by job description and salary, it is often this third aspect of his life—the crude economics of living on the periphery as an agent of the center—that can cause him to be disloyal to his first role.

The conflicting pressures of life and access to earning opportunities in the teak forest make it difficult to differentiate "good" versus "bad" actors, actions, or attitudes. The networks for illegally exporting teak out of the region—parallel to legal methods in much of the personnel, skills, and connections required—are so deeply embedded in the culture and structure of the teak forest economy that it is difficult to imagine their ever changing. And while the SFC claims, rightly so, that the amount and value of stolen wood is only a small percentage of its total production, the *thousands* of people involved in *thousands* of incidents of forest crime are a powerful indicator that something is not right in the system.

COUNTERRESISTANCE: THE FIELD FORESTERS' TACTICS

Clearly, field foresters have to be prepared to protect themselves from attacks of various kinds. And to a certain extent, the SFC provides them with some "tools." But sometimes these very tools work against the foresters. Chapter 5 contained a description of the MALU program, in which the mantri is advised to ask the village head (*lurah*) to join forces in protecting the forest from the local people. Some mantris maintained that this worked best with lurahs who had been recruited from the ranks of retired or former ABRI or state police,[18] while others found these lurahs to be the most difficult to work with, having their own agendas: "Some lurahs ask for wood during the *operasi*—'just a little' for this or that. We can't win; if we help them we are wrong, if we don't, they won't help us." Where retired military or policemen practice their own empire building, the efforts of the mantris and others involved in forest security are all but lost.

Some field foresters deal with the psychological pressures of their positions by devising systems to convince local people to protect the forest. They place bounds on the degree and manner of their interactions with local people. Some attend social functions, take part in the festivities, make traditional donations (*nyumbang*) to the hosts but refrain from drinking alcohol, or keep a mandor on guard in the forest during the celebration. Some are able to elicit concessions from their superiors to benefit the community, such as a piece of land on the forest's edge for a volleyball court. Such limited concessions may make the community grateful to the SFC and to the mantri, but usually fall short of stopping theft. In the few villages where the SFC has invested heavily in broad-based village development, people reportedly go to extremes to assist the SFC (Teguh, personal communication, February 1986).

Some field foresters attempt to talk with forest laborers or villagers, to visit them at home, and thus to show respect to their families. They play other paternalistic roles, as expected of them as patrons. One asper said he takes occasional walks through the forest and talks with fuelwood collectors, not telling those who don't know his real status, but letting them think he is a mantri. Sharing a cigarette with them, he indicates his indifference to their cutting firewood, but that he expects them to take care of the rest of the forest (*titip hutan*). His motive, of course, is to encourage them to inform the SFC of any efforts to steal teak. Their motive is to collect as much firewood as they can without trouble from the forester.

Village-level informants are paid by field foresters to report on actual or planned teak appropriation and hiding places. Not all villagers see all informing as abhorrent. Depending on the local consensus and history of interaction with the forestry departments, they may view it as the informer's way of survival. Many informers work both sides of the fence, extending information about proposed police actions they hear of to the villagers. In some people's view, given the jumble of roles and public appearances, informing is no more dishonest than the actions of foresters and forest villagers involved in various networks or modes of teak extraction. Forest laborers are granted favors—such as access to regular employment—by local foresters; they then feel obligated (or are pressured) to repay these favors with information. Some foresters remark explicitly on their expectations that people will feel obligated; others are not as open unless someone should lose sight of his dependence on the forester and get involved in theft or graze animals in reforestation plots. Other kinds of favors include the forester not reporting a small plot of land farmed in the forest, allowing someone to cultivate a patch of forest land not yet slated for reforestation, and not reporting the discovery in the forest of charcoal kilns or saplings cut for fuelwood. Many villagers find themselves both dependent on the foresters and disdaining their dependence.

Whether adapting policy with "good" or "bad" intentions, field foresters must shield their actions from their superiors. Policy is supposed to be made at the top and the forest district, the unit, and the central offices do not condone changes made in the field. To keep certain information from his superiors, the field forester must prevent district and provincial forest officials from passing through parts of the forest where local practice does not conform with policy. When the field forester is deeply involved in illegal activities, he may purposefully misreport the local situation. One social forestry researcher in Central Java, a recent graduate of a prominent university's forestry department, found a hectare of healthy forest that had been reported as empty land and slated for reforestation. Because the site was far from the road, never visited by officials, and adjacent to a tract of other land slated for reforestation, the mantri's superiors never knew there were standing trees. The mantri was progressively selling off the trees and then selling access rights to wealthy local farmers who recognized that the land beneath those trees was more fertile than the land they had been cropping for generations. Access to these forest plots was allegedly selling for more than Rp. 100,000 per quarter-hectare plot, nearly half a mantri's monthly salary, or nearly four times a mandor's monthly salary (Teguh 1985:95; Teguh, personal communication, April 1985).

The survival strategies of field foresters clearly run the gamut in their interactions with people in different power contexts. The range of competitors for control (or at least survival) in the forest includes village leaders, the foresters' superiors in the forestry hierarchy, villagers as partners-in-crime or partners in crimebusting, and the legends in which they all play living parts. Indeed, this competition for control in ideology and in practice is what takes the science out of scientific forestry and replaces it with art.

DISCOVERY AND COVER-UP

When a network is discovered, when superior foresters suspect foul play by field foresters, or when the SFC decides to "sweep" a village suspected of teak theft, everyone involved reverts to their "front-stage" roles whether or not they are among the individuals caught. The mantri receiving payoffs for ignoring nocturnal teak transport through his territory, the hamlet or village head whose people are undeniably involved, the military man from town who has a charcoal distribution business, and the villagers who cut, saw, hide, and deliver the teak to intermediaries—all revert to a set of roles and the type of expected public behavior that belie the intricacies of the complex circumstances.

Field foresters and field military men must participate in BRIMOB sweeps. Hamlet or village officials have more delicate positions to play. In order to show their support for the state (which would oust them if they resisted too openly), they must placate the teams arriving on the village scene by appearing to cooperate. At the same time, they must not appear too willing to desert the villagers. In this they are aided by the requirement that the SFC notify the village head before an operation, in recognition of the village head's jurisdiction. Prior notice allows the village head to warn the villagers, who may hide either illicit wood stocks or themselves. When the team arrives, the village head can also arrange to be out; the team is not supposed to search a village without his presence and on-site permission.

The extent of the village head's cooperation depends on the degree to which he feels he must accommodate the SFC, his own involvement in the network, how desperate he believes his villagers are for employment and income, and how he perceives his obligations to outsiders and insiders. Although he is elected by the local people,[19] the village head is approved by officials higher up in the state apparatus, preventing him from completely disregarding the SFC. As ABRI, the police, and the regional government become increasingly involved in forest security operations, the village head is harder pressed to protect his villagers by openly refusing the SFC entry. If the village head is a former member of ABRI or the national police (as many contemporary village heads are), a colleague may be sent to appeal to his ABRI loyalties. When the odds are against deterring the sweep teams, village officials can only register their resistance to the search by reverting to administrative foot-dragging—a postponement of the inevitable. The following account of a raid, related by a hamlet head and his family, illustrates the mixed nature of one village leader's resistance to SFC pressure.

The team came here, but they couldn't all be paid off because they were a big team from Semarang [the provincial capital of Central Java]. There were members of the army and the police; the only representative of forestry was a mantri. They drove right up to my house in a small truck, came into the house and met my wife. I hid in the bedroom with my youngest son. They asked my wife and her daughter where the [family's] father was, and they said in the fields. They kept telling her she had to go get me, but she said she wasn't sure where I was. One picked up a cattle whip and tapped her on the shoulder with it as he talked. She didn't like that very much but didn't say anything, just looked at him. My daughter finished eating—very slowly—while the team waited. Finally, Mother (*Ibu*) went out toward the fields, the long way out the back of the house, walking slowly and looking for me. As she went, she stopped in all the houses along the way, telling the men to run and hide, not to stay home. Eventually I slipped out of the back of the house, carrying my parang, and hid near the spring. When she returned to the house without having found me, the team told her if she didn't find me they would take her to Blora [the district capital] and put her in jail. She went out again and this time found me. They didn't do anything to me. They just needed my permission to enter the village because it is my territory.

The foresters proceeded to poke long sticks into the ground and found boards and posts near the river banks and under the dry-fields. They confiscated two trucks' worth of wooden boards and unsawn logs. The only person they arrested was my neighbor, who happened to be making a buffet cabinet at the time of their arrival. He was caught red-handed with ten unregistered teak boards, which got him a three-month sentence in the Blora jail. Except for the first night, he said, it wasn't so bad. The first night they were kept at the local ABRI post and only given a fistful of rice to eat. In Blora, there were about 300 men in the jail from all over the province, all arrested for "teak theft." Fifteen of them shared a room 10 meters by 10 meters. They were fed well and were allowed to have visitors.

The hamlet head had no choice, ultimately, in whether the integrated team would enter the village. They would enter, sooner or later. Unlike Saminists or peasant uprisers, the hamlet head recognized the power of his ad hoc opponent, the state, as do most of the villagers. It is a completely different game now: the stakes are higher and prescribed outcomes are more rigid. He also recognized the context in which he recounted the story to me: we talked in the kitchen, in the presence of his wife, his daughter, and the neighbor who had been arrested. His own reluctance was an important part of the story.

Although village officials cannot avoid the pressures of the state and the foresters, the village head's position is such that local people need to believe he or she tries to protect them.[20] The following description of a power struggle between the head of a forest village and a mantri illustrates the protective posture that many villagers, particularly poor ones, believe the ideal lurah should take.

> Our lurah has lots of personal power, passed on to him from his father, who was the village head before him. He didn't dare hit someone because he would hurt them. And no one dared cross him. Any forestry official from a mandor all the way [up the ranks] to an asper who crossed the village head, or who punished or captured a thief without going through the village head, wouldn't keep his job. Once when a mantri arrested someone without the lurah's permission, the lurah became very angry and called the mantri in. After asking about the incident he said to the mantri "That thief is your own kind and a poor man at that. You should be aware of that before arresting him. Do you still want to work?" The mantri answered yes, and the lurah said, "Fine, but don't work around here." Not long after, the mantri was moved.

In a subsequent interview, this lurah confirmed these events and expressed the viewpoint (and official position) that his jurisdiction is the people, while the foresters' jurisdiction is the forest. Problems of defining jurisdiction arise when people are in the forest doing things the foresters say are illegal. On such occasions, the above lurah says he considers the person, and warns them if they are caught once or twice. After the third incident the person is told to do community work for several days. A fourth time may "cause problems." And yes, he recommends people for transmigration. Often, transmigrants happen to have been forest thieves who have been caught repeatedly.

Everyone involved in the authorized or unauthorized production and trade in teak at some time finds him or herself facing contradictions seen as inherent and inevitable parts of the system. While villagers may be most likely to disdain or despise outsiders such as members of the sweep squads, other forest policeman (PCK), indiscreet intermediaries, or unsympathetic village leaders, villagers are less likely to blame their fellow villagers and mandors if they are caught. People say that they need to be flexible because everyone may have to work together again. Capture is, in one sense, one of the risks of the game. Even the village head who is forced by his position to turn people in is preferred to a leader who is an unswaying ally of a rigidly interpreted law and order.

More than the village officials or the forest villagers, field foresters involved in illegal activities are forced to revert to character in the event of a raid. They have no excuses: If they knew of illegal activities they should have reported them; if they did not know they are incompetent—their job is to know. Saving face (and their jobs) requires identification of people involved while hoping that those identified do not implicate them.

Even if the field forester is charged, he will be fired or jailed only in the most extreme circumstances. When a mantri or another official is involved in a theft incident, or a series of them, he is confined to desk work for two or more years or transferred to another location where the temptations are not as formidable. The SFC generally protects its employees, particularly those who have achieved the rank of civil servant.

In sum, both foresters and villagers find themselves "patrolling middle ground" (Turton 1986:36), in the sense that the public and private roles they play adapt to changing circumstances. They are, in effect, functions of time-and-place-specific repertoires of control and resistance.

RESISTANCE AND DESPERATION

The teak forest's culture of resistance often brings discord as well as pride. The most direct victims of discord are women and children, just as they are only indirect benefactors of the duping of foresters. To be sure, there are times when women and children share directly in the self-congratulation that accompanies a successful sham. They also benefit from the acquisition of wood to build or rebuild a house or a piece of furniture. Women and children are the subsistence resisters who collect firewood and sell nontimber products seasonally to make ends meet. They slash saplings and stand them up against living trees until they dry. Children generally graze the family cattle in the forest; while tending cattle in off-limits young teak stands (where more grass grows), they risk confrontations with the foresters.

Women's pride is tempered by hardship. If the women are at home when forest police come searching for stolen wood, they front for the men, they answer the questions. In Java (as in many parts of Africa and other places), it is the women who keep the family going when the husband falls into self-destructive behavior. Gambling sucks up the profits of illicit teak sales. Peer pressure to participate is strong, especially among younger men. Women talk about men losing Rp. 20,000, Rp. 60,000, or Rp. 95,000 in a single night's games, coming home the next day to sell cows, jewelry, or the walls of the house to pay their debts.

Some women are spared shouting, slapping, and stomping-out scenes because marriage brings the man to his senses and he avoids gambling. Others face the heartbreak and the strains on stretched budgets from their wedding days at age eighteen or nineteen until they or their spouses die or leave. I met women who had been forced into prostitution by their husbands to pay gambling debts, and whose further earnings from this other kind of exploitation were then lost in games of dice or cards. Other women chose prostitution because no other income-earning opportunities were as lucrative in the short term, and everything else they owned had been sold by the gambling-addict husband.

Outsiders encourage the participation of the poorer villagers in the culture of resistance by encouraging and financing its addictive and dependent elements. Illicit teak network operators are not only outlets and contacts for the sale of teak, but are often entrepreneurs or associates of those who manufacture or import cheap alcohol, moneylenders who extend credit to gamblers, and pimps who control prostitution. This is but another form of labor control, ensuring both the villagers' need for easy cash and dependence on the black market sources of employment and income. Once in place, this culture perpetuates itself as long as there are no significant changes in the villagers' need of the income from teak appropriation—that is, in the structures of employment and income opportunities. As long as the villagers view their illegal activities as rewards for winning a game—in addition to being a source of subsistence—and continue to view the moneylenders as benefactors, this culture of resistance will persist.

In villages where religious values are strong enough that gambling, prostitution, and drunkenness entice few people, loss of access rights and inability to make ends meet have given rise to religious or mystically inspired resistance "movements" (Sartono 1973; Shiraishi 1989). The Saminists, who still exist today in a few villages of the teak forest, provide one example of traditional values. All cultures of forest-based resistance, religiously inspired or not, include the villagers' beliefs that they are victims of a system imposed and represented by field foresters. Their daily confrontations with foresters and what the foresters represent obscure the traps of the counterculture emerging in response. In the confusion, it becomes difficult to separate survival strategies from political statements; it becomes difficult to identify enemies and allies.

The role played in teak counter-appropriation by underground commercial interests forces us to step back from Scott's model (1985) and reconsider the nature of forest-based resistance in Java's teak zone. Recall this comment by Scott:

> Seen in the light of a supportive subculture and the knowledge that the risk to a single resister is generally reduced to the extent that the whole community is involved, it becomes plausible to speak of a social movement. Curiously, however, this is a social movement with no formal organization, no formal leaders, no manifestoes, no dues, no name and no banner. . . . Multiplied many thousandfold, such petty acts of resistance by peasants

may in the end make an utter shambles of the policies dreamed up by their would-be superiors in the capital. [Scott 1985:35–36]

The rice growers Scott lived among had no highly organized networks backing them, unlike those of Java's teak zone. But is it the existence of the networks alone that causes people to cut and sell the teak, to resist state efforts to control the species? I think not. If the networks were all to be discovered and disbanded, teak would still be salable—its value would probably tempt others to buy and sell. Legal institutions such as house selling are also structured in such a way that they make teak theft attractive to various social groups, some with a great deal of local or regional power. And private teak-processing industries, whether far from or near the forest, exert a great deal of pressure on the available resources. The elimination of these numerous legal outlets for teak is not possible. Radically different solutions must be considered.

Meanwhile, the people of the teak forest still need wood for housing, for furniture, fencing, and fuel. Other woods are neither available in abundance nor desired by people preferring the durability of teak; most can't afford or refuse to buy wood. This calls into question the logic of ameliorative SFC policies such as selling wood from Kalimantan as a measure to reduce teak theft. The fact remains that until local people have an immediate economic interest in keeping teak growing, they are unlikely to protect it. Whether they actively resist by taking part in the networks, or avoid confrontation by refusing to report their active neighbors, or simply continue to collect wood for their subsistence needs from the nearby forest, most teak forest villagers have no incentive to help the state monopolize access to the most valuable forest resource on Java.

CONCLUSION: TIPPING THE BALANCE

Forest-based peasants and state foresters are caught in conflict over control of the major forest species of Java. The struggles result from a shortage of legal income-earning opportunities and an abundance of claimants and pursuers of access to teak. Without the political ability to change the whole monopoly system, villagers as well as field foresters act on the basis of daily needs and have been forced to sell their teak to outsiders who profit from the weaknesses of everyone involved at the field level.

At the local level, villagers and field foresters act out a larger symbolic drama of legitimacy and resource-based power. As in other clashes over ideology or power, the people in the thick of things are only partially playing their own game. While each side does have field-level personnel, these individuals also have personal interests that diverge from those of their patrons and supporters.

The multiple loyalties and contradictory interests are poised in delicate balance. If the field foresters use too much state power and pressure, the villagers and their backers can implicate key players on the SFC "team." On the other hand, when the villagers appear to be "winning"—stealing teak in large quantities in rowdy gangs of fifty or one hundred, or in constant small thefts by individuals—the forest police squads and their military and police allies descend with a vengeance. Each side is resisting the other. Both sides are really allies, in a sense, influenced by external actors and institutions, but joined by their common interest in maintaining a forest to exploit. And for both sides, teak "theft" and forest control are matters of cultural perspective.

PART FIVE

Conclusion

EIGHT

Toward Integrated Social Forestry

This book constitutes an argument against the custodial-paramilitary approach to forest management in a region characterized by a dense and growing population, by severely skewed distribution of privately owned rural resources, and by insufficient employment opportunities outside of forestry or agriculture. Continued deployment of coercive forest controls—especially in the absence of programs to involve the poorest forest villagers in forest management—will only further antagonize and alienate the rural population. The state's own control policies have pushed forest villagers away from the state and toward state-defined "illegal" alternatives for forest land use and forest species disposal. The future portends increasing economic, social, and political costs to the SFC, the confounding of the SFC's other efforts to "develop" forest village economies, and continued forest destruction and degradation. Similar outcomes may be expected in other regions of the world where state control of forests or forest lands has failed to ameliorate forest degradation and has exacerbated poverty among forest-dependent people.

Although restricted forest access and increasing village resource concentration have caused degraded forests, this does not mean that open forest access would result in a high-grade forest. Some joint management strategy is needed, but it must be responsive to the needs of the village poor. Moreover, the value of teak and other hardwoods is not likely to decline in the future—which is both good news and bad news for the SFC. In addition, social forestry programs alone will not solve foresters' problems. More important is an integration of the principles of social forestry into the entire forestry structure and the replacement of integrated rural repression by targeted rural development with real participation by forest villagers.

Such an endeavor would require consideration of the origins of peasant resistance, a theme this book has pursued from several different perspectives. I have argued that peasant resistance to state control of the forests derives from the progressive criminalization of customary rights of forest access and use since wood was sought to expand the fleets of mercantile capitalists and, in particular, since the emergence of a legitimizing ideology of scientific forestry under the colonial state in Java. The policies, regulations, methods, and creeds of scientific forestry—in terms of both the international settings whence they derive and the national interpretations of these methods and creeds—constitute the essence of a culture of forest control. They form a "moral economy of the forester," to paraphrase James Scott (1976), in that forest protection is the ultimate goal justifying any manner of tactics to achieve it. However, those who profess this creed, and those who cling to this moral economy, do so in a vacuum of sorts. Foresters are not ignorant of the social and political storms brewing in the villages adjacent to their precious resources, but they have remained largely opposed to radical changes in the structures and processes of forest management unless the forest has been given up for lost.[1] Foresters are thus constrained by their own laws, their own ideologies, and their own history. They are, in effect, victims of the fear and terror they helped create in the distant and recent past. Violence begets violence only until too many have died; then violence gives way to secret wars and silent insurgency.

The case studies from forest villages in Java empirically illustrate two complementary aspects of peasant resistance to contemporary, centralized forms of resource control. The first is the expression of village solidarity in facing common external enemies. This solidarity creates a culture of conspiracy without acknowledging crime as defined by outside individuals or institutions. Such a conspiratorial atmosphere can be powerful enough to draw into itself allies and sympathizers from the quarters of those confronting it. The capacity of resistance mechanisms to create ambiguity among resource controllers results from the complex and intertwined social relations of individuals and the social history of regions and management institutions. Claims and counterclaims lead directly, however gradually, to resource decline.

One might argue that the so-called moral economy underlying the forest peasants' various cultures of resistance is also caught in a vacuum of time. The gloss of solidarity does not penetrate to all levels of social relations—hence, the multiplicity of roles and ideologies that individuals profess under particular circumstances. The veneer merely covers highly divided communities whose members' acts of resistance derive from a range of motives. For middle and better-off peasants, especially elites, and for field foresters, the expectations of loyalty from competing interests lead to contradictions of individual experience and action. The poorest villagers are well aware that they have the most to lose whatever the outcome of the struggles for control of forest resources. Because many poor forest villagers are caught in a reproductive squeeze (de Janvry 1981), the cultures of resistance can and are being manipulated by outsiders who create a different sort of dependence, promising an equally bleak future. The illicit harvesting of teak for sale to black market traders may not substantially change the villagers' proportion of surplus from the production of teak; the poor villagers remain the exploited, but they have access to more income-earning opportunities. The counter-appropriation of teak impinges severely on the prospects for sustained-yield management, already illustrated by the supplements to long-term logging plans in some of the acknowledged "best" forests. Similarly, the de facto conversion of forest land to agricultural land, without legal title and always at the risk of confiscation, does not bode well for the rehabilitation of deteriorating lands.

The question of the consciousness of the criminal nature of their acts becomes almost moot in the face of villagers' reasons for resistance. Whether a form of protest or a last-ditch effort at subsistence, people do not care that their forest activities are crimes against the state. Their forms or repertoires of resistance are merely contextualized in the political, economic, and ideological circumstances of the times. As a result, the bandit as opponent of controversial power and authority will remain a culture hero as long as his or her village loyalties are not abandoned, and is unlikely to disappear from capitalist societies as long as noncapitalist social relations remain part of the structure of authority. The more people's formal and informal forest access depends on their individual negotiations with field foresters, the more likely they will be to disregard formal regulations of forest control.

All the historical evidence suggests that most of the kinds of changes in forest cover that foresters pejoratively call degradation derive from a specific interpretation and interest in what that forest should be, who it shall serve, and how it shall be used. Forestry has not only evolved as a science, therefore, but also as a political-economic system for resource control.

Up to this point we have been looking backward, at the origins of forest access control and resistance, to explain contemporary conflicts and forest quality. Now let us consider some of the prospects for a program of constructive change in the management of Java's forest. The most recent social forestry program in Java aims to release some of the state's traditional controls and to engage forest-based communities in the management of the forests. The ultimate question is: Can it work?

THE ROLE OF THE STATE IN DEVELOPING THE SOCIAL
AND NATURAL ENVIRONMENT

In Indonesia, social forestry is yet another form of state intervention and custodianship. State intervention in Indonesian development, however, is inevitable. The fourth Five-Year Plan for Indonesia declared it a national objective to distribute more equitably the benefits of development. Government officials concede that they have prioritized such macroeconomic goals as increased foreign exchange earnings, the intensification of rice production, and the political-ideological goals of training all bureaucrats and employees of the state—and many clients of the state—in the "appropriate," New Order ideology, known as "P-4."

Forestry has been no exception. Since 1984 state forestry development programs, stimulated by international interest and subtle political prodding, began under the rubric of the PMDH program. In late 1985 pilot projects for social forestry were conceived after a year of diagnostic research, and in 1986 a trial group of foresters was trained in community organizing techniques. Forest villagers were to be given longer tenures over tumpang sari lands, more input into their contracts with the SFC, and extended usufruct rights to the fruit of fruit trees (as opposed to their wood) planted on the forest lands—all of which were unprecedented actions in the history of state forestry on Java. The objectives of the program were to build trust between foresters and local people, to improve the economic circumstances of the farmers in the vicinity of the forest, and by so doing to improve the forest's chances of restoration, rehabilitation, or reforestation.[2] In 1987 the project shed its pilot status, and the policy became the strategy of choice for the reforestation of the SFC's most degraded or "empty" lands.

What seems doubtful, unfortunately, is the project's capacity to achieve its social objectives. The ultimate goal of the SFC is to reforest the 15 to 25 percent of the state forest lands today classified as empty or severely degraded. Until now, SFC policies have aimed directly at reforestation in the expectation that other goals, such as reduced erosion and flooding, will follow and the general socioeconomic situation will be ameliorated.[3] But in spite of a new rhetoric of social forestry, the means of achieving environmental stability or amelioration—through improving the economic circumstances of the rural poor—has been almost forgotten.

Improving poor forest villagers' incomes is meant to reduce their dependence on the forest, or at least to reduce their resorting to illegal forms of forest use. Field "social" foresters are supposed to organize the poor in forest villages and mobilize them in reforestation efforts by giving them more of a stake in the success of reforestation. People's shares have been increased by lengthening the terms of tenure in

tumpang sari areas, by widening the rows of forest species so that preferred agricultural crops can be grown for longer periods of time, by
allowing them to plant SFC-provided fruit trees on the forest lands at
predetermined intervals, and by giving them tenure rights to the fruits
of those trees for as long as they protect the forest species and remain
members of the forest farmer's group. Tree tenure rights are to last only
as long as the planned lifetime of the major forest species planted in the
reforestation tract. The program was designed in the belief that the
achievement of the social goals would facilitate the achievement of the
environmental goals.

The objectives and targets of the social forestry development project
seem straightforward enough. However, although on the surface major
concessions in forest access rights for villagers seem to have been given
policy support, no changes have been made in the structure of access—it
must still be made through a forester, whose choices of participants are
necessarily made in a short time frame, without access to the kinds of
local-level data—a socioeconomic survey, for example—that would facilitate an informed decision. Nor have there been any real changes in the
economic, social, and political bases of power or the structure of power
relations between either the villagers and the foresters or among various
classes and interest groups within the villages. No measures have been
taken to prevent sabotage or failure of the project's ultimate objective of
improving *poor* forest villagers' incomes and, *by so doing*, reforesting the
empty lands. The SFC and its institutional predecessors have been very
successful at putting trees in the ground. They have been less successful
at keeping them there, largely because most forest villagers' economic
circumstances have remained precarious. While antagonistic relations
between foresters and villagers have been alleviated to a large degree,
the issues of forest access and access control remain problematic.

STRUCTURE OF ACCESS TO THE "NEW" SOCIAL
FORESTRY PROGRAM

As Wood observes (1979:6), "state intervention cannot replace the entire
structure of accumulation from agriculture . . . it can only at best constitute an incremental addition to the existing pattern of present allocation
and thus its impact will be determined by the social forces which already
exist in the region." More than ever, access to the new social forestry
program (and, by default, access to the forest) depends on one's access to
the mandor or the mantri.

But the connections of the mandor and mantri to the village have
traditionally not been with the poorest forest villagers, except in certain
logging and reforestation areas in the teak forests where landless laborers

live and work near the magersaren. The mandors and mantris typically make their village-level connections through the villages' formal administrative leaders such as the lurah and the secretary; the village security organizations (LKMD and HANSIP); religious leaders such as *modin* (religious officials), *kyai* (teachers), or priests and ministers; or through informal leaders such as wealthy peasants, landowners, and traders; and their friends and family.

In former days these people would have been called patrons, and in some ways they still are. The nature of their patronage has been changed by recent developments such as the continuing commercialization of agriculture, which has been discussed at length by Scott (1972, 1976, 1985) and Adas (1981). These patrons are still powerful in their control of economic resources and opportunities for wage employment. Thus, the typical forester-village links are with people who can exert economic, political, or social control over other villagers. And this is exactly what field foresters have been encouraged to do by their superiors: we saw above that Indonesian forest development policy recommends that the foresters make inroads into the village society through its formal and informal leaders (Perum Perhutani 1982).

Having made their connections through these channels, the foresters have built up, not surprisingly, loyalties and obligations to village power figures (whom I will call patrons hereafter). They may have been extended hospitality in the patrons' homes, been introduced to their clients (the poor villagers) who eventually become forest laborers, and incurred obligations to do favors for patrons who have talked to the poor villagers about the religious, economic, or political importance of using the forest as the government wants them to. The class loyalties of these field foresters are often deeper than the professional web of reciprocal favors and obligations they have constructed, as many field foresters are sons of field foresters or village officials, or are married to the daughters of field foresters or village officials.

In response to the obligations they incur, field foresters feel pressure to exchange what they have access to themselves, namely, forest land, positions of control in forest farmers' groups, and privileged roles in the marketing of produce cultivated on the forest lands. Not only does this alleviate the forester's personal and professional debt, but it sometimes aids the forester in completing his work. The rural patrons have ties to the local people, and power over some of them that the forester does not have (although some mandors act as patrons just as any rural landlord might). If the rural patron's heart is in the right place, or he can turn an additional profit from his access to a forest plot, or both, the forester's task may be simplified. The "only" thing sacrificed, in the forester's mind, is the method of approaching the poor, who are more difficult to reach than the class of rural patrons. Despite the good intentions of those field foresters who wish to help the poor, a morass of strongly felt personal and professional obligations often prevents field foresters from directing the benefits of the new program to the poorest of the poor in forest villages. However, in truly social forestry the means—or the process of eliciting participation—*is* the desired end.

The degree of power held by the villages' formal and informal leaders may impel the forester to work through them. Their power is buttressed by the weight of the state (as discussed in chapter 5), which has taken pains in the last twenty years to extend its power and influence down to the village level through the formal village leaders (Hart 1986). Thus it is both structurally and ideologically difficult, if not impossible, for the field forester to bypass the lurah and his circle. In addition, a forester's failure to succumb to the micropolitical and psychological pressures (of obligation) can result in the village patrons' insidious or outright sabotage of the foresters' efforts. This may be done by their failure to support the project, by speaking out against it, or by insinuating that the foresters' intentions are dishonorable. They may also achieve the same end (usurping control of allocated forest plots) through "helping out" poor villagers—who do not have the means to invest large amounts of capital or labor (or time)—by taking over control of the land, financing the inputs, and reaping the yields for themselves.

In such instances, which research shows are not uncommon, poor forest farmers might receive either a small share of the crop (if it is sharecropped) or, more often, irregular wages from the patrons who hire them as laborers. These wages are invariably insufficient to live on, and the displaced forest farmers seek additional income by gathering and selling fuelwood, stealing teak, gathering young teak leaves, taking care of someone's cattle and grazing them in the forest, or engaging in other illegal activities on the forest lands. They may then take part in efforts to destroy the SFC's newly planted trees because they need continued wage-earning opportunities on a patron's forest land. The result is that the social objectives of the project are not met, and the environmental goals are sabotaged.

PROBLEMS WITHIN THE ACCESS STRUCTURE

Field foresters have their own professionally generated contradictions to deal with in making social forestry programs work. Even before they are trained as foresters, they observe that the professional functions of field foresters are to plant, maintain, and protect trees (and wildlife in some forests). Their training reinforces this self-perception. They have never seen themselves as channels for redistribution of rural incomes. Many are committed to economic development, but, like Indonesian officials in other sectors, the bounds of their actual roles in rural development end somewhat fuzzily at the point of providing the primary service for which they have been groomed—production and protection of the state's forest resources (read "trees") in Java.

Every field agency has its own personality, and as a relatively autonomous state enterprise, Perhutani has a deserved reputation for exercising corporate efficiency and rapid bureaucratic processing when it wishes to. At the same time, as in any agency or company, matters that are opposed by various middle administrators are subject to bureaucratic slowdowns and foot-dragging—in other words, bureaucratic resistance.

Part of the problem of functional identity lies in the priorities of superior forestry officials when they tour the field. Forest managers, who all have to answer to higher-level managers, want to see results, and "results" to foresters means trees in the ground, growing. The repertoire of questions fired at a manager's "men" rarely, if ever, include questions such as "Are the poorest forest villagers' circumstances improving?" or "Have benefits from these forestry programs remained with the poor villagers?" and "Which people are participating in the project, and why?" The real issue in social forestry, after all, is not whether people are involved—people will always be involved—the issue is *which* people are involved, how, and why. However, the importance of differentiating who, how, and why has not yet been institutionalized in the forestry structure, in the foresters' professional ideology, or in the social forestry program.

What is ironic about this situation is that SFC foresters in planning and policy-making offices or in the field articulate the connection between poverty in forest villages and degradation of the forest resource. The papers cited in chapter 5 represent only a portion of the policy papers, case studies, and conference proceedings that discuss the relationship between rural poverty and forest degradation. But when the time comes to actually plan or implement concrete programs for forest village development, the foresters depend on "Band-Aid" formulas. Fortmann (1989) observed that field foresters planning forestry development programs (particularly on privately owned lands) are plagued by the "three stranges": "strange trees in strange places for strange purposes." These same stranges plague foresters trying to involve people on state forest lands. The problem in both cases has been that the planning programs aim to get trees in the ground rather than to get the household economies of the rural poor off the ground. Instead of using forest resources to help redistribute economic resources in the village, alleviate poverty, and protect their trees, the foresters allocate money for social forestry but do not ensure that local programs meet their social goals. For an efficient business organization, this approach is uncharacteristically inefficient.

Another unusual aspect of the program is that members of the forestry profession—which has had to be more long-sighted and future-oriented than many other professions—feel pressured by time. While foresters have never let short-term production goals deter them from planting trees that would be harvested eighty to one hundred years hence—"barring political conflict," as they say—they succumb easily to the temptation to mark a project a failure if the trees are not in the ground within three months of the designated time. They are so committed to planting trees on schedule that they will go to any length—no matter that in the process they plant the seeds of failure by eliminating local interest in keeping the trees in the ground. Such an orientation to tangible goals is not unique to the Java social forestry program—it is the bane of social forestry and other state interventions worldwide.

A typical scenario: A field forester had involved poor people in the original program, but they dropped out. The forester knows that his boss or, worse, someone higher up is planning to view the new project within days. The trees are not yet in the ground. Therefore, the forester's first strategy is to deploy all his men (if a mantri, his mandors, if a mandor then his assistants and "clients") to find people, anybody, to plant the trees. If they agree, they are rewarded with rights to the plots. On such short notice, not only is the forester more likely to go to the upper crust of the village, with whom he has better ties, but also the poorer villagers are unable to halt their regular income-earning activities to take part in a program with deferred benefits. So the likelihood is that better-off villagers will become the forest farmers. After the official tour is over, the wealthy farmers retain their claim on the forest lands and the program proceeds, sometimes with the poorest people as the laborers.

If, as may also be the case, the forester has poor relations with the rich as well as the poor villagers, or it is the height of the peak labor-absorbing season on agricultural lands, he may not be able to enlist the aid of any forest villagers. In such cases, numerous examples of which were related to me and other researchers, the forester deploys his own men and their wives and children to get the trees in the ground. (One lurah's wife said, "Even Bu Mantri [the mantri's wife] was out there planting with the others the night before the unit manager's tour of duty.") Shortly afterward, the official entourage of jeeps comes through. The head man sees the trees in the ground, has a pleasant and polite conversation and a meal with the mantri, and leaves; everyone smiles. But the basic problem of how to *keep* those trees in the ground remains unresolved.

CONTRADICTIONS IN THE FIELD FORESTERS' ROLES

Further complicating matters are the contradictory roles that each field forester (mantri or mandor) must assume. There has been a contradiction of sorts in field foresters' roles since Indonesian independence: Indonesian foresters do not want to be as ruthless as their colonial predecessors. This contradiction, which began to intensify in the early days of the Prosperity Approach, has reached its height since the launching of the new social forestry program. Now there are higher-ups (many of them representatives of foreign donor agencies) asking questions that seem to contradict each other: "Are the trees in the ground, growing?" and "Are the poor people getting the benefits from these programs?" These are the questions they should be asking, but does the field forester have the tools to be able to answer yes to both questions?

At the same time that growing international concern with social forestry prompted the diagnostic research (approximately 1984), growing national concern with the diversification of sources of foreign exchange prompted the intensification of the integrated approach to forest policing. Thus, at the same time the foresters were expected to get friendly with the village poor, they were also expected to put on their paramilitary hats more frequently, and by so doing to instill fear in local forest thieves, including the village poor. In an abstract manner, these intense contradictions were not regarded as new developments, for the forest management structure, particularly the branch concerned with forest security, has always regarded the foresters' approach as two-pronged: a combination of "repressive" and "preventive" forest security measures. And though a "two-pronged approach" may sound fine on paper, it has been frustrating and sometimes impossible for field people to implement such policy.

STRUCTURAL FACTORS PRECLUDING THE INVOLVEMENT OF THE POOR

One of the main reasons that the poor are less likely to become or remain involved in social forestry projects is a lack of initial capital. For the first year of the project, the SFC subsidizes a portion of the forest farmer's costs by providing fertilizer at 30 percent of the cost and deferring the payments on this fertilizer until the harvest. The fertilizer has the added benefit of feeding the primary forest species that will dominate the plot until the trees are harvested and the reforestation process begins again. High-yielding varieties of maize were introduced to the project and made mandatory in most pilot sites, sidestepping one of the initial tenets of the program: the farmers' right to participate in the decisions about crops to be planted. Indeed, agricultural crops in tumpang sari were always the farmer's domain. For the first harvest, the cost of high-yielding varieties (HYV) seeds was borne by the SFC. In subsequent years they had to be purchased.

Despite these input supports, no supports were provided to alleviate the burdens of financing the most costly factor of production—labor. The explanation for this decision was that the average Javanese peasant does not calculate his own labor power in the traditional equation of costs and benefits of investment in agriculture. This is only partially true. It is possible for the peasant household with members who earn wages outside of agriculture (whether locally or outside the area) to invest labor in a social forestry project with deferred income. This is also possible for the middle or well-off peasant with some accumulated capital in the form of stores of rice and maize from previous harvests, or capital goods (such as gold jewelry or livestock) that can be sold to finance investment in agriculture—the benefits from which will be deferred until harvest. However, for those rural people who do not find themselves in such circumstances, the prospects of involvement in such projects are not bright.

Research shows that some forest areas, particularly the degraded forest lands and forest lands that have not been successfully reforested for ten to thirty years, require tremendous quantities of labor just to prepare the land for initial cultivation. My observations and the calculations of certain mantris and other researchers or field workers showed that some 50 to 90 person-days of preparation for planting were required per quarter-hectare. Assuming that the forest farmer is to perform this labor himself (most designated forest farmers in the program were men), participation would require withdrawing from the labor market for about two to three months, and not being remunerated for this labor until the first harvest, about fourteen weeks after the maize was planted. Effectively, payment was deferred some five or six months.

What if all or part of the land preparation were done by hired labor? Depending on the task, whether it was performed by a man or a woman, and the location of the forest village (wages for agricultural labor vary widely throughout rural Java), the labor cost of land preparation could amount to as much as Rp. 90,000 per quarter-hectare (including the cost of meals during work). For a poor forest villager whose family of five can barely subsist on Rp. 24,000 a month, hiring labor is out of the question.

In short, without other sources of income to subsidize their social forestry activities, without inexpensive credit, and without some kind of organization to strengthen and protect them from the inevitable "assistance" of the wealthy village patrons, poor and powerless people simply cannot participate in social forestry projects. And if they do try to participate in the projects at their outset, how long will this last? Private land is increasingly being transferred to the better-off villagers because of the indebtedness of the poor; similar patterns have been observed in the transfer of access rights to tumpang sari land. The current social forestry projects do not enable the poor to overcome the historical trajectory that has entrenched them in their poverty.

IDEOLOGICAL OBSTACLES TO SUCCESSFUL SOCIAL FORESTRY PROJECTS

Having earlier examined the foresters' ideology of conservation and custodianship of the state's forest resources as well as the peasants' cultures of resistance and autonomy, we may now clarify the interaction between these two ideologies, or, more accurately, the failure of the foresters' ideology to meet the ideological expectations of the forest villagers.

Poor forest villagers are more likely to retain the types of ideological orientation identified with peasants, particularly their "multi-stranded" conception of the roles of rural patrons who are to protect them, provide credit, provide employment in slack periods, and help them operate in an increasingly alien world.[4] Even when these peasants have become semiproletarians, as discussed in chapter 7, they still tend to maintain a portion of this peasant consciousness (Mintz 1979). I have suggested that they transfer some of their peasant values and expectations from the traditional patrons of village society to the relatively new patron of forest village societies, the SFC. They still expect (and need) credit, protection, employment in slack periods, and so forth. Given this tendency, it is clear why they choose not to regard the SFC as an institution (which might be and is impersonal), but rather to identify the SFC with its agents—to "personify" the institution—by regarding the field foresters as their modern patrons. What they would expect from a working relationship with the foresters, therefore, is something along the lines of a traditional patron-client relationship with mutual rights and obligations.

The foresters, on the other hand, are constrained in delivering the expected patronage to the village clientele because of the constraints on their decision-making powers imposed by the dynamic of the bureaucratic corporation they are part of. At the same time, they are all too aware of their positions in the village society, the deference paid them as officials, the economic expectations of them as members of an upper class, and the strong cultural pressures on them to assume the roles of patrons.

The wealthiest peasants living in the forest village have been structurally capable of assuming many of the ideological concepts of capitalist agriculture. One indirect result of their experience as rural capitalists is their capability of understanding the SFC's strategy for production, even though they might take offense at the methods the state and its agents employ. Being patrons themselves, or rural farm managers, their survival is not dependent on the patronage of others, although they may enjoy the patronage of urban middlemen or the state in the form of power accorded them for having successfully embraced the capitalist dynamic of the New Order (Hart 1986). In other words, wealthy peasants—some might call them farmers—are strategically positioned to enjoy the best of both worlds. They understand the peasant ideology and use it to their advantage. They also understand the capitalist and power dynamics of the state and the SFC, and use these to their advantage.

A trend toward more capitalist forms of agriculture among the wealthier classes in forest villages was documented before the implementation of the most recent form of state intervention in social forestry and clearly existed outside the villages where earlier forms of social forestry were put in place in the early 1970s (SFT 1985). It is thus not really necessary for field foresters to "teach" rural people to become market oriented; those who can afford to be, are. Wealthy peasants are most capable of making the necessary connections and bearing the risks. When the foresters bring in new technologies, such as new agroforestry techniques, fertilizers, and high-yielding seeds, an effective rural demand in all likelihood already exists, primarily among the better-off classes. The problem becomes, therefore, not a matter of disposing of the new technologies, or dropping them off and hoping that sooner rather than later they will be dispersed throughout the society, but rather how to target their initial disposal so that they are within the reach of the poorer forest villagers. Again, the issue comes down to the principal question raised in the beginning of this chapter, and the concept that has guided much of this discussion: *Who has access?* Access, in this case, to the foresters and their new technology.

Another way of posing this question is to question the compatibility of the various ideologies that have been thrown together into the development pot. These ingredients have been stirred, and stirred, and stirred again, for at least two decades, but they still lie one on top of the other, like oil and water, no matter how vigorously the stirring is done. Perhaps it is time to admit that the state's style of bureaucratic behavior, particularly through an agency whose primary function and motivating source is revenue generation, is simply not compatible with the complex components of the lives of forest-based peasants. The more bureaucratic and efficient the state becomes at producing forest products for itself, the more divorced it becomes from the daily realities of peasant economy that it is inextricably wound up with.

This contradiction is most obvious in the SFC's conception of its sectoral function—to produce and maintain control over production and protection of forest lands. The SFC will provide forest-related employ-ment to forest villagers, it will to a certain extent provide forest-related and nonforest-related income-earning opportunities, and it will offer teaching to forest villagers about "the meaning and function of the for-est," even in villages where the forest is totally degraded. It is possible; though more difficult, to cross over into the bureaucratic territories of other government agencies or bureaucracies. For this reason, the provi-sion of seedlings for tree crops that are categorized as plantation crops (coffee, rubber, clove)—and thus under the Ministry of Agriculture—is a more complicated procedure than providing forest crop seedlings. More-over, provision of institutionalized credit by the SFC itself is strongly resisted on the basis of this argument of intended mandate.

To what extent are these refusals to extend beyond the sectoral bounds dividing the territory of state administrators' valid excuses? Why, for example, did the SFC willingly provide the farmers with seeds for HYVs of maize for the first season of the social forestry project, but hesitate to provide coffee, rubber, or clove seedlings? In the first case, the SFC supported a government program to increase food production and to achieve self-sufficiency in maize. External pressures pushed the SFC to aid in this task, but not without (well-founded) complaints that its field foresters were not trained to teach forest farmers how to plant the HYV maize (which came with the typical package of fertilizers, pesti-cides, and timing instructions). At other times, in other projects, the SFC has dabbled in the realm of the Department of Livestock by providing forest villagers with goats and chickens, or in the realm of the Depart-ment of Agriculture by constructing erosion-controlling check-dams on private lands. It has drawn the line at provision of rural credit, particu-larly for the poor peasants who need it the most, but who can offer nothing in the way of collateral. The SFC is unwilling, as an institution, to take on the patronage role of credit provider. This is particularly true when the possibility exists that the credit will be used for consumption purposes rather than directly for production.

This does not mean that its agents do not get involved in the business of extending credit. Again, perhaps because of the field foresters' sensi-tivity to their constituents' conception of them as patrons, but also be-cause of the pressures on them to get trees in the ground, some field foresters lend forest farmers the money they need to pay labor, buy inputs, or support themselves through the waiting period of the first season. As individuals, the foresters are constrained as to how much they can afford to lend. However, as local residents and power figures, they are better able to judge who is a good credit risk and who they exert enough influence over—as rural patrons—to be trusted with their own personal funds. Unfortunately, there is always the risk that a wealthy peasant will learn that the SFC is financing the efforts of one or more poorer peasants, and request a loan, directly or indirectly calling up the forester's felt obligations to him or compelling the forester to "be fair" in distributing the credit. Of course, it is unfair of the better-off peasant to siphon off potential credit from those who need it more, but that reality may never be addressed by those constrained by ideology and obligation. The question remains, is the SFC as an institution not responsible for extending credit even though its field employees feel they should be? Further, how can other lending institutions be involved in the forestry issue in a nonthreatening, supportive manner?

ADMINISTRATIVE SOLUTIONS OR RESTRUCTURING?

The potential for an administrative solution to the development of forest villages seems slim, largely because many of the problems lie beyond the reach of any administrative solution that does not alter the balance of power in the village. But such changes would require the state—or the forestry agency—to make a complete reversal of the trajectory it has followed for almost two centuries and to oppose the theme and structure of development in Indonesia today. Furthermore, the state would have to overturn the established structures of rural power and overcome the forces of rural class formation—an impossible effort.

Nonetheless, the alleviation of some of the social problems in forest villages—problems of poverty and powerlessness—seems feasible and will reduce forest degradation. A first step would be to reorient the forestry organization to be more responsive and open to the range of rural problems related to the forest. The current social forestry program is attempting this, although teaching foresters to learn from villagers is easier said than done. At the village level, forest villagers need to organize to obtain services for forest farming and other forest-related activities. The poorest ones need an economic base, particularly in the early years, and support to follow through on activities they may initiate under state guidance. The role of the state should be to try to implement villagers' suggestions, listen to their problems, and help them develop alternative and locally appropriate solutions. Villagers, even more than the state, face formidable ideological and structural obstacles in efforts to change their fates, and are likely to remain disdainful and distrustful for several years into any such project.

The poor of forest villages could be organized to provide transport of logs and other forest products out of the village, or to take part in their processing.[5] While major land reform is unlikely, and the 2-hectare holding sizes called for in the 1960 land reform do not seem useful for Java, production on forest lands might be reorganized. Clearly, credit is needed, and an appropriate system for inexpensive credit must be developed if the poorest forest villagers are to participate. Transferring long-term tenure rights to better-off peasants and justifying this by citing the availability of seasonal laboring opportunities for the poor villagers skirts the issue of economic empowerment of the village poor. Finally, some consideration will eventually have to be given to the notion of real joint management of forest lands—degraded and robust.

More research and policy changes—and probably more mistakes—are needed to identify the appropriate solutions. Social forestry has to extend beyond the borders of forest villages and village forests and beyond the confines of the field forester-village relationship; it must embark upon a more comprehensive understanding of the articulation of forestry policies within the state structure, the structure and nature of forest production itself, and the impacts of structural changes on poor rural people's access to and demand for forest resources. An integrated social forestry would include the multistage study of the social organization of forestry and be a more appropriate approach to understanding and implementing change than the programmatic and sectoral approach of social forestry today. Moreover, it would not be limited to participation by forestry agencies alone. The challenge of village development requires a broader base of knowledge, experience, responsibility, and participation.

The SFC has reached a turning point, poised to make historic choices about means and ends. Its forest security mandate has always been described as two-pronged: preventive and repressive. But the type of development that is called for in the forest villages of Java, particularly the poorest villages in the richest teak forests, is not as passive as "preventive" implies, and will ultimately fail in other, more violent ways if repression is the only real effort made. It is time for the SFC and the other forestry agencies on Java to commit themselves not to a more aggressive style of repression, but to an aggressive style of development, of directed and sincere development of the forest poor. It just might keep those trees in the ground, growing.

APPENDIX A: A "LONG VIEW"
OF THE RESEARCH DESIGN

Is not history, as the dialectics of duration, in its own way an explanation of the total reality of social life? And therefore, an explanation of the present? In this respect, the lesson it teaches us is a warning—to be on our guard against the event, not to think merely within the short-term, not to think that those actors who make the most noise are the most authentic; there are other, silent ones. But who does not already know that?

FERNAND BRAUDEL, "History and the Social Sciences"

This book is grounded in the traditions of both historical sociology and regional political ecology. Though I had not read Piers Blaikie's first major book until I returned from the field in late 1985, I was greatly influenced by his approach to the social analysis of natural resource degradation. At the time I had not yet written a theoretical chapter integrating the issues I encountered in the field with those I had anticipated beforehand. I had, however, formulated a rough conception of combining political economy theory and analysis with the anthropological-human ecology methods I used in much of my fieldwork. Blaikie's *The Political Economy of Soil Erosion* provided a model for doing just that. Though I could not apply his model to my research design, it reinforced my view of the importance of understanding resource use and degradation from different perspectives and levels of analysis.

In structuring this as a study grounded in history, I have followed the Tillys (1975) by tracing the concept of forest access control, detailing its contemporary forms of expression in policy and action, and examining its nuances over time and space. I also explore the related concept of forest-based resistance in two contemporary contexts. The decision to study the evolution of control over three centuries and to focus on forms of resistance in the present and recent past was primarily a practical methodological one.

For the powerful participants in social and environmental interactions—the states, their agents, the ruling classes, and the international organizations—the social historian has access to a wealth of tangible materials: records, documents, diaries, and other articulate reconstructions of the past by those who experienced it and who shape the historical record as they wish it to be remembered. The reconstruction of the distant historical experiences of the less powerful majority—peasants, laborers, and others struggling for forest access—is more difficult. Peasants file few reports, write few letters, issue no legal guidelines or justifications for community and household uses of the environment. In Java, there is a recognition of customary or *adat* law, but debates rage over the interpretation of formalized versions of this law because analysts have effectively frozen it in time, depriving it of its characteristic flexibility. Both the written and unwritten records of the past require an exploration of not only the events but also the actors' likely perceptions of those events. Through these perceptions they reveal the interests that explain the essence of their actions. The difficulty of interpreting the unwritten perceptions of forest villagers in the past has led me to analyze contemporary people's accounts of their history, thus restricting my discussion of the cultures of resistance to the present and the recent past.

The study did not start out as a study of control and resistance, per se. I started by asking "Why and how do people use forests in Java?" Only later did I narrow my focus to: "What causes conflict over forest use between the state and forest villagers in Java?" This question began to intrigue me as a result of my earlier studies in Java and Kalimantan. In the mid-1970s, I spent several years studying rural women's nonfarm employment in rural Yogyakarta. Two and a half of these years were spent living in one Javanese village. While the focus of the current study of Javanese forest villages was not women, these two and a half years, and the other year and a half spent writing and thinking about them, gave me a strong empirical grasp of rural social relations and employment in rural Java. Interaction with rural researchers in other parts of Java at the time, particularly those associated with the Agroeconomic Survey in Bogor and the Population Institute at UGM gave me a broader comparative basis on which to later build my understanding of rural people's forest use.

In 1979 I joined a Man and the Biosphere research team and went to East Kalimantan to study the social and environmental impacts of the trade in "minor" forest products. In this latter project, I was first inspired by my anthropologist colleagues to think about the decisions individuals make about using forests under changing socioeconomic and environmental circumstances. This experience led to the primary research interest that I was to pursue over the next few years: the role of local or regional history in shaping the contemporary resource management structures and the social relations in which individuals' actions and decisions are embedded.

Hoping to benefit from my experiences in both Java and Kalimantan, I decided to study people's uses of forests in Java. I was challenged by the fact that a highly differentiated rural social structure would influence the ways the Javanese used forests, compared to the less differentiated Dayak villages I had encountered in Kalimantan. The role of the state in forest management was more direct as well, and turned out to be more pervasive than I had thought when I first embarked on the project. My goal was to go beyond my usual view "from the bottom," combining village-level fieldwork with views from "the top" and from the past.

While preparing to go to the field, I was offered the opportunity to coordinate field research for a social forestry project funded by the Ford Foundation. I accepted the offer, excited about the opportunity to work with Indonesian academics (mostly foresters, ecologists, and biologists), and about having easier access to the State Forestry Corporation itself.

In setting up this research, it was not long before I realized that conflict and confrontation characterized most interactions between forest villagers and officials of the SFC. Foresters all had tales to tell of their personal experiences in facing off with villagers in the forest. Many had joined the service after being environmentalists as students or because their fathers had been foresters; all those who worked in the field found themselves acting more like police than environmental managers. At the same time, social scientists working in rural Java talked of the deep mistrust and misunderstanding they had observed between foresters and villagers.

The different views I wished to take required the collection of data in diverse settings, using a variety of methods. Overall, I applied the principles of grounded research (Glaser and Strauss 1967) to guide my decisions on the kinds of data needed: as the research unfolded I decided what needed to be quantified, and who to target as additional key informants. The actual research was divided into three stages.

The first stage was a year-long field study (October 1984 to October 1985) during which I lived and collected data in two forest villages in Central Java and visited some twenty other forest villages. During this time, I met periodically with the eleven researchers involved in the social forestry diagnostic research in eleven villages in Central and West Java, including one of my study villages, and one who was located in a village in South Sulawesi. In our meetings we compared findings and coordinated methods and data-collection goals for the project as a whole. This was a learning experience in itself. Many of the participants were faculty from the forestry schools at Gadjah Mada University and the Bogor Agricultural Institute. Although they had spent considerable time in Java's forests, most of them had never lived in forest villages or tried to understand the people's perspective on access to the forest. Most were neither social scientists nor social foresters (yet). Through their changing views and new understandings as the research progressed, I was helped to better understand the differences in the perspectives of the forest people and those who studied or managed the forests for the state.

In collecting village-level data, my own residence in the villages and the assistance I received were critical. My main research assistant, Nuning, was "assigned" to work with me by her colleagues in an NGO (nongovernment organization) called Dhworowati whose assistance I had sought before beginning fieldwork. Though privately daunted by the prospect of being in the forest (she later confided), she threw herself into the project and proceeded to become a top-notch field researcher. I had other assistants from Dhworowati and from Gadjah Mada but their involvement in the study was much less intimate: illness, love, or other work commitments eventually drew them all away.

Nuning and I lived in separate households in Kalianjat, she full-time from January through September 1985, I full-time from January through April, one week a month from May through August, most of the month of September, and part of October. I made several visits to my second village in the teak forest of Kabupaten Blora in January, February, and March, and lived there most of the time from May through August, and for several weeks in September and October. For May through most of July, I had an assistant from UGM; he left for another job in mid-July and I continued the work there on my own.

Because their activities are considered illegal, I do not identify the villages, hamlets, or reforestation "base camps" from which specific data were collected in this study. Nevertheless, all the methods used by villagers to appropriate teak or convert the forest to agriculture presented here are common knowledge among foresters. Teak forest dwellers are not as secretive about their activities as one might think they would be, largely because the "culture of resistance" is an integral part of the personality of the region.

The most important sources of village-level data were semistructured interviews about daily events and people's uses of the forest, and oral histories. My assistant and I spent some days together in the field, some days working separately. When the situation was conducive, I became a participant-observer. I have to admit that I never actually chopped down a teak tree, and I never carried bundles of fuelwood, fodder, or leaves on my back, although I accompanied people doing all these things. Other data sources included household income studies of eight purposively selected families during six and four months in each hamlet, time allocation studies of a stratified random sample of twenty-four families in Kalianjat, and household surveys in each hamlet of random samples of seventy-four households (one-third of Kalianjat's households) and fifty-six households (two-thirds of the teak forest hamlet's households). For additional background information, we also interviewed the twenty-four households in Kalianjat that had participated in the time allocation study if they had not been randomly selected in the sample (these data are not included in the tables in chapter 6). My assistant and I conducted interviews in Indonesian and the local dialect of Javanese; to collect quantitative data we used only local Javanese. The Javanese dialects in the two villages/districts were mutually unintelligible. Until I became familiar with the dialect in the first research village, my assistant acted as an interpreter; thus at the beginning of the fieldwork, we spent more time together. In the second village I worked primarily in Javanese; the surveys were also conducted in the local dialect of Javanese.

During the first year of fieldwork, I also collected documents and conducted in-depth interviews with key managers and administrators in the State Forestry Corporation of Java, as well as forest rangers, mantris, and mandors in forest villages other than those selected for intensive village research. This was possible during trips from one site to another, when we would often travel off the direct route to visit foresters formerly assigned to one of the two study sites. Virtually every activity was a research activity—every visit with foresters or occasion to accompany foresters somewhere became a source of information. Due to the generally confrontational nature of the relationships between foresters and villagers, it was impossible to simultaneously act as a "participant-observer" with both foresters and the residents of a village.

While it did not occur to me at the time, upon reflection I have realized how access controls were imposed on me by some of the key people who controlled forest and forest village access. They began upon my arrival in Jakarta when I was told that my original plans to do research in East Java, where the largest teak forest area was found, had been refused. I would have to work in Central Java only. (Because I had not requested research permission for West Java, I could not select one village in West Java and one in Central for my study when I agreed to work with the social forestry project.) Because Central Java was the province where the SFC had been "born," the geographical restriction did not seem to be a problem. As it turned out, my research design for the field was seriously affected by the controls placed on my access. I had planned to work in Bojonegoro (East Java) or another highly productive teak forest district as a whole management unit having prime forests, degraded forests, and high rates of forest "crime." The SFC took me on a tour of seven Central Java forest districts—pine and teak—to locate a site. In the course of this tour, I was generally told by forest district managers and their assistants that no conflict existed within their district and that it was not suitable for my study. Meanwhile, my official escort talked constantly with me and with the foresters we encountered in the field about past and present confrontations with mobs and individuals.

Local forest police talked about the difficulties of getting people to co-operate with them on a variety of issues. Yet forest district managers were so loath to direct me to their problem areas that it finally took the intervention of a Jakarta-based forest administrator to place me in a forest site that they had been unable to reforest for more than thirty-five years. The site was, incidentally, located in one of the forest districts where I had been told there were no problems. It was not, however, in the heart of the teak forest about which I knew there was a considerable history that I needed to tap.

This process of gaining research access generated another type of field problem, which I had anticipated but was unable to avoid: village resistance to my research. In the village where the State Forestry Corporation placed me, I experienced the same type of mistrust and underwent a period of testing similar to what new foresters must experience. For the first month, longer with some individuals, I had to "prove" that I was neither a spy for the State Forestry Corporation nor the grandchild of the first Dutchman who leased forest lands in that area, but an American university student interested in learning the nature and extent of the villagers' forest dependence. In this, again, I was indebted to the efforts and sincerity of my research assistant in integrating herself as a member of the village and thus helping me to integrate as well.

Because of the difficulties anticipated and experienced by the SFC's placing me in a village, the second forest village in which I lived was the home of a friend in the heart of the teak forest. This village was not directly adjacent to degraded forest lands, but was interesting for several reasons. First, it was in the heart of a highly productive teak forest district to which I had been denied earlier access. Second, the selected hamlet was isolated but currently had very limited access to forest employment due to the logging rotation schedule of the district. Finally, it was near another village notorious for its open involvement in underground teak marketing, information about which was available through local villagers and the field foresters working in the subdistrict. I lived in an isolated hamlet in this village after getting the approval of local and regional officials.

Frequent visits to other districts and discussions with SFC employees ranging from forest district managers to drivers, added to my knowledge about teak "theft" and policing methods. Dhworowati placed several of its members in a forest village in Jepara; from their interviews and my own interviews with local foresters, villagers, and activists in that area, my understanding of the dynamics of the under- and aboveground teak trades was enhanced.

The second stage of research focused on field foresters. I conducted unstructured interviews and took part in group problem-solving sessions in addition to participating in two social forestry training programs (January 1986 and February 1987) for forest guards and forest work foremen. The first session involved thirty days of daily interaction with forest guards from all over Java, in a setting where they were encouraged to talk about forest management, police methods, and their side of forester-village relations in their own forest territories, before "social forestry" became a pilot program in the SFC. These intensive interactions provided some data impossible to collect in quantity during the field studies. In the second session, I spent approximately one week with a set of foresters being trained at the main forestry training school in Java in Madiun. After this, I spent a week in each of two social forestry pilot sites, one of which was adjacent to Kalianjat, the other in a teak forest in western East Java. I also met and interviewed several of my fellow social forestry researchers, two of whom were actively involved in coordinating pilot projects in Central and West Java. In each of these visits I was able to check data and fill in gaps in interviews with forest administrators in Jakarta.

The third stage of the research was historical research. In this I depended most heavily on the Dutch forestry journal *Tectona* (published from 1908 to 1955), as well as some articles in Dutch cultural journals, colonial reports, and other studies on the nineteenth and twentieth centuries. Because of funding and time constraints, I relied primarily on materials available at Cornell University and in the Forestry library at the University of California at Berkeley. *Tectona* was a valuable source of data, in that many colonial foresters interested in Java's forest history published in this journal. Many articles, particularly those by E. H. B. Brascamp, appended excerpts from the archives, thus providing a primary data source within a secondary source. Some statistics, not available in the journals at these institutions, were collected from the Royal Tropical Institute, Amsterdam, during a brief visit to the Netherlands.

Although not all these data are presented in this book, all contributed to my understanding of the dynamics of forest management and use. By alternating my focus from the local scenes to the big picture, I have tried to illustrate the harmony and discord between centers and peripheries, between structure and individual action, between state and peasant ideologies. The result is an analysis of Java's forests as seen from above and below; not comprehensive, as such a view would be impossible, but representing a few facets on the prism of forest-based experience and perception.

APPENDIX B:
GLOSSARY

abangan	Adherent of syncretic or traditional peasant values—nominally Muslim, heavily influenced by Hindu-Buddhist or traditional Javanese beliefs
ABRI (Angkatan Bersenjata Republik Indonesia)	Indonesian Armed Forces
aci	Cassava flour
adat	Custom, customary law
Administrateur (KKPH or ADM)	Forest district manager, highest field manager; manages forest district bureaus and field people; approves district's plans for reforestation, logging, research, forest recreational facilities; forestry equivalent of district head (bupati)
Ajun Administrateur	Assistant forest district manager
aksi sepihak	Unilateral actions carried out by PKI
aksi kedua	Second police action by the Dutch returning after World War II
aksi pertama	First police action by the Dutch returning to reclaim the Indies after World War II
asper (Asisten Perhutani)	Forest ranger; supervises mantris, has territorial, planning responsibilities; forestry equivalent of subdistrict head (camat)
badan perjuangan	People's paramilitary organization (during the revolution)
bandar	Equivalent of a dealer in various gambling games

bau	Literally, "shoulder"; in contemporary usage, 0.7 hectares of land
bibrikan	Clearing land or forest little by little
blandong	Woodcutter, logger
blandongdiensten	Corvée labor in forests required of forest villagers who owned or had access to private and communal agricultural land
bludruk	Stroke (apoplexy)
bosdistrict	Unplanned teak forest district during Dutch colonial administration
BRIMOB	Mobile brigade, security units consisting of army, police, and forest police to search villages suspected of teak "theft"
BTI (Barisan Tani Indonesia)	Indonesian Peasants Front
bujang	Bachelor, dependent
bupati	District head, equivalent of Dutch-era regent
camat	Subdistrict head
cemplongan	A wage-labor system for reforestation
cerita silat	Comic book stories (contemporary)
daerah hulu	Upriver
Darul Islam/Tentara Islam Indonesia (DI/TII)	Darul Islam/Islamic Army of Indonesia; an armed political group in the 1950s that wanted to make Indonesia an Islamic state
Departement van Civiele Magazijnen	Department of Civil Warehouses
Departement van Landbouw, Nijverheid, en Handel	Department of Agriculture, Industry, and Trade
desa	Village (may refer to kelurahan or pedukuhan in local usage)
desahoofd	Village head under Dutch
Dienst der Wildhoutbosschen	Junglewoods (nonteak) Forest Service
Dienst van het Boschwezen	Forest Service (Dutch)
Dinas Kehutanan	Forest Service (since 1967)
Djatibedrijf	State Teak enterprise (1930–38)
Domeinverklaring	Dutch decree in 1870 that all land not claimed as private land belonged to the state

DPR (Dewan Perwakilan Rakyat)	People's Congress
dukun	Traditional healer or person with supernatural powers
dukun bayi	Midwife
Forest lands	A legal classification made by the Indonesian government, referring to all lands under the jurisdiction of the Ministry of Forestry. Because this is a political classification (based on the land's potential and national land use objectives, as well as political criteria originating under the Dutch colonial government), not all lands thus classified meet the ecologist's definition of *forest*.
gaplek	Peeled, sliced, and dried cassava
geding	Measurement in Kalijurang, equal to 62 kilograms of (usually) unhulled rice; measure is no longer in general use
gendong	A woman's load, carried on the back or in front, tied on by a long shawl, usually knotted at the shoulder
gondorekum	Rosin made from pine resin
gotong-royong	Mutual assistance
gouvernement	The government
gugur gunung	System for making wet-fields by chipping away at hillsides
Gunzyuseisanbu	Department of War Production (Japanese Occupation)
halus	Refined (in manner)
HANSIP	Acronym for *Ketahanan Sipil*, or civilian security police; usually village or neighborhood "police" made up of village residents appointed by the village head
houtvester	The head of a planned forest division (Dutch administration)
houtvesterij	Planned forest division (Dutch administration)
hutan	Forest
hutan rakyat	People's forest
jaman	Era, period

jaman aman	The safe period; refers in Kalianjat to the end of the DI occupation of their forest, and the end to the fighting
jaman berontakan	Time of uprisings, upsets
jati	Teak
Jawatan Kehutanan	Forest Service (1945–66)
kabupaten	District (administrative)
kali	River
kampung	Village, neighborhood
kayu perkakas	Lumber, sawlogs
kebun	Garden, yard
kecamatan	Subdistrict (administrative)
kelurahan	Village
kepala kelompok	Work group head, for loggers or tumpang sari farmers
kepala kontrak	"Head" of tumpang sari farmers
kerja bakti	Village services or labor performed for village without pay
ketupat	Ritual rice wrapped in young coconut leaves
krama	High Javanese; the language of deference
kraton	Palace, esp. palace of the Javanese king
kyai	Islamic religious teacher
Laskyar rakyat	People's militias during the revolution
lipet	Ritual rice wrapped in young coconut leaves
LKMD (Lembaga Ketahanan Masyarakat Desa)	Village Security Institution, made up of heads of key village-level sectors; all village-level development is supposed to be administered by this group
lungguh	Appanage lands, lands granted by the king
lurah	Village head
magersaren	A living compound for forest laborers consisting of twelve houses, one of which is occupied by a mandor; usually includes a building to be used for Islamic worship (*langgar*)
MALU (Mantri-Lurah)	Forestry program aimed at promoting cooperation between forest guards and village heads

mancanegara	Outer territories (of Java); farthest states from center of Mataram power
mandor	Forest labor foreman, lowest rung on the forestry bureaucracy; supervises blandongs, reforestation labor, resin tappers; often doubles as forest police
mantri (KRPH) (Kepala Resort Polisi Hutan)	Forest guard; supervises mandors, has territorial and some management responsibilities; forestry equivalent of village head
Marhaen	Proletarian, have-nots (Soekarno's term); as an acronym, refers to the PNI youth group
Marhaenis	Person who works for the poor; for the proletarian
masak tebang	Age-class category of forest plantation trees past the optimal harvest age
masyarakat	Society, people
mengarak	Captured
modin	Islamic religious official
nasi oyek	"Rice" made from cassava
negaragung	"Core" or central territory of traditional Javanese kingdoms
ngoko	Low Javanese; the everyday language
NU (Nahdatul Ulama)	Islamic organization
numpang	Dependent; someone who occupies or cultivates another's land
nyumbang	To donate money or goods to the host family of a ritual feast
operasi	Village wood sweeps
opziener	Overseer; forest ranger, Dutch equivalent of *asper, sinder*
Ordre Baru	New Order (1966–present), Soeharto's own term for his regime after overthrowing Soekarno
Ordre Lama	Old Order (1958–65), Soeharto's term used in reference to the Guided Democracy period of Soekarno's regime
Paal, palen	Linear measure, equal to 1,506 meters
Pancasila	The Five Principles, ideological basis of the modern Indonesian state
pantong	Fee paid for permission to transport teak

parang	A machete-like bush-knife
Pasukan Wanara	Troops from Forestry who participated in Indonesian revolution
PCK (Polisi Chusus Kehutanan)	Forest police, at the mantri level
PDI (Partai Demokrasi Indonesia)	Indonesian Democratic Party
pedukuhan	Hamlet
pegawai negeri	Civil servant
pegawai perusahaan	Company employee, employment status in SFC second to civil servant
pekarangan	Home garden; yard
Pemuda Marhaenis (MARHAEN)	PNI youth group
Pemuda Rakyat	The People's Youth, a communist youth organization
penduduk liar	Squatters (lit.: "wild settlers")
penebangan liar	Unauthorized forest cutting (lit.: "wild cutting")
penyarad	Wood hauler (refers to laborer guiding the oxen or water-buffalo that actually drag the teak)
peraturan pemerintah	Government regulation
Perjan (Perusahaan Jawatan)	Government agency and nonstock company
Persatuan Wanita Kehutanan	Organization of foresters' wives in the 1960s
Persero (Perseroan)	Stock company owned by the state, managed by the minister of finance
persil	Parcel of land; in Kalianjat used to refer to all land formerly leased for plantations (*tanah erfpacht*)
Perum (Perusahaan Umum)	Public enterprise, owned by the state, a government nonstock company with its own budget
Perum Perhutani	State Forestry Corporation
pesanggem	Tumpang sari farmer
pikul	A man's double load, each weight tied on either end of a yoke, carried across one or both shoulders; also, formerly, 100 catties (approximately 150 pounds) of goods
PJJ (Patroli Jarak Jauh)	Long distance patrol, a forestry security team for village "sweep" operations

PKI (Partai Komunis Indonesia)	Indonesian Communist Party
PLP (Petugas Lapangan Pertanian)	Agricultural extension agent
PMDH (Pembangunan Masyarakat Desa Hutan)	Forest Village Community Development Program; a community forestry program initiated in 1981
P.N. (Perusahaan Negara)	State enterprise, financed directly out of the government's general budget (not autonomous)
P.N. Perhutani	State Forestry Enterprise (1962–69)
POLHUT (polisi hutan)	Forest police (usually refers to mandor level, can be mantri-level police)
PPP (Partai Pembanguan Indonesia)	Indonesian Development Party (Islamic)
priyayi	Aristocrat, upper-class person, person of high office or status
Ratu adil	The Just King, expected by followers of millenarian movements to return to Java and bestow peace and harmonious relations on the land
rawan	Troublesome, dangerous
RPKH (Rencana Pengaturan Kelestarian Hutan)	Ten-year forest management plans
romusha	Forced labor under the Japanese
Rp.	Rupiah (Indonesian unit of currency)
RTZ (Ringyo Tyuoo Zimusyo)	Forest Service (Japanese Occupation)
Sangyobu	Department of Economic Affairs (Japanese Occupation)
SARBUKSI (Sarekat Buruh Kehutanan Seluruh Indonesia)	Forestry Workers Union of Indonesia
SBK (Sarekat Buruh Kehutanan)	Union of foresters
SARBUMUSI (Sarekat Buruh Muslim Seluruh Indonesia)	Islamic Workers Union of Indonesia
sawah	Wet-fields
sawah pusaka	Inherited wet-fields

sega jagung	Corn-rice; maize processed to look like rice kernels and cooked with or without real rice as a staple food
SFC	State Forestry Corporation (Perum Perhutani)
sikep	Term for landholder in Java before the mid-nineteenth century; "one who holds the burdens in the land"; also term used by Saminists to describe themselves
slametan	Ritual feast
SM (stapel meter)	Stacked meter, a stere, a measurement for firewood pieces 1 meter long, stacked 1 meter high and 1 meter deep
Staatsdomeinverklaring	*See* Domeinverklaring
sukarela	Voluntary
sunan	Sultan (abbreviated form of *susuhunan;* used in eastern Mataram—Surakarta area)
susuhunan	Sultan (title for sultan of eastern Mataram in the Surakarta area)
tanah air	Homeland
tanah bengkok	Salary lands for village officials
tanah erfpacht	Land leased by Dutch colonial state to planters
taungya	Burmese term for tumpang sari
tegalan	Dry-fields
TNI (Tentara Nasional Indonesia)	Indonesian army (name during the revolution)
tournee	Field inspections, tourney
tulang punggung	Backbone (spine)
tumpang sari	Reforestation system under which farmers are permitted to plant agricultural crops between the rows of primary forest species for one to two years; their "payment" for reforesting the plot is the usufruct rights to that land and intercropped species
tumpeng	Rice prepared for ritual by shaping into a mound
undang-undang	Laws

VOC (Vereenigde Oost-Indische Compagnie)	The United East India Company
wayang kulit	Shadow plays
Zoosenkyoku	Department of Shipping (Japanese Occupation)

APPENDIX C: STATE CONSOLIDATION OF FOREST LANDS, 1839–1985

		Nonteak Forest		
Year	Teak Forest	Reserved	Unreserved	Total
1839	746,864		397,017	1,143,881
1840	845,070		676,102	1,521,172
1841	794,266		715,565	1,509,831
1842	781,792		719,648	1,501,440
1843	671,565		745,503	1,417,068
1844	622,803		612,823	1,235,626
1845	623,029		779,524	1,402,553
1846	634,143		780,885	1,415,028
1847	611,916		775,215	1,387,131
1848	591,050		643,215	1,234,265
1849	586,514		634,823	1,221,337
1850	600,122		632,453	1,232,575
1851	567,304		634,688	1,201,992
1852	469,415		757,955	1,227,370
1853	469,030		763,307	1,232,337
1854	461,613		698,351	1,159,964
1855	393,958		609,308	1,003,266
1856	238,280		658,388	896,668
1857	237,690		650,530	888,220
1858	263,773		594,906	858,679
1859	274,432		555,216	829,648
1860	274,432		577,669	852,101
1861	271,484		583,112	854,596

(continued)

Year	Teak Forest	Nonteak Forest		Total
		Reserved	Unreserved	
1862	475,380		705,790	1,181,170
1863	521,580		883,196	1,404,776
1864	641,854		1,550,220	2,192,074
1865	677,961		1,252,580	1,930,541
1893	653,943		n.a.	
1894	654,517		n.a.	
1895	654,500		n.a.	
1899	655,904		n.a.	
1900	655,279		n.a.	
1901	645,231		n.a.	
1902	637,811		1,200,000	
1903	643,818		1,200,000	
1904	643,830	n.a.	n.a.	
1905	649,247	n.a.	n.a.	
1906	654,241	n.a.	n.a.	
1907	666,027	n.a.	n.a.	
1908	667,700	n.a.	n.a.	
1909	673,573	n.a.	n.a.	
1910	671,913	872,000	n.a.	
1911	683,137	938,932	1,486,300	3,108,369
1912	679,764	998,404	883,300	2,561,468
1913	686,190	1,024,700	890,100	2,600,990
1914	686,373	1,025,650	890,000	2,602,023
1915	713,474	1,196,154	943,800	2,853,428
1916	721,818	1,264,800	916,000	2,902,618
1917	727,398	1,271,600	911,000	2,909,998
1918	726,576	1,276,615	865,613	2,868,804
1919	735,282	1,396,960	861,800	2,994,042
1920	737,400	1,482,000	708,000	2,927,400
1921	732,985	1,470,890	700,000	2,903,875
1922	734,738	1,575,798	n.a.	
1923	747,126	1,564,073	n.a.	
1924	768,089	1,538,688	n.a.	
1925	770,418	1,623,906	818,200	3,212,524
1926	765,422	1,649,000	770,000	3,184,422
1927	766,820	1,637,000	603,000	3,006,820
1928	767,938	1,654,852	575,000	2,997,790
1929	788,234	1,648,862	572,055	3,009,151

(continued)

Appendix C *(continued)*

Year	Teak Forest	Nonteak Forest		Total
		Reserved	Unreserved	
1930	799,104	1,665,175	582,500	3,046,779
1931	798,090	1,706,319	540,800	3,045,209
1933	801,052	1,772,481	316,300	2,889,833
1934	818,084	1,790,519	399,400	3,008,003
1935	817,782	1,812,462	407,100	3,037,344
1936	814,474	1,821,055	402,300	3,037,829
1937	814,826	1,869,952	370,000	3,054,778
1938	815,416	1,905,855	349,300	3,074,571
1939	813,525	1,898,629	345,046	3,057,200
1940	824,049	1,941,013	342,000	3,107,062
1946	852,700	1,954,900	442,000	3,249,600
1950	824,049	1,941,013		2,765,062
1951	824,049	1,941,013		2,765,062
1952	886,424	2,008,272		2,894,696
1976	854,145	1,979,343		2,833,488
1982	1,053,250	1,990,930		2,833,488
1985	1,049,236	1,938,986		2,988,222

SOURCES: Koloniaal Verslag 1849–1902; Verslag van den Dienst van het Boschwezen in Nederlandsch-Indie 1903–1939; Verslag van den Dienst van het Boschwezen in Indonesie 1940–1946; Pocketbook of Statistics for Indonesia, 1958–1967; Perum Perhutani 1986.

NOTE: Figures for 1839 to 1865 were converted from squared *palen* to hectares, using the measure of 1 linear *paal* = 1,506 meters. In the original documents forest land categories from 1839 to 1865 are given as (a) land covered entirely in teak, (b) land partially covered in teak but primarily covered in other species, and (c) nonteak forests. The (a) figure is given here as "Teak Forest," and the other two categories are combined under "Unreserved Nonteak Forests." From 1866 to 1892, the Koloniaal Verslager often failed to mention the area of the forest, particularly the nonteak forest. What was reported regularly was the area leased out to the private logging companies, but the unleased area was not listed.

Changes in the area of forest included in any category reflect diverse events. In 1912 several hundred hectares of teak forest land were converted to rubber production. As more nonteak forest was measured and mapped, it was brought into the reserved

(continued)

forest area and the area of unreserved forest lands was reduced. In some years, land considered no longer suited or better suited to teak production would be brought into the teak forest area.

The terms "reserved" and "unreserved" were not used after all these forests were claimed by the Indonesian state in the early 1950s.

APPENDIX D:
TEAK PRODUCTION, 1896–1985

	Sawlogs (Cubic Meters)			Firewood (Stacked Meters)		
Year	Forest Service	Contractors	Total[a]	Forest Service	Contractors	Total[a]
1896		132,184	140,151		279,722	280,713
1897	2,218	126,905	135,903	1,818	327,932	329,795
1898	6,163	129,988	139,953	5,314	240,914	246,295
1899	4,100	133,189	146,186	9,292	295,011	306,019
1900	3,018	114,624	124,167	10,074	303,384	318,458
1901	5,151	134,756	149,905	7,547	389,934	405,879
1902	7,906	152,352	171,868	15,498	365,150	381,151
1903	10,177	96,011	117,801	29,828	324,050	355,443
1904	20,587	150,553	179,744	73,937	437,169	513,176
1905	36,379	168,122	213,038	135,076	436,207	572,979
1906	49,709	161,598	217,975	196,937	443,670	632,081
1907	54,568	180,504	245,285	251,186	514,418	766,414
1908	78,576	147,694	242,039	334,627	487,311	825,465
1909	108,652	142,530	263,039	416,263	472,215	890,898
1910	116,815	166,749	294,018	364,935	530,100	896,684
1911	116,863	154,881	278,838	368,874	583,056	952,985
1912	121,152	118,873	247,072	416,648	530,565	948,527
1913	144,678	117,877	269,946	532,494	644,417	1,176,971
1914	136,525	87,168	229,468	600,719	525,545	1,127,132
1915	86,627	80,918	172,719	444,124	450,078	894,202
1916	109,106	73,336	186,202	670,424	503,132	1,173,580
1917	183,678	74,278	261,176	1,043,147	488,018	1,531,395

(continued)

	Sawlogs (Cubic Meters)			Firewood (Stacked Meters)		
Year	Forest Service	Contractors	Total[a]	Forest Service	Contractors	Total[a]
1918	155,712	58,588	217,807	785,323	441,593	1,227,235
1919	137,058	45,362	188,483	594,054	347,947	955,429
1920	151,657	55,556	214,718	868,436	462,747	1,354,763
1921	188,481	64,476	255,234	796,750	527,512	1,324,263
1922	69,097	43,030	115,167	106,012	262,323	668,901
1923	86,148	33,100	118,980	506,012	262,323	768,335
1924	134,500	30,000	167,000	725,000	n.a.	
1925	208,203	38,100	251,276	958,767	205,180	1,163,947
1926	202,740	29,700	232,500	714,608	156,000	904,428
1927	255,209	37,200	292,409	903,741	172,000	1,076,741
1928	283,000	32,200	320,400	998,000	131,000	1,135,400
1929	503,101	27,552	531,873	1,730,289	131,567	1,861,975
1930	360,477	19,791	381,072	998,223	67,958	1,066,181
1931	344,300	9,620	355,279	921,985	42,872	964,857
1932	227,096	2,731	230,636	585,184	5,314	590,498
1933	262,012	1,987	264,522	547,775	2,266	550,041
1934	265,656	2,815	268,775	636,917	932	637,849
1935	236,341	279	237,143	602,993	846	603,842
1936	258,336	448	259,167	686,923	773	687,712
1937	441,093		441,093	863,484		863,484
1938	441,618		441,618	875,003		875,003
1939	504,984		504,984	984,074		984,074
1940	512,472		512,472	891,664		891,664
1941	685,888		685,888	1,003,186		1,003,186
1942	456,000		456,000	1,787,000		1,787,000
1943	917,000		917,000	1,219,000		1,219,000
1944	908,000		908,000	2,182,000		2,182,000
1945	357,000		357,000	1,596,000		1,596,000
1946	165,911		165,911	1,195,096		1,195,096
1947	158,720		158,720	1,295,407		1,295,407
1950	397,000		397,000	1,045,000		1,045,000
1951	444,000		444,000	907,000		907,000
1952	526,000		526,000	1,136,000		1,136,000
1953	534,000		534,000	1,251,000		1,251,000
1954	509,000		509,000	834,000		834,000
1955	572,000		572,000	1,143,000		1,143,000
1956	541,000		541,000	1,118,000		1,118,000

(continued)

	Sawlogs (Cubic Meters)			Firewood (Stacked Meters)		
Year	Forest Service	Contractors	Total[a]	Forest Service	Contractors	Total[a]
1957	572,000		572,000	1,032,000		1,032,000
1958	514,000		514,000	1,008,000		1,008,000
1959	503,000		503,000	1,086,000		1,086,000
1960	420,000		420,000	999,000		999,000
1961	414,000		414,000	958,000		958,000
1962	434,000		434,000	820,000		820,000
1963	478,000		478,000	1,001,000		1,001,000
1964	464,000		464,000	685,000		685,000
1965	439,000		439,000	629,000		629,000
1969–70	545,633		545,633	1,009,000		1,009,000
1970–71	594,066		594,066	550,858		550,858
1971–72	494,753		494,753	694,658		694,658
1972–73	562,022		562,022	717,349		717,349
1973–74	604,952		604,952	1,004,520		1,004,520
1981	576,300		576,300	178,900		178,900
1982	690,800		690,800	227,900		227,900
1983	716,400		716,400	200,400		200,400
1984	758,200		758,200	203,300		203,300
1985	777,500		777,500	236,300		236,300

SOURCES: Koloniaal Verslagen 1896–1900; Verslagen van den Dienst van het Boschwezen di Nederlands Indie 1903–1939; Verslagen van den Dienst van het Boschwezen di Indonesie 1940–1946; Departement Pertanian Indonesia 1973; Perum Perhutani 1986.

[a]Totals include unregulated cutting permitted to villages and some individuals.

NOTES

CHAPTER ONE
Structures of Access Control

1. See, among others, Pelzer 1945, 1978, 1982; Manning 1971; Kartawinata 1977; Adicondro 1978; Jessup 1980, 1989; Vayda 1981; Colfer 1983; Peluso 1983; Dove 1983, 1984, 1986.

2. Guha and I were working on our manuscripts at approximately the same time. His book was published while this manuscript was being copyedited. As a result, it was impossible to make as many specific comparisons to the present work as I would have liked.

3. This is known as the doctrine of "neutral competence," or nonpartisan technical competence; see Kaufman 1956.

4. An abundant literature on participation and its relationship to top-down bureaucratic structures exists; see, for example, Cohen et al. 1979; Fortmann 1980; Korten and Uphoff 1981; Whyte 1983. On the general nature of core-periphery relations, see Wallerstein 1974 or Shannon 1989; on the effectiveness of natural resource bureaucracies, see Kaufman 1967, Selznick 1966, and West 1982.

5. A sample of studies on these topics would include the following. Peasant resistance against state policy in Southeast Asia, particularly in Indonesia, has been discussed by The (1967, 1968); Benda and Castles (1969); King (1973); and Scott (1985). Though it is the most recent, Scott's (1985) book on the Malay peasantry has already become a classic. Recent discussions of arson as protest have been written by Elson (1984); Peluso (1985); and Teguh (1985); murder and rebellion are the subject of research by Sartono (1973); Scott (1976); and Adas (1981).

6. The deflection of discontent and an ideology of solidarity may be deployed by states toward certain societal groups as well, as in Anderson's 1983 description of Indonesian state ideology concerning the economic activities of the Chinese.

7. Chambers (1983:12) based these lines on the following old English rhyme: "They clap in gaol the man or woman / Who steals the goose from off the common / But let the bigger knave go loose / Who steals the common from the goose."

8. In addition to the works on peasant resistance cited ealier in the text, see also Tilly and Tilly 1981, and the special edition of the *Journal of Peasant Studies on Everyday Forms of Peasant Resistance,* 1986, edited by Scott and Kerkvliet; on forest-based resistance, see Guha 1985, 1990. But more has been done on labor control and ideological control (hegemony) than on other aspects of forest access control; see, for example, Mintz 1979; Scott 1985; and Stoler 1985. These writers did not study peasants in forested areas or living near state forest lands, although Scott 1976 talks about peasants' access to "the free resources of nature."

9. This analysis covers general forest policy and use only through 1985. Since 1986, new policies have been tried in villages near Java's most degraded forest lands. It is too early to determine what the sociopolitical outcomes of these policy initiatives will be. Despite these changes, however, in most forests, the old policies are still in effect, so this analysis retains a policy value beyond the historical; see chapter 8.

10. The Department of Agraria and the Ministry of Forestry do not agree on either the total percentage of Java's land under forests or the total land area of Java. According to the Department of Agraria, 19.6 percent of Java's 12,590 million hectares are forest land, but the Ministry of Forestry states that Java's total land area amounts to 13,219 million hectares (GOI/IIED 1985b:35–36).

11. Recently, some forests classified as "protection" forests (*hutan lindunq*) have been changed to "limited production forests" where low impact uses, such as resin collection, will be carried out. The organizational and political-economic implications of this decision are discussed in chapter 5.

12. The lower value overall is only partly because so much of the nonteak forest is protection or limited production forest. The value of nonteak forest varies widely by species. Rosewood, for example, was the most expensive wood on the world market in 1985. The value of pine forest varies across its lifetime, depending on its intended end-use and lifetime; from age 11 years its resin is tapped for industrial purposes, while after age 20 it may be logged.

CHAPTER TWO
Gaining Access to People and Trees

1. Here, van Hogendorp addresses the residents of Batavia, as Jakarta was called under the Dutch. Dirk van Hogendorp first came to Java in 1784, in the service of the United East India Company. In 1791 he became Resident of Jepara, and he later assumed positions of greater power within and outside of the Indies. Considered a liberal, he believed that the free market in Java was the best way for the Netherlands to profit from her colony. See *Encyclopaedie van Nederlandsch-Indie* 1918, s.v. "Hogendorp."

2. Wood was sought not only for the needs of foreign ships in Batavia but also for use in Java's other ports of call (Brascamp 1921a:134).

3. Regents were regional administrators appointed by the Dutch. Before and

after the Dutch rule, the local term for a regent was *Bupati* (today, the head of a District or Kabupaten).

4. I do not call the VOC the "Dutch" East India Company because although the organization was an enterprise based in what is now Holland, neither all its investors nor its personnel were Dutch; in its structure, the company anticipated the multinational corporations of our time (Ricklefs 1981:25).

5. See Pigeaud 1962; Onghokham 1975; Breman 1980; Moertono 1981.

6. The Hindu-Buddhist Singasari kingdom, believed to have been centered in the teak forest near the border of present-day Central and East Java, ended with the reign of Kartanegara in 1292 (Vlekke 1960). The Majapahit kingdom, centered at today's Trawulan near Mojokerto, reigned in Central and East Java from approximately 1294 to 1478. When the Dutch began to arrive on Java at the end of the sixteenth century, the Islamic sultan of Mataram, seated near today's Kartasura, had already seized control or was allied with rulers in much of the island. Before the arrival of Islam, Javanese rulers were referred to as kings, since then, *sultan* has been used. When Mataram split into two sultanates, the rulers of eastern Mataram used the title *susuhanan* or *sunan.*

7. These heartland territories within the realm of the Mataram empire of Java were called *Negaragung;* the outer territories were called *Pasisiran* (maritime or coastal territories) and *Mancanegara* (external territories).

8. Pigeaud (1962) merely mentions that a class of "untouchables" is referred to in the fourteenth-century text of the *Negarakertagama;* other writers have been more explicit about their outcast status. For general information on the Kalangs, see *Encyclopaedie van Nederlandsch-Indie* 1918, s.v. "Kalangs." The *Encyclopaedie* suggests Veth (1875–82), among other sources on the Kalangs. Altona, in his thesis about the origins of teak on Java (1922:457–507; 1923:237–63), also discusses the Kalangs. As this book went to press, I became aware of F. Seltmann's *Die Kalang; Eine Volksgruppe auf Jave und ihne stamm-mythe* (Stuttgart, 1987), but time constraints prevented me from integrating Seltmann's material into this analysis.

9. The story of the waxing and waning of Dutch trading power, and the initial forays of the United East India Company into what is today the Indonesian archipelago, are detailed in Boxer (1965), especially pp. 84–112.

10. The susuhunan was concerned in part that the rice he provided the Dutch would end up in the hands of his enemies, the Bantamese and the Balinese (Brascamp 1921b:349).

11. The number of Kalangs then living in these districts is difficult to cite accurately because the taxes were not rendered per family but per group of families. The estimates range from approximately 3,000 families to 8,000 families. Moreover, we do not know how many Kalangs constituted a typical family.

12. The last we hear of the "forest-dwelling people" (*bosvolkeren,* most likely the Kalangs) is from Daendels, in his edicts of August 21, 1808. He allowed Kalangs and other forest dwellers who built ships, carriages, and carts greater forest access to cut wood.

13. Many of the Europeans were likely mestizos (Shiraishi, personal communication, 1990).

14. In Java today, *blandong* is used in reference to woodcutters among both

villagers and forestry personnel. As Boomgaard points out, nineteenth- and twentieth-century foresters and historians called all woodcutters of the VOC period "blandong," although archival materials reserve the term for those wood-cutters in Rembang subject to the blandongdiensten.

15. Cf. Raffles's (1817:181) comment that some 100,000 people a year were under the jurisdiction of the Board of Forests; this does not mean that all were employed in logging activities.

16. It is not clear if Boomgaard's figures cover only those the archives refer to as "blandong" (forest laborers in Rembang), or include forest laborers in the forested regions of Tegal, Pekalongan, Cirebon, and Pemalang.

17. Boxer (1965:304) explains the value of Dutch coins as follows: "The Dutch guilder or florin . . . contained 20 stuivers, and may be regarded as the equivalent of the English florin. . . . For the first half of the seventeenth century, the Spanish-American rial-of-eight [Spanish real] was widely used in the East by the Dutch both as real money and a unit of account, being usually converted at about 48 stuivers and considered as the (slightly overvalued) equivalent of the rijks-dollar (*rijksdaalders*) (2.5 florins)."

The first Coinage Act after Dutch resumption of power in 1817 maintained the money standard set by the English: 10.37 grams of fine silver were equal to one guilder (van Laanen 1980:16).

18. A similar drop in the buffalo population was experienced in the coffee regions of Priangan where peasant growers had to deliver their quotas to Jakarta, hauling the loads by buffalo (Breman 1980).

19. Apparently, however, enough forest remained in the coastal residency of Jepara so that in the ensuing 150 years, much more could be depleted. Du Quesne van Bruchem (1939:103–4) made an interesting study comparing a 1776 report on the forests of Jepara with the state of the forest in 1925. Although his estimates of forest area are rough, calculated by the amount of distance that could be covered in the times cited by the early report's author, his results are nevertheless provocative. From the territory in 1925 comprising the forest district of Pati, including parts of Kudus, Jepara, and Pati regencies, he calculated nearly 50,000 hectares had been converted to village territories, pasture, and agricultural land since 1776. Thus from an estimated area of 70,000 hectares, the forest had been reduced to 22,600 hectares.

20. In comparison, when the sultanate of Bantam was abolished by Raffles in 1813, the sultan was given a yearly salary of 10,000 Spanish dollars (at the time equal to rijksdaalders) by the British government (Vlekke 1960:263).

CHAPTER THREE
The Emergence of "Scientific" Forestry

1. The path the Dutch followed was not much different than that taken by the British in India (Guha 1985, 1990) and others in Southeast Asia who tried various logging methods and the management ideas of European and Chinese entrepreneurs. See Mekvichai 1988 and Hafner 1990 on Thailand; Adas 1981 on Burma.

2. Although the Dutch lost the Anglo-Dutch War, the English returned their colonies to them in 1816; see Vlekke 1960:270–71.

3. Some of the ideas implemented by Daendels had been suggested earlier by van Hogendorp, but had not been implmented at the time (Furnivall 1944:65).

4. This rule was alternately enacted and rejected over the next sixty years; in the forest laws of 1865, villagers' access to sawlogs was eliminated.

5. The Cultivation System was introduced by Governor-General van den Bosch and in effect in Java from 1830 to 1870. The system—or systems, as they varied greatly by region and by crop, were forms of organizing the production of agricultural crops for the state. While in some locales peasants and factory laborers producing export crops were to be paid, in others it was often a system of compulsory labor for state enterprise. The state profited greatly from the Cultivation System(s) in the early years but its implementation had long and depressing consequences for the people's welfare and development in many regions. In other regions, the peasants actually profited from the system. On the regional aspects of the Cultivation System and its effects, see Vlekke 1960:288–96; Fasseur 1975; Breman 1980; and Elson 1984.

6. Ordonnantie van 10 September 1865, Staatsblad no. 96: Reglement voor het beheer en de exploitatie der houtbosschen van de Lande op Java en Madura.

7. Daendels's directives were issued September 4, 1810, and February 5, 1811. To this day, a similar regulation for the taxation of privately grown and marketed teak trees is enforced by the State Forestry Corporation.

8. Guha (1985) describes the same perspective and the same time frame for the rise of scientific forestry in India.

9. These Germans came from the hertog of Nassau (Koloniaal Verslag 1849:137).

10. The Dutch in Java were not the only ones turning to Germany for education in the relatively newly formulated "science" of forestry. Aspiring foresters from the other Dutch and English colonial services, and from free nations such as Sweden, Norway, Russia, and Japan, were sent to German forestry schools. German foresters migrated to other countries to develop principles of forest management and to cement these principles into the legal structures of their adopted states (Fernow 1911:176, 262, 273–74, 295, 310, 316–17, 332, 355, 378, 394, 450, 486).

11. Besluit 7 July 1875, Indies Staatsblad no. 126.

12. Besluit 10 September 1874, Staatsblad no. 214.

13. The work period coincided with the usual months of the dry monsoon, that is, April through September or October.

14. Staatsblad no. 189, 1864, increased the wages of group leaders to 20 cents and cutters to 12 cents; for other changes in wages, see Cordes 1881:216.

15. The allotments were 1¼ catties of rice and ¹⁄₁₀ catty of salt.

16. Hence, Boomgaard's estimates of the number of corvée laborers employed under Daendels probably also fall short of the actual number of people involved in the blandong system in the course of a year.

17. These leaders were likely called *jago,* literally, "rooster" or "cock," which, loosely translated, means "tough guy."

18. *Woestegrond* referred to agricultural land long abandoned to fallow by people who moved or died without heirs.

19. There were some exceptions, instances in which all land was either privately or communally owned; see Bergsma 1880:186.

20. In nonforest villages, communal lands were worked only by the landowning families who owed tribute or taxes (sikeps) (Onghokham 1964:5). Because numpangs in forest villages under the blandong system paid taxes with their labor, they were given access to the communal lands.

21. It is not known whether there were traditional (*adat*) means by which landowners who had forfeited their private rights to land could reclaim them.

22. Staatsbladen nos. 495, 221, 65, 168, and 63, respectively (Soepardi 1974a:52).

23. Bamboo is not considered "woody."

24. All woods found in Indonesia that were not teak were called "jungle woods." Today the SFC classifies forests as "teak" (jati) or "nonteak" (bukan jati).

25. One SFC argument for maintaining certain lands under teak is its vigor under environmental conditions that are not particularly good for agriculture.

26. At least one community of Kalangs remained distinct until recently—a group who lived in Kota Gede, south of the Yogyakarta *kraton*. These Kalangs, however, had been palace artisans, wood carvers, and urban dwellers, attached to the palace and disengaged from the forest proper for centuries.

27. See Jasper 1918; Onghokham 1964, 1975; The 1968a, 1968b, 1969; Benda and Castles 1969. King (1973) offers a theoretical framework for the analysis of the Samin movement and other forms of peasant unrest in nineteenth-century Java. The following discussion is drawn from these authors.

28. This attitude prevails in the teak forest today among non-Saminists and confounds efforts to encourage cattle stalling.

29. The Dutch said the irrigation project was too expensive at the time, but the minister of colonies later said that the decision to suspend it had made Rembang Residency the most backward region of Java.

30. Differences in Saminist belief from the generally accepted *abangan* peasant tradition of Java were clear: Saminists did not believe in the plethora of spirits or perform the rituals of what might be called the abangan mainstream. However, their emphasis on the maintenance of simple life-styles and values, respect of the land and people's role in tilling it, and on the family were reminiscent of abangan peasant values.

31. Later, in the same region as the Saminist movement, other forms of protest, resistance, or organized opposition arose against the Forest Service's constraints imposed on the heavily burdened peasants—notably the Sarekat Islam (SI) movement and the young Indonesian Communist Party (PKI). On the formation of Sarekat Islam, see Takashi Shiraishi 1989; on the early Communist Party in Java, see McVey 1965.

32. *Wong sikep*, meaning "those who embrace" was what the Saminists called themselves. *Sikep* was also used in reference to a person who had the kind of rights in land accompanied by corvée labor, including the founders of a village who first cleared the forest for agriculture (Onghokham 1975).

33. All forest district heads (*houtvesters*), assistant district heads, and forest rangers (*opzieners*) were Dutch.

34. Opium was legal in the Dutch East Indies at this time, but the government had a monopoly on it. The sale of opium was restricted to the opium farmers who bought the "farms" for particular regions at government auctions. The government not only punished unauthorized sellers but also sought illegal buyers of the drug. Seeking out these "criminals" was the task of the notorious and intensely hated opium police. It was not uncommon to punish illegal possession by public whipping (Rush 1983:53–64).

35. Some forest cultivators managed to resist the most persistent of land-swapping forest officials and today their heirs are still cultivating these forest enclaves.

CHAPTER 4
Organized Forest Violence

1. On the ideology of the Indonesian revolution, see Kahin 1952; for the role of youth in compelling social and ideological change during the Japanese period and the revolution, see Anderson 1972. Benda (1956) and McVey (1965) describe some political and ideological influences on Javanese thinking in the late colonial period. Wertheim (1956) observes transition in Indonesian society from a longer sociological perspective.

2. Soekarno served as president of the Republic of Indonesia from 1945 to 1966. Analysts divide his regime into three periods: the revolution (1945–49), the period of "Constitutional Democracy" (1950–58), and the "Guided Democracy" (1959–65), when the democratic process was far weaker. By the time of Guided Democracy, changes in the structure of government had begun to set the stage for the post-Soekarno period. On the transition from Constitutional to Guided democracy, Feith (1962) remains one of the best sources. Since Soeharto came to power, the 1958–65 period has been known as "The Old Order" (*Ordre Lama*). Soeharto's government is known as "The New Order" (*Ordre Baru*).

3. I restrict my discussion of the Japanese and revolutionary periods to those events and individuals related to forestry. For an excellent description and analysis of Javanese politics in these two periods, see Anderson 1972. The classic discussion of the Indonesian revolution is offered by Kahin (1952).

4. *Structure* here refers to the age-class structure, that is, the percentage of trees in a forest management district or throughout the forest within certain age-classes. The age-classes of teak, an 80-year rotation tree crop, are 10 years long. Thus, age-class 1 includes teak trees aged 1–10 years, age-class 2 includes teak trees aged 11–20 years, and so on. Fast-growing pine (*Pinus merkusii*) is kept on the plantation for only 18–30 years, and each age-class is only 5 years long. Thus pines in age-class 1 are 1–5 years old, in age-class 2, they are 6–11 years old, and so on.

5. A longer view of teak production, though some of the figures are crude, is provided in Appendix D.

6. Calculated from Soepardi (1974a:109), and rounded off.

7. The complaint about people's conflicting views of their own and the Forest Service's claims on the forest is reflected throughout the writings of Soepardi and of the Departemen Kehutanan.

8. Two days after the Japanese surrendered, the Indonesians declared their independence from the Dutch. When the Dutch refused to recognize Indonesia's independence, the revolution (1945–49) ensued.

9. For a detailed account of the Indonesian-British interactions, see Anderson 1972, especially chap. 7. For a discussion of the Indonesian perspective, see Kahin 1952.

10. During the war, the territory of what would later be known as Indonesia was divided between the Indonesian Republicans, and the returning colonial Dutch.

11. Masjumi was an Indonesian Islamic organization that later developed into a political party.

12. It is unlikely that *all* of the twenty-seven districts surveyed could have been marked off in this manner, particularly given the other revolutionary conditions and the symptoms of civil war starting to affect the forests, namely, the Darul Islam activity in West and West Central Java and the Communist party (PKI) activity throughout the island. Foresters of the wrong political denomination, or in some places, any government foresters, were killed with no questions asked when they ventured into certain forest districts.

13. Except for a brief time in 1964, when it was made a ministry. In the aftermath of the events of 1965–66, Forestry once again became a Directorate General in the Ministry of Agriculture.

14. *Peraturan pemerintah* (Government regulation) no. 64, 1957.

15. Ideologies and actions at the time tended to be taken as whole packages, one inseparable from another, requiring wholesale support of a platform and efforts to implement that platform.

16. Foresters sympathetic to the DI or PKI parties or who simply wanted to help forest villagers approached the issue of forest land control in ways condoned by their parties' philosophies. The PNI was largely aligned with the PKI until about 1964, when unilateral actions were begun, as discussed later in this chapter.

17. The Barisan Hizbullah was established in December 1944 by the Japanese, who intended to deploy the group in the event of Allied attack on Java. Activist Muslim youths were recruited and began training in February 1945 (Anderson 1972:26). Masjumi was organized by the Japanese in 1943 as a coordinating organization "to encompass and unify the notoriously fissiparous elements of prewar Islam" (Anderson 1972:28). It later became the major right-wing Islamic party.

18. It is not clear whether written reforestation contracts were made between the Forest Service and the farmers as they are today.

19. Mortimer (1974:278) points out that the PKI initiated a drive to integrate and organize the non-estate/non-forest squatters peasantry into the party's activities only in 1958 and 1959. This "go-down" (to the village) movement included rural research as well as organizational activities.

20. I received several photocopied pages of this report as part of a paper that a forester was writing for the *Sejarah Kehutanan Indonesia;* the quote did not appear in the final published version, probably because it reflects favorably on the radical foresters' perspective.

21. By comparison, the central government had only 807,000 employees in 1960 (Ricklefs 1981:227). In 1959 SOBSI claimed that 531,946 central government employees belonged to one of the forty SOBSI member unions, one of which was SARBUKSI (Hindley 1967:14).

22. Although these numbers are likely exaggerated, as was the practice among most political parties at the time, they do provide an indication of the numbers of people influenced or at least contacted by peasant organizations at this point in Javanese history.

23. One may only speculate on the extent of changes had the communists gained greater power in the government. In China, wildlands have been allocated to the members of collectives for growing trees and forage. The collective owns the land while the commune members are allowed to plant the land only in trees and forage crops. Field crops are not permitted. Deeds of ownership (of the wildlands so allocated) are issued by the state (Chen 1981).

24. It seems strange that SARBUKSI members, many of whom would have had significant environmental training, were not more vocal on these points; in fact, they may have been. No internal documents of this organization, no newsletters or policy papers, were available for this analysis, so my sources are confined to official forestry accounts of the period, interviews with foresters and villagers who remember the period, and newspaper accounts. All of these sources, of course, may simply not have known of alternative forest management plans in the works, or chosen not to report them.

25. Cepu sawmill operated before the war; it was rebuilt with foreign aid. The other sawmills were at Brumbung, Randublatung, Bojonegoro, Saradan, Madiun, and Benculuk. In 1956 and 1957 Eximbank also financed sawmills in Samarinda, Balikpapan, and Niceran (all in Kalimantan) (Departemen Kehutanan 1986, 2:52).

26. This level of production was not significantly less than before the war and probably far exceeded the amount of production intended by Becking.

27. Large-scale exploitation of Indonesian forests outside Java did not begin until 1967. Soekarno tried to follow a policy of restricting (or forbidding) extensive foreign investment in Indonesia to avoid debt and dependence. When Soeharto became president, one of his first acts was to enact Foreign Investment Law no. 1, giving a green light to foreign capital and Western international development organizations.

28. Besides the wood sold at regional and local auctions, each forest district officer is allowed to sell a certain amount of wood at his own discretion. This type of distribution is called "out of hand" (literally "under the hand," but with no negative connotation).

29. The origin of these maps remains unclear. Accounts of the arrival of the Japanese claim that maps and other working tools that might assist the Japanese were destroyed during the "scorched-earth policy."

30. Irrigated land has always been considered by the state to be of higher status and value, indicated by higher taxes and greater number of privileges and obligations that fell to owners of irrigated land. See Bergsma 1880 for various versions of this rule in different residencies; see also Dove 1984, 1985.

31. Peraturan Pemerintah no. 51, 1960.

32. Undang-undang Darurat Nomor 1, tahun 1956, Kementerian Agraria.

33. Mortimer (1972:295–328) offers an excellent account of the unilateral actions and the events preceding and following. Much of the following discussion comes from Mortimer's recounting of the events of this period.

34. The *aksi sepihak* marked the first real application of a class-based strategy in the countryside, and this sudden class orientation—a switch from the dependence on traditional vertical loyalties in the countryside—may have been the reason it failed (Mortimer 1974).

35. The Land Reform Law of 1959–1960 is discussed further in chapter 6.

36. In the newspaper accounts of this period, every few days new reports came in of starving peasants.

37. According to Mortimer (1972), this setback for the PKI was the result of one of its own "mistakes," made throughout Java. Many top-level (Jakarta-based) officials and intellectuals were PKI or sympathetic to PKI; many workers and peasants joined the organization. But many middle-level management people—in the provinces and districts—were opposed to PKI or allied with landowning interests and the interests of the right and center parties. When the aksi sepihak went into effect, the opponents of PKI reacted strongly to PKI actions and activities, and enlisted the loyalty of their networks of "clients" and allies.

38. ANSOR was the *Nahdatul Ulama* ("NU," a contemporary Muslim party) youth group; MARHAEN was the youth group of the PNI.

39. Various analyses of the 30th of September movement have been made. See, for example, Wertheim 1966 and 1979; Anderson and McVey 1971; van der Kroef 1971; Mortimer 1972; Crouch 1973. Crouch (1973:18–20) provides a comprehensive list of previous publications in English on the movement.

CHAPTER 5
State Power to Persist

1. Pancasila, or "The Five Principles," on which the national government of Indonesia is based, form the ideological basis for all laws and policies of the nation. These principles are: (1) belief in one Almighty God, (2) national consciousness, (3) humanism, (4) social justice, and (5) democracy. The last *sila* used to be translated as "The Sovereignty of the People," but this phrase is rarely used anymore.

2. *Perusahaan Negara* (or P.N.) also literally translates as "state enterprise."

3. By Presidental Directive no. 75/1969.

4. There are three types of state enterprises: Perum, Perjan, and Persero. Perum (which, though an acronym for *Perusahaan Umum*—literally, "public enterprise"—is owned entirely by the state) has been defined in the text. Perjan

is an acronym for *Perusahaan Jawatan*, and is a government agency and nonstock company part of the government budget. Persero is a shortening of *Perseroan* ("a stockholding corporation"); however, the minister of finance, representing the government, is the sole shareholder in state enterprises that are perseroans (Junus 1984:174).

5. West Java had been left out of the original Perum Perhutani because the province showed less potential for profitable forest exploitation than Central and East Java where 84 percent of the land designated for teak production was located. Teak produced in East and Central Java is the island's highest quality. Because of soil and climatic differences, teak grown in West Java is by and large harvested after forty years and priced far below teak grown in East or Central Java. After forty years, the teak in this region is more susceptible to disease (Sumitro 1985:11). West Java was added to the SFC in 1978 because its operation under the Forest Service was draining monies from the Development Budget, rather than contributing them. Given the SFC's success, due partially to the "more conducive" political/business atmosphere, the ministry believed West Java's forests could be better managed by the SFC.

6. While most of the forest lands of the Special Region of Yogyakarta are under the *Dinas Kehutanan* (Forest Service), the SFC has a regional planning office in the city of Yogyakarta, and a small local office that manages some production forest lands. The Dutch also had a special relationship to the forests in the territory still partly controlled by the sultan of Yogyakarta, and in some of the "sacred" forests belonging to the Sunan of Solo. The details of these agreements, however, are beyond the scope of this discussion.

7. Java's forest lands are managed by four institutions: the State Forestry Corporation (*Perum Perhutani*), the Forest Service (*Dinas Kehutanan*), the Directorate General of Nature Conservancy and Forest Protection (*PHPA*), and the Baduy traditional management region. The Baduy autonomously administer their forests under Baduy *adat* (customary) law. Located in Kabupaten Banten, the Baduy region in West Java has been accorded special status since the Dutch colonial period; see Iskandar 1985.

8. In 1984–85, when I conducted field research, the exchange rate averaged about Rp. 1,650 to the dollar. A kilo of medium-quality hulled rice cost approximately Rp. 225 in the marketplace.

9. "Sacred ideology" is Charles Barber's term. Barber's fieldwork in Java coincided with mine in 1985 and 1986, and many of our ideas on the SFC were developed in conversations in the field and the United States. Although we purposefully conducted separate analyses, some overlap is inevitable, given our common approach to the issues and our common experience and access to materials in Java; see Barber 1989.

10. The PKI has been outlawed since 1965; the DI/TII troops and the radical elements of the Masjumi party that backed DI/TII are also outlawed. Nonetheless, certain areas in Java are still considered "red" (tending toward a PKI or related type of ideology) or "green" (tending toward Muslim ideologies, and often supporting the PPP in the elections).

11. GOLKAR is an acronym from *Golongan Karya*, which translates as "func-

tional group." To rid itself of what are considered the bad or weak points of the previous political period, GOLKAR defines itself as "not a political party."

12. Kaufman (1967:178–79) discusses how these same attitudes and feelings are incorporated in the training of foresters in the U.S. Forest Service.

13. Basic Agrarian Law of 1960 and Basic Forestry Law no. 5, 1967.

14. Policy dictates that animals may not graze in forests aged ten years or under; in practice the limits vary from restrictions in forests aged five years or under to prohibition of grazing in all forest age-classes.

15. Some informants are paid in cash, some in favors such as first choice in selection of tumpang sari plots or preferred location in logging. Depending on the local circumstances, informants may be despised by their neighbors if they are found out. In some cases, informing is recognized (although disdained) as some people's manner of surviving.

16. This branch of the forest police was formed in 1962 by Keputusan Presiden 1962 no. 372. Until the advent of the New Order and more consolidated control of the forest lands, the PCK was largely ineffective. The political and ideological battles of the early 1960s tied their hands. Forest police often had to confront individuals in the military, the regular police, and powerful criminals (the "jagos" of the New Order) who cut teak in truckloads and openly drove out of the forest. Under the New Order, the common ideology of power is beginning to draw together the security forces of the state.

17. Possession of firearms in Indonesia, except for certain types of hunting guns, is restricted to members of the military, the national police, and forest police of mantri level or above.

18. These formulas, and the analysis of Javanese numerology based on birthdays, are described in the *Kitab Primbon: Betaljemur Adammakna* (1977).

19. Other instances of friction and action against the BRIMOB squads are described in chapter 7.

20. There are exceptions, however, which require interdepartmental negotiations and special permission. In Jember, for example, the SFC produces some coffee; it also cultivates some cloves in Central Java. When the plantation versus tree crops issue came up in the course of one Social Forestry planning session (September 1985), it was cited as the reason that the forest farmers could not be permitted to intercrop and have tenure over fruit or coffee trees on state forest lands. A legal advisor to the session pointed out that if the farmer owned the tree, the SFC would not be out of line with the law. More at issue were the questions of giving up the land on which those trees would be planted, and of the implications of tree tenure arrangements.

21. In teak forest districts, teak leaves are often the most common form of natural wrapping used in marketing; they are also used most frequently in wrapping or presenting food used in rituals. In other parts of the island, banana leaves are more commonly used.

22. This restriction applied to all forests until 1986, with the initiation of a pilot social forestry project allowing farmers to plant certain kinds of fruit trees. Nevertheless, the restrictions on species held even within this new program, so that the SFC's timber crops would not be shaded by broad-canopy fruit trees.

23. In mountain villages where labor opportunities in plantation or private agriculture are more numerous, foresters generally label labor conditions "in shortage" when other sectors offer higher wages to the laborers who might work as loggers for the SFC. Labor shortages are also blamed when forest lands slated for reforestation are so degraded that not even the poorest laborers are willing to work them in exchange for access to intercropping land.

24. In 1964 the Directorate General of Forestry was elevated to ministerial status for a brief period. In the initial years of Soeharto's government, it reverted to a Directorate General, but in 1981 it again became a ministry.

25. These characteristics qualify the SFC as a "state within a state" as Robison (1986) calls Pertamina, the Indonesian oil corporation.

26. In one working day, each chainsaw operator does the equivalent of ten man-days by manual sawyers (Hasanu 1983:134–37).

27. "Teak conversions" refers generally to any kind of processed teak: lumber, veneer, parquet, doors, or furniture. The SFC produces only simple teak conversations, including the first four listed here. Note that the SFC monopoly on teak marketing extends only to raw logs.

28. Robison (1986) reports that 60 percent of the capital invested in Indonesia is from domestic sources.

29. Those in Gresik, Surabaya, and Madiun. Three others are in Cepu, Randublatung, and Jatirogo. Only Randublatung is a village.

30. Age-class, as used here, refers to the management system used for the aggregation of trees by age. Teak, for example, currently has an eighty-year rotation period, and is divided into 8 ten-year age classes. Based on this system, every year one-eightieth of the teak forest is slated for harvest, or in every decade one-tenth of the forest is supposed to be cut and reforested. Age-classes 9–12 are either old-growth plantations or natural growth. These tracts were not cut sooner because of remote location or other managerial considerations.

31. Recently, the SFC has changed the projected age of harvest for some teak plantations from eighty to forty or sixty years. These shorter-rotation forest districts tend to be younger stands, and those most heavily damaged during the war and postwar periods. In general, they only produce 10–20 percent the volume of the province's biggest producers (PERSAKI 1985).

32. Thinnings in age-classes 3–4 have some economic value, but compared to the value of other age-classes their value is minimal.

33. Forest land is kept under taungya for two to three years, and 20 percent of productive teak land is in age-class 1. Given the repeated reforestation of many areas, an estimated 6–10 percent of productive teak forest land is controlled by reforestation laborers.

34. In some nonteak forests where soils are good for agriculture, reforestation land has been controlled by absentee owners (SFT 1985; Peluso 1986).

35. *Cemplongan* is planting by wage labor, where the laborer does not get access to forest land for intercropping but is paid a wage for each task he or she performs. Piecework tasks include clearing underbrush, digging the holes, transporting, and planting seedlings. Because agricultural crops are not planted between the trees, weeds are a major problem in cemplongan reforestation areas.

Laborers are paid once a year for two years to clear the undergrowth, but many seedlings are choked.

36. Forest locales with good soil where tumpang sari labor is in shortage are rare, although I spent a week at one in March 1987. Near the coast and surrounded by small industries, the forest lands are overrun with thick secondary growth. According to the local mantri, just to clear and plant a quarter-hectare plot in the first year of cultivation required an investment of some Rp. 150,000— all of which was paid for by the farmer. This advance capital requirement deters some people who would like to participate.

37. The term is also a play on words, like many acronyms. In Indonesian *malu* means "shy," "embarrassed," or "shame."

38. But military affiliation was no guarantee of cooperation. Foresters in Cepu, Bojonegoro, and Tuban all gave examples of security difficulties in villages where a former ABRI village leader was either directly involved in the black market for teak or protecting other villagers involved.

CHAPTER 6
A Forest Without Trees

1. RPH = *Resort Polisi Hutan,* as defined earlier, "Forest Police Resort." I refer to Kaliaman forest lands as "Kaliaman forest" or RPH Kaliaman. Kaliaman is a pseudonym, but the Kabupaten (Brebes) and the KPH (Pekalongan Barat) names have not been changed.

2. Kaliaman suffered an unusually long dry season in 1981–82.

3. The terms "rainfed" and "simple irrigation" are often misleading. The Indonesian government uses these terms to indicate that the sawah has not been "technically" irrigated, meaning that state-sponsored or large-scale irrigation works have not been constructed. "Rainfed" is used sometimes pejoratively, to indicate the speaker's low opinion of the simple irrigation system and to imply the backwardness of the construction compared to the technical superiority of the state. Landowners, however, also have an interest in maintaining that their land is classified rainfed—to prevent the taxes from going up.

4. Including 21 hectares of salary lands for officials.

5. The first three of these are included in the village record's "other" category. The fourth is the former plantation land discussed above.

6. The exception is Stoler (1975), who did a now classic study of the economic value of home gardens to poor households in a wet-rice producing district.

7. Hunink and Stoffers (1984) differentiate three types of tegalan: (1) "fields," on which food or other crops are grown exclusively, (2) "mixed gardens," on which food crops are mixed with tree crops and the former cover more than 50 percent of the land, and (3) "forest gardens," on which tree crops predominate. All three categories were found in Kalianjat. Both the Commissie voor het Adatrecht (1911, 2:96–97) and Bergsma (1880:75–76) listed various local terms for the types of land called "tegalan" and "pekarangan."

8. Many villagers expressed the areas of their land in units called *wadrad.* We were given several explanations of the actual size of a wadrad. The most logical,

given the data and what we had learned from our experience with certain sample households' landholdings, was the explanation given by the hamlet head. He claimed a wadrad was a square 4 meters by 4 meters. Another villager said that the word had been locally altered from a Dutch term *kwadrant*, meaning "quadrant," similar to the Dutch word for square, *kwadraat*. Short of measuring every plot of land in the sample, it is impossible to know for sure. Some inaccuracy in the figures presented is thus expected.

9. Table 6.3 includes 2.5 hectares of persil land.

10. The Indonesian government classifies anyone with less than 0.10 hectares of land as landless.

11. Parents and their married children living in the same house but cooking rice separately are counted by Indonesian census-takers as two households (*soma*).

12. We heard of only two cases in parts of the village not selected for quantitative data collection where sharecropping arrangements had been made between nonrelatives.

13. The lurah rents out 10 hectares of dry land for Rp. 10,000 a year. Although the lurah's term is only eight years, he has rented the land out for ten years.

14. In past and present development efforts, both these terms were used to refer to labor performed for the good of the community, even though *kerja bakti* refers back to the village services performed under the feudalistic system in colonial and precolonial Java. But where it could be argued that construction of a roadway, a meeting hall, or the preparations for a village feast performed in the spirit of mutual cooperation benefited most everyone, the voluntary activities required by the foresters do not "benefit" the forest farmers, and the farmers know this. In general, volunteer forest labor is for constructing things that help the foresters control the forest territory and people, such as shelters, supervising paths, and guardhouses.

15. The term "man-days" is used where male labor is specifically meant. Where both male and female labor is meant, the term "person-days" is used. Women generally take more time to clear and hoe land. Some women interviewed hire men or work with their sons clearing and hoeing; some do only the second, refining, hoeing of a field; others do the whole job themselves.

16. Whereas in the teak belt of eastern Central Java and western East Java, collection and sale of teak leaves is a common female occupation, generally without stigma.

17. Men and women carry loads differently. A pikul as used here refers to the shoulder-pole (yoke) on which ropes are hung on both ends, allowing the carrier—a man—to carry a double load. A gendong is carried by women on their backs. A pikul usually allows the carrier to carry burdens of greater weight than does the gendong, but because of the great bulk of teak leaf bundles, the need to prevent them ripping (a whole leaf is one wrapper), and the difficulties of carrying these by pikul, gendongs of teak leaves are both bulkier and heavier.

18. Petty traders are usually women as in most of Central Java; among the Sundanese of West Java, men are usually the traders.

19. Corn-rice (*sega jagung*) used to be made more frequently by Kalianjat villagers, but has largely been replaced by dry-field or paddy rice. Villagers said making the corn into rice-shaped kernels required too much work and takes too much fuel.

20. I tend to think that the "lurahs" that people refer to were powerful local leaders—*jagos* or patrons—who controlled people through magic, charismatic personalities, the ability to fight, and perhaps their connections to other villages, like wet-rice villages, where people needed to rent cattle from the Kalianjat people. The nature of the village's precolonial relationship to the principalities is not clear.

21. At the same time, the writers of the *Adatrechtbundels* (Commissie voor het Adatrecht 1911:97) recommended that the state select the village lands to be exchanged for forest consolidation in accordance with the current use rights and clearing rights.

22. At the time of the survey (1867–1869), Brebes was part of Tegal Residency.

23. Originally conceived of as the amount of land one man and his family could cultivate or "shoulder" (*bau* literally means "shoulder"), the bau is today considered 0.7 hectares of land. Older villagers occasionally still use this in referring to land areas, but official measures are now cited in hectares.

24. Tumpeng is a mountain of rice, while lipet and ketupat are various forms of rice wrapped in leaves and steamed.

25. Transfer-of-ownership rules were hardly followed in cases of inheritance and some sales, however. To avoid the inevitable fee, people just remembered the division of lands among heirs and paid the village secretary for their shares. Village land registries all over Java still contain the names of long-dead original landowners.

26. The following papers were found in the name of Mr. Van de Laar at the Kantor Agraria Brebes: Akte Pemilikan (Act of Ownership) 13 September 1939, Persil 393 Ledoek, 86 hectares, returned 24 November 1966, certificate of measurement 23-8-1890; Persil 500 Kali soeren, certificate of measurement 13-8-1892 no. 60, 95 hectares, 6868 m², Akte Pemilikan 15 September 1939 no. 283; authorization 10-12-1899 no. 45, certificate of measurement 23-8-1890 no. 137; Persil 436 Kali Teloe, 239 hectares, 2550 m², returned 15-9-70; certificate of measurement 4 December 1893 no. 59; Cadastre form no. 31 [for all three parcels]. Although the forms stated dates returned, these are only the formal dates on which the land was registered as returned. Since the beginning of the war, the plantation land was left idle. Part of it, where secondary forest began to regenerate, was occupied by DI.

27. Villagers tell of their former neighbors whose bellies were slit up the middle, who were stretched between trees bordering the paths where they lived, whose throats were cut, or who were tied to railroad tracks minutes before the arrival of a train.

28. This "voluntary" planting may have been the result of PKI and PNI influence in P.N. Perhutani. People today call it *jaman jati sukarela*, literally meaning, "the voluntary teak time."

29. Some people from other villages around Kaliaman forest, however, continued to graze large livestock in the forest.

30. This district was first called "Bumiayu Forest District" but its name was changed to West Pekalongan Forest District after a few years.

31. Interviewed October 1985.

CHAPTER SEVEN
Teak and Temptation

1. My assistants and I lived in villages in the forest districts of Pati and Cepu. I also visited Blora, Bojonegoro, Tuban, and Randublatung forest districts and spoke at length with forest villagers, forest farmers, pesanggem, and foresters at various levels of district administration.

2. This accounts for 44 percent of the total agricultural land.

3. These and other statistics (except those I calculate in the text or the notes) are taken from Kabupaten Blora 1982.

4. Cf. Sayogyo's calculation of 22 kilograms of rice per capita per month to meet basic needs. This means some would be consumed, some sold to purchase others foods. A family of five would need nearly 4 kilograms of rice per day, most of which would be cooked, to remain above this nutritional poverty line.

5. Even if the full one-eightieth of the forest lands supposed to be under reforestation are included in the total agricultural land, the percentage represented by tumpang sari land is still less than 1 percent of the total.

6. Tanah bengkok are offically village lands given to the village officials in lieu of a monetary salary. Most, but not all, villages have them.

7. As of 1988 magersaren were phased out of the SFC program.

8. In either case, forests are generally cut down in the Outer Islands to accommodate transmigrants.

9. Recall the blandongs of the nineteenth century: those coming from farthest away were given rice and salt rations.

10. Javanese women are considered better money managers than men and are usually in charge of the household finances (Geertz 1961).

11. According to population statistics in Kabupaten Blora (1982:24), 49 percent of the population was between the ages of 15 and 49 in 1982.

12. Some mandors or mantris try to increase their interest by demanding money from anyone building a new house. One villager claimed a mandor asked him for Rp. 50,000 when he started building his house, a kind of unofficial building permit. This would have nicely augmented the mandor's Rp. 225,000 monthly salary. In this case, the villager was asked by a mandor in a neighboring territory rather than the one in his own. The mandor in his own district simply turned a blind eye to the construction. When the villager refused to pay the mandor, the mandor insisted he sign a piece of paper saying he was building a new house. If he needed to, the mandor said, he would make use of the document to prove the villager was building a house without permission.

13. This type of power alliance is not limited to coercion at the village level; Robison (1986) documents its emergence at the national and provincial levels.

14. The mysterious killings (*penembakan misterius* or *Petrus*) took place from about 1982 to 1984 and were carried out by government-sponsored death squads, partially in response to the complaints of the middle and upper classes affected by the rising petty crime rates.

15. One could argue that the ultimate quality of *halus* ("refined") was never meant to apply to villagers, but only to the residents of the court cities and the servants or families of the nobles. Close to the court cities of Yogyakarta and Solo, however, the description "halus" is accurately applied to many villagers.

16. For a detailed discussion of the procedures by which arrests for forest crimes are made and brought to trial, see Barber 1989.

17. Cf. Kaufman 1967.

18. See Hart 1986:43.

19. These elections are held under surveillance and often tight controls. As a result, upper-level officials can impede the chances of candidates who seem unwilling to bend in the direction of the state. See Ward 1974:176–91; Hart 1986:42–43; Pemberton 1986.

20. In some villages, however, villagers distrust the village head, and their opposition may include efforts to unseat him.

CHAPTER EIGHT
Toward Integrated Social Forestry

1. The Java social forestry program discussed here, for example, was limited from the outset to the most degraded forest lands, many of which had no physical hope of being returned to any kind of forest cover, let alone to teak production.

2. For details of the project and its development, see Barber 1989; Peluso and Poffenberger 1989.

3. The traditional forestry viewpoint that trees prevent erosion and regulate water more efficiently than other vegetative covers has recently been challenged by the work of Hamilton and King (1983).

4. The following discussion is influenced by Wood (1979), who offers a similar comparison concerning the participation of peasants and farmers in agricultural projects in India.

5. One attempt at involving rural people in log transport in the teak forest has been attempted, but the operation is dominated by the village's lurah and his cronies (Radite 1985).

REFERENCES

A NOTE ON SOURCES

In addition to the published references listed below, I consulted the following colonial reports: Koloniaal Verslagen, 1849–1902 (multiple issues); Verslagen van den Dienst van het Boschwezen in Nederlandsche-Indie over het jaar 1921–22, 1927, 1929, 1933–36, 1938–39 (five volumes); Verslagen van den Dienst van het Boschwezen in Nederlandsche-Indie 1903–39 (multiple volumes); and Verslag van den Dienst van het Boschwezen in Indonesie 1940–46. I also consulted the newspapers *Harian Rakyat, Harian Benteng,* and *Kompas.*

PUBLISHED REFERENCES

Adas, Michael
    1981   From avoidance to confrontation: Peasant protest in precolonial and colonial Southeast Asia. *Comparative Studies in Society and History* 23:3:217–47.

Adicondro, George
    1979   The jungles are awakening. *Impact* (September): 310–15.

Altona, T.
    1922   Djati en Hindoes: Oorsprong van het djatibosch in Bodjonegoro. *Tectona* 15:457–507.
    1923   Djati en Hindoes (Oorsprong van Tectona grandis op Java)— vervolg. *Tectona* 16:237–63.

Anderson, Benedict R. O'G.
    1963   The Javanese concept of power. In *Culture and Politics in Indonesia,* ed. Claire Holt, pp. 1–70. Ithaca, N.Y.: Cornell University Press.
    1972   *Java in a Time of Revolution.* Ithaca, N.Y.: Cornell University Press.
    1975   Millenarianism and the Saminist movement. In *Religion and Social*

Ethos in Indonesia, ed. James Mackie. Clayton, Victoria: Monash University.

1983   Old state, new society: Indonesia's New Order in comparative historical perspective. *Journal of Asian Studies* 42:3 (May): 477–96.

Anderson, Benedict R. O'G., and Ruth McVey

1971   *A Preliminary Analysis of the October 1, 1965 Coup in Indonesia.* Ithaca, N.Y.: Cornell Modern Indonesia Project.

Barber, Charles

1989   State, People and the Environment: The Case of Forests in Java. PhD dissertation, University of California.

Beck, H. J. L.

1923   De houtvoorziening uit de wildhoutbosschen op Java. *Tectona* 16:411–34.

Becking, J. H.

1926   De houtvoorziening van de inlandsche bevolking. *Tectona* 19: 904–13

1946   De wederopbouw van den Dienst van het Boschwezen in Indonesie. *Tectona* 36:86–161.

Benda, Harry J.

1956   *The Crescent and the Rising Sun.* The Hague: Van Hoeve.

Benda, Harry J., and Lance Castles

1969   The Samin movement. *Bijdragen tot de Taal-, Land- en Volkenkunde* 125:207–40.

Benda, Harry J., James K. Irikura, and Koichi Kishi (eds.)

1965   *Japanese Military Administration in Java: Selected Documents.* Southeast Asia Studies, Translation Series, no. 6. New Haven: Yale University.

Bergsma, W. S.

1880   Eindresume van het bij Gouvernementsbesluit dd. 10 Juli 1867, No. 2, Bevolen Onderzoek Naar de Rechten van den Inlander op den Grond op Java en Madoera. Vol. 2. Batavia: Ernst & Co. and Landsdrukkerij.

Billah, M. M., L. Widjajanto, and A. Kristyanto

1982   Segi Penguasaan Tanah dan Dinamika Sosial di Pedesaan Jawa (Tengah). In *Dua Abad Penguasaan Tanah: Pola Penguasaan Tanah Pertanian di Jawa dari Masa ke Masa,* eds. Sediono M. P. Tjondronegoro and Gunawan Wiradi, pp. 250–86. Jakarta: PT Gramedia.

BPS (Biro Pusat Statistik)

n.d.   *Pocketbook of Statistics for Indonesia, 1958–1967.* Jakarta: Biro Pusat Statistik.

1981   *Statistik Indonesia, 1980–81.* Jakarta: Biro Pusat Statistik.

1988   *Statistik Indonesia, 1988.* Jakarta: Biro Pusat Statistik.

BKPH Statistics

1986   Extrak Risalah Hutan RPH [Kaliaman] 1983–1985. Typescript.

Blaikie, Piers

1985   *The Political Economy of Soil Erosion in Developing Countries.* London: Longman.

Bloch, Marc
1966   *French Rural History: An Essay on Its Basic Characteristics.* Berkeley: University of California Press.
Boomgaard, Peter
1987   Forests and Forestry in Colonial Java, 1677–1942. Paper presented at the Conference on the Environmental History of the Pacific, Canberra, Australia.
De boschpolitie op Java onder het binnenlands bestuur
1923   *Tectona* 16:163–69.
Boxer, C. R.
1965   *The Dutch Seaborne Empire, 1600–1800.* New York: Alfred A. Knopf.
Brascamp, E. H. B.
1917   Hoe Daendels Boschgangers behandelde, die hunnen plicht niet vervulden. *Tectona* 10:207–8. (Reprint of article from *Bataviasche Koloniale Courant* van Vrijdag den 10den van Oogstmaand 1810, no. 32.)
1920   Houtleveranties onder de Oost Indische Compagnie I. Stichting van een comptoir te Japara en de opperkoopman Dirk Schouten als eerste Resident in 1651. *Tijdschrijft voor Indische Taal- Land- Volkenkunde* 59:5:432–70.
1921a   Houtleveranties onder de Oost Indische Compagnie IV. Houtleveranties te Japara onder den Resident B. Volsch in het jaar 1652. *Tijdschrijft voor Indische Taal- Land- Volkenkunde* 60:144–60.
1921b   Houtleveranties onder de Oost Indische Compagnie V. Rijckloff van Goens als ambassadeur naar den Soesoehoenan van Mataram om vrijen uitvoer van houtwerken te bekomen in het jaar 1652. *Tijdschrijft voor Indische Taal- Land- Volkenkunde* 60:345–72.
1922a   Houtleveranties onder de Oost Indische Compagnie VI. De instelling van vaste houtcontingenten in het contract van 8 November 1733 met den Soesoehoenan. *Tijdschrijft voor Indische Taal- Land- Volkenkunde* 61:131–49.
1922b   [Untitled.] *Tijdschrijft voor Indische Taal- Land- Volkenkunde* 61:150–79.
1922c   Regeling van het Indische boschbeheer in 1865 bij de wet. *Tectona* 15:1095–1110.
1923   Het contract met den Soesoehoenan van 5 October 1705 en de Houtleverantie. *Tectona* 16:636–42.
1924a   De eerste regeling van den houtaankap in de Preanger van 1684. *Tectona* 17:907–15.
1924b   De bosschen in het Kolonial Verslag van 1849. *Tectona* 17:916–23.
Braudel, Fernand
1972   History and the social sciences. In *Economy and Society in Early Modern Europe: Essays from ANNALES,* ed. Peter Burke. New York: Harper & Row.

Breman, Jan
1980   The village on Java and the early-colonial state. Rotterdam: The
            Comparative Asian Studies Programme at Erasmus University.
            Published in 1988 in the *Journal of Peasant Studies.*
Bunker, Stephen
1985   *Underdeveloping the Amazon: Extraction, Unequal Exchange, and the
            Failure of the Modern State.* Urbana: University of Illinois Press.
Cernea, Michael M.
1985   *Units of Social Organization Sustaining Alternative Forestry Development
            Strategies.* Washington, D.C.: Agriculture and Rural Development
            Department, The World Bank.
Chambers, Robert
1983   Concept and issues paper: People and common property resources
            in land. Paper prepared for Ford Foundation Staff Meeting, Cairo,
            May 9–13.
Chen Zhimin
1981   State wildland rights consolidate the responsibility system. *Chinese
            Forestry* (May). Translated by Nick Menzies.
Cohen, John, Gladys Culagovski, Norman Uphoff, and Diane Wolf
1979   *Participation at the Local Level: A Working Bibliography.* Ithaca, N.Y.:
            Cornell University Rural Development Committee.
Cohen, Stanley
1986   Bandits, rebels, or criminals: African history and Western crimi-
            nology. *Africa* 56:4:468–83.
Colfer, Carol J. Pierce
1983   Change and indigenous agroforestry in East Kalimantan. *Borneo
            Research Bulletin* 13:2:75–85.
Commissie voor het Adatrecht (comp.)
1911   *Adatrechtbundels I, II, III.* The Hague: Martinus Nijhoff.
Cordes, J. W. H.
1881   *De Djati-bosschen op Java; hunne natuur, verspreiding, geschedenis en
            exploitatie.* Batavia: Ogilvie & Co.
Crouch, Harold
1973   Another look at the Indonesian "coup." *Indonesia* no. 15 (April):
            1–20.
Crummey, Donald
1986   *Banditry, Rebellion, and Social Protest in Africa.* London: J. Currey;
            Portsmouth, N.H.: Heinemann.
Dagh Register
1631, 1643, 1679, 1680, 1681
            Dagh-Register gehouden int Casteel Batavia vant passerende
            daer ter plaetse als over geheel Nederlandts India. (door F. de
            Haan.) Batavia: Landsdrukkerij; The Hague: Martinus Nijhoff.
Dana, Samuel T., and Sally K. Fairfax
1980   *Forest and Range Policy, Its Development in the United States.* New
            York: McGraw-Hill.

de Janvry, Alain
  1981   *The Agrarian Question and Reformism in Latin America.* Baltimore
           and London: Johns Hopkins Press.
Departemen Kehutanan
  1986   *Sejarah Kehutanan Indonesia.* 2 vols. Jakarta: Menteri Kehutanan.
Departemen Pertanian Indonesia
  1968   *Statistik Kehutanan Indonesia.* Jakarta: Departemen Pertanian.
  1973   *Statistik Kehutanan Indonesia.* Jakarta: Departemen Pertanian.
Departement van Landbouw, Nijverheid en Handel
  1911–1929 Jaarboek van het Departement van Landbouw, Nijverheid en
           Handel in Nederlandsch-Indie. Weltevreden: Landsdrukkerij.
Dienst van het Boschwezen
  1903–1936 *Verslag van den Dienst van het Boschwezen in Nederlandsch-Indie over
           het jaren 1903–1936.* Weltevreden, Batavia: Landsdrukkerij.
  1948   *Verslag van den Dienst van het Boschwezen in Indonesie over de Periode
           1940 t/m 1946.* Buitenzorg: Archipel Drukkerij.
Direcktorat Djendral Kehutanan
  1968   *Statistik 1968.* Jakarta: Perusahaan Kehutanan Negara, Perhutani.
Djamali Asikin, and Zulfi R. Pohan
  1985   Studi kasus Social Forestry di Mayangan, Pamanukan, Jawa Barat.
           In *Studi Kasus Social Forestry Berbagai Aspek Tentang Hubungan In-
           teraksi Masyarakat Dengan Hutan di Jawa Barat,* ed. Tim Social For-
           estry Indonesia. Jakarta: Perum Perhutani dan Yayasan Ford.
Djokonomo Darmosoehardjo
  1985   *Pengamanan Hutan Perum Perhutani.* Jakarta: Perum Perhutani.
  1986   *Penguasaan Teritorial oleh Jajaran Perum Perhutani.* PHT 50–Seri
           Umum 23. Jakarta: Perum Perhutani.
Djuwadi
  1985   Hasil Penelitian Social Forestry di Desa Kemiriombo (BKPH
           Ngadisono-KPH Kedu Selatan). In *Studi Kasus Social Forestry Ber-
           bagai Aspek Tentang Hubungan Interaksi Masyarakat Dengan Hutan Di
           Jawa Tengah,* ed. Tim Social Forestry Indonesia. Jakarta: Perum
           Perhutani dan Yayasan Ford.
Dove, Michael R.
  1983   Theories of swidden agriculture and the political economy of
           ignorance. *Agroforestry Systems* 1:85–99.
  1984   Government versus peasant beliefs concerning Imperata and
           Eupatorium: A structual analysis of knowledge, myth, and agricul-
           tural ecology in Indonesia. Working Paper, Environment and Pol-
           icy Institute, East-West Center, Honolulu, Hawaii.
  1985   The agroecological mythology of the Javanese and the political
           economy of Indonesia. *Indonesia* no. 39 (April): 1–36.
  1986   *Swidden Agriculture in Indonesia.* Berlin: Mouton.
du Quesne van Bruchem, L. L. G.
  1938a   De bosschen der tegenwoordige houtvesterijen Kedoengdjati en
           Semarang in 1776 en in 1930. *Tectona* 31:821–38.

1938b   De bosschen van Mantingan ten noorden de Blorasche grens in 1776 en thans. *Tectona* 31:865–75.

1939   De djatibosschen der houtvesterij Pati in 1776 en thans. *Tectona* 32:91–107.

Elson, R. E.
1984   *Javanese Peasants and the Colonial Sugar Industry: Impact and Change in an East Java Residency, 1830–1940.* Southeast Asia Publications Series, vol. 9. Published for the Asian Studies Association of Australia by Oxford University Press.

Encyclopaedie van Nederlandsch-Indie
1918   2d ed. The Hague: Martinus Nijhoff; Leiden: N.V. v/h E. J. Brill.

Everts, F. E. C.
1933   Het djatibedrijf en de partikuliere handel. *Tectona* 26:268–70.

Fasseur, C.
1975   *Kultuurstelsel en Koloniale Baten: De Nederlandse Exploitatie van Java 1840–1860.* Leiden: Universitaire Pers. [2d ed., 1978.]

Fernow, Bernard
1911   *The History of Forestry.* 3d ed. Toronto: University Press.

Fortmann, Louise P.
1980   *Peasants, Officials and Participation in Rural Tanzania: Experience with Villagization and Decentralization.* Ithaca, N.Y.: Cornell University Rural Development Committee.

1989   Great planting disasters: Pitfalls in technical assistance in forestry. *Agricultural and Human Values* 5:1–2:49–60.

Fortmann, Louise P., and Sally K. Fairfax
1985   American forestry professionalism in the Third World: Some preliminary observations on effects. In *Women Creating Wealth: Transforming Economic Development,* ed. Rita S. Gallin and Anita Spring. Washington, D.C.: Association for Women in Development.

Fowler, George A., Roggie Cale, and Joe C. Bartlett
1974   *Java: A Garden Continuum.* Hong Kong: Amerasian.

Furnivall, J. S.
1944   *Netherlands India: A Study of Plural Economy.* Cambridge: Cambridge University Press; New York: Macmillan.

Gaventa, John
1980   *Power and Powerlessness: Quiescence and Rebellion in an Appalachian Valley.* Urbana: University of Illinois Press.

Geertz, Clifford
1963   *Agricultural Involution: The Processes of Ecological Change in Indonesia.* Association of Asian Studies Monographs and Papers, no. 11. Berkeley: University of California Press.

Geertz, Hildred
1961   *The Javanese Family: A Study of Kinship and Socialization.* New York: Free Press of Glencoe.

Glaser, Barney G., and Anselm L. Strauss
1967   *The Discovery of Grounded Theory: Strategies for Qualitative Research.*
          Chicago: Aldine.
Goffman, Erving
1959   *The Presentation of Self in Everyday Life.* New York: Doubleday.
GOI/IIED (Government of Indonesia and International Institute for
Environment and Development)
1985a   Government Regulations concerning Perum Perhutani. Trans-
          lated by the Government of Indonesia and the International Insti-
          tute for Environment and Development Policy Review Team. Ja-
          karta. Typescript.
1985b   Report on Phase I of "A review of policies affecting the sustain-
          able development of forest lands in Indonesia." Jakarta.
Graff, G. S. de
1899   Moeten zoveel mogelijk alle Djatibosschen blijven bestaan? *De
          Indische Gids* 21:908–18.
Guha, Ramachandra
1985   Scientific forestry and social change in Uttarakhand. *Economic and
          Political Weekly* 20 (November): 1939–52.
1990   *The Unquiet Woods: Ecological Change and Peasant Resistance in the
          Indian Himalaya.* Berkeley: University of California Press.
Haan, Frederick de
1910–12   *Preangan: De Preangan Regentschappen onder het Nederlandsch Bes-
          tuur tot 1811.* 4 vols. Batavia: G. Kloft.
Hafner, James A.
1990   Forces and policy issues affecting forest use in Northeast Thai-
          land 1900–1985. In *Keepers of the Forest: Land Management Alterna-
          tives in Southeast Asia,* ed. Mark Poffenberger, pp. 69–74. West
          Hartford, Conn.: Kumarian Press.
Hamilton, Lawrence, and Peter N. King
1983   *Tropical Forested Watersheds: Hydrologic and Soils Response to Major
          Uses or Conversions.* Boulder, Colo.: Westview Press.
Hart, Gillian
1986   *Power, Labor, and Livelihood.* Berkeley: University of California
          Press.
Hasanu Simon
1983   Analysis "interrelationship" antara pembangunan kehutanan den-
          gan pembangunan masyarakat desa. Master's thesis, Gadjah Mada
          University, Yogykarta.
Hatley, Ron, Jim Schiller, Anton Lucas, and Barbara Martin-Schiller
1984   *Other Javas away from the Kraton.* Clayton, Victoria: Monash Univer-
          sity.
Hay, Douglas
1975a   Property, authority and the criminal law. In *Albion's Fatal Tree:
          Crime and Society in Eighteenth-Century England,* ed. Douglas Hay,

Peter Linebaugh, John G. Rule, E. P. Thompson, and Cal Winslow, pp. 17–64. New York: Pantheon

1975b Poaching and the game laws on Cannock Chase. In *Albion's Fatal Tree: Crime and Society in Eighteenth-Century England*, ed. Douglas Hay, Peter Linebaugh, John G. Rule, E. P. Thompson, and Cal Winslow, pp. 189–254. New York: Pantheon.

Het gouvernement en de djatibosschen in Soerakarta
1917 *Tectona* 10:697–98.

Hindley, Donald
1967 *The Communist Party of Indonesia*. Berkeley: University of California Press.

Hobsbawm, Eric J.
1959 *Primitive Rebels: Studies in Archaic Forms of Social Movement in the 19th and 20th Centuries*. Manchester, Eng.: University Press.

Holleman, J. F. (ed.)
1981 *Van Vollenhoven on Indonesian Adat Law: Selections from "Het Adatrecht van Nederlandsch-Indie Vol. I, 1918; Vol. II, 1931."* The Hague: Martinus Nijhoff.

Humphrey, C. R., and F. Buttel
1982 *Environment, Energy, and Society*. Belmont, Calif.: Wadsworth.

Hunink, R. B. M., and J. W. Stoffers
1984 Mixed and forest gardens on Central Java: An analysis of socioeconomic factors influencing the choice between different types of landuse. Working Paper, Geografisch Instituut. Utrecht: Rijksuniversiteit.

Irwin, Graham
1967 *Nineteenth-Century Borneo: A Study in Diplomatic Rivalry*. Singapore: Donald Moore Books.

Iskandar, Johan
1985 Hasil Penelitian Social Forestry di Daerah Baduy, Banten Selatan, Jawa Barat. In *Studi Kasus Social Forestry Berbagai Aspek Tentang Hubungan Interaksi Masyarakat Dengan Hutan Di Jawa Barat*, ed. Tim Social Forestry Indonesia. Jakarta: Perum Perhutani dan Yayasan Ford.

Ives, Edward D.
1988 *George Magoon and the Down-East Game War: History, Folklore, and the Law*. Urbana: University of Illinois Press.

Jasper, J. E.
1918 *Verslag betreffende het onderzoek in zake de Saminbeweging ingesteld ingevolge het Gouvernements Besluit van 1 Juni 1917, Nr 20. (The Jasper Report)*. Batavia: Landsdrukkerij.

Jawatan Kehutanan Indonesia
1956 Laporan Jawatan Kehutanan. Jakarta: Jawatan Kehutanan.

Jessup, Timothy C.
1980 Report on forest-cutting activities of the Apo Kayan Kenyah in Sungai Barang, East Kalimantan, Indonesia. Typescript.

1989   Minor Forest Products in the Apo Kayan: History, Trade, and Ecology. Draft of PhD dissertation, Rutgers University.

Jonge, J. K. J. de, and M. L. van Deventer
1863   *De Opkomst van het Nederlandsch gezag in Oost-Indie. Verzameling van onuitgegeven stukken uit het Oud-koloniaal archief.* Vol. 2. The Hague.

Junus Kartasubrata
1985   Forest policy, legislation, and administration in Indonesia. *Nederlands Bosbouw Tijdschrift.*

Kabupaten Blora
1982   *Kabupaten Blora dalam Angka: 1982.* Blora, Indonesia: Kantor Statistik.

Kahin, George McT.
1952   *Nationalism and Revolution in Indonesia.* Ithaca, N.Y.: Cornell University Press.

Kano, Hiroyoshi
1982   Sistem Pemilikan Tanah dan Masyarakat Desa di Jawa pada Abad XIX. In *Dua Abad Penguasaan Tanah: Pola Penguasaan Tanah Pertanian di Jawa dari Masa ke Masa,* pp. 26–85. Jakarta: PT Gramedia.

Kantor Agraria Brebes
1939   Arsip-arsip tanah erfpacht Desa Kalinoesoeh, District Boemiayu, Regenschap Brebes, Residensie Pekalongan.

Kartawinata, Kuswata
1977   A report on a study of floristic, faunistic, and other ecological changes in the lowland rainforest after destruction by man in East Kalimantan. In *Transactions of MAB-IUFRO Workshop on Tropical Rainforest Research,* ed. E. F. Brunig. Chair of World Forestry Special Report No. 1. Hamburg.

Kaufman, Herbert
1956   Emerging conflicts in the doctrines of Public Administration. *American Political Science Review:* 1057–73.
1967   *The Forest Ranger: A Study in Administrative Behavior.* Baltimore: John Hopkins Press.

Kerbert, H.J.
1919   Geschiedkundig overzicht van de houtvervreemdingspolitiek op Java. *Tectona* 12:603–70.

Kerkvliet, Benedict J. Tria
1990   *Everyday Politics in the Philippines.* Berkeley: University of California Press.

King, Victor T.
1973   Some observations on the Samin movement of North-Central Java. *Bijdragen tot de Taal-, Land- en Volkenkunde:*129:457–81.

Kitab Primbon Betaljemur Adammakna
1977   Yogyakarta: Soemodidjojo Mahadewa.

Korten, David, and Norman Uphoff
1981   Bureaucratic Reorientation for Participatory Rural Development. NASPAA Working Paper No. 1. NASPAA and USAID.

KPH Cepu
   1983a   Laporan Hasil Kerja KPH Cepu. District report. Cepu: Perum
              Perhutani Unit 1.
   1983b   RPKH Cepu. Subdistrict report. Cepu: Perum Perhutani Unit 1.
KPH Pekalongan Barat
   1985   *Tarip Upah Tahun 1985*. Slawi: KPH Pekalongan Barat.
Kumar, Ann
   1980   The peasantry and the state in nineteenth-century Java. In *Indone-
              sia: The Making of a Nation*, ed. J. C. Mackie. Canberra: Australian
              National University Press.
Lombard, Denys
   1974   La vision de la forêt à Java (Indonesie). *Etudes Rurales* 53–54–55–
              56 (Jan.–Dec.): 473–85.
Lugt, Ch. S.
   1933   *Het Boschbeheer in Nederlandsche Indie*. Oonze Koloniale Landbouw
              (series), ed. J. Dekker. Haarlem: H.D. Tjeenk Willingk & Zoon
              N.V.
McVey, Ruth
   1965   *The Rise in Indonesian Communism*. Ithaca, N.Y.: Cornell University
              Press.
   1982   The Beamtenstaat in Indonesia (1977). In *Interpreting Indonesian
              Politics: Thirteen Contributions to the Debate*, ed. Benedict Anderson
              and Audrey Kahin. Ithaca, N.Y.: Cornell Modern Indonesia Proj-
              ect.
Manning, Chris
   1971   The timber boom: With special reference to East Kalimantan.
              Bulletin of Indonesian Economic Studies 7:3 (November): 30–61.
Mantel, Kurt
   1964   History of the international science of forestry with special consid-
              eration of Central Europe: Literature, training, and research
              from the earliest beginnings to the nineteenth century. In *Interna-
              tional Review of Forestry Research*, Vol. 1, ed. John A. Romberger
              and Peitsa Mikola, pp. 1–37. New York: Academic Press.
Meiggs, Russell
   1982   *Trees and Timber in the Ancient Mediterranean World*. Oxford: Claren-
              don Press.
Mekvichai, Banasopit
   1988   The Teak Industry in Northern Thailand: The Role of a Natural-
              Resource-Based Export Economy in Regional Development. PhD
              dissertation, Cornell University.
Menzies, Nicholas Kay
   1988   300 years of Taungya: A study of long-term stability in an
              agroforestry system. *Human Ecology* 16:4:361–76.
Meyier, J. E. de
   1903   Het Boschwezen en de politie. *De Indische Gids* 25:1:709–15.

Mintz, Sidney W.
 1979   The rural proletariat and the problem of the rural proletarian
           consciousness. In *Peasants and Proletarians: The Struggles of Third
           World Workers,* ed. Robin Cohen, Peter C. W. Gutkind, and Phyllis
           Brazier. New York: Monthly Review Press.
Moertono, Soemarsaid
 1981   State and Statecraft in Old Java: A Study of the Later Mataram
           Period, 16th to 19th Century. Cornell Modern Indonesia Project
           Monograph Series (Publication No. 43). Ithaca, N.Y.: Cornell
           University.
Mortimer, Rex
 1972   *The Indonesian Communist Party and Land Reform, 1959–1965.* Clay-
           ton, Victoria: Centre of Southeast Asian Studies.
 1974   *Indonesian Communism Under Sukarno.* Ithaca, N.Y.: Cornell Univer-
           sity Press.
Myrdal, Gunnar, and Seth S. King
 1972   *Asian Drama: An Inquiry into the Poverty of Nations.* New York: Vin-
           tage Books.
Newby, Howard
 1975   The Deferential Dialectic. *Comparative Studies in Society and History*
           17:2 (April).
De nieuwe houtvervreemdingspolitiek
 1935   *Tectona* 28:73–78.
Onghokham
 1964   Saminisme: Tinjauan sosial-ekonomi dan kebudayaan pada gera-
           kan tani dari awal abad ke-20. Skripsi sarjana muda, Fakultas Seja-
           rah Indonesia, Universitas Indonesia, Jakarta.
 1975   The Residency of Madiun: Priyayi and Peasant in the Nineteenth
           Century. PhD dissertation, Yale University.
 1976   The inscrutable and the paranoid: An investigation into the
           sources of the Brotodiningrat affair. In *Southeast Asian Transitions:
           Voices from Social History,* ed. Ruth T. McVey. New Haven: Yale
           University Press.
Palte, Jan
 1983   *The Development of Java's Rural Uplands in Response to Population
           Growth.* Yogyakarta: Gadjah Mada University Press.
Peluso, Nancy Lee
 1983   Markets and merchants: The forest products trade of East Kali-
           mantan in historical perspective. Master's thesis, Cornell Univer-
           sity.
 1985   *Forest and People in Kalinusu, Central Java, or, "Border Issues": A
           Social Forestry Case Study.* Jakarta: Perum Perhutani and The Ford
           Foundation.
 1986   Overview report on social forestry research in Java. Prepared for
           The Ford Foundation, Jakarta, and Perum Perhutani.

1987   Social forestry in Java: Can it work? Consultant's report to the Ford Foundation, Jakarta and New York.

1988   Rich Forests, Poor People, and Development: Access Control and Resistance in Java. PhD dissertation, Cornell University.

Peluso, Nancy Lee, and Mark Poffenberger

1989   Social forestry on Java: Reorienting management systems. *Human Organization* 48:4:333–43.

Pelzer, Karl

1945   *Pioneer Settlements in the Asiatic Tropics.* New York: Pacific Institute.

1978   *Planter and Peasant: Colonial Policy and the Agrarian Struggle in East Sumatra, 1863–1947.* The Hague: Martinus Nijhoff.

1982   *Planter Against Peasant: The Agrarian Struggle in East Sumatra, 1947–1958.* The Hague: Martinus Nijhoff.

Pemberton, John

1986   Notes on the 1982 general election in Solo. *Indonesia* no. 41 (April): 1–23.

PERSAKI

1985   Pemugaran kawasan hutan Jawa Tengah. Paper prepared for PERSAKI Seminar. Semarang.

PERSAKI Cabang Jawa Tengah

1985a   Pemugaran kawasan hutan Jawa Tengah. Paper presented to PERSAKI Seminar in Madiun, March 2. Typescript.

1985b   Suatu Tinjauan Tentang Daur Jati di Jawa. In *Proceedings Seminar Daur Jati,* pp. 39–118. Yogyakarta: Persaki Cabang Yogyakarta.

Perum Perhutani

1981   *Memori Serah Terima Direksi Perum Perhutani.* Jakarta: Perum Perhutani.

1982   *Proceeding Lokakarya Pembangunan Masyarakat Desa Sekitar Hutan (PMDH), Yogyakarta, 29–31 March 1982.* Jakarta: Perum Perhutani.

1984   *Bosordonansi Jawa Madura 1927; Bosverordening Jawa Madura 1932; Undang-Undang No. 5 Tahun 1967.* Publication No. 1.199.287. Jakarta: Perum Perhutani.

1985   *Buku I: Materi Rapat.* Proceeding Rapat Paripurna Perum Perhutani Tahun 1984 (Jakarta, 13–15 December 1984). [Publication] No. 2.62.311. Jakarta: Perum Perhutani.

1986   *Perum Perhutani 1981–1985.* Jakarta: Perum Perhutani.

1987   *Memori Serah Terima Direksi Perum Perhutani, 1981–1987.* Jakarta: Perum Perhutani.

Perum Perhutani, Biro Perencanaan Unit I Jawa Tengah

1983   Potensi hutan jati Unit I Jateng. Salatiga: Biro Perencanaan. Typescript.

Perum Perhutani, Unit I

1983   *Buku Saku Statistik Unit I, 1979–1983.* Central Java: Perum Perhutani.

1984   Laporan Evaluasi Hasil Kerja Tahun 1984: Untuk Bahan Rapat

Paripuna Direksi. [Publication] No. 1.48.111. Semarang: Perum Perhutani Unit I Jawa Tengah.

Pigeaud, Theodore G. Th.
1962   *Java in the Fourteenth Century.* Vol. 4. The Hague: Martinus Nijhoff.

Pinchot, Gifford
1947   *Breaking New Ground.* New York: Harcourt, Brace.

Prastowo Hendro
1983   Peningkatan manfaat hutan dan pembangunan masyarakat lingkungan. Semarang. Typescript.

Prochaska, David
1986   Fire on the mountain: Resisting colonialism in Algeria. In *Banditry, Rebellion, and Social Protest in Africa*, ed. Donald Crummey, pp. 229–52. London: James Currey; Portsmouth, N.H.: Heinemann.

Radite, Djoko Suharno
1985   Hasil penelitian Social Forestry di Desa Tanggel (BKPH Tanggel-KPH Randublatung). In *Studi Kasus Social Forestry Berbagai Aspek Tentang Hubungan Interaksi Masyarakat Dengan Hutan Di Jawa Tengah,* ed. Tim Social Forestry Indonesia. Jakarta: Perum Perhutani dan Yayasan Ford.

Raffles, Thomas Stamford
1817   *The History of Java.* Vol. 1. Reprinted 1965, London: Oxford University Press.

Raintree, J. B.
1985   Agroforestry, tropical land use and tenure. Background paper for the International Consultative Workshop on Tenure Issues in Agroforestry, 27–31 May. Nairobi, Kenya.

Reber, Lindsay
1966   The Sulu world in the eighteenth and early nineteenth centuries: An historiographical problem in British writings on Malay piracy. Masters' thesis, Cornell University.

Reid, Anthony
1984   The precolonial economy of Indonesia. *Bulletin of Indonesian Economic Studies* 20:2 (August): 151–67.

Republik Indonesia
1989   *Nota Keuangan dan Rancangan Anggaran Pendapatan dan Belanja Negara Tahun 1988–1989.* Jakarta: Republik Indonesia.

Ricklefs, M. C.
1981   *A History of Modern Indonesia.* Bloomington: Indiana University Press.

Robison, Richard
1986   *Indonesia: The Rise of Capital.* Canberra: Asian Studies Association of Australia.

Romm, Jeff
1985   Developing models for effective analysis of forest policy. Paper prepared for conference on renewable resource problems in Asia, June 24–28. Sapporo, Japan.

Rush, James
    1983   Social control and influence in nineteenth century Indonesia:
                Opium farms and the Chinese in Java. *Indonesia* no. 35 (April):
                53–64.
Sartono Kartodirdjo
    1972   Agrarian radicalism in Java: Its setting and development. In *Cul-
                ture and Politics in Indonesia*, ed. Claire Holt. Ithaca, N.Y.: Cornell
                University Press.
    1973   *Protest Movements in Rural Java: A Study of Agrarian Unrest in the
                Nineteenth and Early Twentieth Centuries*. London: Oxford Univer-
                sity Press.
Schrieke, B. S.
    1957   *Indonesian Sociological Studies*. Vol. 2: *Ruler and Realm in Early Java*.
                The Hague.
Schuitemaker, J. P.
    1950   *Bos en Bosbeheer of Java*. Groningen: J.B. Wolters.
Scott, James C.
    1972   The erosion of patron-client bonds and social change in rural
                Southeast Asia. *Journal of Asian Studies* 23:1:5–37.
    1976   *The Moral Economy of the Peasant: Rebellion and Subsistence in South-
                east Asia*. New Haven: Yale University Press.
    1985   *Weapons of the Weak: Everyday Forms of Peasant Resistance*. New
                Haven: Yale University Press.
Scott, James C., and Benedict Kerkvliet
    1986   *Journal of Peasant Studies Special Issue on Everyday Forms of Peasant
                Resistance*.
Selznick, Phillip
    1966   *TVA and the Grass Roots*. New York: Harper & Row.
SFT (Social Forestry Team)
    1985   *Studi Kasus Social Forestry Berbagai Aspek Tengtan Hubungan Interaksi
                Masyarakat Dengan Hutan di Jawa Tengah dan Jawa Barat*. Jakarta:
                Perum Perhutani dengan Yayasan Ford.
Shannon, Thomas Richard
    1989   *An Introduction to the World System Perspective*. Boulder, Colo.: West-
                view Press.
Shiraishi, Takashi
    1989   *An Age in Motion: Java 1913–1926*. Ithaca, N.Y.: Cornell Univer-
                sity Press.
Shiva, Vandana, H. C. Sharatchandra, and J. Bandyopadhyay
    1982   Social forestry—No solution within the market. *The Ecologist*.
                2:4:158–68.
Skocpol, Theda
    1979   *States and Social Revolutions: A Comparative Analysis of France, Rus-
                sia, and China*. Cambridge: Cambridge University Press.
Soedarwono Hardjosoediro
    1979   Forestry under conditions of population pressure in Indonesia.

    In *Development Studies Center Monograph No. 17*. Canberra: Australian National University.

Soentoro, William L. Collier, and Kliwon Hidayat
1976 Land markets in rural Java. Village Studies Workshop, 26–27 August. Los Banos, Philippines. Typescript.

Soepardi, R.
1974a *Hutan dan Kehutanan Dalam Tiga Jaman*. Vol. 1. Jakarta: Perum Perhutani.
1974b *Hutan dan Kehutanan Dalam Tiga Jaman*. Vol. 2. Jakarta: Perum Perhutani.

Soesilo H. Prakoso
1953 Hutan dan Masyarakat. Rimba Indonesia 3:1–2:9–21 (excerpted from *Almanak Pertanian* 1953).

Stoler, Ann Laura
1975 Garden use and household economy in rural Java. *Bulletin of Indonesian Economic Studies* 14:2:85–101.
1985 *Capitalism and Confrontation in Sumatra's Plantation Belt, 1870–1979*. New Haven: Yale University Press.

Sumitro, Achmad
1985 Daur Ditinjau Kembali. In *Proceedings Seminar Daur Jati*, pp. 1–16. Yogyakarta: PERSAKI Cabang Jawa Tengah.

Sutherland, Heather
1979 The Making of a Bureaucratic Elite: The Colonial Transformation of the Javanese Priyayi. Southeast Asian Publications Series, Vol. 2. Singapore: Heinemann Educational Books for the Asian Studies Association of Australia.

Tarrant, James, et al.
1987 *Natural Resources and Environmental Management in Indonesia: An Overview*. Jakarta: United States Agency for International Development.

Taussig, Michael
1980 *The Devil and Commodity Fetishism in Latin America*. Chapel Hill: North Carolina University Press.

Teguh Purwanto
1985 Hasil penelitian Social Forestry di Desa Sukobubuk (BKPH Muria Patiayam-KPH Pati). In *Studi Kasus Social Forestry Berbagai Aspek Tentang Hubungan Interaksi Masytarakat Dengan Hutan Di Jawa Tengah*, ed. Tim Social Forestry Indonesia. Jakarta: Perum Perhutani dan Yayasan Ford.

The Siauw Giap
1967 The Samin and Samat movements in Java: Two examples of peasant resistance. (Part I). *Journal of South-east Asia and the Far-East* 2:303–10.
1968 The Samin and Samat movements in Java: Two examples of peasant resistance. (Part II). *Journal of South-east Asia and the Far-East* 1:107–13.

1969   The Samin movement in Java: Complimentary remarks. *Journal of South-east Asia and the Far-East* 1:63–79.

Thompson, Edward P.
1963   *The Making of the English Working Class.* London: Victor Gollancz Ltd.
1975a   The crime of anonymity. In *Albion's Fatal Tree: Crime and Society in Eighteenth-Century England,* ed. Douglas Hay, Peter Linebaugh, John G. Rule, E. P. Thompson, and Cal Winslow, pp. 255–344. New York: Pantheon.
1975b   *Whigs and Hunters: The Origins of the Black Act.* London: Allen Lane.

Tilly, Charles
1978   *From Mobilization to Revolution.* Reading, Mass.: Addison-Wesley Publishing Company.

Tilly, Charles, and Louise Tilly (eds.)
1981   *Class, Conflict, and Collective Action.* Beverly Hills, Calif.: Sage Publications

Tilly, Charles, Louise Tilly, and Richard Tilly
1975   *The Rebellious Century: 1830–1930.* Cambridge, Mass.: Harvard University Press.

Tinjauan Serikat Buruh Kehutanan
1949   Typescript.

Turton, Andrew
1986   Patrolling the middle ground: Methodological perspectives on "Everyday forms of resistance." *Journal of Peasant Studies* 13:2 (January): 36–49.

van der Chijs, J. A.
1891   *Nederlandsch Indisch Plakaatboek 1602–1811.* Vol. 8, 1765–1775. Batavia: Landsdrukkerij; The Hague: Martinus Nijhoff.
1896   *Nederlandsch Indisch Plakaatboek 1602–1811.* Vol. 15, 1808–1809. Batavia: Landsdrukkerij; The Hague: Martinus Nijhoff.

van der Kroef, Justus M.
1971   Interpretations of the 1965 Indonesian coup. *Pacific Affairs* 43:4.

van der Laan, E.
1933   Debat prae-advies, "Het Boschwezen als werkgever." *Tectona* 26: 317–20.

van Doorn, Z.
1932   Een stukje welvaartspolitiek in onze hand. *Tectona* 25:804–7.

van Laanen, J. T. M.
1980   *Changing Economy in Indonesia.* Vol. 6: *Money and Banking 1816– 1940.* Amsterdam: Royal Tropical Institute.

van Steenis, C. G. G. J.
1981   *Flora.* Jakarta: P.T. Pradnya Paramita.

Vayda, Andrew P.
1981   Research in East Kalimantan on "Interactions between people and forests": A preliminary report. *Borneo Research Bulletin* 13:1:3–15.

Vlekke, Bernard H. M.
1960   *Nusantara: A History of Indonesia.* Chicago: Quadrangle Books; The Hague: W. van Hoeve.

Wallerstein, Immanuel
1974   *The Modern World-System: Capitalist Agriculture and the Origins of the European World-Economy in the Sixteenth Century.* New York: Academic Press.

Ward, K.
1974   *The 1971 Elections in Indonesia: An East Java Case Study.* Monash: Centre for Southeast Asian Studies, Monash University.

Warren, James F.
1975   Trade, Raid, Slave: The Socioeconomic Patterns of the Sulu Zone, 1770–1898. PhD dissertation, Australian National University.

Watts, Michael J.
1983   *Silent Violence: Food, Famine and Peasantry in Northern Nigeria.* Berkeley: University of California Press.

Weber, Max
1978   *Economy and Society,* ed. Guenther Roth and Claus Wittich. Berkeley: University of California Press.

Wertheim, Willem F.
1956   *Indonesian Society in Transition: A Study of Social Change.* The Hague: W. van Hoeve.
1966   Indonesia before and after the Untung Coup. *Pacific Affairs* 39 (Spring–Summer).
1979   Whose plot?—New light on the 1965 events. *Journal of Contemporary Asia* 9:2:197–215.

Westoby, Jack
1987   *The Purpose of Forests: Follies of Development.* Oxford: Basil Blackwell.

Westra, J. G.
1933   Het djatibedrijf, de partikuliere handel en de consument van djatihout. *Tectona* 26:270–73.

White, Benjamin
1983   "Agricultural Involution" and its critics: Twenty years after. *Bulletin for Concerned Asian Scholars* 15 (April–June): 2:18–31.
1989   Agrarian and non–agrarian bases of inequality in nine Javanese villages. In *Agrarian Transformations: Local Processes and the State in Southeast Asia,* ed. Gillian Hart, Andrew Turton, Benjamin White with Brian Fegan and Lim Teck Ghee, pp. 266–302. Berkeley: University of California Press.

Whyte, William Foote
1983   Participatory approaches to agricultural research and development: A state-of-the-art paper. Special Series on Agriculture Research and Extension. Ithaca, N.Y.: Cornell University Rural Development Committee.

Winslow, Cal
1975 Sussex smugglers. In *Albion's Fatal Tree: Crime and Society in Eighteenth-Century England,* ed. Douglas Hay, Peter Linebaugh, John G. Rule, E. P. Thompson, and Cal Winslow, pp. 119–66. New York: Pantheon.

Wolf, Eric R.
1957 Closed corporate peasant communities in Mesoamerica and Central Java. *Southwestern Journal of Anthropology* 13:1:1–18.

Wood, Geof D.
1979 The access problem and class formation: Some reflections on the Kosi Development Region. Paper written for the "Post-fact Evaluation of a Water Resources Project" Symposium. Bihar College of Engineering, Patna University, Patna, Bihar, January 22–25.

Zwart, W.
1930 Over boschzaken in Rembang omstreeks 1860. *Tectona* 23:971–82.
1934 Houtskoolbedrijf, een nieuw verschiet voor onze slecte djati-gronden. *Tectona* 27:631–33.
1936 Een ontevredenheidsbetuiging aan den Semarangschen houtvester in 1894, of: De gespannen verhouding tusschen boschwezen en binnenlandsch bestuur in dien tijd in het bosch district Semarang-Vorstenlanden, of: Episoden uit den strijd om de zelfstandigheid van het Boschwezen tegenover het Binnenlandsch-Bestuur. *Tectona* 29:266–300.
1938 Uit de boschgeschiedenis van Java en Madoera, III: Over de scheepsbouw en scheepsbouwhout ten tijde van de Compagnie. *Tectona* 31:78–98.

INDEX

Access control. *See* Forest access control

Access qualifications: forest land in Kaliaman, 173–75, 190; for forest-related employment, 179–82, 208–11; and income, 163; to land in teak zone, 204; for non-forest employment, 182–85; to persil lands, 178–79; resistance to, 200; for rural employment, 163–64; for social forestry, 237, 239–46, 247; to tumpang sari land, 173, 174, 175

Access rights: to forest products, 59, 60, 67, 69; to land, 61, 210; sale of, 225; to wasteland, 59, 60

Adat, interpretations of, 252

Agrarian Law, 1870. *See* Domeinverklaring

Agrarian war, 1965–66, 103, 116–21, 123, 147

Agroforestry: on state lands, 149–50; types of, 286 nn. 20, 22

Aidit, 117, 118

Aksi sepihak, 117, 118, 119, 120, 121; and forest land, 119, 120; and PKI membership, 284 n. 37; as a rural strategy, 284 nn. 33, 34

Bandits, forest: as cultural heroes, 237; in nineteenth century, 68; politicization of, 112, 113; as a survival strategy, 15; and symbolic resistance, 14

Becking, 96, 114

Black market, teak, 201, 202, 211–16, 221–22, 223, 226; dynamics of, 256;

and G30S, 120; as a medium of control, 237; and species control, 212

Blandong, 40, 277–78 n. 14, 278 n. 16; contemporary wages of, 209, 210; forest access of, 206; illegal activities of, 211, 215, 216; numbers employed in colonial period, 49; rights to wood products, 137. *See also* Blandongdiensten; Forest labor; Kalangs

Blandongdiensten: burdens of, 77; as a cause of migration, 58, 61, 62; end of, 55, 56, 62; as a means of access to land, 61, 62; origins of, 40; self-realized, 105; under Raffles, 55–56; village administration of, 56, 57, 60

Bottom up history, 20, 253, 257

BTI, 101, 105, 117, 119, 120, 193; activities near forest lands, 106; membership, 107

Bureaucracy, natural resources, 18, 24, 44, 275 n. 4. *See also* Scientific forestry

Buurman, W., 63

Capital accumulation: and forest access control, 18; through livestock, 186; and tumpang sari land, 175–76

Charcoal production, in teak zone, 207

Clearcutting. *See* Forest production: clearcutting

Collective action, repertoires of, 12, 13, 122; Soekarno period, 116–17, 119, 120–22. *See also* Collective violence; Forest violence; Repertoires of resistance